LARGE-SCALE DISTRIBUTED SYSTEMS AND ENERGY EFFICIENCY

**WILEY SERIES ON PARALLEL
AND DISTRIBUTED COMPUTING**

Series Editor: Albert Y. Zomaya

A complete list of titles in this series appears at the end of this volume.

LARGE-SCALE DISTRIBUTED SYSTEMS AND ENERGY EFFICIENCY

A HOLISTIC VIEW

Edited by

Jean-Marc Pierson

WILEY

Published by John Wiley & Sons, Inc., Hoboken, New Jersey
Published simultaneously in Canada

For general information on our other products and services or for technical support, please contact our
Customer Care Department within the United States at (800) 762-2974, outside the United States at (317)
572-3993 or fax (317) 572-4002.

Wiley also publishes its books in a variety of electronic formats. Some content that appears in print may not
be available in electronic formats. For more information about Wiley products, visit our web site at
www.wiley.com.

Library of Congress Cataloging-in-Publication Data:

Pierson, Jean-Marc.
  Large-scale distributed systems and energy efficiency : a holistic view / Jean-Marc Pierson.
      pages cm – (Wiley series on parallel and distributed computing)
  Includes bibliographical references and index.
  ISBN 978-1-118-86463-0 (hardback)
  1. Data processing service centers–Energy conservation. 2. Electronic data processing–Distributed
processing–Energy conservation. 3. Computer networks–Energy conservation. I. Title.
  TJ163.5.D38P54 2015
  621.39–dc23
                                                              2014025598

Printed in the United States of America

10 9 8 7 6 5 4 3 2 1

We do not inherit the Earth from our Ancestors,
we borrow it from our Children.
To all who contribute to a sustainable future.

CONTENTS

3 GREEN WIRED NETWORKS   41

Alfonso Gazo Cervero, Michele Chincoli, Lars Dittmann, Andreas Fischer, Alberto E. Garcia, Jaime Galán-Jiménez, Laurent Lefevre, Hermann de Meer, Thierry Monteil, Paolo Monti, Anne-Cecile Orgerie, Louis-Francois Pau, Chris Phillips, Sergio Ricciardi, Remi Sharrock, Patricia Stolf, Tuan Trinh, and Luca Valcarenghi

4 GREEN WIRELESS-ENERGY EFFICIENCY IN WIRELESS NETWORKS   81

*Vitor Bernardo, Torsten Braun, Marilia Curado, Markus Fiedler,
David Hock, Theus Hossmann, Karin Anna Hummel, Philipp Hurni,
Selim Ickin, Almerima Jamakovic-Kapic, Simin Nadjm-Tehrani,
Tuan Ahn Trinh, Ekhiotz Jon Vergara, Florian Wamser,
and Thomas Zinner*

PREFACE

Jean-Marc Pierson

University Paul Sabatier Toulouse 3, France

The focus and context of the book is on energy efficiency in large-scale distributed systems. These systems consist of thousands of heterogeneous elements that communicate via heterogeneous networks and provide different memory, storage, and processing capabilities. Examples for very large-scale distributed systems are computational and data grids, data centers, clouds, core and sensor networks, and so on. The target audiences of the book are manifold: from IT and environmental researchers to operators of large-scale systems, up to small and medium enterprises (SMEs) and startups willing to understand the global picture and the state of the art in the field. It helps in building strategies and understanding upcoming developments in the rapid field of energy efficiency to speedup transfer of technologies to industries.

This book is one major outcome of the European Cooperation in Science and Technology (COST) Action IC0804. The COST Action instrument is a 4-year funding scheme in European research framework aimed at helping the development of networks of researchers.[1] The funding goes mainly to four main objectives: (i) to organize meetings on a specific field with experts of the members' countries and to foster closer cooperations; (ii) to help exchanges of researchers through short-term scientific missions (STSM), for a duration of 1 week to several weeks; (iii) to develop the young researchers' skills in the field through the organization of annual training schools; and (iv) to shape and rethink the research agenda on the field. One important information at this stage is that COST Actions do not fund research directly: individual projects still rely on European and national funding agencies.

The COST Action IC0804[2] finds its root in 2008. It was started in May 2009 and finished in May 2013. The COST Action IC0804 investigated energy efficiency in large-scale distributed systems. These systems include, among others, wired and wireless networks, high performance computing, cloud and desktop computing, and smart grids. The scientific outcome of the Action has been numerous and will be detailed in the rest of this book. At the end of the Action duration, 23 European countries, and 7 non-European institutions, were members of the Action. About 150 researchers participated on the various Action activities, coming from academy and industry (including IBM, Microsoft, Intel, Yahoo, Ericsson, and EDF and also various SMEs and startups originated during the 4 years). Twenty-four STSM have been organized, and altogether more than 76 joint publications have been released.

---

[1]www.cost.eu.

[2]www.cost804.org.

All the chapters of this book represent a part of these results and are collaborative works involving several institutions from many different countries.

ACKNOWLEDGMENT

The editor wants to thank all the researchers who made this book appear, especially the leading editors of the 10 chapters: Giuseppe Anastasi, Georges Da Costa, Christina Herzog, Karin Anna Hummel, Sebastien Lafond, Jason Mair, Chris Philips, Shrisha Rao, and Sebastien Varrette, for their involvement in driving, selecting, organizing, and editing the contributions from more than 50 researchers. Thanks, of course, to all contributors of this book for their time, engagement, and willingness that it becomes true. Finally, thanks to the European Cooperation in Science and Technology (COST) Office who partly funded the works presented herein.

1

INTRODUCTION TO ENERGY EFFICIENCY IN LARGE-SCALE DISTRIBUTED SYSTEMS

Jean-Marc Pierson[1] and Helmut Hlavacs[2]

[1] *IRIT, University of Toulouse, France*
[2] *Faculty of Computer Science, University of Vienna, Austria*

1.1 ENERGY CONSUMPTION STATUS

The demand for research in energy efficiency in large-scale systems is supported by several incentives [1Â–3], including financial incentives by government or institutions to energy efficient industries/companies [4-5]. Indeed, studies such as [6] reported already in 2006 that the information technology (IT) consumption accounts for 5% to 10% of the growing global electricity demand and for a mere 2% of the energy while data centers alone account for 14% of the information and communication technology (ICT) footprint. It was projected that by 2020, the energy demand of data centers will represent 18% of the ICT footprint, the carbon footprint rising at an annual 7% pace, doubling between 2007 and 2020 [7]. The study of Koomey [8] in 2011 highlights that the rise of energy consumption is not as bad as expected in 2007: between 2005 and 2010, the electricity demand for data centers increased by (only) about 56% worldwide instead of the projected doubling and even as low as 36% in the United States. Altogether the electricity used worldwide for operating data centers in 2010 accounted for about 1.3% of total electricity use.

The past 5 years have witnessed the increase of research focusing especially in energy reduction. While being a major concern in embedded systems since decades, the problem is quite new in the large-scale infrastructures where performances have been for long the sole parameters to optimize. The motivation comes from two complementary concerns: first, the electrical cost of running such infrastructure is equivalent nowadays to the purchase costs of the equipment during a 4-year usage [9]. Second, electricity providers are not always able to deliver the needed power to run the machines, capping the amount of electricity delivered to one particular client.

Modern usage of ITs relies on the existence of large data centers, high-performance infrastructures, and performance networks, core and mobile networks.

Cloud computing is one of the major evolutions in IT in the past decade. It mainly relies on data centers, some hosting thousands of servers. In 2010, Google was hosting already 900,000 servers (almost 1 million must be the case today, and is estimated to be even more than 1.5 million). In 2013, Microsoft's CEO Steve Ballmer claimed hosting more than 1 million servers. Amazon is guessed to have about the same number of servers. For 1 million servers, at about 200 W per server, plus something like 50 W for cooling and electricity distribution losses, it represents a total power consumption of 250 MW, which is likely 2 TWh/year. However, in [8], it is shown that less than 1% of electricity used by data centers worldwide was attributable to Google's data center operations: The big players are often cited as examples, but they represent only a few percentage of the problem. When they exhibit better energy efficiency, it must be remembered that most other companies have less advances and the average is far from these big players.

While, traditionally, supercomputers have been mainly compared by their raw performance measured now in PFlops (petaflops), they are now also assessed based on their energy efficiency. The ranking of supercomputers by their energy efficiency places great emphasis on their energy consumption through the number of GFlops (gigaflops) they can achieve per watt. For instance, the Tianhe-2 machine, the leading one of the top performance list (Top500[1]), delivers a computing power of over 33 PFlops and shows an energy efficiency of 1.9 GFlops/W; while the CINECA machine, which tops the green list (Green500 list[2]) with an energy efficiency of 3.9 GFlops/W, delivers a low computing power of less than 2 PFlops. Nevertheless, it can be noted that supercomputers are getting greener, or more exactly, their energy efficiency is continuously increasing, while their energy consumption itself is nevertheless growing. Despite this trend, it will be difficult to achieve exascale computing for 20 MW by 2020, the limit given by the US Department of Energy (DoE).

Network operators are among the most power-consuming players. Telecom Italia [10] estimated that its consumption represented 1% of the Italian total power consumption in 2011 (compared to 0.7% in 2008). Similarly, British Telecom estimates 0.7% to be its share of electricity usage in the United Kingdom (2.3 TWh), same as that of NTT in Japan. These numbers account not only for networks but also for associated infrastructures to operate them. For instance, for Telecom Italia, 65% of electricity is consumed in the networks (wired and mobile) and 10% by their data centers. However, these numbers do not account for the equipment at final clients. In France, a study from

---

[1]top500.org.
[2]green500.org.

IDATE [11] shows that the total electricity consumption of the telecom is 8.5 TWh in 2012 (for 6.7 TWh in 2008). The share is 40% for wired and mobile networks, 6% for data centers, 24% for the ADSL boxes at client places, and, finally, 18% for the fix and mobile phones themselves. We can notice that the total energy consumption of the internet boxes at clients' home is estimated to be 3.3 TWh in 2012 (40 millions of boxes).

The share of power consumption in servers is evolving continuously, because of the improvement in electronics for individual components. Processors (central processing unit, CPU) and memory account together for about 54% of the total consumption, with a rough 37% share for CPU and 17% for memory while the other components are consuming less: Peripheral Component Interconnect (PCI) slots (23%), motherboard (12%), disk (6%), and fans (5%) [12] (see Chapter 2 for details). When graphics processing unit (GPU) are present, they can represent up to a tremendous 50% share of the total consumption. It is, therefore, not surprising that most of the efforts have been put on reducing the power consumption of processors and memory. However, despite the urge for proportional computing already demonstrated in 2007 [13], the current servers are not consuming proportionally to their usage. This makes a lot of work trying to switch off components (consolidation in clouds) or using them at lower speed and capacity (dynamic voltage frequency scaling (DVFS) for CPU, Low Power Idle (LPI) for network cards, disk spin down for hard disk) very valuable. It should be noted that the situation is improving: 5 years ago, a server was consuming as much as 50% of its peak power when idle. Now this drops to 20%, and the peak power itself is decreasing. One can wonder if the works based on the nonproportionality of power consumption will still be interesting in the future. We believe that the delay is still long enough to see achievements in this dimension and also that the aforementioned researches may be used in conjunction and transferred at lower levels (at the components architecture), to allow for actual proportional computing.

One must not forget also the impact of cooling in the global consumption, especially in data centers or large-scale networking equipment rooms. The power usage effectiveness (PUE), promoted since 2007 as a criteria for assessing the power efficiencies of infrastructures, is the ratio between the global power usage to the power usage for IT. While it was common to have a PUE of 2 or more (meaning that as much electricity was used for the infrastructure – mainly cooling and distribution losses) the state-of-the-art values are now at about 1.5 or 1.6. Still 50–60% of power is used for cooling IT equipment. However, as outlined earlier, many data centers do not operate with state-of-the-art solutions, and their PUE are more likely to be at about 1.8 or 1.9 [8].

Energy concerns have been integrated in many works at the different levels of the IT stack: hardware, network, middleware, and software levels in large-scale distributed systems, being high-performance computing (HPC), clouds, or networks.

In the following, we exhibit some actions undertaken at these levels, in particular in the scope of an European-funded initiative.

1.2   TARGET OF THE BOOK

The focus and context of the book is on large-scale distributed systems. We will not study embedded systems in this book. Also we are not investigating hardware-specific optimization for energy saving. Instead, we focus in this work on energy-efficient computation and communication in large-scale distributed systems. These systems consist of thousands of heterogeneous elements that communicate via heterogeneous networks and provide different memory, storage, and processing capabilities. Examples for very large-scale distributed systems are computational and data grids, data centers, clouds, core and sensor networks, and so on.

The target audiences of the book are manifold: from IT and environmental researchers to operators of large-scale systems, up to small and medium sized enterprises (SMEs) and startups willing to understand the global picture and the state of the art in the field. It helps in building strategies and understanding upcoming developments in the rapid field of energy efficiency to speedup transfer of technologies to industries [14].

1.3   THE COST ACTION IC0804

This section introduces the European Cooperation in Science and Technology (COST) Action IC0804. The COST Action instrument is a 4-year funding scheme in European research framework aimed at helping the development of networks of researchers.[3] The funding goes mainly to four main objectives: (i) to organize meetings on a specific field with experts of the members' countries and to foster closer cooperation; (ii) to help exchanges of researchers through short-term scientific missions (STSM), for a duration of 1 week to several weeks ; (iii) to develop the young researchers' skills in the field through the organization of annual training schools; and (iv) to shape and rethink the research agenda on the field. One important information at this stage is that COST Actions do not fund research directly: individual projects still rely on European and national funding agencies.

1.3.1   Birth of the Action

The COST Action IC0804[4] finds its root in 2008. It started in May 2009 and finished in May 2013. The idea of the Action started with eco-awareness during the previous years among colleagues around the world. This topic appeared in both national and international research agendas and scientific interests.

First, the ecological concerns came more and more on the agenda of many funding institutions, raising the foundations for some research projects in various countries and then at the European level. At the European level, the Environmental Research themes were still not investigating the issues related to the electricity consumption in the IT.[5] In FP7 (Framework Program 7), the Energy theme[6] is concerned with the energy consumption and production. The Environment theme of the FP7[7] focuses its actions on

[3]www.cost.eu.
[4]http://www.cost.eu/COST_Actions/ict/Actions/IC0804
[5]ec.europa.eu/research/environment/themes/themes_en.htm.
[6]cordis.europa.eu/fp7/energy/.
[7]cordis.europa.eu/fp7/environment/.

environmental issues and climate change but nothing is done on the ICT side. For the ICT theme, the COST Action fitted into Challenge 1 on pervasive and trusted network and service infrastructure and in Challenge 6 on mobility, environmental sustainability, and energy efficiency.[8] Altogether, these programs raised a number of projects with at least eco-awareness. The Action IC0804 served as a means to coordinate focused initiatives. As for examples, the Virtual Home Environment (VHE) project, a specific subproject of the European Network of Excellence (NoE) Euro-FGI (Design and Engineering of the Future Generation Internet) has been carried out on energy-efficient home networking. In the FP7 call, the AIM[9] and the BE-AWARE[10] projects were among the first ones to investigate complementary approaches to energy awareness.

Second, conferences specialized in distributed systems, clusters, or grids saw the emergence of research papers in the field of energy efficiency and energy awareness (topics that have finally become part of their calls for research papers). When done separately, the researches are likely to contradict each other, leading to the idea for a common forum and exchange place. Energy has thus become a fixed topic in the distributed systems community research. Also, researchers working outside the field of energy efficiency and savings may want to gain more information about the energy consumption of their distributed systems, especially of large scale or cluster likes. They want to be guided in some good practices so as to use alternative eco-aware solutions if the performance and costs of these are satisfying. The common fear is the critical loss of performance while trying to reduce the ecological footprint. The COST Action aimed to show that efficient energy aware solutions exist. The work carried out in the course of the Action, summarized in the rest of the book, shows that this is achievable.

1.3.2 Development of the Action

The COST Action IC0804 investigated energy efficiency in large-scale distributed systems. These systems include, among others, wired and wireless networks, HPC, cloud and desktop computing, and smart grids. The scientific outcome of the Action have been numerous: a brochure on hardware leverages for energy reduction; some methodologies to monitor and model the energy consumption of hardware and software components under the constraints imposed by power meters (accuracy, frequency); concrete techniques and their analyses for energy savings (from using Power On/Power Off, DVFS, idle states of components, to algorithmic and rethinking of algorithms, and management of the platforms); outline of the need for self-management of infrastructures; trade-off analysis, including not only the electricity price but also other costs (CO_2, quality of experience (QoE), human resources, management efforts of organizations, etc.).

1.3.2.1 Numbers and Facts about the Action. At the end of the Action duration, 23 European countries and 7 non-European institutions were members of the Action. About 150 researchers participated on the various Action activities, coming from academy and industry (including IBM, Microsoft, Intel, Yahoo, Ericsson, and EDF and

---

[8]cordis.europa.eu/fp7/ict/programme/challenge6_en.html.
[9]http://www.ict-aim.eu/.
[10]http://www.energyawareness.eu/beaware/.

also various SMEs and startups originated during the 4 years). Twenty-four STSMs have been organized, and altogether more than 76 joint publications have been released.

1.3.2.2 Concrete Actions Toward Eco-Friendliness. In this section, we highlight some of the results that can be awarded to the Action. This section is not designed to provide a summary of the research results obtained but rather gives the opportunity to have a glimpse of a selection of them. All the works cited here are collaborative works involving a minimum of two institutions from two different countries. Some of them will be detailed in the upcoming chapters, while the reader can refer to the individual research papers for the others.

- *Hardware*. Energy efficiency is directly related to the efficiency of individual components. Therefore, it is very important to follow the actual development of technologies. Tremendous efforts are spent on improving electronics, and more energy-efficient new technologies are coming out regularly. Still, energy proportional computing [4404806] is not in place, and it is still worth investigating how to use the different possible status for a component (power off, standby, idle, etc.) and for every component: CPU, memory, network, disk, and accelerators (including GPU and cells, for instance). Hardware improves at a fast pace. Future hardwares are moving towards dedicated pieces of hardware instead of the current "able to do all, perfect for nothing" approach. Future is going towards high-scale dedicated infrastructure such as data mining (such as Google and Facebook) for which newly dedicated hardware will be available. From a software point of view, this means that in the future, new possibilities will arise as decisions will be more complex due to software requirements.

- *Monitoring*. Concerning the monitoring of energy consumption, we have witnessed a change from ad-hoc solutions at the beginning of the Action to more industrial solutions at the end, including the raise of the ACPI 4.0 norm, defining that in the future, components will be able to tell about their energy consumption individually. We also saw that the accuracy and the frequency of measurements play a large role in the evaluation of the solutions: Power meters have to be carefully studied and/or chosen before starting any serious experiments. Currently, mostly ad-hoc solutions are provided for monitoring data centers, wired network devices, and wireless networks using external measurement devices to get energy readings and derive models from these readings. Differences in hardware manufacturing require different models. Thus, more information from manufacturers would fasten the model creation step as well as classification of devices in terms of energy consumption characteristics. Often, the required information about measurements is missing in distributed monitoring, which makes it hard to compare results.

  During the course of the Action, a joint methodology has been put in place between two teams (France and Spain), which proposed an analysis and evaluation of different external and internal power monitoring devices to validate the accuracy of the equipment in terms of power dispersion and energy consumption. This experimental study is completed by some results for a variety of benchmarks that exercise intensively the main components (CPU, Memory, hard disk drives (HDDs), and network interface controllers (NICs) of the target platforms. This study has been the first one to carefully deal with the monitoring of energy consumption of computing servers and to correct several wrong assumptions on this topic: internal wattmeters do not register neither an equal energy consumption nor a similar power dispersion. Thanks to the high sampling rate and to the different measured lines, the internal wattmeters allow to better visualize some power fluctuations. However, a high sampling rate is not always necessary to understand the evolution of the power consumption during the execution of a benchmark [15].

- *Modeling the Energy Consumption.* Several techniques exist and have been used within the course of the Action; some very simple and some complicated machine learning or neural networks based. One basic observation is that the accuracy of the model has to be related to the scale of the utilization of the model. For instance, a simple model could easily give a 5–10% accuracy at almost no cost (linear combination of power and load), which is sufficient for actions on the system at the cloud level, done generally at the scale of minutes or more. At the operating system level, models have to be more precise because actions on the system (for instance, using DVFS) are in the order of milliseconds, but at the same time, this accuracy must not come at the cost of complexity and time, because the operating system has to react quickly. When it comes to model the applications and not the system, some tools (for instance, the ectop and valgreen software suite [16]) have been developed for estimating the power consumption of applications.

  A very important and difficult research topic addressed by members of the action was understanding how specific applications affect power usage of servers they are executed on. This problem became particularly relevant in the advent of many-core processors, dynamic power states management techniques, and a variety of applications ranging from mobile devices, through virtualized environments, to petascale HPC codes. To solve this problem, colleagues worked on the analysis of applications using information coming from the system (performance counters, Input/Output status, temperature, etc.) and correlated these using statistical methods. Proposed methodology and models enabled estimation of power usage of servers and single applications without the use of power meters [17Â–21] and modeling application profiles in simulations tools [22]. Methods for application clustering and classification at runtime were also proposed [20, 23].

  We also witnessed that only a few works are intended to evaluate and model the power consumption of virtual machines.

- *Taking Actions at the Communication Layer.* On the side of the networks, the potential of energy is also very huge, either in wired or in wireless networks. For instance, in wireless networks, working on energy savings between end-users and base stations has more value than working in the core network: The numbers make the savings.

  Concerning wireless networks, researchers investigated in [24] the energy consumption of various wireless network technologies such as WiFi and

WiMAX, in particular considering network interfaces of end systems when receiving data from cloud services. Other researchers analyzed the trade-off between QoE and energy consumption for receiving high-quality video streams via wireless mesh networks as well as WiFi access networks [25]. On the basis of that work, a novel power saving algorithms for continuous media applications (optimized power save algorithm for continuous media applications, OPAMA) over IEEE 802.11 WiFi networks has been developed and evaluated [26].

In [27], Aleksic et al. present joint work assessing the feasibility of using a core network approach where no switching is performed at the Internet Protocol (IP) layer, but end-to-end data connections between ingress and egress nodes are realized by means of digital and optical resources at the transport layer. They introduce an analytical model for estimating the average number of required transport switch ports for different topologies, in order to assess both scalability and power consumption of three particular realizations of these static optical core networks. The results show that the concept of a static optically transparent core network promises high energy efficiency and scalability to several tens of nodes.

Another example of the front of networks is the work on developing an algorithm to solve the resource assignment problem in virtual networks (also known as virtual network embedding) with a focus on energy efficiency. In particular, the approach tries to achieve higher consolidation of resources, thereby allowing to power off part of the substrate network [28].

- *Taking Actions for Data Centers.* Beyond classical approaches for reducing energy in data centers focusing on one aspect of the problem (machines, scheduling, operating system, communication layer, etc.), some colleagues joined efforts to start research on energy efficiency of large-scale distributed systems taking into consideration the thermal aspects. To this end, they took a holistic approach including modeling of application profiles, thermal-aware resource management policies, and appropriate metrics to evaluate efficiency. This joint work was on the basis of the CoolEmAll project.[11] The main goal of that project is to decrease energy consumption of data centers by allowing data center designers, planners, and administrators to model and analyze energy efficiency of various configurations and solutions. The project provides models of data center building blocks and tools that apply these models to simulate, visualize, and analyze data center energy efficiency. Both building blocks and the toolkit take into account the aspects that have major impact on actual energy consumption: hardware characteristics, cooling solutions, application profiles, and workload and resource management policies. In addition to common static approaches, the proposed platform enables studies of dynamic states of data centers based on changing workloads, management policies, cooling method, and ambient temperature. To our knowledge, this is the first such holistic approach to date. Especially, combination of detailed application analysis, workload management and scheduling simulation, and heat transfer simulation are not

---

[11]coolemall.eu.

available in concurrent solutions. Results have been presented in several joint publications [17, 22, 29, 30].

While all data centers have common problems to be addressed (such as thermal aspects), we also witnessed a huge difference in handling energy efficiency between cloud and HPC systems. While the first one deals with service-level agreement (SLA) and allows for its degradation, HPC system tends to be more conservative, that is, allowing less energy saving leverages.

- *Taking Actions for Cloud Computing*. Solutions for cloud computing are already on the market, some developed in startups issued from the Action members (Eco4Cloud,[12] EasyVirt[13]). Even if more precise allocation of virtual machines on the data centers can achieve better energy savings, already existing solutions can save a lot, about 40–70% of energy costs. For a specific example as results of STSMs, collaborations on energy/resource-efficient management of cloud computing infrastructures started between partners on the long term. They propose to tackle the problem in a hierarchical manner, where they structure all possible adaptation actions into the so-called escalation levels [31]. In [32], Maurer et al. devise an approach for self-adaptive and resource-efficient decision-making considering the three conflicting goals of minimizing the number of SLA violations, maximizing resource utilization, and minimizing the number of necessary time- and energy-consuming reconfiguration actions. Their approach is based on automatically detecting workload volatility in the virtual machines' demands and reaction based on rules. They introduce categorization and present cost- and volatility-based methods for self-tuning. Evaluation shows that in most cases, the self-adaptive approach outperforms the static approach. In [33], the work is extended to include different allocations strategies (vector packing, best fit, Monte Carlo, etc.).

- *Taking Actions for High-Performance Computing*: In HPC, guaranteeing high performance at all costs is a challenge. Savings are less important in terms of percentage (5%, for instance) but the size of the infrastructure is so large that the final energy savings are large as well. Here it is important to understand that a small saving at large scale has more value than large savings at small scale. Exascale will not be achievable without a significant work on energy efficiency of solutions for HPC.

Many organizations have departments and workgroups that could benefit from HPC resources to analyze, model, and visualize the growing volumes of data they need to conduct business. Up to now, most HPC systems are built on general-purpose multi-core processors that use the x86 and power instruction sets. This trend is about to change with the massive investments (several billions of dollar) voted by leading countries in 2012 to build an exascale HPC system by 2019 while staying below a power budget of around 20 MW. Such a platform requires a maximal power consumption of 0.1 W per core. In order to achieve this ambitious goal, alternative low power processor architectures are required

---

[12] www.eco4cloud.com.
[13] easyvirt.fr.

and two main directions are currently explored: (i) general-purpose graphics processing unit (GPGPU) accelerators or (ii) processors (ARM, Intel Atom, etc.) primarily designed for the mobile and embedded devices market. Building on preliminary results exhibited from the European Mont-Blanc project[14] in an Action meeting that investigates the second approach, partners from Luxembourg and Poland cooperated to compare the performance and energy efficiency of cutting-edge high-density HPC platform enclosures featuring either very high-performing processors (such as Intel Core i7 or E7) yet having low power efficiency, or the reverse, that is, energy-efficient processors (such as Intel Atom, AMD Fusion, or ARM Cortex A9) yet with limited computing capacity [34].

- *Automating Actions.* At large scale, it is obvious that most of the actions that have to be undertaken must be automatized. Autonomic computing is key for achieving the adoption of energy savings mechanisms. Most of the approaches described earlier and in the rest of the book are relying on this concept, more or less integrated in a holistic work.

1.3.2.3 European Projects Related to the Field. During the development of the Action, a number of FP7 European projects have been initialized in the field of energy efficiency in large-scale distributed systems. Most of them have involved some members of the COST Action community. Without entering in the details of the projects themselves, the focus were on data centers (GAMES, FIT4GREEN, ALL4GREEN, COOLEMALL, primeEnergyIT), clouds (EUROCLOUD, ECO2CLOUD), HPC (Mont Blanc), and networks (EARTH, ECONET, TREND). Several results presented in this book have originated from these researches funded by the European FP7 program and developed during the course of the Action.

1.3.3   End and Future of the Action

The Action was completed in May 2013. Researchers are continuing their investigations, building on their experience gained here. Some follow-up may appear on sustainable ultrascale computing and on the smart grid problem. The main lessons learnt from the Action can be summarized as follows:

- Energy efficiency by itself is a very broad subject, encompassing hardware-related aspects and middleware, networking, and software issues. A holistic view is necessary to capture the whole picture. Unfortunately, this broad view is difficult to achieve because it requires a similar broad knowledge for the researchers as well as for the development of automation.

- Knowledge and precision of models are very important in order to describe, address, and, finally, propose solutions for better energy efficiency. While strong mathematical models help to optimize the system theoretically, it can be noted that simple solutions based on easy-to-deploy heuristics have proven to be very effective on real application domains.

---

[14]www.montblanc-project.eu/.

- Developed tools for assessing the energy consumption and taking actions for reducing it exist, at middleware, software, or network layers. Their acceptance in communities is the major challenge for the coming years.

- Electrical power dissipated in data centers and networks is huge. Low hanging fruits for saving energy are still here in production sites while research has demonstrated the effectiveness of actual solutions. The lack of formal standardization and regulation in this field is a major problem [35].

- While individual hardware components become more and more energy efficient, their proliferation and the foreseen data deluge makes the problem of energy consumption more and more serious.

- As the infrastructure grows, trade-off between energy consumption and performance becomes a key issue. With a million-core machine, resilience, fault tolerance, and the expected redundancy represent opposite objectives to energy efficiency: the fight will be even more exciting.

- The link with electrical power production (in particular renewable or clean energy) is mandatory. Smart grid development will help to solve this issue. However, it must be understood that the electricity production with renewable energy is (and will be for a certain future) far from being sufficient to power a very large data center.

1.4 CHAPTERS PREVIEW

The rest of the book is organized around the major topics that have been investigated during the course of the Action.

Chapter 2 covers the technological possibilities at the hardware level and infrastructure level for energy efficiency. It discusses individual components (CPU, memory, etc.) and the global view, including large-scale infrastructure, including power supply and cooling.

Chapter 3 focuses on wired networks. After highlighting the significant energy consumption of existing wired communication networks, this chapter will examine various means of operating such networks more efficiently. The chapter examines the components that make up wired communications network and their differing characteristics between the access and core, as well as patterns of traffic behavior. Once this is done, the chapter focuses on static (network planning) and dynamic (traffic engineering) schemes that can be used to reduce the energy consumption of the network. The chapter also pays attention to a number of challenges/open research questions that need to be resolved before the implementation of such schemes. These include issues with migration and resilience. Finally, a summary draws out the key themes that have been covered.

Chapter 4 deals with wireless networks. It exhibits the metrics and the trade-offs used in these networks. It discusses the methodology for measuring or profiling the energy consumption of mobile devices and the infrastructures. It explains the different access networks Long Term Evolution(LTE), Wireless Local Area Network(WLAN) their impact in terms of energy consumption linked with the notion of quality of services. Wireless sensor networks and ad-hoc networks [vehicular ad-hoc networks

(VANET), mobile ad hoc network (MANET), opportunistic networks, delay tolerant network (DTN)] conclude this chapter.

Chapter 5 is interested in power modeling techniques and tools. It provides a broad discussion of the techniques involved in performance-based power estimation modeling, as well as the driving motivation for the use of estimation models over the alternative hardware metering devices. A discussion on the impact of providing power consumption feedback to users is given. Power modeling for single core, multi-cores, multiprocessors, and distributed systems (especially for clouds) is discussed.

Chapter 6 discusses green data centers, from their design to their operations. It describes the possibilities of energy reduction in data centers, taking into account the servers, and also the infrastructure of the data center (cooling, heating, power distribution, etc.) and the interconnect inside the data center. Solutions at architectural and middleware levels are presented.

Chapter 7 is investigating the side of energy efficiency in HPC, in particular taking into account the high utilization of HPC platforms, the hybrid architectures (including GPU), and the race for performances towards exascale.

Chapter 8 aims at providing an overview on resource management, in particular in cloud computing, in particular aspects related to the SLA enactment, economic issues, and virtualization technologies and a theoretical part on scheduling, including exact solutions, centralized heuristics, and distributed solutions.

Chapter 9 exhibits the advances on energy efficiency solutions for peer-to-peer (P2P) systems and applications with special focus on file sharing applications and epidemic protocols.

Chapter 10 concludes the book with a discussion about sustainability for large-scale computing systems: environmental, economic, and standardization aspects are outlined and open the book to less technical aspects but still mandatory to effect the transfer of researches to industry and society.

ACKNOWLEDGEMENT

This work was partially supported by the COST (European Cooperation in Science and Technology) framework, under Action IC0804 (www.cost804.org).

REFERENCES

[1] COST European Cooperation in Science and Technology. ICT COST Action IC0804 on Energy efficiency in large scale distributed systems. Available at http://www.cost.eu/COST_Actions/ict/Actions/IC0804.

[2] Cameron KW, Pruhs K, Irani S, Ranganathan P, Brooks D. Report of the science of power management workshop; 2009. Available at http://scipm.cs.vt.edu/SciPM-ReportToNSF-Web.pdf.

[3] U.S. Environmental Protection Agency ENERGY STAR Program. Report to congress on server and data center energy efficiency; 2007. Available online www.energystar.gov/ia/partners/prod_development/downloads/epa_datacenter_report_congress_final1.pdf. Accessed 2014 Oct 16.

[4] Naegel B. The Data Center Journal, Energy Efficiency: The New SLA, Dec; 2008. http://datacenterjournal.com/index.php?option=com_content&task=view&id=2352&Itemid=43.

[5] Barroso LA and Holzle U. IEEE Computer, The Case for Energy-Proportional Computing, 40; 2007. http://www.computer.org/portal/site/computer/index.jsp?pageID=computer_level1 &path=computer/homepage/Dec07&file=feature.xml&xsl=article.xsl.

[6] Bertoldi P, Atanasiu B. Electricity consumption and efficiency trends in the enlarged European Union; 2006. Available online re.jrc.ec.europa.eu/energyefficiency/pdf/eneff report 2006.pdf. Accessed 2014 Oct 16.

[7] The Climate Group. SMART 2020: enabling the low carbon economy in the information age. Technical report; 2008. A report by The Climate Group on behalf of the Global eSustainability Initiative (GeSI), http://www.theclimategroup.org/_assets/files/Smart2020Report.pdf

[8] Koomey J. Growth in data center electricity use 2005 to 2010; 2011.

[9] Koomey JG, Belady C, Patterson M, Santos A. Assessing trends over time in performance, costs, and energy use for servers; 2009.

[10] Bianco C, Cucchietti F, Griffa G. (2006) Energy consumption trends in the Next Generation - Access Network-a Telco perspective http://www.polisave.polito.it/greennet/docs/TlcEnergy Trends.pdf Accessed 2014 Oct 16.

[11] IDATE. 2010, http://www.fftelecoms.org/sites/default/files/contenus_lies/007.15_idate_ presentation_conference_de_presse.pdf. Accessed 2014 Oct 16.

[12] Fan X, Weber W-D, Barroso LA. Power provisioning for a warehouse-sized computer. ISCA '07: Proceedings of the 34th Annual International Symposium on Computer Architecture. New York (NY): ACM; 2007. p 13–23.

[13] Barroso LA, Holzle U. The case for energy-proportional computing. IEEE Comput 2007;40(12):33Â–37.

[14] Herzog C, Lefevre L, Pierson J-M. Green IT for innovation and innovation for green IT: the virtuous circle. In: Hercheui MD, Whitehouse D, McIver W Jr., Phahlamohlaka J, editors, *ICT Critical Infrastructures and Society, 10th IFIP TC9 International Conference on Human Choice and Computers (HCC); 2012 Sep 27Â–28. Number 386 in IFIP AICT*. Amsterdam: Springer; 2012. p 79–89. Available at http://www.springerlink.com. Accessed 2014 Oct 16.

[15] Diouri MEM, Dolz MF, Glück O, Lefèvre L, Alonso P, Catalán S, Mayo R, Quintana-Ortí ES. Solving some mysteries in power monitoring of servers: take care of your wattmeters! Energy Efficiency in Large Scale Distributed Systems conference (EE-LSDS); Vienne, Autriche; 2013.

[16] Cupertino LF, Costa G, Sayah A, Pierson J-M. Energy consumption library. *Energy Efficiency in Large Scale Distributed Systems*, Vienna, Austria, April 2013. Lecture notes in computer science. Springer Berlin Heidelberg; 2013. p 51–57.

[17] Cupertino LF, Da Costa G, Sayah A, Pierson J-M. Valgreen: an application's energy profiler. International Journal of Soft Computing and Software Engineering, SCSE'13 Conference, Volume 3(3):(on line), March 2013.

[18] Costa GD, Hlavacs H. Methodology of measurement for energy consumption of applications. 2010 11th IEEE/ACM International Conference on Grid Computing (GRID); 2010. p 290–297.

[19] Witkowski M, Oleksiak A, Piontek T, Węglarz J. Practical power consumption estimation for real life {HPC} applications. Future Gener Comput Syst 2013;29(1):208–217.

[20] Jarus M, Oleksiak A, Piontek T, Węglarz J. Runtime power usage estimation of HPC servers for various classes of real-life applications, Future Generation Computer Systems Volume 36, July 2014, P 299–310, ISSN 0167–739X, http://dx.doi.org/10.1016/j.future.2013.07.012.

[21] Landry G Chetsa T, Lefevre L, Pierson J-M, Stolf P, Da Costa G. DNA-inspired scheme for building the energy profile of HPC systems. E2DC - 1st International Workshop on Energy-Efficient Data Centres - 2011; Madrid, Europe; 2012.

[22] Piatek W. Dcworms - a tool for simulation of energy efficiency in data centers. In: Pierson J-M, Da Costa G, Dittmann L, editors, *Energy Efficiency in Large Scale Distributed Systems*, Vienna, Austria, April 2013. Lecture notes in computer science. Springer Berlin Heidelberg; 2013. p 118–124.

[23] Da Costa G, Pierson J-M. Characterizing applications from power consumption: a case study for HPC benchmarks. International Conference on ICT as Key Technology for the Fight Against Global Warming (ICT-GLOW); 2011 Aug 29-Sep 02 (electronic medium). Toulouse: Springer; 2011. Available at http://www.springerlink.com. Accessed 2014 Oct 16.

[24] Bernardo V, Curado M, Staub T, Braun T. Towards energy consumption measurement in a cloud computing wireless testbed. *Proceedings of the 2011 1st International Symposium on Network Cloud Computing and Applications, NCCA '11*. Washington (DC): IEEE Computer Society; 2011. p 91–98.

[25] Hock D, Bernardo V, Zinner T, Wamser F, Hummel KA, Curado M, Pries R, Braun T, Tran-Gia P. Evaluating the trade-off between energy-efficiency and QoE in wireless mesh networks. 4th International Conference on Communications and Electronics (ICCE 12); Hue, Vietnam; 2012.

[26] Bernardo V, Curado M, Braun T. Enhancing IEEE 802.11 energy efficiency for continuous media applications. In: Pierson J-M, Da Costa G, Dittmann L, editors. *Energy Efficiency in Large Scale Distributed Systems*, Vienna, Austria, April 2013. Lecture notes in computer science, Springer Berlin Heidelberg; 2013. p 203–217.

[27] Aleksic S, Van Heddeghem W, Pickavet M. Scalability and power consumption of static optical core networks. Global Communications Conference (GLOBECOM), 2012 IEEE; 2012. p 3465–3471.

[28] Botero JF, Hesselbach X, Duelli M, Schlosser D, Fischer A, De Meer H. Energy efficient virtual network embedding. IEEE Commun Lett 2012;16(5):756–759.

[29] Berge M, Da Costa G, Kopecki A, Oleksiak A, Pierson J-M, Piontek T, Volk E, Wesner S. Modeling and simulation of data center energy-efficiency in coolemall. In: Huusko J, Meer H, Klingert S, Somov A, editors. *E2DC'12 Proceedings of the First international conference on Energy Efficient Data Centers*. Volume 7396 of Lecture notes in computer science. Springer Berlin Heidelberg; 2012. p 25–36.

[30] Vor Dem Berge M, Da Costa G, Jarus M, Oleksiak A, Piontek W, Volk E. Modeling data center building blocks for energy-efficiency and thermal simulations. International Workshop on Energy-Efficient Data Centres, Co-located with E-Energy (E2DC); 2013 May 21 (electronic medium). Berkeley: Springer; 2013. Available at http://www.springerlink.com.

[31] Maurer M, Brandic I, Sakellariou R. Adaptive resource configuration for cloud infrastructure management. Future Gener Comput Syst 2013;29(2):472–487.

[32] Maurer M, Brandic I, Sakellariou R. Self-adaptive and resource-efficient SLA enactment for cloud computing infrastructures. 2012 IEEE 5th International Conference on Cloud Computing (CLOUD); 2012. p 368–375.

[33] Borgetto D, Maurer M, Da Costa G, Pierson J-M, Brandic I. Energy-efficient and SLA-aware management of IAAS clouds. Proceedings of the 3rd International Conference on Future Energy Systems: Where Energy, Computing and Communication Meet, e-Energy '12. New York (NY): ACM; 2012. p 25:1–25:10.

[34] Jarus M, Varrette S, Oleksiak A, Bouvry P. Performance evaluation and energy efficiency of high-density HPC platforms based on Intel, AMD and ARM processors. In: Pierson J-M, Da Costa G, Dittmann L, editors. *Energy Efficiency in Large Scale Distributed Systems*, Vienna, Austria, April 2013. Lecture notes in computer science. Springer Berlin Heidelberg; 2013. p 182–200.

[35] Herzog C. Standardization bodies, initiatives and their relation to green IT focused on the data centre side. Energy Efficiency in Large Scale Distributed Systems (EE-LSDS); 2013 April 22-24; LNCS. Vienna: Springer; 2013. Available at http://www.springerlink.com. Accessed 2014 Oct 16.

2

HARDWARE LEVERAGES FOR ENERGY REDUCTION IN LARGE-SCALE DISTRIBUTED SYSTEMS

Davide Careglio[2], Georges Da Costa,[1] and Sergio Ricciardi[2]

[1]*Institute for Research in Informatics of Toulouse (IRIT),
University of Toulouse, Toulouse, France*
[2]*Department of Computer Architecture (DAC), Universitat Politècnica de
Catalunya – BarcelonaTech (UPC), Barcelona, Spain*

2.1 INTRODUCTION

2.1.1 Motivation for Energy-Aware Distributed Computing

In the past years, the Information and Communication Society (ICS) has experienced unprecedented growth in the amount of information being processed, stored, and transferred over the Internet. This is due to the ever increasing number of connected users and demand for rich contents (cloud computing and big data applications, social networks and photo sharing, on-demand video streaming, etc.) that require huge bandwidths and computational/storage capacities. Large-scale distributed systems and network equipment are, therefore, growing in performance and size to support the demand and offer more and more connectivity and services to their clients. It has been estimated that the Internet (including both operational and embodied energy of servers, networking, end users equipment, and mobile telecommunication infrastructures) requires a mean value of 240 GW of power [1], which corresponds roughly to 12.6% of the electrical power produced worldwide. Furthermore, from 2011 to 2015, the total Internet traffic will be three times larger [2], equivalent to a monthly traffic of $60\,EB$ of data ($1\,EB = 10^6\,TB$), and in the same time span the number of users connected to the Internet will pass from 2.1 to 3 billions [3, 4].

Apart from the enormous costs that operating such infrastructure involves and the new business opportunities that are being created, the information and communications technology (ICT) growth has severe impacts on the environment. In fact, it directly influences the energy consumption and, in general, resource exploitation, as well as greenhouse gases (GHG) emissions, which are related to pollution and climate changes such as global warming. It has been estimated that in 2007, the ICT was responsible for 2–3% of the world's GHG emissions (including only the use phase), which is as much as the aviation industry [5]. ICT-footprint initiative [6] shows that data centers, personal computers, and network electricity consumption was at $930\,TWh$ in 2012, growing at a rate of 6.6% every year. Compared to the worldwide electricity production, ICT share rose from 4% in 2007 to 4.7% in 2012.

This is due to the fact that traditionally, there has been a dearth of eco-awareness in the computing industry. Moore's law, 3D lithography, and future memristors has or will allow to pack higher and higher number of transistors in devices, but it has not been compensated at the same pace by a decrease in the energy consumption. Instead, greater capacity and capability have invariably taken precedence over eco-concerns. Despite the fact that the energy dimension was taken into account since several years in mobile and embedded systems, the total collective costs of large-scale distributed technologies have not traditionally prioritized ecological concerns. Ecological impacts constitute a silent cost which until recently has largely been ignored. But recent studies charged from government institution are going to consider energy efficiency procedures mainly for server and data centers.

Central to this approach is the recognition that environmental resources need to be effectively managed as an integral part of every computation – just as processing cycles, storage, and bandwidth are currently routinely managed in every computation.

This chapter provides the summary and references on existing and future leverages to adapt the underlying hardware infrastructures of large-scale distributed computing systems in order to decrease their energy consumption.

The chapter is intended to be used by researchers, as well as companies and general public, to drive their research fostering activities toward energy-aware solutions for large-scale distributed computing systems.

The chapter consists of several sections, each addressing one hardware component, such as the central processing unit (CPU), main memory, storage (disk and flash), motherboard, network interface, and fans. This chapter also includes a section discussing existing energy-aware practices in large-scale systems. Leverages are available at several levels, from such subsystems to changing the state of whole computers (using suspend-to-disk or suspend-to-ram and powering on and off [7]).

The above breakdown of resources is based on recent [8] studies by Google that show the following breakdown of power in a server with a local disk:

CPU	37%
Memory	17%
PCI slots	23%
Motherboard	12%
Disk	6%
Fan	5%

Another study performed by Lim et al. [9] obtains results similar to the above.

2.2 PROCESSOR

2.2.1 Context

Power-related issues are considered as one of the most important aspects of designing modern processors because it affects many aspects of the entire system. When discussing power issues, we need to consider different aspects of the problem.

- *Energy Consumption.* How much energy (power multiplied by time) the system consumes when it executes a given piece of work (workload). This parameter mainly affects battery life of mobile systems and the cost of operation of other systems such as servers, data centers, and cloud facilities.
- *Power Consumption.* How much power the processor (or the system) consumes at a given time. This parameter affects the power delivery subsystem and, in many cases, the cooling system, because the die must not exceed its maximum temperature because of physical and reliability limitations.
- *Power Density.* The distribution of power consumption to different subsystems. This parameter has a significant impact on the internal design and the maximum achievable temperature of certain parts of the system. This aspect is out of the scope of this chapter.
- *Dynamic Power versus Idle Power.* The dynamic power is defined as the power the system consumes while working, while the idle power is defined as the power the system or subsystem consumes while not doing any active work (idle). Idle power starts to be very significant in modern architectures. Many techniques proposed to reduce leakage power, all of them require significant latency when moving from sleep mode to active mode.

The processor is very sensitive to each of these aspects of power management; in many systems, the processor consumes a significant part of the entire system's energy consumption, and therefore, the cost of operating and cooling it can be very significant.

More specifically, the amount of heat the processor produces is proportional to the power it consumes, and the power consumption (P) of a processor is given by $P = \alpha * f * V^2$, where α is a constant that depends on the technology; therefore, it depends on its frequency (f) and voltage (V). Thus, in order to prevent the system from overheating, we may need to reduce its frequency, which will consequently affect the performance.

As a result, the power consumption of a processor impacts the direct and indirect costs of the system as well as its performance, making power consumption a major issue in any modern CPU design. However, controlling power consumption only through hardware mechanisms was found not to be optimal, so many hybrid hardware (HW) and software (SW) techniques were developed, such as AMD's PowerNow! and Intel's SpeedStep. These techniques help to control the voltage and the frequency of the processor as a function of the workload being executed, such as the dynamic voltage scaling (DVS). One of the most common techniques to control the different aspects of the power-related issues in processors and the entire system was developed as a consortium between Intel, Microsoft, HP Phoenix, and Toshiba and is called *advanced configuration and power interface* (ACPI).

2.2.2 Advanced Configuration and Power Interface (ACPI)

The ACPI specification [10] is quite complicated and contains 700 pages that cover many SW- and HW-related issues. In this chapter, we focus only on the main features that impact the operation modes of the CPU (processor) and include three mechanisms, namely, thermal control zone, performance state (P-state), and CPU's state (power state).

2.2.2.1 Thermal Control Zone. ACPI defines a set of events to prevent the system from getting overheated. These events include "Trip_points," which are dynamically defined events that indicate to the OS to change the speed of the fan or the speed of the CPU, and a "critical-shutdown" event that indicates that the system MUST shut down immediately to prevent damages [11].

2.2.2.2 C-States. They control how deep the CPU "sleeps" when it is not active. The deeper the CPU goes, less leakage power it consumes but it also significantly increases the latency of the system to wake-up. Thus the ACPI defines four states (as we will see later, HW companies extended it):

- C0 is the operating state, it consumes dynamic power;
- C1 (Halt) is the state where the processor is not executing anything but can come back at C0 in a few cycles (but the saving is minimal);
- C2 (Stop-Clock) is a deeper sleep state that consumes less leakage power than C1 at the cost of a slower wake-up (this state is optional and usually not implemented);
- C3 (Sleep) offers improved power savings with respect to the C1 and C2 states. The worst-case wake-up latency for this state is provided via the ACPI system

firmware, and the operating software can use this information to determine when the C3 can be used and when higher states must be used to guarantee critical response time.

All modern processors extend the notion of C3 to further refinements. For example, I7 (Intel) implements the notion of C6 state. But from the ACPI point of view (SW/HW interfaces), only three of them exist and the rest are handled by HW only.

2.2.2.3 P-States.
P-States indicates how fast the processor should run when in C0 state. System can define a table of frequency/voltage operational points and operating system (OS)/SW can define at what operational work the system will work:

- P_0 is the max frequency/voltage state;
- P_1 is a state where frequency and voltage are reduced;
- P_n, in general, is a state where frequency and voltage are reduced compared to P_{n-1}.

The way OS handles P-States is by applying dynamic learning algorithms. It samples the system for every given period of time (usually 100 ms) and determines the utilization of the system during that period of time. If it finds that the system was "busy" most of the time, it reduces its P-State (faster); if it finds that the CPU was in a sleep state most of the time, then it increases its P-State (slower). By doing that, the systems tries to optimize between the power it is consuming and the performance it can get. These possibilities allow for potential large energy savings [12, 13].

2.2.3 Vendors

2.2.3.1 Advanced Micro Devices (AMD).
Recent Advanced Micro Devices (AMD) processors use PowerNow! and Cool'N'Quiet technology. These two technologies provide means to change processor frequency and voltage. PowerNow! is aimed at laptops, and Cool'N'Quiet is aimed at desktop and servers.

AMD also implements the Turbo Core technology [14], which aims at optimizing the usage of multicores by tuning their frequency when some cores are idle. It has a target of a given maximum power, and when power consumption is lower than the threshold, it boosts the frequency of one core while reducing idle cores frequency of a few hundred megahertz.

2.2.3.2 Intel.
Recently, much information was published [15] regarding the power management of the new I7 processor's family. This section extends the discussion on some of these features to provide a better picture on how power is managed in modern cores.

The implementation of the Throttling mechanism in I7 is not well documented, so we will focus the discussion on the implementation of CoreDuo-2 as appeared in [16]. Here two mechanisms were discussed, the two levels mechanism and the dynamic throttling mechanism.

The two levels mechanism (implemented in P4 family) defines two operation points: "normal" and "halt." While in "normal" mode, the system works in the corresponding P_n state. When the system reaches Max-temp trip point (which is usually at 90 or 100°C), it indicates the OS to change the state to halt. While in "Halt" state, the system waits until it cools down below a specified point and changes to "normal" again. If, for any reason, the system reaches the critical-shutdown point, the HW shuts the system down immediately to prevent any damage [11].

The more sophisticated mechanism employed is dynamic throttling; at any operational point, the system defines two trip points, upper and lower. When the temperature crosses the upper trip point, an HW mechanism forces the system to slow down (redefine the values of the P-state table), and when the temperature crosses the low-trip point, it allows the system to work faster (limited by max frequency).

I7 Core extends the implementation of the C-states and defines a new state called *C6* (because it is not exposed to the ACPI and is purely handled by HW). The states implemented by the I7 Core are the following:

- C0. When the microprocessor is in the active state (some P-State);
- C1. No instructions are being executed; the controller turns off the clocks of all clocks domains pertaining to the core pipeline. Clock gating is accomplished by logically ANDing the clock signal of a particular clock domain with a conditional control signal;
- C3. The core phase-locked-loops (PLLs) are turned off, and all the core caches are flushed. A core in C3 is considered an inactive core. The time it takes for the core to wake up is significantly longer that it does for C1 because the PLLs are linear-feedback-based control systems, which need to be turned back on. Time must be allocated for the PLLs to lock (stabilize) to the correct frequency and return to the "full speed." Besides, the time it takes to the system to return to full utilization is even longer, because of the cold start of the cache memories;
- C6. The most power efficient state, the core PLLs are turned off, the core caches are flushed, and the core state is saved to the last-level cache (LLC). The power gate transistors are activated to reduce leakage power consumption of a particular core to near to 0 W. A core in idle state C6 is considered an inactive core. The wake-up time of a core in the idle state C6 is the longest one, because the core state must be restored from the LLC, the core PLLs must be relocked, the power gates must be deactivated, and the caches start from clean state.

It is worthwhile to note that waking up from C6 may consume significant power, so the system needs to make sure that the power it saves by entering a C6 state is greater than the power it wastes for entering and exiting the state. To prevent unwanted fluctuations, the I7 Core includes an auto-demote capability that uses intelligent heuristics to optimize the use of this aggressive state.

I7 Core also presents a revolutionary approach on how to manage P-states and the overall thermal budget of the core. Intel discovered [17] that when only a single core is active, it never uses the entire power and thermal envelop allowed for the four CPU die. Thus, they introduced the notion of "Intel Turbo Boost Technology" that allows a core to increase its frequency above the maximum allowed frequency (the official frequency of the core) if thermal and power head rooms allow it.

Intel processors also propose a new technique for capping their power. This technique called *RAPL* (*Running Average Power Limit*) is proposed by Intel as a standard. It is currently implemented for Intel processors, but the goal is to implement it for other processors vendors and also other hardware (e.g., memory). This standard proposes common interface for thermal and power point of view. It provides an Application Programming Interface (API) to access the instantaneous thermal values and power consumption, as well as threshold over which those two values should not rise.

2.2.3.3 Apple. Even if Apple is not a chip manufacturer, it is currently the only one to provide a tool for its current OS (MacOSX) for stopping a core on a multi-core processor.

2.2.3.4 International Business Machines Corporation (IBM). Some IBM processors have a low power mode called *Winkle*, which consumes no watts at all. Current sleep modes achieve 15% reduction in the power consumption when implementing an immediate return to execution and achieve 85% of reduction when a latency of 2 ms is allowed to wake up from the sleep mode. In the Winkle low power mode, a 100% reduction in power is achieved, at the expense of a 10-ms delay needed to come back to a running state from the Winkle state. IBM provides in its documentation [18, 19] references of possible working frequencies and voltages for POWER6 and POWER7 series and their corresponding power consumption. Those documents also provide data concerning IBM solutions (fan monitoring and control, thermal control, etc.).

2.2.3.5 Godson. Godson-3B [20] is a Chinese homegrown processor launched in 2011, which has been designed to be used inside Chinese supercomputers. Its main goal is to reach high performance within a low power budget. It achieves this goal with a reduced frequency (1.05 GHz) that performs its 128 billion floating-point operations per second by using only 40 W. This processor uses a hierarchical mesh network to connect its eight cores.

2.2.4 General-Purpose Graphics Processing Unit (GPGPU)

While traditional data centers are not using GPU (graphics processing units) or cells, a current trend for most powerful supercomputers is to use such alternative hybrid architectures (combining CPU with cells/GPU) to deliver ever more processing power. CPUs have a limited number of cores and are optimized to perform serial operations, while GPUs have several thousands of smaller and more efficient cores optimized for parallel operations (natively conceived for massive computations on millions of pixels). When used in a generic way, graphical units are called *GPGPU* (*general-purpose graphics processing units*).

In the Green500 list (June 2013), which provides a ranking of the most energy-efficient supercomputers in the world (sorted by Mflops per Watt), the top end of the list is dominated by heterogeneous supercomputers, those that combine two or more types of processing elements together, such as a CPU/GPGPU. Even if the top one supercomputer (the CINECA consortium supercomputer, in Italy, Eurora,[1] which combines Intel CPUs and nVIDIA GPGPUs, is the most energy-efficient supercomputer in the world (3200 Mflops/W), it only ranks #467 (175.7 TFlop/s Rmax) in the Top500 list (June 2013) of the most powerful supercomputers in the world. However, very large-scale supercomputers can achieve high energy efficiency; it is the case of the world top one supercomputer in the Top500 list, the Tianhe-2[2] of the National University of Defense Technology in China, which reaches 33,862.7 TFlop/s Rmax and rates #8 in the Green500 list (1900 MFlops/W).

The main problem with a GPGPU is when it is idle, because it is not possible to switch off a GPGPU card. Once installed, a GPGPU will consume an important minimal amount of power (not less than 50–60 W). Recently, both AMD and Nvidia started to address the GPGPU-switching-off problem.

AMD Dynamic Switchable Graphics (DSG) allows to shut down transparently the GPGPU. This mechanism is only used in a laptop. In this case, the laptop has two graphic elements, an IGP (integrated graphic processor), which is simple slow but consumes nearly nothing, and a GPGPU. AMD DSG allows to use either of the two graphic elements depending on the load. The GPGPU is connected to a PCI-E link that stays awake even when the GPGPU is switched off (consuming around 50 mW). This mechanism is transparent for the OS, for which it seems that the GPGPU is always there. At run time, video drivers for both IGP and GPGPU are always in the OS. The video drivers decide which of the two components to use. When instructions are sent to the GPGPU, it wakes up and treats them. This choice is done at the driver level. It is possible also to stop this mechanism and to choose to use either the GPGPU or the IGP. Once treated, the GPGPU directly send the result to the IGP framebuffer.

Nvidia Optimus works on the same principle but without the transparency of having the PCI-E proxy always on. In this case, there is only one driver that will receive rendering instructions. Depending on the context (i.e., application), either it will send them to the IGP or it can wake up the GPGPU and use it for rendering. It is not possible to deactivate this system.

2.2.5 ARM Architecture

Not perse a vendor, lot of investments were done around energy-efficient ARM processors. One of the main power-related improvement concerns the Big.LITTLE ARM technology [21]. It encompasses the same die two cores, one is slow but with low power consumption (ARM A7) and the other is faster with higher power consumption (ARM A15). By migrating workload between these two cores, the OS can optimize power consumption depending on workload. A step further has been announced in July 2013 when Fujitsu announced having licensed this technology by integrating an A7 core and an A15 core with four GPGPU ARM-Mali cores. It is now also possible to switch on/off one

---

[1]Eurotech Aurora HPC 10-20, Xeon E5-2687W 8C 3.100GHz, Infiniband QDR, NVIDIA K20.

[2]MilkyWay-2, TH-IVB-FEP Cluster, Intel Xeon E5-2692 12C 2.200GHz, TH Express-2, Intel Xeon Phi 31S1P.

of these two cores. Using such architecture can ease the way to achieve proportional computing [22].

2.3   MEMORY (DRAM)

2.3.1   Context

According to [8, 9], the central memory (random-access memory, RAM) is one of the largest power-consuming subsystems in a typical server with a local disk, accounting for 17% of the total energy consumption. Moreover, CPU and memory are the main contributors to the dynamic power, while other components have very small dynamic range.

In this chapter, we only focus on DRAM (dynamic random-access memory), which is the common memory used in servers.

2.3.2   Power Consumption

To know the power consumption of a DRAM module, it is necessary to understand the basic functionality of the device. DRAM needs periodic refresh to keep the charge (bit) in the capacitors of the integrated circuit. The master operation of the DRAM is controlled by clock enable (CKE) line. If CKE is LOW, the input buffers are turned off. To allow the DRAM to receive commands, the CKE must be HIGH, thus enabling the input buffers and propagates the command/address into the logic/decoders on the DRAM.

During normal operation, the first command sent to the DRAM is typically an active (ACT) command. This command selects a bank and row address. For every ACT command, there is a corresponding precharge (PRE) command. The ACT command opens a row, and the PRE closes the row.

In the active state, the DRAM device can perform READs and WRITEs.

- *Background Power*   During normal operation, the DRAM always consumes background power. When CKE is LOW, most inputs are disabled. This is the lowest power state in which the device can operate. When CKE goes HIGH, commands start propagating through the DRAM command decoders, and the activity increases the power consumption.
- *Activate Power*   To allow a DRAM to READ or WRITE data, a bank and row must first be selected using an ACT command. Following an ACT command, the device uses a significant amount of current to decode the command/address and then transfer the data from the DRAM array to the sense amplifiers. When this is complete, the DRAM is maintained in an active state until a PRE command is issued.
- *Write and Read Power*   After a bank is open, data can be either read from or written to the DRAM. The two cases are similar.
- *I/O Termination Power*   This is the power consumed by the output driver or on-die termination.

- *Refresh Power*   Refresh is the final power component that must be calculated for the device to retain data integrity. DDR3 memory cells store data information in small capacitors that lose their charge over time and must be recharged.

2.3.3   Energy Efficiency Techniques

Current solutions are mainly based on lowering the voltage of DRAM that can reduce the power use of the CPU–memory subsystem quite significantly. Common DDR3 runs in the range of 1.25–1.6 V operating at 1600 MHz. In contrast, DDR4, which is still far to be produced in mass, requires less energy (1.05–1.2 V) and operates up to 3200 MHz.

Other solutions exploit the multiple power states such as active, standby, nap, and power-down of the DRAM manufacturers. The chip must be in the active state to service a request. The remaining states are in order of decreasing power consumption but increasing time to transition back to active. Energy efficiency can be improved by placing the chips in a lower power state when not used. The challenge is to understand the characteristics of memory access patterns in a cache-based memory architecture and how those patterns affect the design of power-management controller policies to control the transition among power states.

Recently, a joint initiative in the European-funded project EuroCloud pushes ARM Cortex A9 processors, linked with 3D DRAM to create 3D server on chip, serving as a basis for energy-efficient data centers.[3]

Other research solutions aim at reducing the refreshing time to lowering the energy consumption, developing delay-hiding energy management mechanisms for DRAM, combining adaptive DRAM temperature and power management with TAP-low, adapting the DRAM row buffer policy in accordance with both locality and activity in memory access patterns, exploring the design space of contemporary DRAM array organizations by varying the number of pages that can be concurrently accessed and the size of the pages, and eliminating over fetch in DRAM systems by activating only the necessary bit-lines (selective bit-line activation, SBA). By reducing the number of memory bank allocated to processes, memory improves the power consumption when the hardware supports switching off memory banks [23].

On the other hand, other initiatives are promoting the use of mobile DRAM devices that produce lower energy consumption per bit and more efficient idle modes at the expense of a reduced peak bandwidth [24].

For a comprehensive survey on architectural techniques for DRAM power management, readers can refer to [25].

2.3.4   Vendors

2.3.4.1   Kingston. Kingston recently dropped its latest "LoVo" (low voltage) HyperX® DDR3 high performance memory product line that will run at anything down to 1.25 V at 1333 MHz, or even 1866 MHz at 1.35 V with its built-in XMP profile. The flagship product, running an ultra-low 1.25 Vat 1600 MHz, is the lowest voltage to date for desktop personal computers (PCs).

---

[3]EuroCloud:http://www.eurocloudserver.com/.

2.3.4.2   *Micron.* Micron's energy-efficient Aspen Memory product line features 1.5-V DDR2 and 1.35-V DDR3 reduced chip count (RCC) modules, specifically designed to lower data center server power consumption.

Micron claims that when the 1.5-V modules, for example, are implemented into data center server systems in place of 1.8-V solutions, the reduced voltage cuts power consumption by 16% outright.

The RCC also affects overall savings. RCC fully buffered dual in-line memory modules (FBDIMMs) deliver the same performance and memory capacity with half the number of components; less heat is generated because there are fewer modules, and so cooling costs are lower.

Micron is introducing a 64-GB load reduced dual in-line memory module (LRDIMM) in DRAM families to meet the ever-growing density requirements of servers. Micron provides 50% higher memory capacity and a performance increase of 33% for server applications. Resulting improvements to system scalability can significantly enhance cloud computing, high performance computing, Web servers, transactional databases, and data analytics while reducing power needs by nearly 10% per dual in-line memory module (DIMM) slot compared to standard modules.

2.3.4.3   *Samsung.* Samsung aims at optimizing the base consumption of its "Green memory" product line. Similar to other vendors, they do not provide dynamic way to reduce energy. Samsung uses 40-nm and 30-nm technology and reduced voltage to reduce this base consumption. The following data can be found in [26]:

Size, GB	Process Technology, nm	Tension, V	Consumption (for a 48-GB server active for 8 h a day), W
1	60	1.8	102
1	60	1.5	66
1	50	1.5	50
1	40	1.5	41
2	40	1.5	34
2	40	1.35	28
2	30	1.35	24
4	30	1.35	14

Samsung has launched the 20-nm class 4Gb DDR3 DRAM memory using 1.35 V (optional 1.25 V), and this memory can cut power consumption by 67%, compared to 50-nm class DDR3 2Gb1.5V, today's most commonly used DRAM server solutions.

2.4   DISK/FLASH

Disk drives are the primary storage medium in today's storage systems. The mechanical disk design is the dominating factor in its energy consumption. In order to be able to quickly serve input/output (I/O) requests, the disk platters must always be spinning. The disk controls the platters' spin and maintains a communication channel with the host. These two factors are the main contributors to the constant portion of the disk energy consumption, which amounts to about two-third of the total energy consumption under load.

Disk drive technology allows three main control knobs:

- Spindle speed
- Seek speed
- Disk power mode.

2.4.1   Spindle Speed

The energy consumption of the spindle motor is quadratic to the platters RPM (revolutions per minute). Therefore, a reduction in RPM has a dramatic effect on the energy consumption. The term DRPM (dynamic revolutions per minute) [27–30] refers to the ability to vary the spindle RPM that allows the disk to serve I/O requests at different RPMs and data transfer rates. Unfortunately, manufacturing disks that support DRPM is not easy and there are no commercially available disk drives that support DRPM.

However, allowing the disk to reduce its RPM during idle is easy, as the disk head can be parked outside the platters during this idle time. Moving the heads outside the platter is required before slowing down the spindle RPM.

Some disk vendors allow the disk RPM to be reduced by about a quarter of its operational RPM (e.g., from 7200 to 5400 RPM when idle), thus reducing the constant energy consumption. In some cases, this can reduce the energy consumption for idle by almost half of the regular idle energy consumption.

2.4.2   Seek Speed

Disk drives can control the disk head acceleration, deceleration, and velocity by applying different currents to the voice-coil motor that moves the disk head. Vendors such as Seagate and Western Digital introduced such mechanisms in their disks. With Seagate's JIT [31] or Western Digital's IntelliSeek™ mode, the acceleration and speed of the disk head is adjusted so that the disk head will arrive at its destination in time for the data to be located beneath the disk head. This is opposed to normal mode, where the disk head may arrive too early, and will wait until the data is beneath the disk head. This method of slowing down the disk head leads to reduced acoustics and energy consumption without any performance degradation.

The SATA specification [32] includes a standard automatic acoustic management (AAM) feature. This feature allows vendors to define various acoustic modes for the disk. Currently, vendors include only two modes, a normal acoustic mode and a quiet acoustic mode. In the quiet mode, the disk performs seek operations at a reduced velocity (compared to normal mode); as a result, the peak energy consumption of the disk drive is reduced.

2.4.3 Power Modes

Power modes mainly have to do with the state of the disk when idle. Various vendors have increased the number of available power modes, for example, unloading and parking the heads, which reduces friction, or slowing down to a low RPM idle mode.

The SATA specification defines an advanced power management (APM) feature, which supports moving a disk from one power mode to another, following a predefined settings (e.g., a given idle period), without the need to receive a specific command from the host. In addition to placing the disk at a lower power mode, recent works focus on putting the communication link between the host and the disk in a lower power mode. This may be very beneficial, as maintaining the communication link consumes a considerable amount of energy — this is especially noticeable when a disk enters a lower power mode but still needs to be able to receive commands, such as a spin-up command, from the host.

A complementary approach to the above is maximizing the idle interval time between non-idle periods [29, 33]. This allows for longer intervals in which the disk can be placed in a lower power mode or turned off. The concept of massive array of idle disks (MAID), where most of the system disk drives are turned off, is the result of this approach [30, 34].

2.4.4 Power Consumption

Typical hard disk drives (HDDs) consume (numbers for a 2-TB Seagate Constellation ES at 7200 RPM, SATA, 140 MB/s transfer rate, 3″5) about 7 W when idle and 10–11 W when busy (read operations being more power consuming). Lower capacity disks consume less power, down to 4.6/9.4/8.2 W (idle/read/write) for a 500-GB HDD. On these disks, for instance, a PowerChoice mode (a proprietary implementation of T10 and T13 Standards [35, 36]) makes the disk power consumption drop down to 0.53 W. Smaller disks (2.5″ form factor), originally intended only for laptops, are now getting much interest for data centers, despite their more limited capacities at comparable performances. They run at about half the power of 3.5″ disks and takes less space in the racks. For instance, the Savvio (15K.2, 15,000 RPM, SAS) offers 146 GB and consumes just 4.1 W when idle.

2.4.5 Solid-State Drive (SDD)

Solid-state drives (SDD) are garnering much interest in the past years. Their most important feature is the improved access time; a multilevel cell (MLC) SSD has an access time of just 0.5 ms, compared with an access time of 15.7 ms for a 7200 RPM drive. Please note that the highest performances coming for SDD access rate can be limited from an application point of view in some cases (see study on the comparison metrics [37]). As no mechanics exist in an SSD drive, the power consumption is only a fraction of the one of a HDD. A typical Seagate SDD (Pulsar, 200-GB, SATA, 300 MB/s) consumes only 0.75 W when idle and 1.3 W in operation. This improved energy performance comes with a higher price and limited capacities, making them not really sustainable in big data centers that host terabytes or petabytes of data.

2.5 FAN

Fans can have an impact during the boot time because, generally, fans start at full speed during the boot sequence and then reduce their speed in case the part they cool is not overheated [38]. This has a large impact on several energy reduction technique that switch down computers when they are not needed because those techniques then need to switch on a potentially large number of nodes together leading to a high power consumption peak.

But even during classical runs, impacts can be high. In [39], authors show that for blades (c7000), consumption by fans can go up to 16–20% of the global consumption.

Fans can be controlled using ACPI commands, which can also provide some information such as the rotation speed.

2.6 POWER SUPPLY UNIT

Most current computers still use an independent power supply unit (PSU). Owing to current technological limitation, their yield are still usually limited at around 80%. In this case, 20% of energy consumed by a computer only heat the computer PSU. Moreover, depending on the load on the PSU, this yield can change.

The 80 Plus[4] initiative tries to improve awareness of the efficiency of PSU by multilevel certification.

80 PLUS Certification	115-V Internal Nonredundant			230-V Internal Redundant		
Percentage of rated load	20%	50%	100%	20%	50%	100%
80 PLUS	80%	80%	80%	N/A		
80 PLUS Bronze	82%	85%	82%	81%	85%	81%
80 PLUS Silver	85%	88%	85%	85%	89%	85%
80 PLUS Gold	87%	90%	87%	88%	92%	88%
80 PLUS Platinum	90%	92%	89%	90%	94%	91%

Recent efforts are done to completely remove PSU by using directly direct current (DC) infrastructure. A 2007 survey[5] showed that 11% of data center operators have tried DC power in the data center.

Impact is rather large and concerns two distinct improvements.[6]

- *Space* A DC data center needs 25–40 less space than an alternating current (AC) one. It is mainly due to the simplification of connection to battery and by removing PSU.

[4]http://www.80plus.org.

[5]http://searchdatacenter.techtarget.com/tip/Does-DC-power-win-the-direct-current-vs-alternating-current-debate.

[6]Greentechmedia 2011: http://www.greentechmedia.com/articles/read/a-roadmap-to-green-it/

- *Efficiency* As shown before, PSU have an efficiency of 80%, and cooling is necessary to remove heat created by this inefficiency. Thus DC shows a gain of around 35% compared to AC.

2.7 NETWORK INFRASTRUCTURE

2.7.1 Current Scenario

The evolution of the routers capacity and energy consumption from 1997 to 2008 is studied in [40]. In the 10-year time span, the bandwidth has increased by a factor of 1000 and the energy consumption has decreased by a factor of 100, meaning that the net energy consumption has increased by a factor of 10. In other words, the technological advancements foreseen by Moore and Gilders' laws have not been fully compensated by a similar growth in the energy efficiency.

However, if we compare the total power consumption of electronic and optical routers/switches reported in [40], we can observe that optical devices consume 10 times less energy than their electrical counterpart.

As an example, an optical cross-connect node (OXC) with micro-electro-mechanical system (MEMS) fabric consumes 1.2 W for a 10-Gbps interface, while an Internet Protocol (IP) router requires 237 W for the same port [40].

Such numbers suggest that the optical networks should be employed whenever possible to reduce the energy consumption. Besides, also inside optical networking, a number of measures can be taken to further decrease the power consumption, including the following:

- Avoid reamplified, reshaped, and resynchronized (3R) regeneration as much as possible: currently, when the optical signal is too degraded, it is 3R in the electronic domain before being inserted again in the optical fibers. This process is particularly energy consuming (60 W per optical channel); therefore, careful planning, designing, and managing should be put in place in order to avoid 3R regenerations as possible for the paths being established.
- Optical amplification (OA) should be used instead to keep the signal in an acceptable SNR (signal-to-noise ratio); however, several OAs are available, being the most common the EDFA (erbium-doped fiber amplifiers), which feature good performance (high gain, low insertion loss, low noise, and cross-talk effects) and amplify the whole C-Band, but have also higher energy consumption than SOA (silicon-based optical amplifiers), respectively, 25 and 3 W.
- Use dispersion compensation fibers (DSF ITU-T G.653, NZ-DSF ITU-T G.655/656) instead of "simple" single mode fiber (SMF, ITU-T G.652), to reduce the dispersion of the optical signal in the fiber and to reduce the number of required optical amplifiers.

Considering the access, metro, and backbone network segments, in the current infrastructure, the vast majority of the energy consumption can be attributed to fixed line access networks.

This is mainly due to the large number of users that are connected to the Internet. Today, access networks are mainly implemented with copper-based technologies such as asymmetric digital subscriber line (ADSL) and very-high-bit-rate digital subscriber line (VDSL) whose energy consumption is very sensible to increased bit rates. The trend is to replace such technologies with mobile and fiber infrastructure, which is expected to increase considerably the energy efficiency in access networks. As an example, an ADSL link consumes about 2.8 W, while a GPON (gigabit-capable passive optical network) requires only 0.5 W (with an improvement of 80% in the energy efficiency). Such ongoing replacement, together with the fact that the number of users connected in the Internet will increase at a slower pace because the vast majority of population in developed countries is already connected, is moving the problem to the backbone networks, which have to transport the users demand for rich contents.

The energy consumption for IP routers is becoming a bottleneck [41, 42]. In 2009, the backbone energy consumption accounted for less than 10% of the overall network energy consumption, but this percentage is expected to increase to 40% by 2017. As an example, in Japan, it is expected that by 2015, IP routers will consume 9% of the nation's electricity [43]. Soon, the so-called "energy bottleneck" may become more significant than the "electronic speed bottleneck"; the Cisco largest multishelf router (CRS-1 92 Tbps) requires 80 racks to carry the networking equipment and has a power consumption of 1 MW.

A way to provide a smooth transition may be represented by the integration between IP/packet layer, optical transport layer, and control layer in the so-called multilayer approach [44, 45]. In the past, these layers evolved with different constraints and without an overall optimization, which has led to the issues we are facing today such as inefficient energy strategy, limited network scalability and flexibility, reduced network manageability, and increased overall network and costumer services costs. It is clear that a technique that is able to provide an optimal solution in several layers can cope better with the variety of possible phenomena in an overall efficient way and can benefit from the advantages of the solution in each layer.

2.7.2 New Energy-Oriented Model

Of course, advancements in the technologies can provide increases in the energy efficiency (energy per bit) of devices, but increased energy efficiency does not lead always to overall reduced energy consumption, as argued in the Khazzoom–Brookes postulate [46, 47]: "increased energy efficiency paradoxically tends to lead to increased energy consumption" (a phenomenon also known as the *Jevons paradox* or, simply, as *rebound effect*). In fact, an improvement of the energy efficiency leads to a reduction of the operating costs, so that the demand may increase and consequently the energy consumption of the networking, possibly overtaking the offset gained by the increased efficiency.

A paradigm shift is required in networks in order to sustain the growing traffic rates for limiting or even decreasing the power consumption. This shift can be accomplished through a number of measures.

- *Energy efficiency* is the first improvement that leads to reduced consumption through technological innovations (such as new materials and new manufacturing processes) without affecting the performance; Such solutions are usually referred as *eco-friendly solutions*.

- *Energy awareness* is the next step toward eco-sustainability; it refers to an intelligent technique that adapts the behavior or performance of the system based on the knowledge of the quantity and quality (energy source) of the energy the equipment is expending.

Apart from energy efficiency and energy awareness, the use of green renewable energy source is a fundamental step for the reduction of the greenhouse gas (GHG) emissions, because a green energy source does not emit CO_2 during its use phase, making it possible to deploy "zero carbon" solutions.

Therefore, to become a reality, green Internet must rely on energy efficiency, energy awareness, green renewable energy sources connected through smart grids, and a system approach studying the whole LCA (life cycle assessment) of new solutions. Such an *energy-oriented approach* defines a comprehensive solution encompassing both energy-efficient devices and energy-aware algorithms and protocols acting in a systemic approach.

Other possible measure is the intelligent designing of ICT premises and energy sources. For example, rather than bringing the electrical power to data centers (with relatively high power losses), it seems more appropriate to move the data centers to the source of renewable power and connect them to Internet with long reach fiber-optic cable. Another alternative is to increase the use of thin clients instead of desktop PCs [48]; a thin client consumes less energy but requires a distributed system and a network able to support it.

2.7.3 Current Advances in Networking

Nonetheless, current router architectures are not energy aware, in the sense that their energy consumption does not scale sensibly with the traffic load. In [49], several router architectures have been analyzed and their energy consumption under different traffic loads have been evaluated. Results show that the energy consumption between an idle and a heavily loaded router (with 75% of offered traffic load) vary only of 3% (about 25 W on 750 W). This happens because the router line cards, which are the most power-consuming elements in a router, are always powered on even if they are totally idle. On the contrary, the energy consumption decreases to just 50% if the idle line cards are physically disconnected. Such a scenario suggests that future router architectures will be energy aware, in the sense that they will be able to automatically switch off or dynamically down-clock-independent subsystems (e.g., line cards, input/output ports, switching fabrics, and buffers) according to the traffic loads in order to save energy whenever possible. Such energy-aware architectures are advocated by both standardization bodies and governmental programs [50] and have been assumed by various literature sources that propose optimization based on smart power-aware routing [51, 52].

For what regards the energy efficiency, the pioneering work in [51] suggested the introduction of sleep mode in networks. When elements are idle, their power consumption is obviously wasteful; turning these elements off reduces the power consumption. Although such functionality may not bring any advantageous when used alone, recent results (see, e.g., [48, 53]) showed that if applied in multilayer scenario, sleep mode can substantially reduce the energy consumption without a corresponding decrease in the network performance. For example, combining traffic grooming (at IP layer) to maximize the utilization of optical transmission links and transparent optical path (at the optical layer) to bypass routers wherever possible (so to reduce the hop count) is an optimal trade-off solution to increase energy efficiency. In such a situation, in fact, the utilization of active interfaces and links are maximized while unused interfaces or even entire router and switch components can be put in sleep mode [52].

Today, energy consumption of Ethernet networks is not greatly linked with bandwidth utilization. So even in low or no usage context, networks equipment consumes energy at high level. Currently, two main techniques have been developed to reduce the power consumption of network interface cards (NIC): Adaptive Link Rate (ALR) and Low Power Idle (LPI).

2.7.4 Adaptive Link Rate (ALR)

In ALR, the idea is to dynamically modify the interface link rate according to the instantaneous traffic (throughput). If, for example, a 10-Gbps legacy interface is transmitting just 1 Gbps of traffic, it automatically fills the channel with stuffing bits in order to always reach the nominal 10-Gbps link rate. With ALR, the interface link rate would be down-clocked to 1 Gbps to match the actual throughput, thus saving energy.

2.7.5 Low Power Idle (LPI)

In LPI, the idea is to always transmit the traffic at the maximum speed, and "sleep" during idle periods, during which just a periodic refresh is sent to not loose the link connectivity (as periodic keep-alive messages). LPI has the advantage to occupy the channel only for the strict time that is needed for the transmission, which will be lower than the corresponding ALR solution, which transmits at lower bitrate, thus occupying the channel for longer time for the same amount of traffic.

However, the effectiveness of LPI strongly depends on the packet arrival distribution; therefore, packet coalescing, buffering, or coordinated Ethernet techniques are required to synchronize the packets and get some gains [54–56].

In order to choose the best local strategy for network interface, a consortium mixing academic and industries was set up by the IEEE, which eventually selected the LPI to be used in the energy-efficient Ethernet compliant NICs and was standardized as the IEEE P802.3az.

2.7.6 Energy-Aware Dynamic RWA Framework

For what regards the energy awareness, anything less than a target of zero carbon emissions throughout the entire ICT system will be pointless because of the Khazzoom–Brookes postulate; with a zero carbon footprint any increase in consumption will still result in a total cumulative zero carbon footprint. In such direction, recent studies propose to include the information on the energy sources in the network operations [44, 57].

At the same time, the market is now offering renewable power supplies (mainly solar panels) for network sites (both nodes and amplifier sites) in such a way that legacy (dirty) energy sources are used only to guarantee power supply without any interruption. Also the deployment of smart grids can provide green renewable energy to telecom networks, and even more advanced techniques to orchestrate services between telecom networks and smart grids control plane can be developed [58].

Accordingly, it is necessary to envisage how the next-generation network architectures and protocols can be modified to meet the purpose of energy-oriented networking. Unfortunately, the rush for achieving energy efficiency has caused that many solutions [59, 60] tend to minimize only the energy consumption of the networks while disregarding the traditional network management goals such as the overall network load balancing. It is instead mandatory to guarantee that the above modifications will not adversely affect the fundamental operators' optimization objectives of keeping the resource usage fairly balanced, to save on each available link sufficient free capacity for demands that may reasonably emerge in the infrastructure operating lifetime, and minimizing the network usage costs, considered as a static way of expressing operator preference to choose some favorite link resources [57]. In the ideal case, new solutions should not only lower the ecological footprint but also increase the offered quality of service such as the connection blocking probability.

Starting from the above considerations, in [57], the authors introduced energy awareness into control plane protocols whose goal is to properly condition all the route/path selection mechanisms on relatively coarse time scales by privileging the use of renewable energy sources and energy-efficient links/switching devices, simultaneously taking advantage from the different users' demands across the interested network infrastructures, in such a way that the overall power consumption can be optimized while the traditional optimization objectives (such as load balancing) are not disrupted. In doing this, they tried to combine all the notable features that a comprehensive energy-aware network model should have and put them together into a general routing and wavelength assignment (RWA) framework.

Specifically, because the RWA problem is known to be NP-complete [61], they introduced a new heuristic method for efficiently calculating (in polynomial times) the routing information subject to power consumption constraints, by taking into account also the specific kind of energy source (dirty or renewable) used for powering the traversed network elements. The selected paths are unlikely to be the shortest ones, but the resulting power savings are substantial, and possible losses on the other optimization objectives are taken into account and considered as negligible.

2.7.7 Energy-Aware Network Attacks

Finally, it is worthwhile to present a new kind of menace that energy awareness introduces. Traditionally, energy awareness and network/site security have developed considerably separately. However, there are areas in common between these two fields. Network attacks, such as DDoS (distributed denial of service), can be put in place to exploit weaknesses in the power saving mechanism of network infrastructure or data centers in order to cause financial damage to the victim by increasing the energy consumption of the sites [62].

Such attacks perform their activity by trying to keep the target system as busy as possible and preventing it to enter a low power consumption state, making it always work at near maximum speed or frequency/voltage. It is important to observe that the more energy proportional a device is, the more it is vulnerable to such types of attacks. Network interface cards, CPUs, and disks, for example, that employ advanced sleep mode techniques to save energy during inactivity periods, can sensibly vary their energy consumption according to their instantaneous working load. Another important observation is that it is not necessary for an attack to gain access to the system in order to be effective under the energy consumption perspective: leveraging on the IDS/IPS (intrusion detection and prevention systems) to make them consume more power will be sufficient to cause economical damage.

REFERENCES

[1] Raghavan B, Ma J. The energy and emergy of the Internet. Proceedings of the 10th ACM Workshop on Hot Topics in Networks (HotNets-X); 2011 Nov; Cambridge (MA); 2011.

[2] CISCO. Cisco visual networking index [online]. Available at http://www.cisco.com/en/US/netsol/ns827/networking_solutions_sub_solution.html. Accessed 2014 Sep 26.

[3] Internet World Stats. Internet world stats online. Available at http://www.internetworldstats.com/emarketing.htm. Accessed 2014 Sep 26.

[4] bluehost. Etforecasts [online]. Available at http://www.etforecasts.com/products/ES_intusersv2.htm. Accessed 2014 Sep 26.

[5] Global Action Plan. An inefficient Truth by the Global Action Plan. Available at http://www.globalactionplan.org.uk/upload/resource/Full-report.pdf. Accessed 2014 Sep 26.

[6] Network of Excellence in Internet Science. Deliverable 8.1 "Overview of ICT energy consumption", FP7-288021, Feb 2013.

[7] Zi C, Zhang C, Lin Q, Qi Z, Gao S. Suspend-to-PCM: a new power-aware strategy for operating system's rapid suspend and resume. In: *Emerging Technologies for Information Systems, Computing, and Management*. Springer New York; 2013. p 667–674.

[8] Fan X, Weber W, Barroso LA. Power provisioning for a warehouse-sized computer. Proceedings of the 34th Annual International Symposium on Computer Architecture; 2007 09–13 June; San Diego (CA); ISCA '07; 2007.

[9] Lim K, Ranganathan P, Chang J, Patel C, Mudge T, Reinhardt S. Understanding and designing new server architectures for emerging warehouse-computing environments. SIGARCH Comput Arch News 2008;36(3):315–326.

[10] ACPI. ACPI specification. Available at http://www.acpi.info/spec.htm. Accessed 2014 Sep 26.

[11] Rotem E, Naveh A, Moffie M, Mendelson A. Analysis of thermal monitor features of the Intel Pentium M processor. TACS Workshop, At ISCA-31; 2004 June; 2004.

[12] Weste N, Eshragian K. *Principles of CMOS VLSI Design: A Systems Perspective*. Reading (MA): Addison-Wesley Publishing Company; 1988.

[13] Chandrakasan AP, Brodersen RW. Minimizing power consumption in digital CMOS circuits. Proceedings of the IEEE 83.4; 1995. p 498–523.

[14] Anandtech. AMD Reveals More Llano Details at ISSCC: 32nm, Power Gating, 4-cores, Turbo? Available at http://www.anandtech.com/show/2933. Accessed 2014 Sep 26, 2014.

[15] Intel IMVP6.5 Core i7 CPU Core Power Design, Texas Instrument [online]. Available at http://www.ti.com/tool/pmp5800. Accessed Dec. 10, 2014.

[16] Naveh A, Roterm E, Mendelson A, Gochman S, Chabukswar R, Krishnan K, Kumar A. Power and thermal management in the intel core duo processor architecture. Intel Technol J 2006;10(02):109–122.

[17] Jon Stokes, Power gating and turbo mode: Intel talks Nehalem at DF. http://arstechnica.com/gadgets/2008/08/power-gating-and-turbo-mode-intel-talks-nehalem-at-idf/ Accessed Sep. 26, 2014.

[18] IBM. IBM EnergyScale for POWER6 Processor-Based Systems; Oct 2009.

[19] IBM. IBM EnergyScale for POWER7 Processor-Based Systems; Apr 2011.

[20] Hu W, Wang R, Chen Y, Fan B, Zhong S, Gao X, Qi Z, Yang X. Godson-3B: a 1GHz 40W 8-core 128GFlops processor in 65nm CMOS. Solid-State Circuits Conference Digest of Technical Papers (ISSCC), IEEE International; 2011.

[21] Greenhalgh P. Big. Little Processing with Arm Cortex.-a15 & Cortex-a7. Technical report. ARM Whitepaper; 2011. http://www.arm.com/files/downloads/big_LITTLE_Final_Final.pdf.

[22] Da Costa G. Heterogeneity: the key to achieve power-proportional computing. *IEEE International Symposium on Cluster Computing and the Grid (CCGrid 2013)*. Delft: IEEE; 2013. p 656–662.

[23] Bathen LAD, Gottscho M, Dutt N, Nicolau A, Gupta P. ViPZonE: OS-level memory variability-driven physical address zoning for energy savings. *Proceedings of the 8th IEEE/ACM/IFIP International Conference on Hardware/software Codesign and System Synthesis*. ACM; 2012. p 33–42.

[24] Malladi KT, Nothaft FA, Periyathambi K, Lee BC, Kozyrakis C, Horowitz M. Towards energy-proportional datacenter memory with mobile DRAM. Proceedings of 39th Annual International Symposium on Computer Architecture (ISCA 2012); 2012 9–13 June; Portland (OR); 2012.

[25] Millal S. A survey of architectural techniques for DRAM power management. Int J High Perform Syst Arch 2012;4(2):110–119.

[26] Kadivar S. Green Memory Moving into the Driver's Seat, At Intel Developer Forum; 2009.

[27] Carrera EV, Pinheiro E, Bianchini R. Conserving disk energy in network servers. Proceedings of the 17th Annual International Conference on Supercomputing, 2003 June; 2003. p 86–97.

[28] Gurumurthi S, Sivasubramaniam A, Kandemir M, and Franke H. DRPM: dynamic speed control for power management in server class disks. Proceedings of the 30th Annual International Symposium on Computer Architecture; 2003 June; 2003. p 169–181.

[29] Li X, Li Z, David F, Zhou P, Zhou Y, Adve S, Kumar S. Performance directed energy management for main memory and disks. *Proceedings of the International Conference on Architectural Support for Programming Languages and Operating Systems*. ACM Press; 2004. p 271–283, New York.

[30] Pinheiro E, Bianchini R. Energy conservation techniques for disk array-based servers. Proceedings of the 18th Annual International Conference on Supercomputing; 2004 June; 2004. p 68–78.

[31] Seagate. Seagate's sound barrier technology (SBT); 2000. Available at http://www.seagate.com/docs/pdf/whitepaper/sound_barrier.pdf. Accessed 2014 Sep 26.

[32] INCITS 361-2002 (1410D): AT attachment - 6 with packet interface (ATA/ATAPI - 6); 2002.

[33] Gurumurthi S, Zhang J, Sivasubramaniam A, Kandemir M, Franke H, Vijaykrishnan N, Irwin MJ. Interplay of energy and performance for disk arrays running transaction processing workloads. Proceedings of the International Symposium on Performance Analysis of Systems and Software; 2003 March; 2003. p 123–132.

[34] Colarelli D, Grunwald D. Massive arrays of idle disks for storage archives. Proceedings of the 2002 ACM/IEEE conference on High Performance Networking and Computing; 2002 Nov; 2002. p 1–11.

[35] incits. SCSI Specification: INCITS Technical Committee T10 subcommittee SCSI. Available at www.t13.org/ Accessed 2014 Sep 26.

[36] incits. SATA Specification: INCITS Technical Committee T13 subcommittee ATA. Available at www.t13.org/. Accessed 2014 Sep 26.

[37] Rydning J, Reinsel D, Janukowicz J. White paper: the need to standardize storage device performance metrics; Sept 2008.

[38] Orgerie A-C, Lefevre L, Gelas J-P. Save watts in your grid: green strategies for energy-aware framework in large scale distributed systems. ICPADS 2008: The 14th IEEE International Conference on Parallel and Distributed Systems; 2008 Dec; Melbourne; 2008.

[39] Itoh S, Kodama Y, Nakamura H, Mori N, Shimizu T, Sekiguchi S. Measuring and Modeling of a Data Center.

[40] BONE project. WP 21 TP Green Optical Networks D21.2b Report on Y1 and updated plan for activities; 2009.

[41] Lange C, Kosiankowski D, Gerlach C, Westphal F, Gladisch A. Energy consumption of telecommunication networks. Proceedings ECOC 2009; 2009 Sep; Vienna, Austria; 2009.

[42] Tucker RS, Parthiban R, Baliga J, Hinton K, Ayre RWA, Sorin WV. Evolution of WDM optical IP networks: a cost and energy perspective. IEEE/OSA J Lightw Technol 2009;27:3.

[43] Nature Publishing Group. Nature photonics. Nature Photonics Technology Conference 2007; 2007 Oct 23–25; Tokyo, Japan; 2007.

[44] Ricciardi S, Careglio D, Santos-Boada G, Solé-Pareta J, Fiore U, Palmieri F. Towards an energy-aware Internet: modeling a cross-layer optimization approach. Telecommun Syst (Springer) 2013;52(2):1247–1268. ISSN: 1018-4864, DOI: 0.1007/s11235-011-9645-7, published online 17 Sep 2011.

[45] Puype B, Vereecken W, Colle D, Pickavet M, Demeester P. Power reduction techniques in multilayer traffic engineering. Proceedings ICTON 2009; 2009 Jun; Säo Miguel, Azores, Portugal; 2009.

[46] Saunders HD. The Khazzoom–Brookes postulate and neoclassical growth. Energy J 1992;13(4):131–148.

[47] Sorrell S. Jevons' Paradox revisited: the evidence for backfire from improved energy efficiency. Energy Policy 2009;37:1456–1469.

[48] Pickavet M, Van Caenegem R, Demeyer S, Audenaert P, Colle D, Demeester P, Leppla R, Jaeger M, Gladisch A, Foisel H-M. Energy footprint of ICT. Broadband Europe 2007, Dec 2007.

[49] Chabarek J, Sommers J, Barford P, Estan C, Tsiang D, Wright S. Power awareness in network design and routing. Proceedings of the IEEE INFOCOM; 2008.

[50] Energy Star. Energy Star, Small network equipment. Available at http://www.energystar.gov/index.cfm?c=new_specs.small_network_equip. Accessed 2014 Sep 26.

[51] Gupta M, Singh S. Greening of the internet. Proceedings of the ACM SIGCOMM 2003; Aug 2003; Karlsruhe.

[52] Muhammad A, Monti P, Cerutti I, Wosinska L, Castoldi P, Tzanakaki A. Energy-efficient WDM network planning with protection resources in sleep mod. accepted for Globecom 2010, ONS01.

[53] Tucker RS, Baliga J, Ayre R, Hinton K, Sorin WV. Energy consumption in IP networks. Proceedings of ECOC 2008; Sep 2008; Brusseles, Belgium; 2008.

[54] Christensen K, Nordman B. Reducing the Energy Consumption of Networked Devices. IEEE 802.3 tutorial; Jul 19 2005.

[55] Kubo R, Kani J, Fujimoto Y, Yoshimoto N, Kumozaki K. Sleep and adaptive link rate control for power saving in 10GEPON systems. Proceedings of Globecom; 2009.

[56] Nedevschi S, Popa L, Iannaccone G, Ratnasamy S, Wetherall D. Reducing network energy consumption via sleeping and rate adaptation. Proceedings of the 5th USENIX Symposium on Networked Systems Design and Implementation, NSDI'08, Apr 2008.

[57] Ricciardi S, Palmieri F, Fiore U, Careglio D, Santos-Boada G, Solé-Pareta J. An energy-aware dynamic RWA framework for next-generation wavelength-routed networks. Comput Netw (Elsevier) 2012;56(10):2420–2442. ISSN 1389-1286, DOI: 10.1016/j.comnet.2012.03.016.

[58] Ricciardi S, Santos-Boada G, Klinkowski M, Careglio D, Palmieri F. Towards service orchestration between smart grids and telecom networks. Energy Efficiency in Large Scale Distributed Systems (EE-LSDS 2013), COST IC0804 European Conference; 2013 Apr 22–24; Vienna. LNCS, Volume 8046, Subseries: Computer Communication Networks and Telecommunications; 2013, X, 299 p 127 illus.

[59] Shen G, Tucker RS. Energy-minimized design for IP over WDM networks. IEEE/OSA J Opt Commun Netw 2009;1(1):176–186.

[60] Idzikowski F, Orlowski S, Raack C, Woesner H, Wolisz A. Saving energy in IP-over-WDM networks by switching off line cards in low-demand scenarios. Proceedings of the 14th Conference on Optical Networks Design and Modeling (ONDM). 2010.

[61] Chlamtac I, Ganz A, Karmi G. Lightpath communications: an approach to high-bandwidth optical WANs. IEEE Trans Commun 1992;40:1171–1182.

[62] Palmieri F, Ricciardi S, Fiore U. Evaluating network-based DoS attacks under the energy consumption perspective: new security issues in the coming green ICT area. International Conference on Broadband and Wireless Computing, Communication and Applications (BWCCA); 2011 Oct 26–28; 2011. p 374–379.

3

GREEN WIRED NETWORKS

Alfonso Gazo Cervero,[1] Michele Chincoli,[2] Lars Dittmann,[3] Andreas Fischer,[4] Alberto E. Garcia,[5] Jaime Galán-Jiménez,[1] Laurent Lefevre,[6] Hermann de Meer,[4] Thierry Monteil,[7] Paolo Monti,[2] Anne-Cecile Orgerie,[8] Louis-Francois Pau,[9] Chris Phillips,[10] Sergio Ricciardi,[11] Remi Sharrock,[12] Patricia Stolf,[13] Tuan Trinh,[14] Luca Valcarenghi[15]

[1]*GÍTACA, University of Extremadura, Cáceres, Spain*
[2]*Optical Networks Lab (ONLab), Communication Systems (CoS) Department, ICT, KTH Royal institute of Technology, Kista Sweden*
[3]*Department of Photonics Engineering, Technical University of Denmark, Lyngby, Denmark*
[4]*Dekanat der Fakultät für Informatik und Mathematik, University of Passau, Passau, Germany*
[5]*Department of Communications Engineering, University of Cantabria, Cantabria, Spain*
[6]*INRIA, University of Lyon, Lyon, France*
[7]*Laboratoire d'analyse et d'architectures des systèmes (LAAS) Centre national de la recherche scientifique, Toulouse, France*
[8]*CNRS, Myriads/IRISA, Rennes, France*
[9]*Copenhagen Business School, Copenhagen, Denmark*
[10]*School of Electronic Engineering and Computer Science, Queen Mary University of London, London, UK*
[11]*Department of Computer Architecture, University of Catalonia, Barcelona, Spain*

Large-Scale Distributed Systems and Energy Efficiency: A Holistic View, First Edition.
Edited by Jean-Marc Pierson.
© 2015 John Wiley & Sons, Inc. Published 2015 by John Wiley & Sons, Inc.

^{12}Le département Informatique et Réseaux (INFRES), Telecom
ParisTech – INFRES, Paris, France
^{13}SEPIA, IRIT, Université Paul Sabatier, Toulouse, France
^{14}Department of Telecommunication and Media Informatics, Budapest University
of Technology and Economics Budapest, Budapest, Hungary
^{15}Istituto di Tecnologie della Comunicazione, dell'Informazione e della
Percezione, Scuola Superiore Sant'Anna, Pisa, Italy

After highlighting the significant energy consumption of existing wired communication networks, this chapter considers various means of operating such networks more efficiently. The chapter examines the components that make up wired communications network and their differing characteristics between the access and core, as well as patterns of traffic behavior. Once this is done, the chapter focuses on static (network planning) and dynamic (traffic-engineering) schemes that can be used to reduce the energy consumption of networks. The chapter also pays attention to a number of challenges/open research questions that need to be resolved before the implementation of such schemes. These include issues with migration and resilience. Finally a summary reviews the key themes that have been covered.

We use the term "wired" to represent any network where the communication channel between nodes is confined to a specific conduit rather than relying on free-space radiation of the signal. This includes systems based on metal conductors as well as glass fiber, with and without in-line amplification. Conversely, we reserve the term "wireless" communication for systems involving radio access. Improving the efficiency of these latter systems is addressed in Chapter 4.

The aim is to make wired networks operate in an energy-efficient way because energy expenditure has become a major concern with the continued development of the Internet [1]. It also has considerable impact on the environment [2]. In the past few years, energy consumption issues have received much attention from the government, general public, and telecommunication operators [3, 4]. Firstly, with the sustained growth of the customer population and greater use of high-bandwidth services such as streaming video, Internet Service Providers (ISPs), and telecom companies have needed to increase network capacity and expand their reach to support these demands. Associated with the use of more powerful and power-hungry network equipment, the operational expenditure, particularly in terms of the cost of electricity, is a significant factor particularly due to the increasing energy prices [5]. Increasing energy usage is also an environmental problem particularly due to the release of carbon dioxide (CO_2) into the atmosphere. It is also a political one, especially as politicians come to terms with the consequences of the anticipated environmental changes.

The power consumption of information and communication technologies (ICT) includes the power consumption of servers, network infrastructure, and end user devices. It accounts for about 2% of the world's power consumption rising to 10% for developed countries such as the United Kingdom [6]. It is anticipated that this will increase notably over the next few years. For example, nondomestic energy consumption is expected to grow by a further 40% by 2020 [7]. Although it seems a small fraction of overall power consumption, the absolute value of 900 billion kWh/year is equal to the power consumption of Central and South America together [2].

Within the field of telecommunications research, energy management can be divided into two segments: wireless networks and wired (fixed) networks. As the operation of (mobile or unattended) user equipment in many wireless networks is limited by battery power, considerable effort has been devoted to devising new energy management schemes for this sector. For example, many energy-efficient schemes have been proposed for wireless ad hoc sensor networks [8, 9]. There is also much ongoing research into energy saving within cellular network infrastructure, including the use of low-energy (and limited functionality) base stations, coding and multiplexing, and exploiting residential wired access points [10]. Conversely, it is generally assumed that wired networks, including fixed user equipment, have access to abundant power, implying there is no need to save energy. Consequently, wired networks' energy consumption is inefficient and, moreover, there is considerable room for improvement [11]. Furthermore, technological advances, particularly in respect to dense wavelength division multiplexing (DWDM), mean that the bandwidth of physical devices is no longer a restriction on the capacity of the Internet; instead, it is limitations in the achievable energy density [1].

Commonly the wired network is considered to be composed of several parts: the access network, the metro(politan) network, and the carrier (core) network. From the point of view of power consumption, research indicates that in the near future, the core network's power consumption may become the most significant element of the overall communications network infrastructure [12]. Therefore, a lot of research is now focused on the regional Tier-2 IP core networks employing various DWDM architectures.

The remainder of the chapter commences in Section 3.1 with an assessment of socioeconomic mechanisms that can be used to promote more energy-efficient use of the wired-network infrastructure. This is followed by a brief review of principle network components and typical wired-network architectures in Sections 3.2 and 3.3, respectively. Section 3.4 then gives consideration to how traffic is evolving both due to the increasing number of users on wired networks and also as a result of additional services being deployed across the Internet. Understanding these changing traffic patterns is essential if networks are to be operated efficiently. Then, we consider a number of energy-saving mechanisms. These are separated into static mechanisms in Section 3.5.1 and dynamic ones in Section 3.5.2. Static mechanisms or network planning [13, 14] consider the energy consumption while planning and configuring the network. Dynamic or traffic-engineering methods make use of a prearranged infrastructure in an energy efficiency way. These approaches include infrastructure sleeping, rate adaptation, and network virtualization. Infrastructure sleeping lets routers and links be switched off or enter a low power consumption state when network traffic demand is light [15]; rate adaptation [16] adjusts the power consumption according to the required transmission rate of the traffic. Finally, network virtualization [17], or network machine migration [18, 19], allows several network component instances to run on the same physical platform when performance requirements permit the saving of energy through consolidation. Despite these various schemes, significant challenges remain. These are considered in

Section 3.6. Finally, Section 3.7 provides a brief summary of the key findings and the issues that still need to be addressed.

3.1 ECONOMIC INCENTIVES AND GREEN TARIFFING

While later sections in this chapter consider design and traffic measures to achieve energy savings in communications networks, the present section deals with economic-, regulatory-, and business-related methods. It is estimated that such approaches, if adopted by users, could achieve a very large impact.

3.1.1 Regulatory, Economic, and Microeconomic Measures

Various measures are available to influence energy usage. We consider several significant examples.

3.1.1.1 Regulatory Dimensions. Communications carriers are universally subject to operating licenses, specified, awarded, and controlled by communications regulators [20]. Electricity and energy production is also, in some countries, subject to regulations, specified, awarded, and controlled by energy regulators [21]. Policies by both categories of regulators must abide to national and international laws or treaties dealing with climate change [22]; however, at this stage, no communications regulators are known to have included yet any mandatory requirements with "green" objectives in their license-awarding schemes. Energy reduction objectives are, therefore, "de facto" implemented by communications equipment manufacturers, to help their clients, the operators, achieve operating cost reductions as well as "green objectives" of their own (e.g., environmental reports to shareholders, regional policies, commitments toward use of specific energy sources). Therefore, in effect, regulatory measures are today driven much more by the communications equipment manufacturers and operators than by national regulators. Industry consortia such as the Groupe Speciale Mobile Association (GSMA) have introduced best practices for energy savings leading later to an International Telecommunication Union (ITU) standard [23].

This is, however, bound to change, as some communications regulators plan to introduce mandatory requirements, especially on ISPs and on public wireless base station operators, whereby technology migration set in the licenses, must be linked to a specified power consumption reduction for a given traffic capacity. Likewise, in a number of countries, some communications operators are seeking energy production and distribution licenses, to be allowed to own and operate energy production facilities serving not only their own needs but also third parties. One motivation is to limit the electricity and cooling prices charged to communications operators by power utilities. Another is to capitalize on the preferential amortization rates for selected green energy production facilities. A third motivation is to earn sometimes incentive-led income from selling excess renewable energy to third parties. Finally, some communications operators are in a competitive strategic positioning game with power utilities around smart grid metering and services [24]. The net effect is that communications operators interact much more with energy regulators, an offer to these a diversification and increased competition among market players.

3.1.1.2 Economic Dimensions.
Traditionally, in economic terms, telecommunications was about user-led traffic and service demands, besides manufacturing output (part of the second economic sector) [25]. The user-led demand as studied in economics did not include content creation, all this being aggregated into utility services, and thus the third sector of the economy (services). Also, in macroeconomics, there are no specific metrics for sustainability.

As a result, the energy consumption driven by communications traffic and services is still treated as a pure substitution between utility services inside the third sector, and not rendered exogenous. The consequence is that, at a macroeconomic level, there is no incentive or ready means to estimate the cross-effects between communications service value and energy pricing. Another consequence is that the relative returns on investments in communication systems and services, and in energy-savings capacity, cannot be assessed. This is bound to evolve, if indeed the knowledge and communications economy will be treated as the fourth sector on its own [25].

3.1.1.3 Microeconomic and Pricing Measures.
The strict definition of rationality is on an individual's preference: the preference relation is rational if it possesses the properties of completeness and transitivity [26]. It means the individual is able to compare all the alternatives and the comparisons are consistent. Furthermore, rationality implies that the individual has complete information of all alternatives and knows about the consequences of the choice; the user also has unlimited time and unlimited computational power to pick the most preferred option. In reality, such a perfectly rational user does not exist. Over the past decades, a large mass of empirical data has shown violations of the rationality assumption [27].

Simon [28] has pointed out that the behavior of most individuals is part rational. Much of the time, the individual does not know all the alternatives. Neither does she/he have perfect information regarding the consequences of choosing a particular alternative both because of limited computational power and because of the uncertainty in the external world. The individual's preferences do not possess the rational prosperities when comparing heterogeneous alternatives. Simon characterized this as "bounded rationality." Model construction under bounded rationality assumption can take two approaches. First is to retain optimization, but to simplify sufficiently so the optimum is computable. Second is to construct a satisfying model that provides good enough decisions, with reasonable computational cost. Neither approach dominates the other [28].

Following the pioneering work of Simon et al. [29] conducted a series of research on various types of judgment about uncertain events. Their conclusion was that people rely on a limited number of heuristics principles, which reduce the complex tasks of assessing probabilities and predicting values to simpler judgment operations. A recent revisit of this analysis [30] proposed a formulation in which the reduction of complexity is achieved by an operation of "attribute substitution" whereby a judgment is said to be mediated by a heuristic.

Costs, benefits, and incentives linked to the adoption of energy savings in communications networks represent a typical attribute substitution and, therefore, dominantly hinge on microeconomic measures at supplier level as well as at user level. The new framework to be considered here is one where the communications suppliers and users alike are not just dealing with traffic and services but are also at the same time suppliers and users of energy, with trade-offs between their two roles [31]. Ultimately, as seen earlier, the communications supplier may also be an energy supplier, and vice-versa, so that at a fundamental level, the microeconomic pricing and revenue are on combined "bundles" of communications and electricity with "attribute substitution."

By a combination of a large number of users, technology improvements, and operator productivity gains, the pure transport and access tariffs for communications have plummeted to low values, while energy costs may soon exceed them. Content-based services will generate certain revenue. Thus the very mix inside the combined "bundles" will change, with energy representing a large component, which only energy savings can reduce.

3.1.2   Pricing Theory in Relation to Green Policies

In this section, we now review pricing principles and introduce the concept of energy-and-communications use bundles and then "green" tariffs as incentives.

3.1.2.1   Pricing Principles. The economic theory of pricing has traditionally been derived for physical goods and from different angles:

1. Either as a static equilibrium between supply and demand, including auctions [32];
2. Or taking in consideration ranked preferences for individual price formation;
3. Or reflecting price dynamics with endogenous fluctuations due to market restructuring.

Most conventional telecommunication pricing schemes have been variants of the above, assuming limited capacity in either bandwidth or transmission capacity; these two assumptions have been made largely erroneous with the advent first of fiber optic transmission, next of advanced radio coding/modulation/spectrum usage techniques, and finally of Internet Protocol (IP)-based networks [25]. More recently, operators, while largely regulated according to the above principles, have determined prices by summing marketing, customer care, and financial costs, thus blurring the picture for users as well as for themselves. Customer segmentation approaches now dominate the pricing and revenue strategies for communications services. Likewise, most electricity pricing schemes have also been variants of the above, assuming limited energy production/generation capacity and/or daily variation patterns of demand [33].

However, at the dawn of telephony services (circa 1880), there were individual tariffs [34]! For quite some years, and in some markets, telephony served mainly some high-level civil servants and privileged people (trade, news), and was a symbol of wealth and social rank. Telephone subscribers were not designated by a number, but by their name; picking up the phone would get the operator, who would then ring and connect

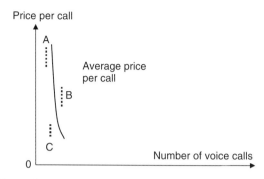

Figure 3.1. Service demands at the dawn of telephony.

the desired party by a polite support staff protocol. As a luxury service at that time, the demand for telephony was limited as was network capacity. Individual demands were price insensitive, which resulted in an inelastic demand curve as shown in Figure 3.1. The supply was scarce and inelastic to prices, as there was no choice or competitive mechanisms: the average price per call was high and anyway the supply stalled because of limited exchange capacity and human operations. Although prices were fixed individually or bundled into packages with fixed numbers of calls, they were extremely high, which resulted in the exclusion of the majority of population from accessing the services due to unaffordability.

In Figure 3.1, A–C represent individual demands, which are limited and price insensitive. The average telephony demand curve at the introduction of telephony is shown as the bold curve, which is inelastic. All voice calls here are assumed for the same destination/distance.

From the beginning, although sets of telephone users and suppliers were restricted, charging patterns began to diverge between flat rates and individual usage-based rates. The number of call attempts, the physical destination, and the call duration were all manually recorded. However, the pricing of the calls was a matter between the telephone company sales person and the customer (who was then not a subscriber); usage, rank, fame, and location were all taken into account, and the settlement was accomplished by a bank note or cash.

This historical recollection is very relevant nowadays in relation to green policies due to a number of fundamental reasons. First, the operators and their users that care about energy savings are initially minorities, also called "early adopters," and the price settlement thus can/should be individualized. Next, as explained in Section 3.1.1, the regulatory vacuum regarding green policy implementations leave space for individual negotiations rather than fixed tariff bundles. One simple reason is that a given user may have a low-energy profile and a high-communications profile, while another might show the reverse, thus impacting the costs, benefits, and incentives at an individual level. Likewise, a communications supplier may have from its infrastructure and service offerings, relatively high energy consumption, but access to low-utility supplier prices, while another might show the reverse picture. This leads to the concept of "individual tariffs" for a communications and energy consumer [34].

TABLE 3.1. Individual Communications and Energy Bundle Tariff Mechanism

---

- Consider one buyer (B) and N sellers $(S(i), i = 1, \ldots, N)$. The buyer signals his/her maximum price p and contract duration T
- Buyer signals his/her service mix and attributes Mix $= (A(j), q(j), j = 1, \ldots, M)$ where "A" denotes a service and "q" the quantity or QoS
- One or several sellers respond
- There is an individual tariff, whenever B and one seller $S(*)$ agree by contract on the provisioning by $S(*)$ to B of the service Mix for duration T at price equal or lower to p
  This contract may be different from the contract for the same service mix for other buyers or sellers respectively

---

An "*individual tariff*" as summarized in Table 3.1 means that each individual sets a tariff for himself/herself for a specific set of communications *and* energy services provided by a supplier or a community, whether this service is user defined or community defined. Even if that individual belongs, say, to an enterprise, the members of the enterprise may have different individual tariffs, simply because their service (contributions and receipts) are different. Even, different users of an identical service (e.g., voice) may value and price it differently, as they decide individually to choose another supplier or belong to different communities. Furthermore, a supplier or community need not own part or the entire transmission infrastructure, sourced competitively from infrastructure owners, especially as this is encouraged by regulators under the "virtual operator" concept. Indeed, this definition omits service provisioning duration, as the duration of the service will be just one attribute in the multiattribute service demand; for example, sporadic uses are possible, just as are long-term ones, but the difference with today is that service duration becomes user defined.

3.1.2.2 Mass-Customized Communication and Energy-Use Bundles.
A pertinent question is "how do early adopters evolve over time?" Twenty years from now, combined advanced communication technologies and smart grid technologies will probably enable people to stay connected anytime and anywhere with access and energy network alternatives. Users will seamlessly roam between networks using yet unknown new services and behave as joint producers and consumers of communications and energy. Hundred percent penetration of access devices over the entire population in most countries will render work more flexible and, individualization of labor, will produce a highly segmented social structure [35].

The total demand will be large, as people can personalize their communications and energy services according to their needs. Furthermore, community proliferation may multiply the effect. However, due to the highly segmented structure, most traditional flat rate tariffs will either not be transparent and appealing enough to users or, if they are made too diverse, users will "churn" (change suppliers) implying high switching costs. These effects will allow flat rates for all to be replaced by mass-customized individual tariffs, provided each user and community has suitable management and monitoring tools for both communications and energy use, allowing in real time (as well as over contract durations) to quantify equilibrium break-even tariffs [36]. This results in

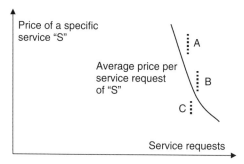

Figure 3.2. Service demand for a mass-customized individual service bundle "S."

price-insensitive individual demands. Although for each specific service, the preference from each user will be different, the average demand across many users again leads to an inelastic price demand curve as illustrated in Figure 3.2. Consequently, we appear to repeat history (see Figure 3.1). However, on closer inspection, the new demand curve is more to the right in terms of the "number of service requests" and much lower in terms of price.

In Figure 3.2, the mass-customized individual service bundle "S" comprises communications and energy. A–C represent individual A's service profile (S, A1, A2, etc.), individual B's service profile (S, B1, B2, etc.), and individual C's service profile (S, C1, C2, etc.). The average demand for service "S" is shown by the bold curve. Note there is a "service proliferation effect" driving the curve slope.

Already today technical means exist to achieve individual tariffs, and the infrastructure industry together with the billing platform industries, have shown that complexity and costs involved in individual user multi-service and multiple access demand monitoring and control are surmountable. In the future, traffic and service aggregation, and filtering coupled with service creation platforms will allow this to be more capable and cheaper both for communications and smart-grid energy services. Although technical details of the eventual implementation are not standardized yet, we can identify possible architectural elements of such a solution using standards [36] as follows:

- The linking of user communications and energy service profiles to the adaptation functionality in the billing/rating system would be carried out at user authentication time in the AAA server.
- In access networks, via the energy grid meters, routers could recognize and tag special packets and process them according to a given code; within this tag may reside a label representing the individual tariff and which would be tied to the access node at which such tariffs are applied.
- The flow label in the IPv6 protocol used to carry quality of service (QoS) features could encode individual tariff information for this packet. This approach offers the advantage that the packet to which this individual tariff code applies does not have to originate in some service node, but only in those who have the decoding key to this field.

- Using the Session Initiation Protocol (SIP), a P-Charging-Vector header is defined to convey charging-related information. The information inside the vector can be prepared and retrieved by multiple network entities during the establishment of a dialog or standalone transaction. In this way, charging-related processing can be session based.

3.1.2.3 *Green Tariffs as Incentives.*

We define here a *"green tariff"* [31], as the contractual price paid by a subscriber to an operator for a set of bundled communications and energy services at a given QoS for a specified duration; this price must reflect both parties' best efforts to reduce CO_2 emissions and pass onto the subscriber a share of the energy and emissions savings from the network. The operator can easily offer "green tariffs" by having a green tariff subscriber base segment, which, against committing to contract for such bundles, allows the operator to earmark a specified percentage of their energy consumption at a network level to technologies with fewer emissions and possibly to the use of renewable energy supplies.

Furthermore, if such green tariffs are made individual (see Section 3.1.2), they provide an incentive for users to specify and adopt a communications and energy service demand profile leading to less waste or unutilized capacity. As this incentive has monetary consequences, there is a strong likelihood that individualized green tariffs would become very important. Their deployment, however, rests on achieving equilibrium (called a sustainable individual green tariff) between users requesting individual green tariffs, and the operators' economic sustainability, as they have to make new investments in communications technology and/or renewable power sources they control. Using a real operator model, it has been shown [36] that by applying recursive Stackelberg equilibrium computations to multiattribute individual tariff contracts covering individualized services, the communications operator could still achieve economic sustainability. This is on a mass-customized basis and applies even for complex services and extreme cases. In addition, the analysis shows that operator profits are not eroded for generic communications services; however, for value-added communications services, the situation is less clear, as investment is also required in content, storage, and competence.

3.1.3 COST Action Results

Research carried out during the COST(European Cooperation in Science and Technology) Action IC0804 focused on the green tariffs and individual communications-and-energy bundles, including wireless access [37, 38]. The operator was assumed to have an energy production and distribution license with alternative renewable energy sources (wind, solar), where excess supply got sold. The main result is to confirm the possible tariff reduction to the user, while maintaining operator's profit margin; the difference between the individual green tariff and the public tariff (for the same service bundle), which is an indicator of the net incentive to the user, is in the order 10–20% [25]. Other results on specific aspects of the same issue are reported in [37, 38]. Nevertheless, the overriding issue is the right sizing of the mutual dependence, and possible combination, of communications operators, electric power utilities, and their customers. Despite now proven advantages in terms of energy savings from individualized end user pricing [39], through the co-creation of value with customers, there remain regulatory challenges [40–42].

3.2 NETWORK COMPONENTS

This section draws upon existing publications and research findings to assess the current and near-future expected energy characteristics of key wired-networking components. It also considers how this profile might change as the Internet continues to develop over the next few years based on the various services it supports.

3.2.1 Router

A router is a device that selectively forwards packets between computer networks. Routers operate at the network layer (Layer-3) of the Open Systems Interconnection (OSI) model. In relation to data, they inspect the headers of data packets they receive on their ingress ports and selectively route them through to a suitable egress port with reference to a routing table.

Router architecture has developed for several generations: from bus-based router architectures with a single processor, through bus-based router architectures with multiple processors and switch-based router architectures with multiple processors, to switch-based router architectures with fully distributed processors [43, 44]. However, a router remains primarily composed of line cards, switch fabric, a management system, and a router processor, often located within the same Line-Card Chassis (LCC) [45].

The line-card is responsible for processing and forwarding packets using its local processing subsystem and buffer spaces for processing the packets arriving along the ingress interfaces (or ports) and awaiting transmission at the egress interfaces. The switch fabric provides the sufficient bandwidth for transferring packets among different line cards. It receives data from the ingress line-card interfaces and switches to appropriate egress one(s). The Router Processor is responsible for maintaining the overall forwarding table and distributing different parts of the table to different line cards. The management system includes functionality for cooling, power control, and alarm handling.

A more powerful router is a multiple-shelf device, which has a functional structure similar to that of the single-shelf router. The principle difference is that it has several LCCs that are connected with one or more Fabric-Card Chassis (FCC) elements [46]. For example, the Cisco CRS-1 multi-shelf routing system typically has 72 LCCs connected via eight FCCs [47]. There are both fabric switches on the FCC and LCC. Generally, the fabric switch employs three-stage switching devices, known as Switch Fabric Elements (SFEs). They are all identical and their operation and behavior are determined by their location. In a single-shelf router, the SFEs are all in the same fabric switch. In the multi-self routing system, the difference is that the switch fabric on the FCC only supports stage 2 switching functionality while the switch fabric on the LCC is responsible for stage 1 and 3 switch functionalities.

The data plane, also called the forwarding plane, is the part of router architecture that is responsible for deciding how to handle the ingress packets by looking up the routing table and then sending them to the appropriate egress interfaces. On the other hand, the control plane is used for routing related control functions, such as generating the network map, the way to treat packets according to the different service classifications and discarding certain packets. In general, the data plane runs on the line cards and the control plane operates on the CPU and main memory. Another important part of the framework is the dynamic interface binding function, which allows different interface resources to be allocated according to the requirements.

Energy-efficient networking means that we aim to transport the same amount of traffic (in bits) with lower energy consumption (in joules) than is currently the case. From the aspect of power consumption, both the node and line equipment should be considered. However, in practice, the consumption of the line equipment is typically omitted [48]. Wavelength division multiplexing (WDM) links account for between 1.2% and 5.8% of the Internet's power consumption, varying with the average access rate [1]. Therefore, the power consumption of the router tends to receive most attention.

The energy consumption of a router is made up of two parts: static and dynamic energy. Static energy is consumed by the LCC, and dynamic energy is consumed by the line cards and is related to the traffic load. For example, in [49], the power consumption of two standard router platforms has been tested with different combinations of line cards and LCCs. The experimental results show that the LCC consumes more than half of the maximum observed power consumption for any combination. From this experiment, we can conclude that switching off the whole router can save more energy than only switching off the line cards because the consumption of the base system is the major contributor to the overall energy consumption.

As monitoring and performing "green" experiments on a wide network is generally unfeasible, some simulation frameworks such as ECofen have been proposed [50]. Such frameworks allow the simulation of large-scale networks and the impact in terms of energy consumption and QoS from on/off or slowdown (Adaptive Link Rate, Low Power Idle) power saving schemes.

Nevertheless, hardware experiments have been made on a French regional platform called GridMip composed of 3 backbone routers, 3 border routers, and 150 nodes. The platform is illustrated in Figure 3.3.

The aim of the experiments was to evaluate precisely what is the consumption of the network equipment during the boot process and how long it takes. This is partic-ularly relevant when considering approaches that aim to switch off routers in order to save energy during "light" operational conditions, as it is necessary to take into account penalty when switching the routers on again.

With a PLOGG wattmeter the power consumption of a Cisco 7600 Border Router (R2) composed of three modules was measured during the boot process as shown in Figure 3.4. This router consumes 785 W. It takes 400 s to switch on a router. From the figure, it is clear to see that the energy consumption is neither constant nor linear during the boot process. Instead, we observe appreciable steps in the energy consumption. This has implications for the accurate modeling of dynamic energy-saving network systems. It also shows that using typical contemporary equipment, there is an appreciable delay before a router can again become operational once it is powered down.

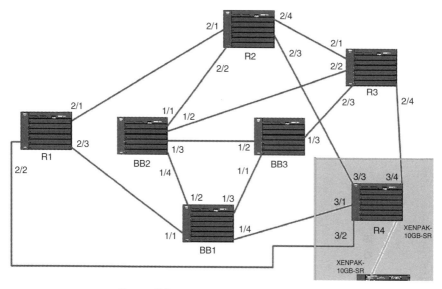

Figure 3.3. GridMip evaluation platform.

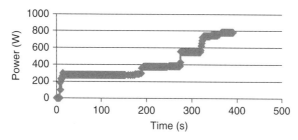

Figure 3.4. Power consumption of a Cisco 7600 border router during the boot process.

A further experiment examined the power consumption of a router module. For this, a 4×10 Gbps module belonging to router R2 was turned off. It was then turned back on 20 s later. When a module is off, it consumes 195 W less. When the module is switched on, there are two phases during the boot process: one from 40 to 80 s which consumes 100 W more and a second phase which consumes 100 W more again as shown in Figure 3.5.

We notice that the powering down of a module is achieved in one step almost immediately. One might also assume that powering up the module would also take one step. However, a module recovers in two phases, with the core module initializing ahead of switching on the ports. The powering on process lasts almost for 50 s.

Finally, the power consumption associated with connected Ethernet ports was examined as shown in Figure 3.6. For this experiment, 18 computers were plugged into the Ethernet module of the router. The right axis represents the number of unplugged

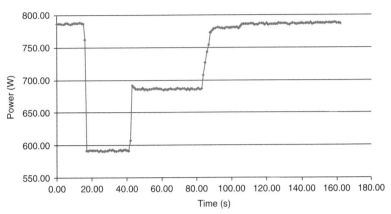

Figure 3.5. Cisco 7600 border router 4 × 10 Gbps interface module: powering down and up after 20 s.

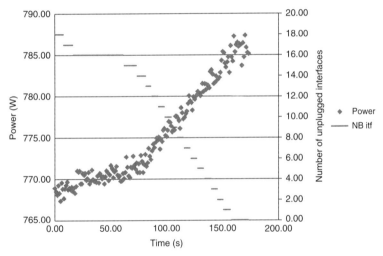

Figure 3.6. Cisco 7600 border router power: physically plugging Ethernet ports.

interfaces (called Nb Itf in the graph). The main objective of this experiment was to observe the energy consumption with as the number of connected (plugged) Ethernet ports was altered.

We see from this experiment that the mean power consumption of a port is 0.94 W and is approximately linear with the number of connected ports.

Experiments such as these are a necessary precursor to the creation of accurate mathematical models such as work exploring energy-performance trade-off in the context of network and data center optimization [51].

3.2.2 Network Interface Card

The role of a network interface card (NIC) has already been introduced in the preceding section where it was referred to as a line-card, forming part of the router architecture. However, this functionality actually exists within any device attached to a network. In a "local area" access network, it is more common to use the term NIC.

In wired networks, researches like [52, 53] show that energy consumption of network devices such as NICs/line cards can be lower if operating rates are reduced. This is due to the fact that devices operating at a lower frequency can reduce their energy consumption by mechanisms such as dynamic voltage scaling (DVS) [54, 55]. By lowering the clock rate of synchronous logic, operation can be maintained at a lower power supply voltage. However, this lowers the switching performance of devices and so must coincide with situations when the processing load is lighter.

The authors of [52] try to find a decision area for which hardware-based technique (Sleeping or Rate Adaptation) can capitalize on operational conditions. To this end, they study the trade-off between links rates and their energy consumption. A uniform (linear energy function) and an exponential (10 Gbps, 1 Gbps, 100 Mbps, 10 Mbps) distribution of rates are used. The latter approach is considered as hardware technologies for these rates already exist (Ethernet technology). We can extract from their results that the uniform distribution of rates is the most suitable one to achieve a greater reduction of links' operations rates and, consequently, a reduction of energy consumption. Moreover, they state that both Sleeping and Rate Adaptation are two effective techniques depending on the energetic profile of networking equipment and network utilization.

One step further, in [56], a study based on [52] in which they compare energy savings in wired networks after applying sleeping and rate adaptation techniques is presented. In this case, they draw some conclusions according to network devices' individual baseline consumption, that is, based only in the amount of energy consumed by a component regardless of its operation rate. For the case in which the baseline consumption of network components is relatively high, it is interesting to keep as few active links as possible (Sleeping). On the other hand, if the baseline consumption of network devices is low, Rate Adaptation technique is more suitable. In the latter case, authors rely on results from [52]. Thus, they assume and use a uniform distribution of rates for their experiments as well.

Otherwise, authors in [57] performed several experiments to measure energy consumption of two different Cisco routers: GSR 12008 and 7507. Both of them include their base systems (chassis plus router processor) and line cards. However, we can extract from the results obtained in this case that the energy function described by line cards consumption takes discrete values and assume its adaptation to a logarithmic distribution of rates.

Rodgers [53], in turn, uses an Intel 82579 Gigabit Ethernet PHY and obtains energy consumption values for 100 Mbps and 1 Gbps links. In this case, several measurements are performed for each of the three different energy levels at which links can be configured: active, idle, and LPI (Low Power Idle from IEEE 802.3az standard). We can extract from these results the value of links consumption when there is no traffic flowing through them (LPI energy level) as a function of their consumption when they are active. Thus, it can be assumed that the energy consumption of a link with a LPI energy level or Sleeping takes values between 5% and 10% out of its consumption if it is configured with an active energy level.

Furthermore, some heuristics are commonly examined, as in [58], with the aim of achieving significant energy savings in the network by progressively switching off both nodes and links after the prior aggregation of traffic flows. Other works indeed solve the problem using Integer Problem Formulation (integer linear programming, ILP) by considering that only links [59] or both links and nodes [60] can be switched off.

3.2.3   Reconfigurable Optical Add-Drop Multiplexer

The ROADM is a known as an "any-to-any" component, which means that it provides a flexible way of adding, dropping or switching any wavelength to any node [61]. When multiple wavelengths arrive at an input interface of an ROADM, one or more wavelengths can be dropped by preselection, and in the output interface, one or more preselected wavelengths are added. What is more, any wavelength can bypass the electronic processing function and pass through the ROADM unhindered to specific ports. As these signals remain in the optical domain, there is little latency. Furthermore, because of its "any-to-any" feature, ROADM technology allows DWDM-based networks to be technology agnostic and thus more flexible [62].

Little work has focused on energy saving within ROADMs, perhaps because they traditionally consume less power than routers. However, a recent example given in [63] looks at using ROADMs more efficiently.

3.2.4   Digital Subscriber Line Access Multiplexer

A digital subscriber line access multiplexer (DSLAM) is a network device often located in the telephone exchanges of the telecommunications operators. It connects multiple customer digital subscriber line (DSL) interfaces to a high-speed digital communications channel using multiplexing techniques.

The DSLAM equipment collects the data from its many modem ports and aggregates their voice and data traffic into one complex composite "signal" via multiplexing. The aggregated traffic is then directed to a Service Provider backbone switch, i.e. a Broadband Remote Access Server (BRAS), at up to 10 Gbit/s data rates. Depending on its device architecture and setup, a DSLAM aggregates the DSL lines over its Asynchronous Transfer Mode (ATM), frame relay, and/or IP network [i.e., an IP-DSLAM using PTM-TC (Packet Transfer Mode – Transmission Convergence)] protocol(s) stack. The DSLAM acts like a switch because its functionality is at Layer 2 of the OSI model. Therefore, it cannot reroute traffic between multiple IP networks, only between BRAS devices and end user connection points. From the BRAS, the DSLAM traffic is then routed across the ISP network to the Internet.

DSL equipment can be a significant source of energy consumption for wired-network operators. One possible approach to decreasing the overall energy consumption is to replace large centralized DSLAMs located at the exchanges with smaller remote units closer to customers. This not only reduces energy consumption but also increases the reach of the access network [64].

3.3 ARCHITECTURES

This section focuses on the architecture of communication networks and the corresponding relationship with energy usage. However, a key dilemma when examining networks, and particularly the Internet, end to end is who pays for the electricity and the potential savings exist.

At the periphery of the Internet sit the end users, residential customers or businesses. In both instances, the customer premises equipment (CPE) is typically powered by an electrical source provided by the end users, for which they pay. Conversely, the access networks are typically operated by ISPs using their own equipment. These networks in turn are connected to carrier networks, maintained by other tier-2 and tier-1 operators that primarily convey the information over large geographical distances using high-performance (and power "hungry") equipment. The Internet is thus a federation of networks with a plethora of providers and consumers.

Interestingly, given the hierarchical "pyramidal" structure of the Internet, the number of networking devices at each tier increases by one or more orders of magnitude as we descend from the tier-1 operators at the tip of the pyramid. This means that the greatest potential energy saving by volume exists at the CPE, where small percentage reductions in energy consumption can amount to substantial savings at a national level because of the vast number of devices involved.

Paradoxically, this arrangement leads to two issues when it comes to saving energy. Firstly, the amount of energy saved at a particular CPE may be regarded by the owner/end user as marginal. Secondly, as the electricity to power these devices is paid for by the end users, there is less incentive to motivate the access and carrier network operators to change their behavior. Despite this, we argue that embracing energy-saving mechanisms detailed in Section 3.5 can still impact on operational expenditure to a degree worthy of consideration.

3.3.1 Access Networks

An access network is that part of a telecommunications network that connects subscribers to their immediate service provider. Traditionally, access networks consist largely of pairs of copper wires, each traveling in a direct path typically between a DSLAM and the customer. The DSLAM connects multiple customer DSL interfaces to a high-speed digital communications channel in the exchange, which provides an access point to the rest of the Internet.

Recently, access networks have evolved to include more optical fiber primarily because of its high bandwidth, low loss, and noise immunity characteristics. Optical fiber already makes up the majority of core networks and has started to "roll out" closer to the customer, until a full transition to fiber is achieved, in order to deliver value-added services over Fiber to the Home (FTTH). One group of optical fiber technologies are passive optical networks (PONs), whereby point-to-multipoint (PMP) fiber links multiple homes to a common optical line terminal (OLT) at the service provider's exchange, using unpowered optical splitters to create a tree-like structure. Indeed Energy Efficient Ethernet Passive Optical Networks (EPONs) are now being deployed, providing cost efficiency and high data rate for the last mile access [65]. A typical EPON is a PMP network with a tree-based topology, where an OLT connects multiple optical network units (ONUs) via optical links. The OLT plays a role of distributor, arbitrator, and aggregator of traffic. In the upstream direction (from ONUs to the OLT), multiple ONUs share a single link and traffic may collide. The OLT distributes the fiber capacity using an upstream bandwidth arbitration mechanism to avoid collisions. In the downstream direction (from the OLT to ONUs), data frames are broadcasted to all ONUs. ONUs filter and accept data that are addressed to them. However, ONUs have to constantly listen and examine downstream traffic, which results in wasting significant energy in the ONU.

3.3.2 Carrier Networks

Generally, the underlying transport technology (Layer 1) of the current Internet uses Synchronous Optical Networking (SONET) or Synchronous Digital Hierarchy (SDH); both architectures transport voice and data in containers in an efficient time-division multiplexed manner over optical fiber. SONET/SDH provide advanced support services such as line monitoring to provide signals for protection switching and so forth. SONET/SDH also allow time-division multiplexing (TDM) circuits to be multiplexed from low speed to high speed into different-sized containers. However, with increasing requirements for service flexibility and reliability and the demand for lower expenditure, ISPs are not satisfied with this "traditional" architecture and are looking for more efficient ways to handle the growing volume of IP traffic. One promising architecture for the next-generation network (NGN) is IP over DWDM because it eliminates the legacy SDH transport layer and so saves equipment costs and reduces energy consumption.

An IP over DWDM network is composed of two layers: the IP layer and an optical layer. This can be abstracted as a structure whereby a node is composed by a set of network equipment, for example, a router and an optical transport switch, typically in the form of a reconfiguration optical add-drop multiplexer (ROADM), that are then interconnected by an optical line system (OLS), which includes optical fiber and amplifiers. In this model, the wavelength continuity constraint is often considered, whereby when an optical connection passes through the optical transport switch, it is required to be on the same wavelength channel from the ingress to the egress. The channel remains in the optical domain and optical–electrical–optical (OEO) conversion is avoided.

The node in an IP over DWDM architecture is composed of a router and an ROADM, which connected to similar devices via a transmission line system. The router is responsible for storing and forwarding packets and the ROADM is used to remotely switch the traffic allowing for adding, dropping, or bypassing the router at the wavelength level without OEO conversion. An example is the Cisco IPoDWDM solution where network nodes are composed of a Cisco CRS-1 multi-self routing system and an ROADM [66]. The original transponders have been combined into the routing system. The ROADM only manages add, drop, and bypass in the optical domain.

3.3.3 Grid Overlay Networks

Grid computing via overlay networks enables a federation of computer resources from multiple administrative domains to coordinate to achieve a common goal. Grids are a form of distributed computing whereby a "super virtual computer" is composed of many networked loosely coupled computers acting together to perform large tasks. For certain applications, "distributed" or "grid" computing can be seen as a special type of parallel computing that relies on complete computers [with onboard central processing units (CPUs), storage, power supplies, network interfaces, etc.] connected to a network (private, public, or the Internet) by a conventional network interface, such as Ethernet.

An analysis of the usage of an experimental grid has been conducted over a 1-year period. On the basis of this analysis, Orgerie et al. [67] proposed a resource reservation infrastructure that takes into account the energy usage. The infrastructure is validated on a large-scale experimental "Grid5000" platform and the gains in terms of energy are presented.

3.4 TRAFFIC CONSIDERATIONS

There is little published data concerning the traffic characteristics of commercial networks, as it is regarded as sensitive. However, some published datasets exist for the Abilene and Géant networks [68, 69]. Figure 3.7 provides just two examples of traffic

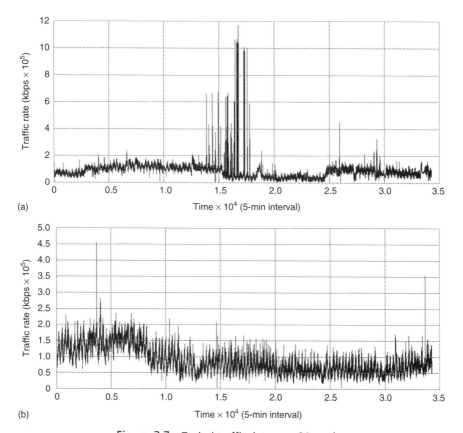

Figure 3.7. Typical traffic data over 24 weeks.

flow between specific source–destination pairs in the case of the Abilene network. The traffic was sampled every 5 min for 24 weeks, omitting weekends. As seen from the figure, traffic varies considerably over time. It is this variation that permits network resources to be switched off when they are not needed.

The variation in traffic over time allows for opportunities when resources can be placed into a sleeping state. Furthermore, the regularity in the autocorrelation pattern lends weight to the idea that the flow of data between given source–destination pairs is temporally predictable [70].

In addition to load variations, traffic can also be differentiated in terms of where it is coming from and going to. For example, within the context of IP over DWDM architectures, there are two types of traffic in every network node: router-terminated traffic and optical bypass traffic [71, 72]. In the former case, the traffic is terminated at the router. The router looks up the routing table at IP layer to decide where to forward the packet. In this scenario, because the packet may be transported in the physical fiber using a different wavelength, the traffic needs an optical to electrical conversion before it processed and forwarded by the router. In fact, the power consumption of optical and electrical transfer in the IP router ports is a major element of the overall power consumption. Therefore, some researchers are considering designing an energy efficiency network by minimizing IP router ports. For optical bypass traffic, in contrast, the router does not process the traffic. Instead, it is transported directly through the intermediate router(s) via preset light paths. As the traffic across the core network is becoming more distributed because of changes in application service deployment, the proportion of bypass traffic is increasing [73]. For example, it is possible that up to 70–80% [66] traffic passing through an optical node is of the bypass type and does not require termination at the router.

3.5 ENERGY-SAVING MECHANISMS

Energy saving in wired networks can be generally divided into static and dynamic mechanisms [4]. Static ones consider network design and configuration with respect to power. The approaches are to design and place network resources in a more energy efficiency way. In contrast, dynamic approaches attempt to make better use of the existing network resources by traffic engineering in response to varying traffic load through infrastructure sleeping, rate adaptation, and so forth. The following section summarizes the state of the art in these two areas.

3.5.1 Static Mechanisms

Static mechanisms mean to design and configure the network from the perspective of power consumption. That is to say, to plan power-aware networks. One approach is to configure the combination of chassis and line cards for lowing the overall power consumption. In [49], the author indicated that the base system (including chassis, switch fabric, and router processor) consumes more than half of the whole power consumption of a router by testing two generic router platforms. Therefore, one method to achieve power-aware networking at the design stage is to minimize the chassis number and to maximize the number of line cards per chassis. Another method is planning the network to reduce the traffic processed by the IP routers. Generally, a packet is transported via 14 routers on an average across the networks [66]. There are two means of transporting packets in the optical layer, lightpath non-bypass and lightpath bypass. The non-bypass lightpath is always terminated at the IP router ports and then transformed into an electrical signal for processing. In contrast, the lightpath bypass approach transports packets through intermediate nodes directly without OEO conversion. Reducing the traffic processed by the IP routers means that the use of bypass lightpaths also minimizes OEO conversions. Eilenberger et al. [71] indicated the power consumption of these two different methods, router-terminated and bypass traffic, for packet transportation. In the former case, it consumes about 10 nJ/bit. Conversely, the traffic processed in the WDM layer consumes less than 1 nJ/bit. Thus, much research has been devoted to exploiting this characteristic.

In [12], the IP-over-WDM network achieves energy efficiency by minimizing the number of IP router ports/interfaces because the ports/interfaces play an important role in the power consumption of networks. It is also the first time that the lightpath bypass approach is taken into consideration for energy saving. The energy-minimized network design uses the lightpath bypass approach to minimize the number of IP router port for reducing the power consumption via OEO conversions. In [13], the paper considers the multi-shelf routing system in an IP-over-WDM network for saving the energy. Both papers employ mixed-integer linear programming (MILP) to build a model for minimizing the power consumption.

Another approach is energy-efficient network design. Here the aim is to devise energy-efficient architectures during the network design state. For example, researchers have proposed an energy-aware design to minimize the energy consumption of all the network components in conjunction for an IP-over-WDM network [13]. Two alternatives were considered: lightpath non-bypass and lightpath bypass. In the former case, IP routers process and forward all the data carried by the lightpaths, while the latter allows IP traffic to directly bypass an intermediate router (which is not the destination node) via a cut-through lightpath. Results showed that lightpath bypass could save significant energy compared with the non-bypass case (between 25% and 45%) because of the reduction of the number of IP routers needed. They also confirm that the total energy consumption of IP routers is much greater than that of the rest of optical network equipment, such as erbium-doped fiber amplifiers (EDFAs) and transponders, accounting for over 90% of the total network power consumption.

3.5.2 Dynamic Mechanisms

Dynamic mechanisms use traffic-engineering methods to make better use of existing resources instead of designing and configuring a network in respect of the power consumption. They react "quickly" to changing conditions such as variations in traffic load. Methods that belong to this class are rate adaptation, infrastructure sleeping, and green routing. We also consider virtualization.

3.5.2.1   Rate Adaptation. Rate adaptation is a mechanism by which a communications device can adjust its processing rate based on the current workload conditions. Many devices have the capacity to operate at a range of processing rates. When the workload is low, a device operates at the low speed, which consumes less power at the same time. Therefore, when the traffic load is low, lowering the transmission speed of device reduces its power consumption. Rate adaptation is described in [15] where it is compared with the infrastructure sleeping. The conclusion is that both the approaches are useful depending on the hardware capabilities of device and network utilization. For example, an ISP could use rate adaptation in the daytime and infrastructure sleeping at night to satisfy the different traffic load requirements. Nevertheless, the ability to perform sleeping and rate adaptation are not supported in existing network devices. Even so, these approaches have been incorporated into the future Ethernet protocol standard such as Energy-Efficient Ethernet (EEE), which was approved in October 2010 [74]. Thus, we should see these approaches receive broad adoption throughout the Internet over the coming years.

A key issue is that current equipment is constrained by technology limitations. Some researchers have explored the trade-off between the amount of energy that could be saved in wired networks and the discrete number of operational rate modes to be implemented in line cards [75]. Results show that it is not necessary to manufacture line cards that support a large number of different operational rate modes, but that a limited number such as four different operational rate modes would be enough to achieve significant reductions in energy consumption. For example, four energy levels are enough to save significant amounts of energy (around 22%). A greater number of energy levels do not result in large savings when compared to the case when an infinite number of energy levels are assumed.

Other researchers have also considered the concept of multi-rate adaptation whereby physical interfaces adapt their rates accordingly with the typical Ethernet values. For example, a 10-Gbps card is considered capable of intermediate transmission speeds of 1 Gbps, 100 Mbps, and 10 Mbps. Consumption of these intermediate rates are then considered, accordingly [76]. The use of "adaptive" link rates can then be applied in concert with "energy-aware routing" and "multilayer traffic engineering" as described in [77, 78], respectively.

The application of adaptive multi-rate techniques and multilayer traffic engineering in hourly intervals can reduce total consumption into a wired backbone to 7% simply by adapting the capabilities of existing systems to the real needs of traffic. This result is obtained from [79] using a theoretical scenario formed of a wired backbone network deployed over five cross connection levels (three aggregation and two core) as illustrated in Figure 3.8. It included a physical coverage 40,000 km^2 (equivalent to the size of Switzerland) and a total volume of 6.3 million connected devices, distributed according to the typical characteristics of urban, suburban, and rural areas.

The deployed network, based on OTN technology, includes 2000 cabinets with nearly 4000 communications interface cards. Total consumption of 53 MW/h was estimated without considering additional cooling systems. The adaptation of the routing and capacity of the links reduces consumption to nearly 2.5 MW on an average, with peaks of up to 4 MW. Given the 1:1 ratio in terms of energy consumption of refrigeration equipment, a decrease in networking energy consumption would see a similar reduction in

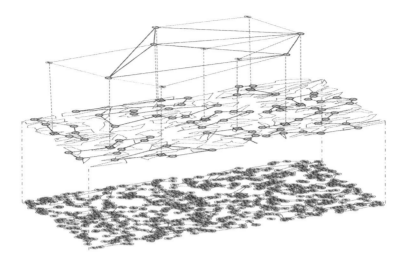

Figure 3.8. Example multilayer backbone network.

the consumption of these ancillary systems. However, as indicated in [80], a reduction of 1 W in the system could reduce the actual overall consumption by 2.42 W, so the total saving could be as much as 5% on an average, with peaks close to 8% as shown in Figure 3.9.

3.5.2.2 *Infrastructure Sleeping.* Infrastructure sleeping means that when equipment is idle, it enters a low power consumption state called standby/sleep while retaining the information for maintaining its operational state when it again wakes up. An example is the "hibernation" state of personal computers.

As a router still consumes about 90% of its full-load energy when it is idle [81], approaches that turn off unneeded devices or permit equipment to enter a coordinated sleep state have more potential for saving energy in a network. Furthermore, because of the well-known daily traffic variations, where load varies in an almost sinusoid manner over the course of each day in response to people's daily activities, the infrastructure sleeping approach can achieve a significant savings. Consequently, considerable research has been devoted to the infrastructure sleeping principle.

In [11], two types of sleeping are identified, uncoordinated sleeping and coordinated sleeping. The former lets the equipment enter a sleep state based on local information, for example, during the interarrival time between packet transmissions. The other takes a global perspective and reroutes traffic via some equipment in order to let other devices enter a sleep state. For example, in [16], the author discussed two mechanisms for sleeping: traditional "wake-on-arrival" and a proposed "buffer-and-burst." The former one wakes up the sleeping device when the new packet arrives. As it takes time for a device to return to the active state, if the packet interarrival time is smaller than the transition time, the energy saving is limited. For "buffer-and-burst" sleeping, the traffic is shaped into burst-by-burst units and stored in a buffer that is processed when buffer is full. This provides longer sleeping periods while the traffic load is low. The results show that the proposed mechanism can obtain significant energy savings while having little impact

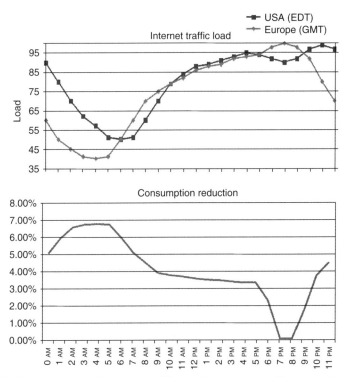

Figure 3.9. Typical averaged Internet traffic load and consumption reduction (using EE techniques).

on the packet loss and delay. A similar approach to buffering or (re)scheduling bursts to improve opportunities to shutdown (sleep)in the context of grids [82] and networks [83, 84] have also been considered.

In [85], Chiaraviglio et al. modeled a network for maximizing the energy saving by switching off idle nodes and idle links. The problem is NP-hard, so in [15], several simple heuristic algorithms are employed, which sort all the nodes depending on the number of links, the amount of flows they accommodate, or using a random strategy to switch off for saving energy. In the simple network scenario, which includes the core, edge, and aggregate networks, it is possible to switch off 30% of links and 50% of nodes. The same author extends their work considering a real-world case in [60]. The problem for minimizing the number of nodes and links for saving energy, given a certain traffic demand, has been solved by ILP for simple networks. The algorithm switches off devices that consume more power in descending order. The results show that it is possible to reduce energy consumption by more than 23%, that is, 3 GWh/year in a real network scenario. In a further example [86], the author took the Italian telecommunications network as reference architecture and evaluated the extent of energy saving if green network technologies were adopted, such as power scaling and standby exploitation. It assumed the network equipment, such as routers, home gateways, and DSLAMs, have three power consumption states: the full load, idle, and standby after making use of green technologies. The power consumption of full-load state and the idle state varies linearly according to the actual traffic load. The power consumption of the standby state is a small fraction of the idle state power. The conclusion of using different green technologies within the reference scenario is that their adoption may save up to 68% power consumed relative to the current approach.

However, these approaches all suffer from the problem that when a router or a link is switched off in a network, they lose the present state of the network and so will trigger routing protocol reconvergence events. The traffic is rerouted along longer paths that may not be acceptable because of congestion, QoS, and the extra delay. Therefore, when making use of the infrastructure sleeping, network connectivity and QoS must be considered to guarantee the reliability of the network.

Recently, there has been a new direction in infrastructure sleeping: to switch off the line-card instead of the whole router. As the disappearance of whole router may trigger reconvergence events and may thus lead to network disruption and discontinuities, some researchers choose to switch off individual line cards and remap the links to other ones. This avoids discontinuities and saves power when the traffic load is light. In [87], routing reconfiguration at different layers is compared: the IP layer (the virtual layer) and WDM (the physical layer) for the purpose of switching off line cards for saving energy. The scheme that reroutes demands in the virtual layer achieves the best saving. Similarly, in [88], it also proposes a scheme to switch off line cards when traffic load is low. Fisher et al. [89] proposed another form of infrastructure sleeping where they shut down the redundant cables and the line cards instead of the whole router during periods of low utilization. The switching off line-card approach may be a good direction to pursue. Nevertheless, in a router, the major source power consumption is the base system (chassis, processor, and switching fabric), which consumes about 50% of the total power consumption [49]. Therefore, to switch off the whole router still yields more substantial energy savings.

Sharrock et al. [51] have worked on introducing the "self-optimizing" autonomic property at the hardware level by applying it to the optimization of data centers' energy costs. They have proposed an approach to describe a compromise between, on one hand, the power consumption of the network infrastructure and on the other hand, the deterioration of the QoS for the applications using this network. Being able to control the dynamic reconfiguration at two levels, at the application level by dynamically reconfiguring QoS profiles and at the hardware level by switching on and off links, modules or routers allows a global management of the data center. Indeed, the use of an autonomic manager allows the administrator to control the energy costs or the performance by varying only one parameter that handles a high-level management policy.

The goal was to deal with the performance/electric consumption dilemma for the network part. This is a challenge for years to come, as the perfect system must take into account the energy consumption of the machines and also the network equipment, the QoS, and financial costs, for example.

3.5.2.3 Sleep-Supporting Protocols. Traditionally, network equipment does not typically possess sleeping state(s). However, recent industry standardization efforts have been proposed for enabling the equipment to operate in a more energy efficiency manner. For instance, the IEEE 802.3az EEE standard has been approved

[74] by the Institute of Electrical and Electronic Engineers (IEEE) in October 2010. EEE provides a hardware support for energy saving, which defines a mechanism to reduce the power consumption when the traffic load is low for a physical layer protocol. Furthermore, the ITU has organized a series of symposia on ICT and climate change [90]; the Alliance for Telecommunications Industry Solutions (ATIS) also set up a specific committee called Network Interface, Power and Protection Committee (NIPP) [91] working on developing standards for network interfaces, with power and protection including reducing the power consumption of equipment.

ENERGY-EFFICIENT PASSIVE OPTICAL NETWORKS. PONs are currently the major contributor to the power budget of fixed optical networks. In a PON, the largest energy consumption is at the customer premises, that is, by the ONUs that account for over 65% of the overall power consumed by PONs [92]. Methods both at the physical layer and at the MAC layer have been proposed to reduce the ONU energy consumption [93]. MAC layer methods are mainly based on the possibility of switching to sleep mode the ONU during low-traffic period. Therefore, strategies based on cycles of sleep and wake periods have been standardized [94]. However, such methods trade energy reduction for increased frame transfer delay. For example, when the ONU is sleeping, it can neither receive nor transmit packets.

For this reason, the concept of variable sleep periods was introduced in [95] to save energy at the ONUs while avoiding service degradation in the presence of traffic with demanding delay requirements. The rationale is simple: each class of service (CoS) is assigned a specific sleep period such that the delay constraint of the specific class is met. If multiple CoS are received by one ONU, the sleep period of the most demanding class is selected. The length of a sleep period can be fixed (i.e., set a priori to a predefined value [96]) or it can vary. In fact, users connected to ONUs may dynamically modify their service subscriptions (e.g., request a video streaming to watch a movie for some hours), possibly changing the overall delay requirements. On the other hand, such changes have a period of hours; therefore, the sleep time does not need to be updated very often. In such a situation, it might be convenient to be able to change the length of the sleep period by either tying it to the downstream frame statistics [97] or having it varying based on the service class delay requirements and to the predicted delay statistics [95, 98].

When focusing on strategies based on variable sleep periods, it becomes crucial to develop effective decision mechanisms for the sleep length. One possibility is to model the implementation of cyclic sleep in a PON using queuing theory. For example, the authors in [4] proposed a model where an OLT–ONU system is assimilated to a polling system with gated service, exponentially distributed frame interarrival time, and generic service time. This model was implemented in OPNET, and its performance was assessed through simulations with a scenario consisting of a 10-GE PON with one OLT linked to connected to single ONU. The OLT is aware of the services subscribed by the ONU in terms of QoS Class, IP packet delay variation (IPDV) and IP packet transfer delay (IPTD) constraints [99], and bandwidth (i.e., data rate) [100]. The values for the delay constraints are related to a generic end-to-end IP network composed of n spans, contributing equally and additively to the considered end-to-end parameters, where the PON is the access span. Each service is defined with its own frame payload size and data rate, defined by studying the real traffic distribution in a network [100–104].

The results show the effectiveness of the model in choosing a value of sleep time that guarantees the IPTD constraint for all the services. By focusing only on the IPTD value, it is not possible to guarantee the IPDV requirements for the strictest service in the first combination; however, the obtained energy efficiency is high, that is slightly below 90%. When the sleep time was calculated as a function of both IPTD and IPDV constraints, the IPTD constraint is again satisfied and, this time, the simulated IPDV is below the maximum allowed time. However, the energy efficiency is lower but is still a respectable 50%.

3.5.2.4 Green Routing. In the current core network architecture, IP routers consume a larger proportion of energy as compared with the underlying synchronous digital hierarchy (SDH) and WDM layers [12, 13, 105]. With the next-generation network (NGN), currently, the industry vision is to employ an IP-over-WDM architecture that eliminates the original SDH transport layer because this lowers the equipment costs and energy consumption [106, 107]. However, in an IP-over-WDM architecture, because there is no traffic grooming in the SDH layer, IP routers are required to perform more IP packet processing, for example, subwavelength grooming, and thus consume more energy. Therefore, in this scenario, the switching off routers or selective interfaces when traffic demand is light has been regarded as a promising strategy and explored intensively in recent years [15, 16].

Energy-aware routing schemes usually follow the following form:

- A physical network topology constructed of routers and links, in which links have a known capacity.
- Knowledge of the amount of traffic exchanged by any source/destination node pair.
- The power consumption of each link and node.
- Find the set of routers and links that must be powered on so that the total power consumption is minimized.
- Flow conservation and maximum link utilization constraints
- Possible QoS constraints – such as end-to-end delay

These approaches naturally lead to some resources being heavily utilized in order for others to be "turned off." To avoid congestion, it is normal to represent links by an "effective capacity."

A typical example is the green distributed algorithm (GRiDA), which exploits link-state routing protocol to disseminate load and power consumption of links [108]. Being reactive, it does not require any knowledge of the traffic demand matrix. A distributed algorithm switches off links when they are underutilized, and their absence in the network does not affect the network functionalities and switches on idle links when capacity is required to guarantee a proper reaction to faults and changes in the traffic demand. A penalty mechanism reduces the risk of undesirable actions. However, the main problem of green routing protocols is that when routers or their interfaces are switched off, they lose the ability to exchange routing protocol signaling messages.

In other words, the logical IP layer topology changes when a node disappears from the network. This can trigger a series of reconvergence events that can cause network discontinuities and disruption. Nevertheless, GRiDA is capable of reducing energy consumption by 50%.

Routers are the most power-hungry devices, followed by the electronic signal regenerators and ROADMs, with the all-optical devices such as optical cross connect (OXC) and optical amplifiers being less power consuming. In the context of Wide Area Networks (WANs), in which network nodes are spread out long distances, such a knowledge may be exploited by a properly crafted energy-aware routing algorithm that routes connections through the NEs, which are currently powered by green energy sources, minimizing the overall greenhouse gas (GHG) emissions of the network. As the renewable energy sources vary with time, it is necessary to have this information updated for each node. In the modern generalized multiprotocol label switching (GMPLS)-controlled optical networks, such updates may be realized by Open Shortest Path First-Traffic Engineering (OSPF-TE) extensions. In [109], such an extension is presented and used to spread the energy-related information through the network on a fixed time interval. Green awareness is enabled by flooding energy source information over the network, which is used in OSPF-TE routing decisions to lower the GHG emissions. Observing the behavior of the proposed algorithm under different scenarios, it is seen that the proposed algorithm can save up to 27% of the GHG emissions (in terms of cost unit) at the expense of a marginal increase in the path length, compared to traditional shortest path routing algorithm. Furthermore, in [110], GMPLS extensions are used to integrate energy efficiency and network resilience. Results show that the electrical port usage can be significantly reduced by using intelligent regenerator and wavelength converter placement strategies. Thus, the scarce usage of electrical ports can help to reduce the power budget of the overall communication system.

Another method for achieving energy savings in excess of 30% in wide-area networks is presented in [111]. The approach applies a limited set of precalculated network topology configurations derived via a genetic algorithm (GA) across the day. The GA determines the minimum set of resources required in order to support a given traffic demand. Information gleaned from Simple Network Management Protocol (SNMP) trap messages, triggered by the use of a link utilization threshold, determine when to switch between configurations. The threshold employs moving average smoothing and is discretely readjusted over the course of a daily cycle based on anticipated basal load variations. By exploiting Multitopology Routing-Open Shortest Path First (MT-OSPF), this approach provides a scalable and flexible means of reconfiguring an infrastructure that avoids routing discontinuities, excessive computational effort, and the exchange of considerable volumes of control information.

Despite the promise of green routing protocols, there remain significant impediments to change. For example, operators have service-level agreements with their customers and are wary of adopting any technology that increases the risk of outages or lowers QoS. Furthermore, resilience typically equates to redundancy. Redundancy implies additional equipment is in "hot" standby for fast protection switch-over in the event of a failure. Therefore, although switching off these "spare" resources saves energy, they may be needed and, if so, they have to be available at very short notice. Consequentially, the overriding commercial interests of the operators may cause them to shy away from new routing protocols and favor energy-saving technologies that are transparent to the IP layer (such as rate adaptation).

ENERGY-AWARE DYNAMIC RWA ALGORITHM. The energy consumption and GHG emissions of the network elements can be taken into account when defining the metric of routing algorithms. In particular, in WDM optical networks, the GreenSpark [112] heuristic has been developed to address the multiobjective routing and wavelength assignment (RWA) problem of minimizing either the power consumption or the GHG emissions while maintaining the connections blocking probability as low as possible. GreenSpark operates online, routing the connections as they arrive. At each new connection request, two stages are performed: in the first stage, the best load-balanced paths satisfying the connection request and QoS constraint are selected (typically, three partially disjoint paths are identified). At the second stage, among such feasible paths, the one that minimizes the power consumption (MinPower) or the GHG emissions (MinGas) is finally chosen to route the connection, according to the objective function selected. Apart from minimizing the power consumption or the emissions, GreenSpark is even able to reduce the blocking probability when compared with a traditional routing algorithm, such as Shortest Path or minimum interference routing algorithm (MIRA). Apart from defining an energy consumption model for an IP-over-WDM network, one of the most significant added values of the framework is the incorporation of both physical layer aspects, such as power demand of each component, and virtual topology-based energy management with integrated traffic grooming, so as to adversely condition the use of energy-hungry links and devices.

ENERGY-AWARE OSPF-TE EXTENSIONS. The information concerning energy consumption of the network elements has to be disseminated across the network routers that can thus determine the best or *greenest* route for each destination by providing each router with complete relevant knowledge of the network. In an autonomous system, a dynamic routing protocol such as OSPF-TE extensions is employed to build the complete map of the network (*link-state* protocol) in each router. However, OSPF-TE does not carry in its link-state advertisement (LSA) messages any information about the current energy consumption of the network elements. Therefore, energy-aware OSPF-TE protocol extensions have been proposed in several works [113–116], together with properly crafted RWA and reoptimization algorithms that exploit such information. Specifically, opaque LSAs have been extended with new type-length-value (TLV) fields, carrying power and CO_2 emissions information. Such LSAs are spread in the network (among the Designated Router/Backup Designated Router and all the nodes) and are included in the LSAs every time a significant change in the energy consumption or emissions occurs (e.g., a change in the energy source powering a device, as an example, when switching from solar panels energy to traditional "dirty" energy source). Results show that the proposed extension helps in reducing the overall network power consumption/GHG emissions when compared to traditional shortest path and pure load-balancing algorithms, at the expense of a limited increase in the blocking probability. However, a network operator should also consider extra network overhead, and the possible additional expenses for obtaining the information from the associated "smart grid" power supply network.

3.5.2.5   Network Virtualization: Virtual Router Migration.   Network virtualization may be seen as one of the basic building blocks of a future Internet. It is expected to overcome the perceived ossification of the current Internet through more flexible management of network resources. Typical network virtualization approaches partition physical routers into an arbitrary number of virtual routers [117, 118]. A virtual router is a logical router that separates behavioral functionality from the physical platform that hosts the entity, including mechanisms and tools for management, configuration, monitoring, and maintenance. Virtual routers provide a means of more effectively utilizing a single physical router. The functions of several small routers can be performed on a single large router that accommodates the virtual router instances. Virtualization is already supported by some commercial routers, such as the Cisco nexus 7000 VDC [119] and the Juniper logical router [120]. They both belong to the class of logical routers. To be more precise, the concept of a virtual router and a logical router are not always the same. A virtual router is a simplified routing instance, which has one routing table, while a logical router can support multiple routing tables at the same time. That is to say, a logical router can contain several virtual routers.

Virtual routers are then interconnected by virtual links, which may span an arbitrary number of physical links in the substrate network. Such an approach allows network administrators to create virtual networks specially tailored toward a certain objectives. These networks may have topologies that differ substantially from the underlying physical network. Moreover, these networks can be created on demand and removed once they are no longer needed. Indeed, one particular advantage gained through virtualization lies in the mobility of virtual resources. As virtualization itself provides an abstraction from actual hardware, virtual resources are no longer bound to a particular hardware instance. Thus, a virtual router can, for example, be moved from one physical router to another physical router. The technical basis for this is the live migration of a virtual machine – that is, moving a virtual machine from one hardware instance to another instance without suspending it [121]. This concept has already been used in data centers and cloud environments [123]. For routers, it has been envisioned as a new network-management primitive [122]. Migrating routers, however, requires more sophisticated migration mechanisms. In particular, some form of traffic redirection is necessary in order to preserve the Network Layer topology and keep existing connections alive. While in a single data center, traffic redirection can be handled transparently by the Link Layer (e.g., via artificial Address Resolution Protocol (ARP) updates), this is not easily possible for routers as prime Network Layer equipment. Migration has to be performed across different subnets. This concept is commonly known as wide-area migration. Again, this has been first introduced for data center scenarios with multiple, distributed data centers [124, 125].

A major advantage of virtual router migration is the possibility to react dynamically to changes to the network whereby virtual routers are moved among different physical hosts without changing the network logical topology. For example, migration can be used as a remediation/recovery mechanism in the face of pending hardware failures or natural disasters [126]. In this case, migration can increase the overall resilience of a virtual network by keeping the network operational even while part of the hardware fails. Another application of virtual router migration is the reconfiguration of available hardware resources. Virtual networks could be created and destroyed in a highly dynamic manner. However, this is a particular challenge for the resource allocation algorithm, as it must cope with the dynamic reconfiguration while avoiding fragmentation of the available hardware resources [127]. The migration must also avoid oscillating states, akin to route flapping, where the act of migration itself causes a change of network state sufficient to trigger a rapid migration back to a preceding state.

Migration is more complex than router virtualization because it needs to solve several problems. The first one is how to minimum the outages when moving the virtual router. As moving a virtual router to new physical platform always leads to some delays, it may cause some network disruption and discontinuities. Specifically, the data plane, which is responsible for forwarding packets, should not be halted during this transfer process. On the other hand, the control plane usually has some form of retransmission mechanism that provides protection from interruptions. It is more tolerant of disruption than the data plane. The second issue is how to realize the link migration after the virtual router migrates to the destination. In the past, an IP layer link corresponds to a physical link. If so, it is hard to realize the virtual router migration, as it is not possible for a physical link to follow the virtual router by unplugging and plugging-in the cable. Thanks to the recent new transport layer technologies, such as the programmable transport network [18], it is possible to allow the physical links between routers to be dynamically connected or suspended according to requirements. For example, when a virtual router moves to the new physical platform, the link to the virtual router can be established by the setting up of a new link in the underlying optical transport network. A third issue is to consider the facilities needed for supporting virtual router migration, for example, whether the destination physical platform has enough interfaces for packet delivery, whether the switch fabric in the router has the ability to process all the required switching tasks after new virtual router have been accommodated, and whether the interfaces can dynamically bind with the data plane.

Some researchers have devoted effort to considering virtual router migration for reducing the impact of planned maintenance because downtime is a primary concern for ISPs. However, these approaches tend to perform the move while the router is "cold," that is, not actively transporting data traffic while the migration takes place. VROOM (virtual routers on the move), on the other hand, supports live migration of logical routers allowing them to move among different physical platforms without causing network discontinuities and instabilities [19]. VROOM has been tested on both software and hardware. The results show that it does not interrupt the data plane and has a short downtime period for the control plane. When number of routes is about 15,000, the migration takes about 30 s on a software testbed and less than 2 s on a hardware testbed. Fortunately, existing retransmission mechanisms within the routing protocols can mitigate the impact of control plane downtime.

Nevertheless, the purpose of VROOM is to reduce the impact of planned maintenance rather than to save energy. It does not consider the events needed to trigger the virtual router migration and the algorithm needed to determine the appropriate physical destination platform for the migration; that is to say, when to move the virtual router and how to choose the appropriate destination physical router with the objective of saving energy. In response, a new dynamic energy management scheme employing infrastructure sleeping and virtual router migration has been proposed [128]. An alternative approach is considered in [129]. It also uses the virtual migration concept to maintain the IP layer topology unchanged. The key difference is that it moves the functionality of line cards within a physical router instead of moving the entire virtual router functionality to another physical platform.

3.6 CHALLENGES

Given the user and economic benefits of adopting "green" energy-saving mechanisms, it is perhaps surprising that the lack of uptake that has taken place. However, network operators have to balance reliability against the potential cost savings. Typically, for a carrier-grade network, it is necessary to restore service delivery within 50 ms. Even for less stringent services, end users (customers) are unlikely to tolerate outages of more than a few tens of seconds, particularly if this situation arises repeatedly. In consequence, operators design their networks with resilience, whereby various backup/alternative paths exist between different parts of the network. In the event of a failure, the presence of these backup paths allows the traffic to be redirected along them to the appropriate destination(s) soon after the failure is detected. However, during normal operating conditions, this equates to spare capacity, which is nonetheless consuming resources.

Operators are also averse to embracing new technologies that lack a clear migration path from the existing deployed infrastructure and may have an unproven "track record." Consequently, it is likely that transparent energy-saving technologies will be embraced, even if the potential benefits are somewhat more modest. These include the roll out of more efficient routers that can interwork seamlessly with existing equipment, thus providing a "plug-in" replacement as and when an upgrade is required. Other "straightforward" approaches include rate adaptation whereby both ends of a point-to-point link can sense the capabilities of the other end and, if supported, adjust the transmission speed or related behavior such as temporary sleeping to take place when the load conditions are suitable.

Of course, the replacement of equipment with similar devices with a better "energy star" rating or dynamic link rate adjustment is only capable of delivering localized improvements. Better energy savings are possible through the global coordination of activities across a network. This requires the adoption of more radical mechanisms, such as green routing and/or virtual router migration. However, at this time, it remains unclear whether the added benefits will outweigh the required capital expenditure, particularly, as has been shown much can be achieved with efficiency improvements within the networking devices, coupled with temporary sleeping and rate adaptation.

3.7 SUMMARY

Designing energy-efficient networking is a challenging task that must involve industrial and academic researchers. Some joint projects such as GreenTouch [130] proposed to increase network energy efficiency by a factor of 1000. Such aggressive approaches must deal with all networking levels from wireless to wired infrastructures and from core to access equipment [131]. Combined improvements in software and hardware must be explored. With the development of the "Internet of Things" machine-to-machine (M2M) communication traffic may grow considerably, even if data rates are smaller, and thus energy costs from M2M will become significant. Key research activities proposed in the area of energy-efficient wired networks have been discussed including a number of contributions of the European COST Action IC0804; however, research in this area remains very much ongoing.

REFERENCES

[1] Baliga J, Ayre R, Hinton K, and Tucker R. Photonic switching and the energy bottleneck. In: *Photonics in Switching*; 2007 Aug 19–22; San Francisco, CA; pp. 125–126.

[2] Fettweis G and Zimmermann E. ICT energy consumption-trends and challenges. In: Proc. of 11th Int'l. Symp. Wireless Personal Multimedia Communications; 2008, Lapland, Finland.

[3] Pickavet M, Vereecken W, Demeyer S, Audenaert P, Vermeulen B, Develder C, et al. Worldwide energy needs for ICT: the rise of power-aware networking. In: 2nd Int'l. Symp. ANTS'08; 2008 Dec; pp. 1–3, Mumbai, India.

[4] R. Bolla, R. Bruschi, F. Davoli, and F. Cucchietti, "Energy efficiency in the future internet: a survey of existing approaches and trends in energy-aware fixed network infrastructures," Commun Surveys Tut, 2011, Vol.13, pp. 1–22.

[5] Paul Bolton, "Energy price rises and fuel poverty", 2010, Available: http://www.parliament. uk/business/publications/research/key-issues-for-the-new-parliament/green-growth/energy -price-rises/. Accessed 2014 Nov 12.

[6] Global Action Plan. An inefficient truth. 2007. Available at http://www.globalactionplan .org.uk/sites/gap/files/An%20Inefficient%20Truth%20-%20Executive%20Summary.pdf. Accessed 2014 Sep 30.

[7] N. E. F. a. 1E. The PC energy report. 2009. Available at http://www.climatesaverscomputing .org/docs/1E_PC_Energy_Report_2009_US.pdf. Accessed 2014 Sep 30.

[8] S. Jayashree and C. S. Ram Murthy, A taxonomy of energy management protocols for ad hoc wireless networks, Commun Mag IEEE, vol. 45, pp. 104–110, 2007.

[9] Prakash V, Kumar B, and Srivastava AK. Energy efficiency comparison of some topology-based and location-based mobile ad hoc routing protocols. In: Proceedings of the 2011 International Conference on Communication, Computing, Security; 2011; Rourkela, Odisha, India.

[10] Deruyck M, Vereecken W, Tanghe E, Joseph W, Pickavet M, Martens L, and Demeester P. Power consumption in wireless access network. In: Wireless Conference; 2010; pp. 924–931.

[11] Gupta M and Singh S. Greening of the Internet. In: Proc. SIGCOMM'03; 2003; pp. 19–26, Karlsruhe, Germany.

[12] Baliga J, Hinton K, and Tucker RS. Energy consumption of the Internet. In: COIN-ACOFT 07; 2007; pp. 1–3, Melbourne, Australia.

[13] G. Shen and R. S. Tucker, Energy-minimized design for IP over WDM networks, Opt Commun Netw IEEE/OSA J, vol. 1, pp. 176–186, 2009.

[14] Wang L, Lu R, Li Q, Zheng X, and Zhang H. Energy efficient design for multi-shelf IP over WDM networks. In: INFOCOM'11, Workshop on Green and Communications and Networking; 2011, Shanghai, China.

[15] Chiaraviglio L, Mellia M, and Neri F. Reducing power consumption in backbone networks. In: ICC'09; 2009; pp. 1–6, Dresden, Germany.

[16] Nedevschi S, Popa L, Iannaccone G, Ratnasamy S, and Wetherall D. Reducing network energy consumption via sleeping and rate-adaptation. In: Proc. NSDI'08, 5th USENIX Symposium on Networked Systems Design and Implementation; 2008; pp. 323–336, San Francisco, USA.

[17] Schaffrath G, Werle C, Papadimitriou P, Feldmann A, Bless R, Greenhalgh A, Wundsam A, Kind M, Maennel O, and Mathy L. Network virtualization architecture: proposal and initial prototype. In: Proc.VISA'09; 2009, pp. 63–72, Barcelona, Spain.

[18] Agrawal M, Bailey SR, Greenberg A, Pastor J, Sebos P, Seshan S, Van Der Merwe K, and Yates J. RouterFarm: towards a dynamic, manageable network edge. In: Proc. SIGCOMM workshop, INM'06; 2006; pp. 5–10, Pisa, Italy.

[19] Wang Y, Keller E, Biskeborn B, van der Merwe J, and Rexford J. Virtual routers on the move: live router migration as a network-management primitive. In: Proceedings of SIGCOMM'08; 2008; pp. 231–242, Seattle, USA.

[20] E. M. Noam, *Telecommunications Regulation Today and Tomorrow*. New York: Law & Business, 1983.

[21] G. Bertram, Restructuring the New Zealand electricity sector 1984–2005, in F.P. Sioshansi and W. Pfaffenberger (eds.) (2006), *Electricity Market Reform: An International Perspective*, Oxford: Elsevier., 203–234.

[22] Department of Energy and Climate Change (DECC), UK Low Carbon Transition Plan Emission Projections, July 2009, Available at http://www.fcrn.org.uk/sites/default/files/UK_low_carbon_transition_plan_2009.pdf

[23] ITU, Standard ITU-T L.1410: Methodology for environmental impact assessment of ICT goods, networks and services. 2011.

[24] European Commission. Towards Smart Power Networks. European Commission; 2012, ISBN: 92-79-00554-5

[25] Pau L-F "The communications and information economy: issues, tariffs and economics research areas," J Econ Dynam Contr, vol. 26, pp. 1651–1675, 2002.

[26] A. Mas-Colell, M.D. Whinston, and JR Green, *Microeconomic Theory*. New York, NY: Oxford University Press, 1995.

[27] E. Shafir, and R. A. LeBoeuf, "Rationality," Annu Rev Psychol, 2002, 53 (1), 491–517.

[28] H.A. Simon, "Rational decision making in business organizations," Am Econ Rev, 1979, 69 (4), 493–513.

[29] A. Tversky, and D. Kahneman, "*Judgment under Uncertainty: Heuristics and Biases*," in, D. Kahneman and P. Slovic and A. Tversky (Eds.), 1974, New York: Cambridge University Press.

[30] D. Kahneman, and S. Frederick, "Representativeness revisited: attribute substitution in intuitive judgment," in *Heuristics & Biases: The Psychology of Intuitive Judgment*, T. Gilovich and D. Griffin and D. Kahneman (Eds.), 2002, New York: Cambridge University Press.

[31] Pau L-F. Green networks and green tariffs as driven by user service demand. In: Hadjiantonis A and Stiller B, editors. *Telecommunications Economics*. Springer Lecture notes in computer science. Volume 7216; 2012; pp. 117–125. DOI: 10.1007/978-3-642-30382-1.

[32] S. Meij, and L-F Pau. *Auctioning bulk SMS/MMS mobile messages*, Comput Econ, Vol 27, no 2–3, 2006, 395–430.

[33] F. Lévêque, *Competitive Electricity Markets and Sustainability*. 2006, New York: Edward Elgar.

[34] H. Chen, L-F Pau. Individual telecommunications tariffs in Chinese communities, in: Huang WW, Wang Y and Day J (Eds), *Global Mobile Commerce: Strategies, Implementations and Cases*. IGI Global (formerly IDEA Group), 2007, ISBN 978-1-59904-558-0. Available at http://www.igi-global.com/reference/details.asp?id=6980. Accessed 2014 Sep 30.

[35] M. Castells, *The Rise of the Network Society*, Vol. 1, 2nd. ed, 2000, Oxford: Blackwell.

[36] Chen H and Pau L-F. Mass customization in wireless communication services: individual services and tariffs. ERIM Research report; 2007 Aug. Available at http://hdl.handle .net/1765/10515. Accessed 2014 Sep 30; bProc. Intl. Conf. on Mass Customization; 2008 Oct; Cambridge, MA; cPiller FT and Tseng MM, editors. Handbook of research in Mass Customization and Personalization (in 2 volumes). Volume 1: Strategies and Concepts; Volume 2: Applications and Cases. World Scientific; 2010. Available at http://www .worldscibooks.com/business/7378.html. Accessed 2014 Sep 30.

[37] Pau L-F. *Optimizing a public 3G/LTE wireless network and associated services for minimum energy consumption or emissions: analysis for "green wireless tariffs"*. In: Pierson J-M and Hlavacs H, editors. Proceedings of the COST Action IC0804 on Energy Efficiency in Large Scale Distributed Systems; 2011. Toulouse: IRIT Publication; pp. 87–91. ISBN : 978-2-917490-18-1; EAN: 9782917490181.

[38] Pau L-F. Energy consumption effects of WiFi off-loading access in 3G or LTE public wireless networks, in Special Issue (SI) on green networking and computing, Int J Bus Data Commun Netw, Vol 9 (2), pp. 1–10, 2013 ISSN: 1548-0631

[39] F.A. Hayek, *Individualism and Economic Order*. University of Chicago Press; Chicago, 1980.

[40] W.J. Adams, and J. L. Yellen, "Commodity bundling and the burden of monopoly," Q J Econ, 1976, 90 (3), 475–98.

[41] Y. Bakos, and E. Brynjolfsson, "Bundling information goods: pricing, profits and efficiency," Manag Sci, 1999, 45 (12), 1613–30.

[42] A.C. Pigou, Discrimination monopoly. Part II, Chapter XVII. in: *The Economics of welfare*. 1920, London: Macmillan and Co.

[43] J. Aweya, "IP router architectures: an overview," J Syst Arch 46, 1999, pp: 483 – 511.

[44] Router architectures. Available at http://www.cs.virginia.edu/~cs458/slides/module09b-routers.pdf. Accessed 2014 Sep 30.

[45] Cisco CRS-1 16-Slot single-shelf system. Cisco data sheet. Available at http://www.cisco .com/en/US/prod/collateral/routers/ps5763/ps5862/product_data_sheet09186a008022d5f3 .pdf. Accessed 2014 Sep 30.

[46] Cisco CRS-1 24-Slot Fabric-Card Chassis. Cisco data sheet. Available at http://www.cisco .com/en/US/prod/collateral/routers/ps5763/ps5862/product_data_sheet0900aecd80340baa .pdf. Accessed 2014 Sep 30.

[47] Cisco CRS-1 carrier routing system multi-shelf system description. Cisco data sheet. Available at: http://www.cisco.com. Accessed 2014 Sep 30.

[48] S. Huang and R. Dutta, Dynamic traffic grooming: the changing role of traffic grooming, Commun Survey Tut, vol. 9, pp. 32–50, 2006.

[49] Chabarek J, Sommers J, Barford P, Estan C, Tsiang D, and Wright S. Power awareness in network design and routing. In: INFOCOM 2008; 2008 Apr 13–18; Phoenix, AZ; pp. 457–465.

[50] Orgerie A-C, Lefèvre L, Guérin-Lassous I, and Pacheco DL. ECOFEN: an end-to-end energy cost model and simulator for evaluating power consumption in large-scale networks.

In: Sustalnet 2011: First International Workshop on Sustainable Internet and Internet for Sustainability; 2011 Jun; Lucca, Italy.

[51] Sharrock R, Monteil T, Stolf P, and Brun O. Autonomic computing to manage green core networks with quality of service (regular paper). In: Energy Efficiency in Large Scale Distributed Systems Conference (EE-LSDS 2013); 2013 Apr 22–24; Vienna. Springer; Switzerland, 2013.

[52] Nedevschi S, Popaa L, Iannaccone G, Ratnasamy S, and Wetherall D. *Reducing network energy consumption via sleeping and rate-adaptation*. In: USENIX NSDI 2008; 2008 Apr 16–18; San Francisco, USA; pp. 323–336.

[53] Rodgers J. Energy efficient Ethernet: technology, application and why you should care. Available at http://communities.intel.com/community/wired/blog/2011/05/05/. Accessed 2014 Sep 30.

[54] Zhai B, Blaauw D, Sylvester D, and Flautner K. *Theoretical and practical limits of dynamic voltage scaling*. In: DAC 2004; 2004 Jun 7–11; San Diego, USA; pp. 868–873.

[55] Weiser M, Welch B, Demers A, and Shenker S. *Scheduling for reduced CPU energy*. In: USENIX OSDI 1994; 1994 Nov 14–17; Monterey, USA; pp. 13–23.

[56] Vasic N and Kostic D. *Energy-aware traffic engineering*. In: e-Energy 2010; 2010 Apr 13–15; Passau, Germany; pp. 169–178.

[57] Chabarek J, Sommers J, Barford P, Estan C, Tsiang D, and Wright S. *Power awareness in network design and routing*. In: IEEE INFOCOM 2008; 2008 Apr 13–18; Phoenix, USA; pp. 457–465.

[58] Chiaraviglio L, Mellia M, and Neri F. *Reducing power consumption in backbone networks*. In: IEEE ICC Workshops 2009; 2009 Jun 14–18, Dresden, Germany; pp. 2298–2303.

[59] Fisher W, Suchara M, and Rexford J, *Greening backbone networks: reducing energy consumption by shutting off cables in bundled links*. In: 1st ACM SIGCOMM Workshop on Green Networking; 2010 Aug 30–Sep 3; New Delhi, India; pp. 29–34.

[60] Bianzino AP, Chaudet C, Larrocca F, Rossi D, and Rougier J-L. Energy-aware routing: a reality check. In: 3rd International Workshop on Green Communications (GreenComm 2010) in Conjunction with the IEEE Global Communications Conference; 2010 Dec 6–10; Miami, USA; pp. 1422–1427.

[61] Tibuleac S. ROADM network design issues. OFC/NFOEC; 2009, paper NMD1.

[62] J. Homa and K. Bala, ROADM architectures and their enabling WSS technology, Commun Mag IEEE, vol. 46, pp. 150–154, 2008.

[63] Morais, RM et al, "Impact of node architecture in the power consumption and footprint requirements of optical transport networks, IEEE/OSA J Opt Commun Netw, Vol:5 Issue:5, May 2013, pp. 421 –436, DOI: 10.1364/JOCN.5.000421

[64] Bhaumik S, et al. Energy-efficient design and optimization of wireline access networks. Technical Report arXiv:1101.2717v1; 2011 Jan. Available at http://arxiv.org/pdf/1101.2717 .pdf. Accessed 2014 Sep 30.

[65] Y Yan, L Dittmann, Energy efficiency in Ethernet passive optical networks (EPONs): protocol design and performance evaluation, J Commun, Vol. 6, No. 3, pp: 249–261, 2011.

[66] Cisco. Converge IP and DWDM layers in the core network. White paper; 2007. Available at http://www.webtorials.com/main/resource/papers/cisco/paper114/ ConvergeIPandDWDMLayersintheCoreNetwork.pdf. Accessed 2014 Sep 30.

[67] Orgerie A-C, Lefèvre L, and Gelas J-P. Chasing gaps between bursts: towards energy efficient large scale experimental grids. In: 9th International Conference on Parallel and Distributed Computing, Applications and Technologies; 2008, Otago, New Zealand.

[68] Abilene™. Available at http://www.cs.utexas.edu/~yzhang/research/AbileneTM/. Accessed 2014 Sep 30.

[69] Géant Network Website. Available at http://www.geant.net. Accessed 2014 Sep 30.

[70] Phillips C, Gazo-Cervero A, and Galan-Jimenez J. Pro-active energy management for wide area networks. In: IET International Conference on Communication Technology and Application (ICCTA 2011); 2011 Jan, Beijing, China.

[71] G. J. Eilenberger, S. Bunse, L. Dembeck, U. Gebhard, F. Ilchmann, W. Lautenschlaeger, and J. Milbrandt, "Energy efficient transport for the future Internet," Bell Labs Tech J, vol. 15, pp. 147–167, 2010.

[72] W. Hou, L. Guo, J. Cao, J. Wu, and L. Hao, "Green multicast grooming based on optical bypass technology," Opt Fiber Tech, vol. 17, pp. 111–119, 2011.

[73] Perrin S. The need for next-generation ROADM networks. Heavy Reading white paper; 2010. Available at http://downloads.lightreading.com/wplib/heavyreading/NG_ROADM_WP_Final.pdf?p_redirone=yes. Accessed 2014 Sep 30.

[74] IEEE P802.3az energy efficient Ethernet. Available at http://www.ieee802.org/3/az/index.html. Accessed 2014 Sep 30.

[75] Galan-Jimenez J and Gazo-Cervero A. ELEE: energy levels-energy efficiency tradeoff in wired communication networks. IEEE Commun Lett, Volume: 17, Issue: 1, 2013, DOI: 10.1109/LCOMM.2012.120312.122176

[76] Gunaratne C and Christensen K. Ethernet adaptive link rate: system design and performance evaluation. In: Proceedings 2006 31st IEEE Conference on Local Computer Networks; 2006 Nov; pp. 28–35, Tampa, USA.

[77] Bianzino, AP, et al.: "A survey of green networking research," Commun Surveys Tut, vol. 14, no. 2, pp. 3–20, 2012.

[78] Bart P, et al. Power reduction techniques in multilayer traffic engineering. In: ICTON 2009: 11th International Conference on Transparent Optical Networks; 2009; Volumes 1 and 2. New York, NY: IEEE; 2009. pp. 41–44, Azores, Portugal.

[79] Paredes A and García AE. Energy efficiency in national Internet networks. Master Thesis in Business and Information Technologies. University of Cantabria; 2012. Available at URL: http://hdl.handle.net/10902/3804. Accessed 2014 Sep 30.

[80] Roy SN. Energy logic: a road map to reducing energy consumption in telecommunications networks. In: IEEE 30th International Telecommunications Energy Conference, INTELEC 2008; 2008, San Diego, USA.

[81] Alimian A, Nordman B and Kharitonov D. Network and Telecom Equipment Energy and Performance Assessment –Test Procedures and Measurement Methodology. ECR Initiative, 2008.

[82] A-C Orgerie, L Lefèvre, "ERIDIS: energy-efficient reservation infrastructure for large-scale distributed systems, Parallel Proc Lett, 21:133–154, June 2011.

[83] Orgerie A-C, Lefèvre L, and Guérin-Lassous I. On the energy efficiency of centralized and decentralized management for reservation-based networks. In: IEEE Global Communications Conference (GLOBECOM 2011); 2011 Dec; Houston, USA.

[84] Orgerie A-C and Lefèvre L. Energy-efficient overlay for data transfers in private networks. In: IEEE International Conference on Networks (ICON 2011); 2011 Dec; Singapore.

[85] Chiaraviglio L, Mellia M, and Neri F. Energy-aware networks: reducing power consumption by switching off network elements. In: GTTI'08; 2008, Rome, Italy.

[86] R. Bolla, R. Bruschi, K. Christensen, F. Cucchietti, F. Davoli, and S. Singh, "The potential impact of Green technologies in next-generation wireline networks –is there room for energy saving optimization?," IEEE Commun Mag (COMMAG), 49, 80–86, 2011.

[87] Idzikowski F, Orlowski S, Raack C, Woesner H, and Wolisz A. Saving energy in IP-over-WDM networks by switching off line cards in low-demand scenarios. In: Conference on Optical Network Design and Modeling; 2010; pp. 1–6, Kyoto, Japan.

[88] Zhang Y, Tornatore M, Chowdhury P, and Mukherjee B. Time-aware energy conservation in IP-over-WDM networks. In: Photonics in Switching'10; 2010, Monterey, USA.

[89] Fisher W, Suchara M, and Rexford J. Greening backbone networks: reducing energy consumption by shutting off cables in bundled links. In: Green Networking '10; 2010; pp. 29–34, New Delhi, India.

[90] T. Kelly and M. Adolph, ITU-T initiatives on climate change, Commun Mag, IEEE, vol. 46, pp. 108–114, 2008.

[91] Aware, Inc. Patent statements and licensing declarations. Available at http://www.atis .org/legal/Docs/PATENTS/ATIS/ATIS-0600007_LBE041_AWARE.pdf. Accessed 2014 Sep 30.

[92] J. Baliga, R. Ayre, K. Hinton, W. V. Sorin, and R. S. Tucker, "Energy consumption in optical IP networks," IEEE/OSA JLT, vol. 27, no. 13, 2009.

[93] L. Valcarenghi, D. Pham Van, P.G. Raponi, P. Castoldi, D. R. Campelo, S.-W. Wong, S.-H. Yen, L. Kazovsky, S. Yamashita, "Energy efficiency in passive optical networks: where, when, and how?", IEEE Network; 26 (6); 2012.

[94] 10-Gigabit-capable passive optical networks (XG-PON): Transmission convergence (TC) specifications. ITU-T G.987.3 Recommendation; 2010.

[95] R. Kubo, J.-I. Kani, Y. Fujimoto, N. Yoshimoto, and K. Kumozaki, "Adaptive power saving mechanism for 10 gigabit class PON systems," IEICE Trans Commun, vol. 2, no. E93.B, pp. 280–288, 2010.

[96] M. Marsan, A. Anta, V. Mancuso, B. Rengarajan, P. Vasallo, and G. Rizzo, "A simple analytical model for energy efficient Ethernet," IEEE Commun Lett, vol. 15, no. 7, pp. 773–775, July 2011.

[97] Fiammengo M, Lindstrom A, Monti P, Wosinska L, and Skubic B. Experimental evaluation of cyclic sleep with adapt- able sleep period length for PON. In: Optical Communication (ECOC), 2011 31th European Conference and Exhibition on; 2011 Sep; pp. 1–3, Geneva, Switzerland.

[98] Valcarenghi L, Chincoli M, Monti P, Wosinska L, and Castoldi P. Energy efficient PONs with service delay guarantees. In: Sustainable Internet and ICT for Sustainability (SustainIT); 2012 Oct 4–5; Pisa.

[99] Network performance objectives for IP-based services. ITU-T Recommendation Y.1541; 2011 Dec.

[100] Y. Chen, T. Farley and N. Ye, "QoS requirements of network applications on the Internet," Inform Knowl Syst Manag, 4, pp. 55–76, 2004

[101] Z. Sun, D. He, L. Liang, H. Cruickshank, "Internet QoS and traffic modelling", IEE Proceedings Software, Vol.151, pp. 248–255, Dec 2004.

[102] Yahoo messenger protocol v9. Available at libyahoo2.sourceforge.net/ymsg-9.txt. Accessed 2014 Sep 30.

[103] P. Seeling, M. Reisslein, and B. Kulapala, "Network performance evaluation using frame size and quality traces of single-layer and two-layer video: a tutorial," Commun Surveys

Tuts, vol. 6, no. 3, pp. 58–78, 2004. Available at http://dx.doi.org/10.1109/COMST.2004 .5342293. Accessed 2014 Sep 30.

[104] Voice over IP –per call bandwidth consumption. Available at http://www.cisco.com/en/ US/tech/tk652/tk698/technologies_tech_note09186a0080094ae2.shtml#topic1. Accessed 2014 Sep 30.

[105] J. Baliga, R. Ayre, K. Hinton, W. V. Sorin, and R. S. Tucker, "Energy consumption in optical IP networks," J Lightwave Technol, vol. 27, pp. 2391–2403, 2009.

[106] D. C. Dowden, R. D. Gitlin, and R. L. Martin, "Next generation networks," Bell Labs Tech J, vol. 3, pp. 3–14, 1998.

[107] G. L. Ragsdale and R. D. Lamm, *Advancements in Photonic Network Architecture Migration: The Evolution and Deployment of Multiprotocol Label Switching MPLS, Generalized Multiprotocol Label Switching GMPLS, and Advanced Optical Switching*," ed: Southwest Research Institute, Office of the Manager National Communications System, Communication Technologies, Inc., USAxs, 2002.

[108] Bianzino A, et al. GRiDA: a Green distributed algorithm for backbone networks. In: IEEE Online Green Communications Conference; 2011 Sep, New York, USA.

[109] Wang J, et al. Green-aware routing in GMPLS networks. In: International Conference on Computing, Networking and Communications (ICNC); 2012; pp. 227–231, Maui, Hawaii, USA.

[110] S Ruepp, *AM Fagertun Energy Efficiency Evaluation of RSVP-TE Extensions for Survivable Translucent WSON Networks*, DTU Fotonik, Technical University of Denmark, 2012.

[111] Phillips C, et al. Pro-active energy management for wide area networks. In: IET International Conference on Communication Technology and Applications (ICCTA); 2011; pp. 317–322.

[112] Sergio Ricciardi, Francesco Palmieri, Ugo Fiore, Davide Careglio, Germán Santos-Boada, Josep Solé-Pareta, "An energy-aware dynamic RWA framework for next-generation wavelength-routed networks", Comput Netw (Elsevier), Volume 56, Issue 10, 2012, Pages: 2420–2442, ISSN 1389-1286, DOI: 10.1016/j.comnet.2012.03.016.

[113] Sergio Ricciardi, Jiayuan Wang, Francesco Palmieri, D Careglio, A Manolova, G Santos-Boada, "Eco-sustainable routing in optical networks", Photonic Netw Commun, 26(2–3):140–149, 2013, DOI 10.1007/s11107-013-0416-0.

[114] Wang J, Ricciardi S, Manolova AV, Ruepp S, Careglio D, and Dittmann L. OSPF-TE extensions for green routing in optical networks. In: Opto-Electronics and Communications Conference (OECC); 2012 Jul 2–6; Volume 17; pp. 411, 412. DOI: 10.1109/OECC.2012.6276497, Busan, Korea.

[115] Wang J, Ricciardi S, Fagertun AM, Ruepp S, Careglio D, and Dittmann L. Energy-aware routing optimization in dynamic GMPLS controlled optical networks. In: 14th International Conference on Transparent Optical Networks (ICTON); 2012 Jul 2–5; pp. 1–4. doi: 10.1109/ICTON.2012.6253843, Coventry, UK.

[116] Wang J, Ruepp S, Manolova AV, Dittmann L, Ricciardi S, and Careglio D. Green-aware routing in GMPLS networks. In: International Conference on Computing, Networking and Communications (ICNC); 2012 Jan 30–Feb 2; pp. 227–231. doi: 10.1109/ICCNC .2012.6167416, Maui, Hawaii, USA.

[117] Bozakov, Z. An open router virtualization framework using a programmable forwarding plane. SIGCOMM Comput Commun Rev 2010, 40, 439–440.

[118] Sherwood R, Gibb G, Yap K-K, Appenzeller G, Casado M, McKeown N, and Parulkar G. FlowVisor: a network virtualization layer. OpenFlow Switch Consortium; 2009

[119] Cisco. Technical overview of virtual device contexts; white paper; 2008. Available at http://www.cisco.com/en/US/prod/collateral/switches/ps9441/ps9402/ps9512/White_Paper_Tech_Overview_Virtual_Device_Contexts.pdf. Accessed 2014 Sep 30.

[120] Kolon M. Intelligent logical router service. White Paper (Juniper Networks, Inc.); 2004.

[121] Clark C, Fraser K, Hand S, Hansen JG, Jul E, Limpach C, Pratt I, and Warfield A. Live migration of virtual machines. In: Proceedings of the 2nd conference on Symposium on Networked Systems Design & Implementation; Volume 2 (NSDI'05), USENIX Association; 2005; Berkeley, CA, USA; pp. 273–286.

[122] Voorsluys W, Broberg J, Venugopal S, and Buyya R. Cost of virtual machine live migration in clouds: a performance evaluation. In: Proceedings of the 1st International Conference on Cloud Computing; 2009; Springer-Verlag; pp. 254–265.

[123] Wang, Y.; Keller, E.; Biskeborn, B.; van der Merwe, J. & Rexford, J. Virtual routers on the move: live router migration as a network-management primitive. SIGCOMM Comput Commun Rev, 2008, 38, 231–242.

[124] Ramakrishnan KK, Shenoy P, and Van der Merwe J. Live data center migration across WANs: a robust cooperative context aware approach. In: Proceedings of the 2007 SIGCOMM Workshop on Internet Network Management, ACM; 2007; pp. 262–267.

[125] Bradford, R.; Kotsovinos, E.; Feldmann, A. & Schiöberg, H. Live wide-area migration of virtual machines including local persistent state. In: VEE '07: Proceedings of the 3rd International Conference on Virtual Execution Environments, ACM; 2007; pp. 169–179, Portland, USA.

[126] Fischer A, Fessi A, Carle G, and De Meer H. Wide-area virtual machine migration as resilience mechanism. In: Proceedings of the Int'l Workshop on Network Resilience: From Research to Practice (WNR2011); 2011; pp. 72–77, Madrid, Spain.

[127] A. Fischer, J.F. Botero, M.T. Beck, H. De Meer and X. Hesselbach, Virtual network embedding: a survey. IEEE Communications Surveys and Tutorials, Vol. 15, pp. 1888–1906, 2013.

[128] Chen X and Phillips C. Virtual router migration and infrastructure sleeping for energy management of IP over WDM networks. In: IEEE International Conference on Telecommunications and Multimedia (TEMU); 2012; pp. 31–36, Heraklion, Greece.

[129] R. Bolla, R. Bruschi, and M. Listanti, Enabling backbone networks to sleep, Network IEEE, vol. 25, pp. 26–31, 2011.

[130] GreenTouch initiative. Available at http://greentouch.org. Accessed 2014 Sep 30.

[131] Gelas J-P, Lefevre L, Assefa T, and Libsie M. Virtualizing home gateways for large scale energy reduction in wireline networks. In: Electronic Goes Green 2012 (EGG); 2012 Sep; Berlin, Germany.

4

GREEN WIRELESS-ENERGY EFFICIENCY IN WIRELESS NETWORKS

Vitor Bernardo[1], Torsten Braun[2], Marilia Curado[1], Markus Fiedler[5], David Hock[3], Theus Hossmann[4], Karin Anna Hummel[4], Philipp Hurni[2], Selim Ickin[5], Almerima Jamakovic-Kapic[2], Simin Nadjm-Tehrani[6], Tuan Ahn Trinh[7], Ekhiotz Jon Vergara[6], Florian Wamser[3], and Thomas Zinner[3]

[1]*Department of Informatics Engineering, University of Coimbra, Coimbra, Portugal*
[2]*University of Bern, Bern, Switzerland*
[3]*University of Würzburg, Würzburg, Germany*
[4]*ETH Zurich, Zurich, Switzerland*
[5]*Blekinge Institute of Technology, Karlskrona, Sweden*
[6]*Linköping University, Linköping, Sweden*
[7]*Budapest University of Technology and Economics, Budapest, Hungary*

4.1 INTRODUCTION

Wireless networks have become more and more popular because of ease of installation, ease of access, and support of smart terminals and gadgets on the move. Energy-efficient wireless network operation is without doubt of high importance, both for infrastructure and for ad-hoc communication. While for infrastructure networks, economic and ecological considerations are predominant and the networking components are often connected to the power grid, ad-hoc networks mainly rely on limited battery-powered components

Large-Scale Distributed Systems and Energy Efficiency: A Holistic View, First Edition.
Edited by Jean-Marc Pierson.
© 2015 John Wiley & Sons, Inc. Published 2015 by John Wiley & Sons, Inc.

and, thus, the network's lifetime and availability is challenged. Similarly, the energy depletion of mobile client devices such as smartphones is a crucial challenge, as they are the user interface to ubiquitous connectivity.

In the overall life cycle of providing *green wireless technology* – from production to operation and, finally, removal – we focus on the operation phase and summarize insights in energy consumption of major technologies. We provide an answer to questions such as how the energy consumption can be characterized, measured, and estimated. Further, we introduce approaches to make wireless networks energy-efficient. A strong focus of this chapter is set on the edge of the network, comprising network access points (APs) and mobile user devices. Here, the energy consumption of the wireless communication modules is still considerably high; thus, there is a need for good understanding of energy consumption and novel approaches to improve energy efficiency. In this setting, we not only summarize well-known challenges but also highlight in particular novel approaches, applications of interest, and results for the included wireless technologies and give pointers to related literature.

Our introduction to the topic on energy-efficient wireless networking provides insights in major measurement methodologies and energy-efficient algorithms. We achieve this by making the following contributions:

- First, we summarize major metrics used to describe energy efficiency in wireless networks. Thus, we briefly list generally applicable metrics such as *energy per information bit* and, then, focus on metrics dedicated to wireless networking in Section 4.2.
- To measure and estimate energy consumption, internal software methods as well as external power meters can be used. We discuss the advantages and disadvantages of major methodologies and exemplify testbeds in Section 4.3.
- Then, we discuss particularities of most important wireless networking technologies: (i) wireless access networks including 3G/LTE and wireless mesh networks (WMNs) in Section 4.4, (ii) wireless sensor networks (WSNs) in Section 4.5, and (iii) ad-hoc and opportunistic networks in Section 4.6. Besides describing major characteristics of these networks in terms of energy consumption and resulting challenges, we take specific perspectives to approach the discussion of energy efficiency, for example, the quality of experience (QoE) versus energy consumption trade-off for access networks, energy-efficient medium access control (MAC) in WSNs, and methods to establish connectivity among a group of mobile devices in an energy-efficient and fair way.

This chapter originates from discussions and joint research work of the *Focus Group on Energy-efficient Wireless Networks* of the European Cooperation in Science and Technology (COST) Action IC0804.

4.2 METRICS AND TRADE-OFFS IN WIRELESS NETWORKS

This section introduces the most popular performance metrics for energy efficiency in wireless networks [1, 2] in Section 4.2.1, followed by a brief discussion on energy consumption versus performance trade-offs in these systems in Section 4.2.2.

4.2.1 Metrics

Energy-aware optimization techniques require metrics to evaluate the real energy savings that can be achieved with a certain solution. First, basic energy consumption metrics are introduced, and then metrics capable of measuring the energy efficiency of a system are discussed.

4.2.1.1 Power and Energy Consumption Metrics. The most obvious and simple metric to assess any system's and network's energy footprint is the total **energy consumption** (E) in joule (J), which can be defined as the product of the average power (P) in watt (W) and the time (t), as follows:

$$E(\text{J}) = P(\text{W}) \times t(\text{s}). \qquad (4.1)$$

The total energy consumption is mostly used to characterize the energy costs associated with a certain operation, but when there is a need to study a single state, the *average power* (P) can also be used as a standalone metric.

4.2.1.2 Power and Energy Efficiency Metrics. Even though the average power and total energy consumption can describe the energy costs, it is important to correlate the network energy consumption (E) with the other network-level parameters [3]. One of the most important system-level metrics, which can be employed in any network system, is *energy per information bit* (Eb). This metric, expressed in joule per bit, describes the relationship between the total number of bits transmitted (I) and the energy consumed (E):

$$Eb[\text{J/bit}] = \frac{E[\text{J}]}{I[\text{bit}]}. \qquad (4.2)$$

While the total energy consumption, the average power, and the energy per information bit metrics can be used in any network system, there are also metrics specially introduced for wireless system. These metrics usually aim to establish a correlation between the energy or power and particular characteristics of the wireless system, such as the number of subscribers or the covered area.

The *power per area unit* metric (Pau) [4] establishes a relationship between the average power used (P) and the size of the covered area (A) and is expressed in watt per meter square:

$$\text{Pau}[\text{W}/\text{m}^2] = \frac{P[\text{W}]}{A[\text{m}^2]}. \qquad (4.3)$$

The *power per subscriber* (Ps) is a metric used to determine the correlation between the average power used (P) and the number of subscribers present in the network (N)

and is expressed in watt per subscriber:

$$\text{Ps[W/subscriber]} = \frac{P[\text{W}]}{N}. \tag{4.4}$$

The presented system-level metrics can be employed within distinct scenarios and technologies; yet once real equipment is used, the results will be further related with the employed hardware. Apart from other components, the energy consumption of the wireless system is strongly related to the energy used by the antenna core components [2]. The *efficiency of an antenna* (η_{Ant}) is defined as the coefficient between the antenna-radiated power (P_{radiated}) and the power needed to support it during operation (P_{input}):

$$\eta_{\text{Ant}} = \frac{P_{\text{radiated}}[W]}{P_{\text{input}}[W]}. \tag{4.5}$$

Chen et al. [2] have also identified the usage of antenna gain information as an alternative way to depict the antenna's efficiency. The *antenna gain* (Gain_{Ant}) describes the antenna's capability to concentrate or direct the power transmitted in a certain direction. It is represented in dBi (decibel relative to an isotropic radiator) and defined as the ratio between the antenna radiation intensity (U) and the antenna power input (P_{input}):

$$\text{Gain}_{\text{Ant}}[\text{dBi}] = 4\pi \times \frac{U}{P_{\text{input}}}. \tag{4.6}$$

The study of energy consumption behavior at multiple levels, namely, system and component levels, will allow superior energy-aware solutions, ranging from higher (e.g., application) to lower level optimizations (e.g., MAC or PHY layers).

4.2.2 Energy Optimization Trade-Offs

The usage of energy optimization techniques might introduce some performance drawbacks in the network. Chen et al. [5] have studied the most significant trade-offs in green wireless networks. Four main trade-offs were identified, namely, trade-offs related to deployment costs, spectrum efficiency, bandwidth management, and delay. More recently, Zhang et al. [6] have also proposed a new metric to establish the fundamental trade-off between QoE and energy efficiency.

Therefore, six important trade-offs in green wireless networks should be considered as follows:

- *Deployment Efficiency/Energy Efficiency Trade-Off.* Correlating the deployment and operation costs, namely, the capital expenditure (CapEx) and the operational expenditure (OpEx), and its relation with the overall energy required to run the network;
- *Spectrum Efficiency/Energy Efficiency Trade-Off.* Establishing a relationship between spectrum efficiency, usually defined as the system throughput per bandwidth unit, and the overall energy consumption needed;

- *Bandwidth/Power Trade-Off.* Defines the relationship between the available bandwidth and the power needed to perform a transmission;
- *Quality of Service (QoS)/Energy Consumption Trade-Off.* Represents the relation between the network-level performance parameters (e.g., delay and packet loss) and the energy needed to transmit certain data;
- *Quality of Experience (QoE)/Energy Consumption Trade-Off.* Represents the relation between the obtained user-perceived quality (QoE) and the energy consumed to achieved it.

Although the use of these trade-offs is not as simple as the use of the metrics presented previously, it is important to take them into account when proposing novel energy-aware enhancements. By understanding and correlating the energy-aware techniques employed and their multiple impacts on the system, it will be possible to obtain superior energy savings while providing sufficient and establishing better performance trade-offs networking performance.

4.2.3 Summary

This section presented the most relevant metrics and trade-offs to be considered when studying the energy efficiency of a wireless communication system. A brief overview about generic energy metrics (e.g., energy or power consumption) was provided together with some wireless-specific metrics, namely, power per area unit and power per subscriber. The introduced trade-offs showed the importance of establishing a proper relationship between the system optimization goals and the user's requirements, because when saving energy, there is almost always some impact on the performance to be considered. In the next section, energy measurement methodologies are presented, which allow to evaluate real systems along the previously introduced metrics.

4.3 MEASUREMENT METHODOLOGY

The recent growth and heterogeneity of wireless technologies have enabled a high usage of networking devices, ranging from infrastructure nodes to end user devices. While infrastructure nodes of wireless networks are, similar to wired networking equipment, mainly powered by the power grid, user devices in mobile settings such as portable computers and mobile phones, and also wirelessly connected sensors, are primarily battery powered. This particularity of wireless networks determines the focus of this section, which is set on understanding the energy consumption of user devices and WSNs. Yet creating mathematical models to estimate the energy consumption in a wireless communication system might be a complex task; with inaccuracies introduced by the assumptions and simplifications required in this approach, it is important to follow proper methodologies in order to accurately measure the energy consumption of real life systems. Additionally, the data obtained through measurements can also be used to improve simulation environments and to perform more detailed energy consumption pattern estimations.

This section gives a brief overview about the most popular empirical techniques to measure energy consumption. First, relevant energy measurement techniques and testbeds are introduced in Section 4.3.1, followed by a discussion concerning the usage of energy estimation techniques in Section 4.3.2. Section 4.3.3 discusses the benefits and problems of using both energy measurement and estimation techniques through an illustrative example.

4.3.1 Energy Measurement Testbeds

We now describe four measurement methodologies for studying the energy consumption of wireless transmission in different scenarios.

4.3.1.1 Generic Measurement for USB Wireless Interfaces. This first methodology proposes a generic approach that is able to measure energy consumption in any multiple wireless access network such as Wi-Fi, WiMAX, or LTE [7]. In order to fulfill the assessment requirements, two major design requirements are defined:

- *High Precision Measurements.* To guarantee a good accuracy of testbed energy measurements, it is vital to use a measurement hardware capable to support multiple samples per second, because energy in small devices (i.e., network interfaces) tends to have slight variations along the observation time.
- *Independent Network Interface Evaluation.* To better understand how the energy consumption is impacted by the network interface, it is essential to measure exclusively the network interface, namely, by assessing the energy utilization in MAC and PHY layers.

The energy measurement testbed was designed to meet the requirements mentioned earlier and to minimize the changes needed in the network interface hardware. The first option was to use an external Universal Serial Bus (USB) network interface, because it is possible to accurately measure the energy consumed solely by the interface, as desired. One of the main issues already reported in previous energy measurement works is the need to provide a stable and continuous voltage to the system [8, 9]. The impact on the voltage drawn when connecting the USB network interface directly to a user device was noticeable in first tests. To overcome this limitation, the USB network interface was connected to an external alternating current (AC)-powered USB hub, which is able to give stable power to the system. The analysis regarding the voltage drawn when employing the external USB hub has shown that voltage drops are always lower than 1% of the total employed voltage, which is negligible in the overall system analysis.

Figure 4.1 depicts the energy measurement testbed setup. Besides the user device, the measurement configuration includes a controller and a high precision digital multimeter. The digital multimeter is a Rigol DM3061 with a maximum sampling rate of 50 K samples/s and a test resolution of 6 1/2 digits. The multimeter is capable of receiving Standard Commands for Programmable Instruments (SCPI) (defined by IEEE 488.2 [10]) and implements the Universal Serial Bus Test and Measurement Class (USBTMC) specification standard interface. By using SCPI commands and USBTMC,

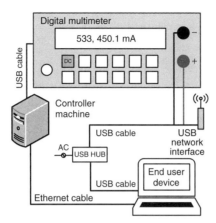

Figure 4.1. Energy measurement setup. Adapted from [7].

the controller is able to control and manage the digital multimeter, which enables accurate and repeatable tests. The controller is also connected to the user device. This entity controls the experiments to be performed in a fast and reliable way and collects all the results from the digital multimeter. As the voltage is stable, all the measurements concerning energy are done by collecting the current values only. The USB cable was intercepted in the common-collector voltage (VCC) cable (i.e., +5 VDC).

In short, the proposed methodology enables the measurement of the energy consumption of a single network interface by employing high precision measurement hardware. By using this methodology, it is possible to study multiple network technologies, which makes it possible to compare and study the behavior of distinct access technologies under different scenarios and conditions. Furthermore, the data collected during the assessments might also be used to support more accurate software-based energy models, namely, for emerging wireless access technologies, as the developed methodology is fully technology independent.

4.3.1.2 Development Boards and Kits. Development equipment allows to isolate the energy consumed for transmission from the consumption of the rest of the system [e.g., central processing unit (CPU) or screen]. Development kits typically expose interfaces to measure the power consumption of, for example, the broadband module or modem under test.

Figure 4.2 shows an example of a measurement setup composed by an Ericsson KRY 901 214/01 development kit provided and a 2G/3G/GPS broadband module (Ericsson F3307). The power consumption is measured using a current probe or measuring the voltage drop over a precision shunt resistor ($0.1\,\Omega$). In the example, the voltage drop is measured with a data acquisition unit (National Instruments myDAQ). The development kit is connected to a test computer using a USB cable appearing as a normal interface. The modem can be further operated with AT commands to access the low layer information such as the radio state. This measurement setup presents high accuracy and details

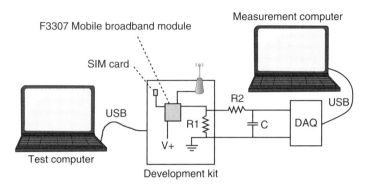

Figure 4.2. A measurement setup based on a development kit.

low layer information, which is useful to understand the impact of the commanding software on the transmission energy (e.g., operating system) [11].

4.3.1.3 *Intercepting Battery Terminals.* As the software running on the devices drastically impacts the energy consumption, directly measuring the power of the mobile device is a common approach. Measurement platforms for mobile devices typically intercept battery terminals to measure the power consumption. These provide aggregated power measurements of network interfaces and other components (e.g., CPU, screen, or sensors). The devices used to acquire the measurements range from laboratory bench multimeters to USB data acquisition units. A widely used power measurement device is the Monsoon Power Monitor [12]. The following aspects need to be considered when employing this measurement technique:

- *Battery Terminal Interception.* A copper tape (or a similar conductor) is placed between the device terminals (V+ and V−) and the battery terminals. The voltage is directly measured from the battery, whereas a shunt resistor is typically used to measure the current. Mobile devices have battery monitoring terminals (e.g., temperature and a communication line), which need to be connected or the mobile device will not switch on.
- *Shunt Resistor Size.* Adding a shunt resistor introduces additional resistance into the measured circuit. However, if the resistor is too small, the drop in voltage is too small for the input offset voltage of the analog conditioning circuit. This can compromise the measurement accuracy. Typical resistors used for these measurements range from 0.01 to 0.1 Ω with a low tolerance.
- *Power Source.* While the battery discharges, the voltage decreases and the current increases. Both the voltage and the current need to be measured if a battery power source is used. Instead, the voltage can be fixed using an external direct current (DC) power supply allowing only measuring the current.
- *Isolating Transmission Energy.* Ideally, one would like to only measure the transmission energy (i.e., the energy spent by the peripheral hardware for transmission). As the operating system running in mobile devices is typically

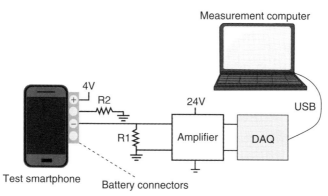

Figure 4.3. The schematic of a mobile device measurement setup that intercepts the battery terminals.

preemptively multitasking, different processes are waking up and consuming resources such as CPU. In order to stabilize the power trace and isolate the transmissions from the rest of the system, the CPU frequency may be fixed and a low priority background process is run in a busy loop [8]. The CPU creates an almost constant power consumption, which enables the isolation of the transmission energy by simply subtracting it. The drawback of this technique is that we cannot distinguish between the CPU load created by the test and the background load.

Figure 4.3 shows an example of a measurement setup used to measure energy consumption in mobile devices. The setup is composed by a low side sensing circuit with a precision shunt resistor (R1 = 0.1 Ω), an isolating amplifier with maximum transmission error of 0.4% (Phoenix Contact MINI MCR-SL-SHUNT-UI), and the data acquisition unit. We added an R2 (33 kΩ) in order to allow the device to switch on.

4.3.1.4 Built-In Sensors and Smart Battery Interfaces. Some vendor-specific development devices are shipped with internal power management integrated circuits that enable power consumption profiling. These allow to separately measure the power consumption of the network interfaces as well as CPU energy consumption. Qualcomm's Trepn Profiler for the Snapdragon processors is an example of such a system [13]. Smart battery interfaces are available in some mobile devices, which provide aggregate current values (e.g., Nokia Energy Profiler [14] or CurrentWidget for Android [15]). The accuracy of these measurements is defined by the battery sensor, which is less than using external physical power measurements [16].

4.3.1.5 Sensors External Measurement Units. Hergenroder et al. [17] proposed an external unit, named Sensor Node Management Device (SNMD), specifically designed to accurately measure the current and voltage of a sensor node with a sampling resolution of up to 20 kHz or even up to 500 kHz in the so-called buffered mode. The SNMD firmware corrects each sampled measurement by an error term, which is obtained in advance. This method reduces the measurement error introduced by the measurement circuit to below 0.5% for any current in the range of 0–100 mA [18], an accuracy range that is definitely sufficient to rely on by any experimental and comparative analyses of sensor network mechanisms. Even though SNMDs are very precise, they represent a high cost hardware-based solution.

4.3.2   Energy Estimation Techniques

While physical power measurements certainly support the evaluation of a system's energy efficiency, performing the measurements is a non-trivial task, which requires some specific knowledge as described in the previous section. Designing and setting up tests, performing the measurements, and analyzing the results is a laborious and time-consuming task. The high cost of the measurement solutions and time limitations (e.g., time to market of applications) stops software developers from investing in these solutions. Thus, applications and system software are often not designed or tested with energy consumption in mind.

Physical power measurements allow device-dependent studies only. As the hardware change between generations can substantially make the energy consumption differ from previous generation devices, the measurements become obsolete quickly. Thus, physical measurements are useful to provide insight and observations, but there is a need for tools and solutions that can complement physical power measurements and enable efficient studies to minimize the energy consumption. This section describes some complementary approaches to physical power measurements for mobile devices and wireless sensor nodes.

4.3.2.1   Measurement-Based Estimation. Energy models abstract the real behavior of the devices by characterizing the mechanisms that consume energy. Some works concentrate on specific mechanisms, whereas others attempt to model the total energy consumption. Here, the focus is on energy models derived from physical measurements used to estimate wireless transmission energy. Yet, theoretical models exist as well [19, 20], which typically investigate the behavior of a specific mechanism of a wireless interface and often suggest guidelines to select parameters for optimizations.

Measurement-based models can be seen as bottom-up approaches, which can be specific to the measured data or generic, depending on the model development approach. The complexity of measurement-based models varies greatly and ranges from simple models characterizing the energy consumption based on some statistical representation of the measurement data (e.g., linear regression) to more complex models employing a finite-state machine (FSM), as described in the following.

Data fitting approaches are often built in two stages. First, the system to be modeled is exercised in a certain manner while collecting physical measurements, and then the collected data is used to create the model. An example is the work by Balasubramanian et al. [21], which models the transmission energy consumption for GSM, 3G, and Wi-Fi. They measure the energy spent to perform bulk data transmissions for different data sizes and build a linear model out of the data. Given the amount of data to be sent in a burst, their model calculates the energy consumed. The data fitting approach is simple, and it results in device- and measurement-specific energy estimation. Yet the proposed model only captures the operation of the system under the conditions that were given during the measurements.

The *finite-state machine (FSM) approach* is a general approach to model energy consumption used to derive the operational states of a system that consume significantly different amounts of power. For example, even if a common wireless interface can be in active or sleep mode, the fact that transmission power substantially increases when transmitting at high data rates can be modeled as an additional state. Power measurements are employed in the modeling phase to select the relevant states, define the transitions between the states, and collect data for the different parameters (e.g., power levels). We illustrate the FSM approach with an example, the EnergyBox [22].

EnergyBox is rooted on wireless interface operation knowledge and measurement data. The tool enables accurate studies of 3G and Wi-Fi transmission energy consumption at the device end. The FSMs built for EnergyBox characterize the 3G network parameters that impact energy consumption and the adaptive power saving mode mechanism specified at the handset driver for Wi-Fi. EnergyBox is focused on studying the impact of the transmission data pattern on energy consumption, thus uses real traffic traces as input. The tool performs trace-based iterative packet-driven simulation: given a packet trace and the configuration parameters, EnergyBox outputs the device states over time. Next, some design decisions are described in the context of EnergyBox.

- *States and Power Values.* In EnergyBox, the states abstract the hardware dependency of measurement-based studies by modeling the mechanisms and interactions that impact the energy consumption. Selecting a reduced number of representative states reduces the model complexity. The FSM states of EnergyBox are derived from the knowledge of the interface operation and a wide range of measurements. The total energy consumption is calculated by associating these states with power levels. Device-specific power-level values are obtained through the measurement platforms. EnergyBox employs fixed power values, which are a convenient simplification in order to feed the model with device-specific measurement data. However, variable power levels are also possible based on some input such as data rate.

- *State Transitions.* State transitions need to model the mechanisms that make a system to change its power consumption. The state transitions are deterministic or stochastic. EnergyBox employs mostly deterministic transitions, which are parameterized allowing the simulation of different interface configurations. Examples of such transitions are the inactivity timeouts used by cellular operators or the adaptive power saving mode timeout to switch between active and sleep states. Stochastic variables can also be used to model the uncertainty of a certain transition, based on the distribution of measurement data, for example.

- *Accuracy Evaluation.* The accuracy of an estimation technique is an important factor to consider, and thus the validation of the model is required. A common approach is to compare the model against physical power measurements. EnergyBox is validated comparing its accuracy against physical power measurements

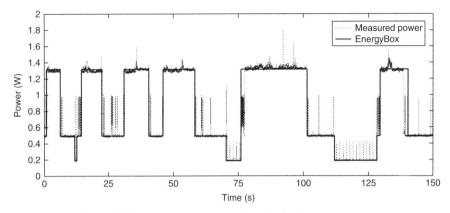

Figure 4.4.   EnergyBox compared to physical measurements.

over a set of real application packet traces. Figure 4.4 shows the accuracy of EnergyBox for a sample Web trace sent via 3G. The accuracy in the example is 99% in terms of energy.

Next we detail energy estimation techniques in the context of WSNs and describe the impact of the estimation model on the resulting estimation accuracy.

4.3.2.2   *Energy Estimation for Wireless Sensor Networks.* The development and operation of energy-efficient WSNs requires to measure or at least to estimate the energy consumption of a sensor node. A simple but expensive approach would be to deploy special measurement devices at each sensor node to measure its energy consumption. This might be too expensive in terms of equipment and deployment costs for large sensor networks. Another approach is to estimate the energy consumption by identifying the states of a sensor node considering the activity of its components. By knowing how long a sensor is in a certain state and what the energy consumption is in each state, for example, by experiments before deployment and operation, it is possible to roughly estimate the energy consumption of a node during its lifetime. This can be done completely by appropriate software recording states and their durations. Simple state-based energy estimation models have already been used in the prominent studies on the common media access control protocols S-MAC [23] and B-MAC [24], yet they have not been evaluated in terms of *accuracy* of their energy estimation model. We discuss now how such software-based energy consumption estimation mechanisms must be designed to achieve the highest accuracy applied to energy-efficient MAC protocols.

THREE STATES MODEL (TSM). The Three States Model (TSM) is the most frequently used model to date for estimating a node's energy consumption as a function of the three states of the radio transceiver, namely, *receive/idle listening*, *transmit*, and *sleep*, cf. [23–25]. The Contiki OS' energy estimation mechanism models the radio's power consumption using this model, but separately tries to keep track of the CPU power consumption, which can vary depending on the low power mode (LPM) it is currently

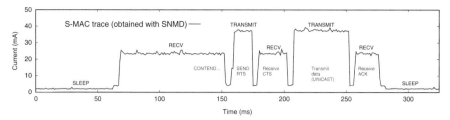

Figure 4.5. Current draw of a sensor node.

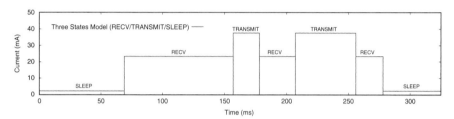

Figure 4.6. Current modeled by the *Three States Model (4.7)*.

operating in. The ScatterWeb[2] OS used in this study put the CPU to LPM as soon as all events have been processed, where the node's current is approximately 1.8 mA, given that the radio is turned off. With the CPU active and the radio off, the node current is roughly 3.5 mA. As energy-efficient MAC protocols generally do not incur intensive computations, we neglected to account for the CPU costs separately and considered the CPU's power consumption to be integrated within the three states of the transceiver.

We, henceforth, employ a model of the energy consumption of major MAC protocol implementations, namely, S-MAC, T-MAC, WiseMAC, and CSMA using the TSM. We let the nodes keep track of the time differences between the transceiver switches, in order to determine how much time has been spent in each state. Figure 4.5 depicts the current draw during the active interval of an S-MAC frame containing an RTS/CTS handshake and a subsequent data packet transmission. Figure 4.6 illustrates how this current draw is approximated by the TSM. The total energy consumed (E) corresponds to the area below the current draw, multiplied by the supply voltage, which is assumed to be constant in the model. Analytically, the TSM can be formulated as equation (4.7). The consumed energy E is calculated as the power level of the node in the receive state P_{rcv} multiplied by the total time spent in this state T_{rcv} and the respective terms for the transmit and sleep states ($P_{slp}T_{slp}$ and $P_{tx}T_{tx}$). This approach is identical to the one applied in [23–25].

$$E = P_{rcv}T_{rcv} + P_{tx}T_{tx} + P_{slp}T_{slp} = I_{rcv}V_{rcv}T_{rcv} + I_{tx}V_{tx}T_{tx} + I_{slp}V_{slp}T_{slp}. \qquad (4.7)$$

Major studies [23–26] calibrate the parameters of their energy model by measuring the currents the nodes draw in the different states and multiplying it with the supply voltage to obtain P_{rcv}, P_{tx}, and P_{slp}. They do so by using either oscilloscopes or high precision multimeters and by measuring the current in each state over a certain timespan. In the

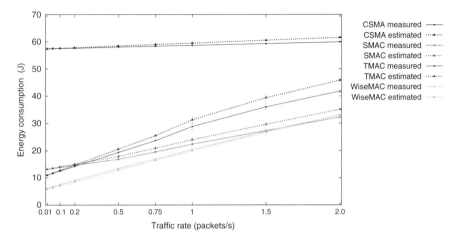

Figure 4.7. Measured versus estimated energy consumption.

first attempt, we pursued exactly the same approach and determined the mean values of I_{rcv}, I_{tx}, and I_{slp} by measuring each state of the *measurement* node using the SNMD for a couple of seconds. The stable mean values were determined to be 23.54, 37.49, and 2.15 mA for I_{rcv}, I_{tx}, and I_{slp}, respectively. We further set the voltage according to the supply voltage of the SNMD to $V_{rcv} = V_{tx} = V_{slp} = 4.06$ V.

Figure 4.7 depicts the mean values of the energy measurements and the estimations for MSB430 sensor nodes being computed with the TSM – using the parameters for P_{rcv}, P_{tx}, and P_{slp} measured in the sample trace. One can clearly see that the estimations fit quite well for low traffic rates but that the gaps between mean estimations and mean measurements become larger with higher rates of packets being sent. For most protocols – especially S-MAC and T-MAC – the energy estimation overestimates the energy consumed by the node with increasing load. This increasing overestimation stems from the fact that the TSM does not account for the transceiver switches. As one can clearly see by comparing Figure 4.5 with Figure 4.6, the current draw decreases to roughly 4 mA when the transceiver is switched to receive or transmit – hence, drawing less current than estimated with the TSM. By defining parameters through example measurement, the impact of the applied traffic load and the frequent transceiver switches as well as the particularities of the MAC protocol are not being taken into account at all. Extrapolating from a short example measurement of a node, hence, leads to suboptimal parameters for the TSM, even when using the same node for parameter calibration and the evaluation of the accuracy.

PARAMETER DEFINITION THROUGH ORDINARY LEAST SQUARES (OLS). Being able to physically measure the current draw of a sensor node *and*, at the same time, obtain the software-based estimation calculated by the node itself offers the opportunity to relate the estimations to the real-world measurements. Using the plethora of experimental data gained in the experiments (in total over 12 GB of measurement data), we reflect upon a method to determine more resilient parameters for the unknown variables

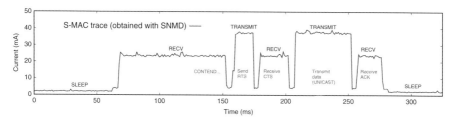

Figure 4.8. Current draw of node B.

P_{rcv}, P_{tx}, and P_{slp} of the TSM. Ideally, the software-based energy estimation running on the node should neither rely on the particularities of a specific MAC protocol nor on the shape or intensity of the traffic. *Ordinary least squares (OLS) regression analysis* yielded the most suitable technique to determine the unknown variables for a linear estimation model with multiple unknown variables. OLS finds the model parameters that minimize the sum of squared errors between the estimations and observations (i.e., the real-world energy measurements captured by the SNMD devices). We formulate a multivariate OLS regression model with explanatory variables T_{rcv}, T_{tx}, and T_{slp}, as well as the physically measured dependent variable E obtained using the SNMD device. The resulting estimation Equation (4.8), hence, simply comprises Equation (4.7) and the error term ε for the residuals. More details can be found in [27].

$$E = P_{rcv}T_{rcv} + P_{tx}T_{tx} + P_{slp}T_{slp} + \varepsilon. \tag{4.8}$$

ESTIMATION ACCURACY OF THE THREE STATES MODEL. In order to determine the accuracy of the OLS-calibrated model, a cross-validation with totally new experimental data is inevitable to omit overfitting effects, cf. Draper and Smith [28]. The determination of the parameters P_{rcv}, P_{tx}, and P_{slp} using OLS regression is achieved based on a first set of experiment runs, the so-called training set. The estimation accuracy results are then gained with a new set of experimental data, the validation set. Figure 4.10 shows that for each traffic rate, the estimation error using the OLS estimator parameters is 4.2–35.9% lower than the corresponding error when using the model parameters defined through example measurement. Across all measurements, the mean absolute estimation error and standard deviation (denoted as $\mu \pm \sigma$) of the TSM with the parameters defined by example measurement equals $3.77 \pm 3.17\%$. When determining the parameters by OLS, we obtain $3.00 \pm 2.55\%$ – hence, achieving an overall reduction of the mean absolute error (MEA) by 21% only by altering the calibration technique.

THREE STATES MODEL WITH STATE TRANSITIONS (TSMwST). With the mean absolute estimation error still in the range of 3% or more, further means to improve the estimation accuracy are required. As Figure 4.8 exhibits, the current draw temporarily drops to approximately 4 mA during the state switches. These state switches remain unaccounted for in the OLS regression model specified in equation (4.8).

The approach of simply counting the transceiver switches and integrating them into the OLS regression model leads to a significant improvement in the estimation accuracy. The number of transceiver switches (from an arbitrary state) to the receive, transmit, or

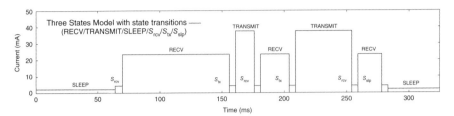

Figure 4.9. Current modeled by the Three States Model with state transitions (4.9).

sleep state was accounted for with the additional regressands s_{rcv}, s_{tx}, and s_{slp}. We refer to this model as *Three States Model with state transitions* (TSMwST) hereafter, as specified in equation (4.9). Figure 4.9 illustrates the model's concept of a node's current draw.

$$E = P_{rcv}T_{rcv} + P_{tx}T_{tx} + P_{slp}T_{slp} + \alpha s_{rcv} + \beta s_{tx} + \gamma s_{slp}. \tag{4.9}$$

According to this enhanced model, the energy consumed by a node is a function of the total time its radio transceiver is in one of the three different states (T_{rcv}, T_{tx}, and T_{slp}) and the three adjustment terms αs_{rcv}, βs_{tx}, and γs_{slp}. The parameters α, β, and γ compensate for the transceiver switches to the states receive, transmit, and sleep.

ESTIMATION ACCURACY OF THE THREE STATES MODEL WITH STATE TRANSITIONS. We calibrated the OLS estimators for the parameters of the second model with the training set and examined the resulting estimation accuracy on the validation set. Across all measurements, the MEA and standard deviation (denoted as $\mu \pm \sigma$) of the software-based estimations using the TSMwST (and the parameters determined by OLS) compared to the physically measured values equals $1.13 \pm 1.15\%$. Comparing this result with the $3.00 \pm 2.55\%$ obtained with the pure TSM (and the parameters determined by OLS), our proposed model enhancement leads to an overall reduction of the MEA by remarkable 62.3%, as also illustrated in Figure 4.10.

Different wireless sensor node instances often exhibit a slightly different behavior with respect to their power consumption levels in the different transceiver states, as quantified for our MSB430 platform and observed in previous studies [25, 29]. We have encountered node pairs of the same node type that differed by more than 4% in their physically measured energy consumption. Hence, even the best *node-generic* software-based energy estimation mechanism can be more than 4%, if its underlying model parameters were not calibrated on a *per-node* basis. Hence, either hardware-dependent deviations have to be tolerated or time-intensive calibration per-node has to be performed, ideally with different MAC protocols and different traffic rates. However, calibrating on a *per-node* basis means that *every single node* needs to be physically measured (e.g., with an SNMD or a high resolution multimeter) ideally with different MAC protocols and different traffic rates. Only this time-intensive calibration leads to the set of *per-node* but *protocol-generic* estimation model parameters to reduce the mean absolute estimation error ($\mu \pm \sigma$) to $1.13 \pm 1.15\%$. To increase the accuracy further, we propose *per-protocol* calibration as an even more accurate estimation approach, which might be useful if researchers know exactly what protocol they intend to use on the MAC layer in advance.

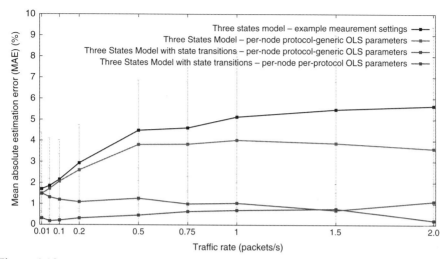

Figure 4.10. Mean absolute estimation error and standard deviation (in %) versus traffic rate (packets per second).

The combined approach of *per-node and per-protocol* calibration obviously leads to the highest accuracy. Across all four protocols and traffic rates, we obtained a mean estimation error and standard deviation $(\mu \pm \sigma)$ of only $0.42 \pm 0.72\%$. Figure 4.10 illustrates the different estimation errors when applying the *per-node and protocol-generic* or the *per-node and per-protocol* calibration approach. Yet, the combined calibration approach has multiplicative impact on the overhead before network deployment, as all nodes need to be equipped with tailor-made estimation model parameters for each protocol.

4.3.3   Energy Measurements versus Estimation

Power consumption measurements on mobile handheld devices have trade-offs between intrusiveness and accuracy. For instance, a software tool can obtain measurements without influencing the actual usage behavior of a mobile device; however, it might not obtain accurate measurements. This section provides the comparison between a *physical measurement tool* and a *measurement-based estimation tool* as an illustrative example.

We analyze two tools introduced at the beginning of this section (Monsoon [12] as a hardware tool and PowerTutor [30] as an internal software tool) and compare the pros and cons of each one. During power measurements, choosing the "right" sampling rate is necessary in a way that the tool collects enough data for the purpose, without influencing the behavior of the system [31]. Therefore, the power measurement process needs to minimize the impact on the battery life during the measurement process as the energy consumption is one of the most influential factors on the end-user-perceived quality in the smartphone [32].

The Monsoon power monitor device contains the power monitor hardware and the power tool software, running on Windows XP and Seven, which can provide robust measurements on any device that uses a single lithium (Li) battery. The measurements are obtained and can be saved with a sampling rate of 5 kHz. The tool supplies the power to the device, thus the device battery is bypassed. The Monsoon external power-monitoring device is typically used for ground-truth measurements [33].

PowerTutor is a smartphone application, developed by a collaboration of academic and industrial institutions, which displays the power consumed by a set of system components such as CPU, network interface, display, GPS, and other applications. The aim of its development was to make the power measurements transparent to the app developers as well as to the users, so that they can take appropriate action to minimize their smartphones' power consumption. PowerTutor receives the current values in milliamperes from the driver and then multiplies the value by the voltage that is basically the phone battery (typically 3.7 or 4.5 V depending on the phone type). PowerTutor estimates the energy consumption of applications and services based on the processing times and is only available for specific phone types. Although these software tools provide the overall picture of the power and energy consumption of the applications being running on the smartphone, the interfaces, CPU, display, and o on, they do not provide ground-truth measurements on all type of devices, but only can provide estimations. We modified the PowerTutor in such a way that it writes the obtained measurements directly to the smartphone's internal storage with a sample rate of 1 Hz. This way, we perform statistical tests.

COMPARISON OF MONSOON AND POWERTUTOR. The choice of the power measurement tool depends on the application to be measured, as the sampling rate of the tools need to be kept limited if they are running on the battery-powered devices as a separate application in the background. We describe now measurements of power consumption during video streaming on the mobile terminals with Monsoon Solutions and obtain ground-truth measurements [34, 35]. We conducted further tests to identify a set of differences between PowerTutor and Monsoon. We installed PowerTutor on the HTC G1, as it is recommended particularly for the Google phones, and in parallel, we connected the Monsoon power-monitoring tool directly to the power supply of the smartphone. This way, we were able to conduct simultaneous measurements and observed the differences between the two approaches. We have found slight inconsistencies between the obtained measurements through Monsoon and PowerTutor. We observed that PowerTutor power measurement values can drop down to zero occasionally as depicted in Figure 4.11. On the other hand, the power consumption values obtained via Monsoon are within the robust 1600–2200 mW range as shown in Figure 4.11. Next, we streamed video (with three different bitrates: 150, 300, and 500 kbit/s) to the device with and without the PowerTutor. In both the scenarios, we recorded the power consumption measurements via Monsoon. We conclude that PowerTutor has consumed extra power within the range 23–59 mW. The descriptive statistics are presented in Table 4.1 for both the scenarios, that is, with and without PowerTutor. Monsoon can provide highly accurate power measurements, yet these measurements are highly obtrusive and cannot be used, for example, in user studies. On the other hand, PowerTutor is minimally intrusive and can provide power models based on the device usage, but it relies on power measurements that are not as accurate as Monsoon because of factors such as unavailability of reliable sensors or low sampling rate. Hence, the measurement tool should be carefully chosen depending on the purpose of the study, and the limits should be reported in any discussion of the results.

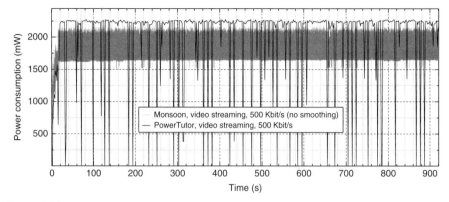

Figure 4.11. Measurements obtained via Monsoon and PowerTutor during video streaming.

TABLE 4.1. Power Measurements Obtained Through Monsoon and PowerTutor in Milliwatts

Rate (kbit/s)	Tool	Max	Min	Standard deviation	Mean	Median	Data Points
			With PowerTutor				
150	Monsoon	2449.3	1351.2	94.0	1786.2	1772.3	4425001
150	PowerTutor	2278.0	0	517.5	2078.8	2227.0	958
300	Monsoon	2404.0	1489.9	94.2	1762.5	1745.0	4375001
300	PowerTutor	2287.0	0	562.3	2047.6	2231.0	453
500	Monsoon	2423.4	1499.1	90.8	1793.6	1776.4	4425001
500	PowerTutor	2278.0	0	649.8	1993.8	2238.0	442
			Without PowerTutor				
150	Monsoon	2198.8	1486.2	110.4	1727.4	1719.6	4425001
300	Monsoon	2170.1	1490.1	107.6	1739.0	1730.0	4425001
500	Monsoon	2201.9	1482.5	99.6	1753.1	1739.7	4425001

4.3.4 Summary

Measuring the energy consumption and deriving the energy efficiency of wireless network components and protocols is a crucial first step toward energy-efficient wireless networking. In this section, we discussed measurements and estimation methodologies based on external and internal measurements. The testbeds presented range from USB interfaces and mobile-battery-powered devices to WSNs. For important sample wireless systems, we detailed the important precautions for measurement and power modeling, such as sampling considerations and achievable accuracy.

The decision between (hardware) power measurement and energy estimation techniques depends on a manifold of considerations. Energy estimation enables simple and fast energy calculations (online and offline) and overcomes some of the major limitations of physical measurements, such as cost, time-intensive setup, and hardware dependency. Moreover, energy estimation techniques provide means to efficiently perform large-scale studies, for example, analyze the energy consumption of a large user trace dataset and can be used in user studies. However, the accuracy of the estimation technique is commonly less when compared to power measurements. This needs to be considered at the time of analyzing the results, and there is a need to consider the energy consumed by the measurement estimation itself. Thus, depending on the requirements of the energy study, either one methodology can followed or different physical measurement methodologies and energy estimation techniques can be used together to complement each other.

4.4   ENERGY EFFICIENCY AND QoE IN WIRELESS ACCESS NETWORKS

The widespread of wireless devices entails an ever-increasing plethora of *wireless access networks* of different kinds. Being wirelessly connected is in the first hand for the benefit of the users. As discussed previously, the convenience comes at the price of limited battery power. In addition, the ever-growing wireless infrastructures consume increasing amounts of energy. Thus, energy saving is of importance for both users and providers, but it may not come at any price: if the *quality of experience* (QoE) gets too low because of energy saving measures, it may entail user churn. For these reasons, energy efficiency must be traded off well against potential quality losses, which is the main point of concern in this section.

Section 4.4.1 provides an overview of recent approaches to increase energy efficiency of mobile long-term evolution (LTE) systems. In particular, several mechanisms that allow an efficient adaptation of the power consumption to the required network resources are summarized. Section 4.4.2 discusses the trade-off between energy consumption, the number of users, and their QoE in a mesh access network. Section 4.4.3 highlights possible energy savings at the user device with a modified resource scheduling. Seen from the perspective of the end user, Section 4.4.4 reveals particular relationships between energy consumption and specific QoE issues for streaming video. A specific-purpose network is targeted in Section 4.4.5. Here, an outlook on environmental access networks is given.

4.4.1   Energy Issues in Cellular Networks

Mobile wireless access networks are increasingly contributing to global energy consumption. Future mobile wireless access, such as LTE networks are no exception. The EARTH (Energy Aware Radio and neTworking tecHnologies) project tackles the important issue of reducing CO_2 emissions by enhancing the energy efficiency of future cellular mobile networks with particular focus on LTE systems. EARTH is a holistic approach to develop a new generation of energy-efficient products, components, deployment strategies, and energy-aware network management solutions in LTE networks. At component level, the various units, including antennas, RF (radio frequency) transceivers, baseband processor, and power amplifiers, are improved to provide envisioned gains for the mobile core and radio access network (RAN) as illustrated in Table 4.2.

Numerical results [42] reveal that for current network design and operation, the power consumption is mostly independent of the traffic load. This highlights the vast potential for energy savings by improving the energy efficiency of cellular networks at low load. Accordingly, techniques and algorithms developed within the EARTH project mainly aim at reducing the power consumption of 4G cellular access networks in low and middle load scenarios. In total, energy savings of 40–60% are possible [43]. Further energy savings can be achieved by combining the proposed methods with other technologies such as DTX, dynamic bandwidth management, and adaptability on system dynamics. However, a well-directed control of the presented mechanisms is required to achieve a reduction of the energy consumption without affecting the user-perceived quality. Controlling the mechanisms is crucial and depends on factors such as network design, user behavior, and technology specifics, both for LTE and for other wireless networks. In the next section, we demonstrated the challenges and potential of such mechanisms for WMNs.

4.4.2 Energy Efficiency and QoE in Wireless Mesh Networks

In the following, we focus on energy efficiency and QoE issues in WMNs. We discuss the trade-off between QoE and energy efficiency in city WMNs as illustrated in Figure 4.12. The evaluation is based on a summary of previous work [44].

4.4.2.1 Evaluation of the Trade-off between QoE and Energy Efficiency in City WMNs. Even though WMN nodes in cites are usually connected to the power grid, network providers still try to minimize the energy consumption and reduce their costs. At the same time, they want to guarantee a good user-perceived quality of the networked services. Accordingly, the QoE of the end user should not be harmed by any reduction of the resources of the WMN. In general, this can be achieved either by controlling the network resources, for example, increasing the number of available mesh gateways, or by controlling the applications, for example, adapting the transmitted content [45]. The implementation of such mechanisms in a wireless mesh environment is rather complicated. On the one hand, fixed bandwidth guarantees are hard to realize because fading or attenuation effects result in a highly variable bandwidth. On the other hand, interference problems may occur when adding more wireless resources which may in the end lead to a decreased network performance.

To demonstrate this challenge, we investigate the trade-off between energy consumption, which depends on the available network resources, the number of supported users, and the perceived application quality. To that end, we conduct measurements in a small wireless mesh network consisting of four mesh nodes, as illustrated in Figure 4.12. The uplink capacity of one relay node to the Internet is regarded as a bottleneck. Hence, adding additional relay nodes (gateways) increases the overall uplink capacity and also the energy consumption. As an application for all users, we consider Web traffic and

TABLE 4.2. Mechanisms Enhancing Energy Efficiency in Cellular Networks

Component	Technology	Technical Approach	Implications and Impact on Energy Efficiency
Antenna [36, 37]	MIMO	• Concurrent transmission on physical layer • Spatial multiplexing	• Higher spectral efficiency • Reduction of error rate/increased capacity • More efficient transmission reduces energy consumption • System supports trade-off between energy efficiency and spectral efficiency
	Beam forming	• Target-oriented antenna arrays	• Spatial selectivity • Interference reduction • Less signal power required
R/F trans-ceiver [36, 38, 39]	Redesign of architecture	• Circuitry and transceiver system level • Power adaptation	• Chips support trade-off between power and performance • Significant reduction of energy consumption for low load situations
Baseband [40]	Micro/pico base stations	• Design of new signal processing algorithms	• Algorithms support trade-off power versus performance • Significant reduction of energy consumption for low load situations
Amplifiers [36, 38, 39]	Operation point adjustments	• Approach specification	• Amplifiers can adapt their operation area • Less power consumption due to more efficient amplifiers
User device [41]	Discontinuous transmission (DTX)	• Deactivation of unused radio components • Micro/short/long timescales	• Less power consumption in idle mode • Significant energy savings in case of low loads • Further savings possible due to not transmitting CRS in short DTX
Mobile core and RAN	Scalability of power consumption	• Bandwidth adaptation • Energy-efficient resource allocation • BS sleep mode	• Improved system efficiency • Improved energy efficiency, in particular for low loads

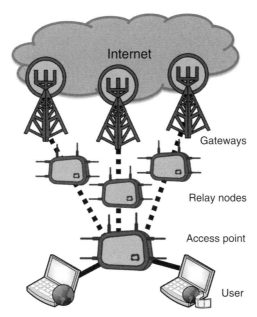

Figure 4.12. City wireless mesh network, multi-hop scenario.

approximate the QoE with the bandwidth/QoE mapping function introduced in [45]:

$$\text{QoE}_{\text{web}}(\text{bw}) = \max \left\{ 1, 5 + 1.5 \ln \left(\frac{\text{bw}}{8 \text{ Mbps}} \right) \right\}. \quad (4.10)$$

The QoE of a Web user is supposed to be in logarithmic relation to the available bandwidth and that a bandwidth of at least bw = 8 Mbps is needed to reach a maximal user QoE of $\text{QoE}_{\text{web}}(\text{bw}) = 5$.

The reference measurements conducted revealed the following issues. First, the power consumption increases linearly with the increasing number of active gateways. Second, the available capacity between the mesh nodes is subject to large variations. An increase of the available resources by increasing the number of gateways from one to three reduced the average available capacity per gateway from 19.15 to 14.58 Mbps. This depends on the placement of the gateway nodes; however, it means that doubling the number of gateways does not necessarily lead to a doubling of the available resources in terms of capacity. In addition, the higher interference leads to higher variations of the available capacity per gateway. In our scenario, the relative gap between the average capacity and the 5% quantile was increased from 14% for the one-gateway case to 42% for the three-gateway case, respectively.

If the available capacity is subject to variations, the resulting QoE will retain this behavior. Hence, we investigate the average QoE and the gap between the average QoE and the 5% quantile of the resulting QoE distribution. Figure 4.13 illustrates the QoE gap for the multi-hop scenario with three gateways. The QoE gap is 0.8186, that is, in 5% of the time, the current opinion score (OS) of a given user can be more than 0.8

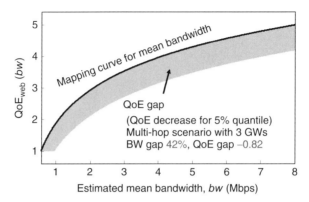

Figure 4.13. Mapping curve mean bandwidth/QoE with QoE gap.

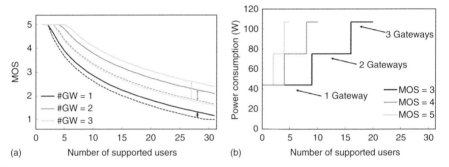

Figure 4.14. Relation between QoE, power consumption, and number of supported users.

worse than the mean opinion score (MOS) of that user. This might be acceptable for an MOS value of 5 and a resulting worst case MOS value of approximately 4.2. However, for an MOS value of 3, this results in a worst case of approximately 2.2, which indicates a higher number of dissatisfied users.

The increased bandwidth fluctuations in multi-gateway scenarios also have a negative impact on the number of supported users with a certain QoE. To study this effect, we first investigate the QoE based on the number of users and the number of used gateways. The results are illustrated in Figure 4.14(a). The bold solid lines represent the case when the average bandwidth in each scenario is regarded, the thin dashed lines represents the 5% percentile case.

As long as the fraction of bandwidth each user obtains is higher than 8 Mbps, the average MOS of the users is 5. For an increasing number of users, the QoE starts to decrease when a certain threshold is reached. From this point, doubling the number of users approximately results in a reduction of the average QoE by 1. Although the decrease can be avoided by adding additional gateways, a lot of resources are wasted because the mentioned interferences lead to a nonlinear relationship between number of gateways and supported users. In particular, this results in a lower minimum quality for three gateways as for two gateways, as illustrated by the 5% quantiles.

Besides the QoE for different numbers of users and gateways, we highlight the number of supported users for a given QoE level and the power consumption of the wireless mesh network. In detail, Figure 4.14(b) illustrates the number of supported users with a certain MOS of 3, 4, or 5 for a given number of gateways and the corresponding power consumption. The power consumption raises almost linearly with the number of gateways and does not depend on the number of users. This is mainly due to the fact that for the access nodes, the energy consumption of the wireless interfaces is negligible compared to the consumption of the overall system. However, the number of users does not increase in the same order of magnitude as the number of gateways. This can be mapped to the following: paying twice the price for power consumption does not necessarily mean to be able to satisfy twice the number of users.

Another important issue besides the application quality is the energy consumption of mobile devices when accessing the network. Current smartphones consume a huge amount of energy while sending and receiving data over the network. Hence, it may be beneficial to reduce the transmission time itself, as investigated in the following.

4.4.3 Reducing Energy Consumption of the End User Device

Huge efforts are currently undertaken to save energy at the mobile end devices. This is reflected by the decreasing power consumption and increasing performance per watt [46] of new devices. Taking the energy consumption profile of smartphones into account, most energy is consumed while sending and receiving data over the network. Thus, mechanisms that reduce the energy consumption of mobile terminals are required. One such a mechanism is DTX, cf. Section 4.4.1. Here, the network determines time intervals where no data is sent to a smartphone and thus allows the smartphone to enter a power saving state while no data is transmitted. This can be combined with data scheduling mechanisms as presented in [47]. The authors propose to adjust resource allocation in multiple user scenarios to avoid long parallel downloads and to allow consecutive short downloads with high data rate [47]. This, however, comes at the cost of additional waiting times before being served. The concept is exemplary illustrated for three users in Figure 4.15. If no additional delays are introduced, the link is utilized similarly for both cases. However, for the second case, the individual downloading durations are reduced.

Without resource scheduling, the available resources are shared fairly among all downloads. As a consequence, the downloading duration per user is increased, because of the reduced resources. On the other hand, a download scheduling on a first come first serve (FCFS) basis might reduce the download duration per task and also might introduce additional waiting times. Hence, the question arises, whether the overall power consumption is reduced compared to the case without scheduling, and whether the overall download duration, which also includes possible waiting times, is increased. We will now study the impact of the scheduling strategy in detail.

4.4.3.1 Evaluation Setup and Performance Metrics. The study is carried out in a WMN. The WMN consists of one wireless AP granting access for the mobile user devices and one mesh node connecting the AP to the WMN's Internet gateway. The

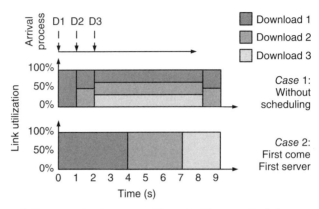

Figure 4.15. Download process with and without a scheduling strategy.

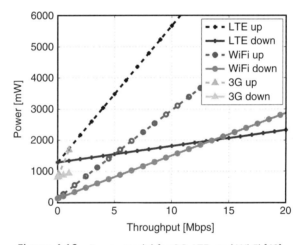

Figure 4.16. Power model for 3G, LTE, and Wi-Fi [48].

mobile users are requesting files with equal or different sizes from a server located in the Internet. On the basis of the order of the requests, a resource algorithm schedules the specific network flows. To determine the energy consumption of the downloads also for other technologies such as LTE, 3G, and Wi-Fi, the model provided by Huang et al. [48] is used.

Figure 4.16 shows the power needed (in mW) depending on the data rate (in Mbps) of the uplink and the downlink for all technologies. A mobile device already consumes a significant amount of energy when 3G or LTE is turned on. In general, LTE provides the highest data rate that is necessary for the emerging high quality applications. Yet it also consumes the most power compared to 3G and Wi-Fi.

4.4.3.2 Performance Results of the Proposed Mechanism. First, we investigate the impact of the FCFS resource allocation algorithm on perceived

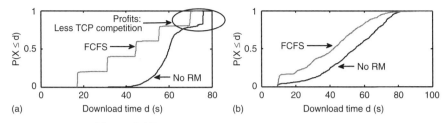

Figure 4.17. CDFs for different download scenarios.

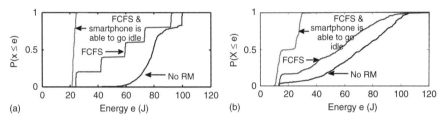

Figure 4.18. Impact if smartphone is able to go idle in transmit pauses in conjunction with FCFS scheduling.

downloading times for two scenarios. We evaluate a scenario with five users that simultaneously try to download the same 5-MB file from a server. Then, we focus on a scenario with a higher statistical variation. The interarrival time for all five download users are distributed exponentially with a mean of 5 s. Further, the users download files with a size of 3 or 6 MB. The available wireless network capacity of the WMN is limited to 3 Mbps. To get statistical significance, the experiments were conducted 100 times. The aggregated results are depicted in Figure 4.17. The results are illustrated as CDF for the download times d. In case of an FCFS scheduling, the download times can be reduced. This is mainly due to less competition between the TCP flows than in the case of "no RM" (no resource management, i.e., without particular scheduling strategy).

A convenient approach for saving energy at the end device is to temporarily suspend their transmissions. Therefore, we consider theoretically how high the savings in energy are if the mobile phone is able to go idle. We compare the results with the energy consumption for terminals that cannot go idle for the cases with and without explicit resource management. The energy consumption per terminal in case of an LTE network are illustrated in Figure 4.18. Again, the results for the static case are depicted in Figure 4.18a, whereas the results for the more varying scenario are illustrated in Figure 4.18b. It can be seen that the FCFS mechanisms with an enabled idle option outperform both the FCFS and the No RM mechanisms. Here, the mobile devices are only activated as long as they are downloading a file. In the lower figure, we can see the effect of different file sizes. The step behavior is the result of energy consumed by the mobile devices for the 3-MB and the 6-MB files.

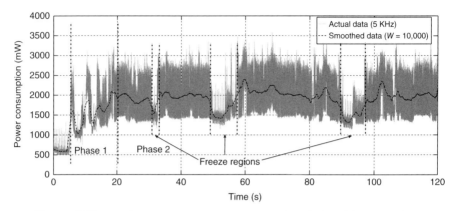

Figure 4.19.   Total instantaneous power consumption during video streaming.

As shown in this section, appropriate resource scheduling mechanisms might reduce the energy consumption of end devices by reducing transmission time. The energy saving potential, however, highly depends on the type of application. During a download, the user typically performs other tasks or does not interact with the device at all. As other components such as the device screen do not depend on the download progress, no additional energy is wasted. This may change by taking other applications such as progressive video streaming into account, as discussed in the following.

4.4.4   Energy Measurements Revealing Video QoE Issues

During the playout of a video, the stream often gets interrupted because of starvation of the playback buffer that is caused by bandwidth and delay variations, affecting the BDP (bandwidth–delay product) and RTT (round trip time). Those short or long pauses during the video stream are referred to as *freezes* or *stalling events* that influence the end user perceived QoE. During a stalling event, typically, no data is transmitted, which on the one hand might result in a reduced power consumption. On the other hand, other components such as the screen consume power leading to an intrinsic need to reduce stalling times and therewith the waste of battery power.

In the following, we investigate whether it is possible to identify video stalling based on the energy consumption of the smartphone using anomaly detection techniques [34, 35]. As detailed in Section 4.3.3, power measurements can be conducted using software internal tools such as PowerTutor or external power-monitoring tools such as Monsoon. More details, as well as a comparison of both tools, can be found in [35]. To achieve a good accuracy of the stalling event estimation, a high sampling rate of power measurements is necessary in order to detect anomalies. If the measurement sampling rate is too low, it might miss the anomalies and thus does not identify stalling. However, oversampling might cause unnecessary high energy consumption because of the excessive amount of system calls to fetch the information on the current drain.

The instantaneous total power consumption during video streaming on the smartphone is given in Figure 4.19. The power consumption values are categorized in to two

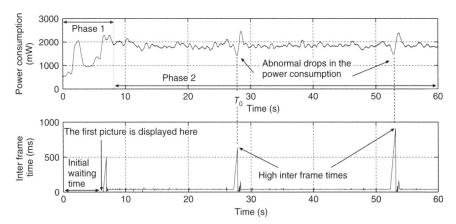

Figure 4.20. Simultaneous interpicture time and power consumption measurements.

parts: Phase 1 and Phase 2. Before Phase 1, the smartphone is in idle state. Phase 1 starts when the user presses the play button and the player requests the video content from the server. Phase 1 duration contains the signaling duration, and it depends on the condition of the link in between the smartphone client and the streaming server. The increases in initial delay extends the duration of Phase 1 and eventually the total energy consumption of the video player. After Phase 1, the instantaneous power consumption values follow a steady-state region in Phase 2, and this second phase continues until the end of the video session. However, in Phase 2, the steady-state behavior of instantaneous power consumption might be impacted by the occasional freezes during the video playout, and we identified these regions as "freeze regions?" We smoothed the high frequency power consumption values obtained via Monsoon with simple moving average (SMA) with varying window sizes (W), where $W = 10,000$ represents a 2 second-long window size. There are two evidences in the power consumption pattern at Phase 2 where the smoothed power consumption values drop down from approximately 2000 to approximately 1500 mW. In parallel, the interpicture times, that is, the time gap in between two consecutively displayed pictures, are obtained via our VLQoE tool [49]. Then, one-to-one mappings between the two parameters (interpicture time and instantaneous power consumption) are obtained using an optimized window size, $W = 7500\,(1.5\,\text{s})$ that yields the highest correlation between those two parameters as shown in Figure 4.20.

The correct choice of internal software-based power measurement tools with minimally obtrusive highly accurate power measurement tool on a mobile device can detect the stalling events through energy measurements. Accordingly, the QoE can be estimated by the device, and appropriate actions to reduce the energy consumption might be performed. The introduced methods have the potential to provide a more energy-efficient QoE monitoring framework that relies on energy measurements instead of a complex instrumentation of network stack and user interfaces.

Until now, we discussed the wireless access networks that are connected to a continuous energy source and the issues related to energy efficiency, and the QoS and QoE for access networks and end device. Next, an outlook on environmental WMNs used to connect weather or climate monitoring stations is given. A main concern these networks face is that they are not connected to the power grid, but are supplied with batteries and have no stable energy supply.

4.4.5   Energy Issues in Environmental WMNs

While environmental WMNs take advantage of wireless communications, they face the challenge of energy supply. In environmental monitoring, in particular, the mesh nodes generally cannot count on energy supplies close by. Thus, they need to be equipped with batteries and will be able to communicate only as long as there is enough charge left. Self-sufficient energy supply means leverage local energy sourcing, for example, through the use of solar panels or windmills. It, furthermore, implies the need to carefully handle power consumption and resource allocation such that communication outages owing to discharged batteries are avoided [50, 51]. The latter has shown to be a QoE issue that is taken very seriously by users [32]. Countermeasures have been proposed, such as a context-aware energy management system for network nodes that are energy self-sufficient [52], a battery-aware scheme for energy-efficient coverage and routing [53], and an energy model for network coding-enabled WMNs based on IEEE 802.11 [54]. In [55], an investigation of the energy consumption behavior from the perspective of a wireless network interface in an ad-hoc networking environment is detailed.

The challenges stated in the works above have been studied in an environmental mesh network deployed in the Valais region of the Swiss Alps for hydrometeorological monitoring [56]. The environmental conditions are challenging and changing, comprising highly varying sunlight conditions and lots of snow throughout the year. This A^4-Mesh network [57] provides researchers quasi-permanent near-real-time remote control of sensors and access to (quite large volumes of) sensor data. Thus, data loss should be avoided by all means. Figure 4.21 shows the network setup, with the distance of each wireless link and the locations of the connected environmental monitoring stations. Energy measurements, in particular, load of the mesh node and charge of the battery (both in Ah), were taken over two periods of several weeks each, one in summer and the other in winter.

Figure 4.22 displays the daily battery load (charge) together with daily usage (discharge) for an arbitrary week in summer and winter. The measurements concern a central node in the wireless mesh network, node 8, and node 3, which is at the edge of the network and acts as gateway for some specific sensors, cf. Figure 4.21. In both figures, at first sight, it seems that there is lacking data for the battery charge. As the battery day load denotes the battery charging by the solar panel module, we can expect activity only when the panel actually generates charge, which explains the lack of recorded data at the beginning and end of each day when sunlight stops hitting the panel. The case is more extreme in winter because of the shorter period of daytime. Moreover, it is interesting to note that the battery day load registers large differences from one day to the next, indicating that depending on weather conditions, the amount of sunlight reaching the panel varies considerably. Although sunny days can be used to bring back the battery to full charge and compensate for periods (days) with poor sunlight, one should always consider daylight statistics of potential deployment locations.

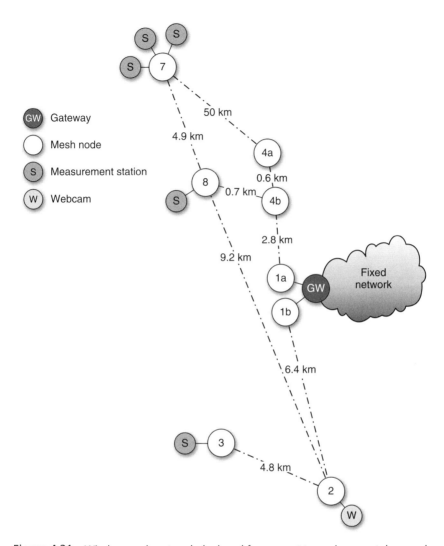

Figure 4.21. Wireless mesh network deployed for support to environmental research.

Comparing the energy usage of the two mesh nodes shows that the central node 8 needs more energy ($\sim$17 Ah in a day) compared to what node 3 consumes ($\sim$12 Ah in a day). The measured data indisputably points out that mesh node 8 is involved in more intensive internode communication using in that way more energy. The impact of the length of the communication link on the required transmit power should also not be neglected, mainly because of higher per-link transmission power. Hence, the design of a wireless mesh network relying on solar energy for its sustainable operation should take into account the role of each individual node in the overall mesh network as well as the node's location, which affects communication distances, and also the amount of usable sunlight in the region.

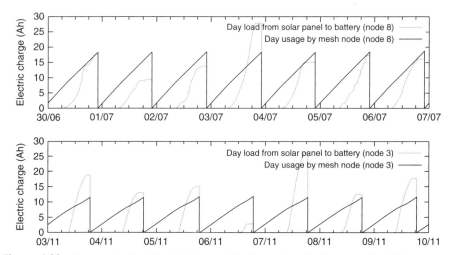

Figure 4.22. Battery day load (in Ah) along with the mesh node day usage (in Ah): measurements are taken at the mesh node 8 and 3 from our real-world wireless mesh network, for a period of 1 week in summer/winter.

4.4.6 Summary

This section discussed the trade-off between QoS and QoE as well as the energy efficiency of access network structures and user devices, starting with summarizing ideas and mechanisms to scale cellular network resources better to the number of users. We found that the power consumption of 4G (LTE) cellular access networks for low and middle load scenarios can be reduced by deploying energy-efficient technologies resulting in energy savings of 40–60%.

We demonstrated the trade-off between QoE and energy consumption of a WMN for an exemplary use case, web browsing. The results illustrate the relationship between the number of customers, their QoE, and the energy consumption of the access network and reveal possible energy savings. Besides energy consumption of the access network, energy savings at the mobile devices is also an important issue. Therefore, resource scheduling mechanisms are candidate technologies for reducing the energy consumption of data transmissions by reducing the download times. In combination with techniques such as discontinuous transmission, which allows to deactivate unused radio components on different timescales, energy consumption for occurring waiting times can be significantly reduced. This, however, changes for applications such as progressive video streaming. Here, the components such as CPU and screen might remain active regardless of the state of the video playback, for example, stalled or smooth playout [58].

Last but not least, environmental wireless access networks that are not connected to the power grid have been discussed. In such a scenario, access nodes are equipped with batteries and solar panels to allow energy harvesting. This type of access network requires a much more sophisticated network design to provide sufficient resources for the supported networking services. Accordingly, various parameters such as length of the communication links, role of the individual nodes, their locations, as well as the amount of usable sunlight have to be taken into account.

4.5   ENERGY-EFFICIENT MEDIUM ACCESS IN WIRELESS SENSOR NETWORKS

Energy efficiency is of highest concern in WSNs. Developed protocols have considered energy efficiency from the beginning, because usually sensor nodes are battery powered and are expected to have long lifetime. Mechanisms developed in WSNs have thus influenced protocols and mechanisms in other (wireless) network environments. The MAC layer is the most important one concerning energy efficiency, because it depends mainly on the MAC protocol when a sensor's transceiver can go to sleep state. The transceiver is the component of a sensor consuming most of its energy, and putting a transceiver into sleep state is by far more effective than adjusting the transmit power.

Many energy-efficient MAC protocols for WSNs have been developed. However, most of those protocols and mechanisms trade energy efficiency for network performance (delay, throughput) and are not able to support varying traffic patterns. This section presents work on energy-efficient WSN MAC protocols (cf. Section 4.5.1), in particular, MaxMAC, which is able to adapt to varying traffic patterns. Measurement in real WSN testbeds demonstrates that it is possible to design both energy-efficient and traffic-adaptive MAC protocols for WSNs (cf. Section 4.5.2).

4.5.1   MaxMAC – An Energy-Efficient MAC Protocol

MaxMAC is an energy-efficient MAC approach, which takes advantage of the substantial work carried out on energy-efficient MAC (E^2-MAC) protocols in the past decade, especially the asynchronous contention-based protocols B-MAC [24], WiseMAC [59], and X-MAC [26].

4.5.1.1   Preamble Sampling. With preamble sampling (also referred to as *low power listening*) introduced in B-MAC and WiseMAC, nodes keep their radios off for most of the time and only wake up for brief periodic duty cycles to poll the channel for a preamble signal once every *Base Interval T* (cf. Figure 4.23). ContikiMAC [60] also applies the WiseMAC preamble minimization to reduce the transmission overhead.

The preamble sampling technique of WiseMAC is already quite efficient in avoiding costly overhearing. However, with sparse traffic, chances are high that the wake-ups of nontargeted receivers do not coincide with those of the targeted receivers. However, with higher traffic and transmissions of queued packet trains, overhearing of preambles and frames can also become an increasing source of energy waste. MaxMAC minimizes overhearing by enriching preambles with target ID information, as illustrated in Figure 4.23. Target nodes turn their radio transceivers on and sense the carrier for *their particular preamble* to receive preamble and frame. Nontarget nodes turn their radios on, extract the target information in the ongoing preamble transmission, notice that they are not targeted, and immediately turn the radio off again. This concept has been applied in X-MAC [26], where nodes send preamble strobes in between which receiver

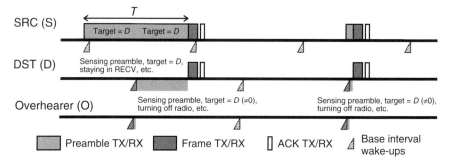

Figure 4.23. Preamble sampling with embedded target address in MaxMAC.

nodes can signal reception readiness with the so-called *Early-ACK*. MaxMAC is the first protocol that merges this concept of integrating a target address identifier into the preamble to reduce overhearing with the highly efficient preamble minimization technique of WiseMAC.

4.5.1.2   Run-Time Traffic-Adaptation Mechanisms.

In contrast to most of today's E^2-MAC protocols, which operate with rather static parameter settings, Max-MAC introduces traffic-adaptation features to instantly react to changing load conditions by altering its behavior at run-time. Similarly as in dynamic frequency/voltage scaling, where the CPU reacts to higher computation load with an increase of the frequency/voltage, a traffic-adaptive E^2-MAC protocol should react to changing load by correspondingly tuning the radio: turning it on more frequently when more traffic has to be handled, keeping it permanently on during load peaks, and turning it off again when the load level permits it.

With E^2-MAC protocols alternating between statically configured sleep in each interval, given that no traffic-adaptation mechanisms are integrated. Latency typically increases sharply, as forwarding nodes need to buffer incoming frames and wait for the next wake-up of their intermediate gateway node, which often sums up to several seconds in multi-hop scenarios. In MaxMAC, nodes change their state and, hence, their behavior, and allocate the so-called *extra wake-ups* when the rate of incoming packets reaches predefined threshold values and release them when the traffic rate drops below these thresholds again, falling back to their initial channel sampling behavior.

Figure 4.24 illustrates the state-based adaptivity mechanism with a source node (SRC) sending packets to a receiver node (destination, DST) with increasing rate. Nodes operate in the *base interval* state per default, polling the channel periodically each base interval T. They alter their state (and behavior) by switching to states S_1 and S_2 when the corresponding thresholds T_1 and T_2 are reached. Thresholds T_1 and T_2 are set to 2 and 6 packets/s in Figure 4.24 but only serve to illustrate the basic concept. Each node keeps estimating the rate of incoming packets, using a sliding window of 1 s (cf. rate estimation graph of DST in Figure 4.24). In case of increasing load, it schedules extra wake-ups in between each base interval, effectively doubling the amount of duty cycles over time. DST communicates its increased wake-up frequency in the ACK. SRC receives this announcement and marks the increased wake-up frequency of DST in its

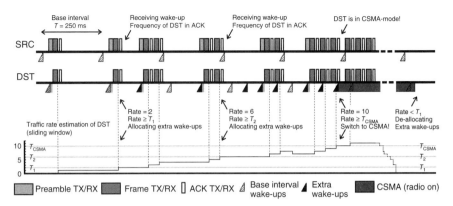

Figure 4.24. Rate estimation, extra wake-ups, and CSMA mode in MaxMAC.

schedule offset table. With the notification sent by DST in the ACK, DST promises to remain in the new state and keep its increased wake-up frequency for a predefined timespan S1_LEASE. For each state in MaxMAC, the LEASE timespans (S1_LEASE, S2_LEASE, CSMA_LEASE) define how long a node promises to remain in the new state when announcing the state change in the ACK. LEASE timespans can be extended in any new ACK transmission. By remaining in a higher state for at least the LEASE duration, fast oscillation between the different states can be mitigated.

With the rate of incoming packets reaching the threshold T_2, DST changes to state S_2, doubles the frequency of wake-ups again, and announces its state change in the ACK (cf. Figure 4.24). As soon as these timespans expire, nodes having received prior state change announcements will assume that the corresponding node has fallen back to its default behavior, polling the channel with the base interval T, which prevents them from transmitting when the target is not awake.

Most E^2-MAC protocols have been designed under the assumption of sparse low rate traffic and, hence, take into account a severe degradation of the maximum through-put compared to non-duty-cycled MACs. They only reach a fraction of that of CSMA. MaxMAC has been specifically designed to achieve a throughput similar as CSMA in situations of increased network activity, which can be seen as best case for the class of contention-based random-access MAC protocols. While the allocation of extra wake-ups helps to achieve a somewhat increased throughput and reduces the latency, the character-istics of CSMA can still not be reached. MaxMAC thus carries the concept of changing the behavior one step further: when the rate of incoming packets reaches a further thresh-old T_{CSMA} (with $T_{CSMA} > T_2 > T_1$), MaxMAC switches to energy-unconstrained CSMA and announces this state change to the sender node (and potentially overhearing nodes) in the ACK. Figure 4.24 illustrates node DST measuring the rate of incoming packets to reach $T_{CSMA} = 10$ packets/s in the right part of the figure. DST, hence, switches to the CSMA state, announcing the state change to SRC in the ACK and promising to remain in the CSMA state for at least the predefined timespan CSMA_LEASE. Within this timespan, SRC can transmit packets without having to wait for a wake-up of DST, as it knows that DST keeps its transceiver on for at least the timespan CSMA_LEASE. With

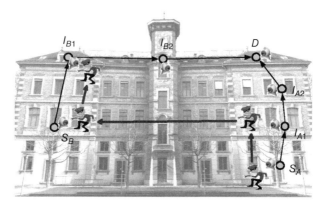

Figure 4.25. Intruder breaking into offices of nodes S_A, I_{A1}, S_B, I_{B1}.

CSMA_LEASE expiring, all nodes having received the prior state change announcement of DST assume that DST has fallen back to the base interval state, which prevents them from transmitting at times when DST is asleep.

4.5.2 Real-World Testbed Experiments with MaxMAC

Our real-world testbed evaluation scenario is inspired by recent work on artificial-intelligence and neural-network-based intrusion detection and office monitoring systems. Figure 4.25 illustrates our application-oriented scenario: the figure displays the testbed with a V-shaped network topology. The nodes in the testbed network are assumed to be part of a distributed office monitoring and intrusion detection system. Each node is assumed to generate sensing information originating from a small CMOS camera and an infrared sensor. On the basis of its sensor values and prior calibration, it detects anomalous behavior as proposed in [61]. The sink node D is again located in the top right corner and is assumed to be connected to the Internet to contact the facility management staff. The events we emulate are described in the following.

All nodes except for the sink are generating *status* messages each 20 s to inform the sink about their alive status (background traffic). In each experiment run, the initial idle period lasts for 100 s. At $t = 100$ s after experiment start, an intruder enters the building in the ground floor and enters the office of node S_A, as displayed in Figure 4.25. Node S_A notices the intruder and generates an image, which is split into 100 packets and sent toward the sink. The node is configured to send two packets per second, hence, the process takes roughly 50 s. The intruder moves up the stairs into the first floor, where he breaks into the office of node I_{A1}, exactly 40 s after visiting the first office. Node I_{A1} detects the intruder and also sends an image toward the sink. After another 40 s, the intruder breaks into the room of node S_B located on the same floor, where the same procedure is triggered. Again, 40 s later, the intruder breaks into the room of node I_{B1} located in the second floor triggering image sending. Finally, the intruder leaves the building. Every node, after transmitting its image data, falls back to its default behavior, generating status messages every 20 s and sending them towards the sink.

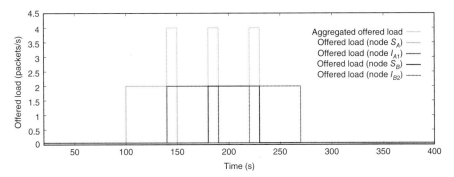

Figure 4.26. Offered load from nodes S_A, I_{A1}, S_B, and I_{B1}.

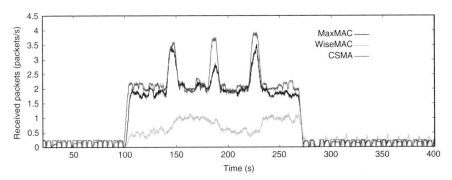

Figure 4.27. Packet reception rate at sink node D.

Figure 4.26 illustrates the shape of the offered load generated by the four sensor nodes in the different rooms of the building. Each node starts transmitting its series of packets when the intruder is in its office. There are overlaps of duration of 10 s where two nodes are concurrently attempting to send their packets toward the sink, as illustrated in the aggregated offered load curve.

Figure 4.27 depicts the rate of received packets by sink node D. The rates were calculated using a central moving average filter of 1 s and computing the average across the results of the 20 experiment runs. In general, WiseMAC obviously manages well to deliver its periodic *alive* status messages to the sink. However, it suffers from major packet loss when the nodes have to transmit the 100 payload messages at a rate of 2 packets/s. With the wake-up interval $T = 500$ ms, each node only wakes up twice per second. As packets have to be forwarded across multiple hops, the rather limited channel contention mechanism and the hidden node problem lead to many packet losses. These are most likely caused by collisions and buffer overflows after failed transmission attempts. The rate of successfully delivered packets from nodes S_A, I_{A1}, S_B, and I_{B1} during the image transmission period does not exceed 1 packet/s on an average, with the major share of packets being lost. After the triggered events, the periodic *alive* status packets sent for every 20 s are again received at the sink without major losses.

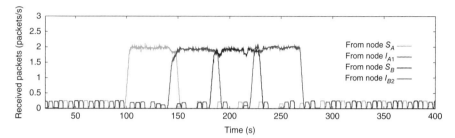

Figure 4.28. CSMA: packet reception rate from nodes S_A, I_{A1}, S_B and I_{B1}.

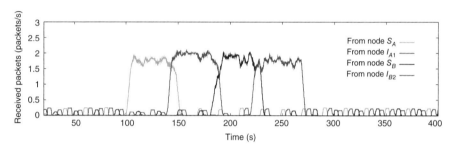

Figure 4.29. MaxMAC: packet reception rate from nodes S_A, I_{A1}, S_B, and I_{B1}.

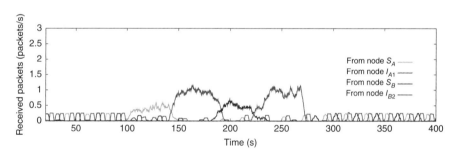

Figure 4.30. WiseMAC: packet reception rate from nodes S_A, I_{A1}, S_B, and I_{B1}.

In contrast to WiseMAC, CSMA and MaxMAC succeed in delivering the periodic *alive* status messages, and also the major share of the 100 packets which are triggered by the intruder. The small time periods when two nodes are delivering their series of packets at the same time is managed best by CSMA. MaxMAC's rate of received packets reaches a slightly lower maximum throughput and also tends to drop some packets when only one event is being handled.

Figures 4.28–4.30 depict the share of packets from each originating node S_A, I_{A1}, S_B, and I_{B1} coming in at the sink node D. Figure 4.28 conveys the superior performance of CSMA with respect to the achieved packet delivery ratio (PDR) (96%). MaxMAC is able to deliver the major portion of packets (89%) but suffers some losses during the

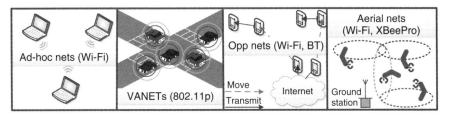

Figure 4.31. Ad-hoc and opportunistic network types and typical technologies.

load peaks, cf. Figure 4.29. WiseMAC suffers heavily from congestion during the load peaks. The rate of 2 packets/s across a couple of hops is not manageable by the protocol and results in buffer overflows and collisions. Nevertheless, it succeeds equally well as MaxMAC or CSMA in delivering the major portion of the periodic *alive* messages.

4.5.3 Summary

This section described the state of the art of energy-efficient and adaptive MAC protocols for WSNs. We have discussed MaxMAC as adaptive and energy-efficient MAC protocol and applied it in a real indoor scenario testbed for intrusion detection. The results show that it is possible to combine energy-efficient and traffic-adaptive protocol operation.

4.6 ENERGY-EFFICIENT CONNECTIVITY IN AD-HOC AND OPPORTUNISTIC NETWORKS

In today's world of information exchange anywhere at any time, heterogeneous infrastructure networks based on a manifold of radio technologies are available. Yet, the ever-increasing need for bandwidth and connectivity asks for the integration of alternative networking technologies in addition to traditional, infrastructure-based ones. Such need is stated by large amounts of traffic because of, for example, multimedia services leveraged by the evolution of smartphones and other smart devices. As a consequence of these demands, offloading the infrastructure by alternative technologies is considered. Additionally, connectivity is still a problem in rural regions of developing countries and when infrastructure networks are destroyed during natural or man-made disasters. Here, ad-hoc and opportunistic networks establish connectivity provided by equal peers, that is, mainly mobile devices. Figure 4.31 visualizes major types of infrastructureless networks that have been introduced in the past. Starting with general ad-hoc networks mainly based on Wi-Fi and concerned with establishing connectivity and efficient routing in the early years, different use cases demanded special solutions. For example, the IEEE 802.11p amendment has been adopted for vehicular ad-hoc networks (VANETs). Other new approaches originating from early ad-hoc networking research are opportunistic networks leveraging Bluetooth or Wi-Fi based networking options for device-to-device communication. Recently, aerial networks have been introduced, which establish ad-hoc network connections between flying unmanned aerial vehicles (UAVs), for example, supported by Wi-Fi ad-hoc and long range technologies for control traffic such as XBeePro.

As end user devices are in these settings often concerned with providing network functions such as relaying of packets and network maintenance, energy-efficient operation of these devices is required to assure a sufficiently long lifetime of the network. Thus, we will ask the question whether the networking technologies are mature enough to cope with this problem and discuss the trade-offs that have to be considered to achieve energy-efficient connection provisioning. Thus, we introduce major technologies, their energy footprint, and methods to increase energy efficiency, as well as typical application fields of ad-hoc (cf. Section 4.6.1) and opportunistic networks (cf. Section 4.6.2).

4.6.1 Ad-Hoc Networking

The original appeal of ad-hoc networking is due to the lack of reliance on an infrastructure, for example, in times of disasters, and the self-organizing nature of the network in a distributed fashion. Research in the area during the past 15 years has, therefore, attempted to show the viability of the ideas in terms of connectivity and message delivery ratio as a function of network capacity (node density and sparseness as a function of mobility). Less research has targeted the important question of energy consumption in ad-hoc networks. One major technology used is Wi-Fi IEEE 802.11a/g/n – operating in infrastructure and ad-hoc mode. Civil use cases of ad-hoc networking based on 802.11 are VANETs, and recently aerial networks of micro UAVs.

A major insight from early studies [62–65] is that ad-hoc networking protocols should target the reduction of energy consumption by avoiding staying too long in an idle listening mode. For example, studies on Symbian and Android phones (N97 and Magic 1, respectively) show that the base consumption for staying connected in the ad-hoc mode of Wi-Fi is considerably high, for example, 0.7 W on the Nokia N97. This is on a par with the amount of energy consumed by the screen. A similar finding is presented in [66], where Nexus One phones are analyzed with respect to their energy consumption during scanning and service set identifier (SSID) beaconing in ad-hoc mode. While the scanning operation is the least energy consuming network operation (4.8% in 24 h), beaconing causes draining of the battery within less than a day.

Another way to save energy is to reduce the number of transmissions and use a way of overhearing communication by many, for example, by using broadcasting or multicasting. The work of Asplund and Nadjm-Tehrani [62] introduces a manycast algorithm termed *Random Walk Gossip* (RWG), which keeps the number of active transmissions to a minimum, thereby saving energy. This protocol was successfully implemented on real devices as well as studied on simulation platforms [63–65]. Implementations of the protocol run on smartphones using the Android as well as Symbian phone platforms.

A major drawback of real implementations of these concepts is that they have to be ported multiple times to new emerging platforms and adapted because of the new energy footprints of networking operations. For example, while it was possible to operate in true Wi-Fi ad-hoc mode with former mobile phones, recent (unrooted and not jail-broken) smartphones do not support this mode any more. We discuss new modes of spontaneous connection establishment in Section 4.6.2. In the following, we summarize major concerns of energy-efficient ad-hoc networking in the use cases disaster and rescue missions.

4.6.1.1   Use Case Establishing Connectivity after Disasters and in Rescue Missions. In disaster scenarios, the major concern is to establish a robust network that maintains connectivity for the time necessary to sufficiently carry out the disaster relief task. Thus, prolonging the network lifetime is a major concern, in particular, in the likely case that some or all ad-hoc nodes are running on batteries.

To study such a situation, a simple model of device energy depletion, including both the idle listening footprint and cost of transmissions on the ad-hoc 802.11 interface, has been added to the NS3 simulator as described by Raciti et al. [67]. In the context of a disaster scenario, it is shown that the lifetime of the network can be extended by 14% with no major loss of performance if each node uses the knowledge about own current energy levels and a local estimation of the normality (or hostility) of the behavior in the nearest environment. This work is based on plugging a module into NS3 whose calibration is based on the actual energy measurements obtained in a small-scale testbed emulating device transmissions [68].

In addition to mobile devices such as notebooks and mobile phones, modern search and rescue missions commence the inclusion of battery-powered micro UAVs. This allows, first, to gather image data of an area and, second, to establish an aerial multi-hop network to transmit over wider distances. These networks are sparse but can make use of sending aerial vehicles to certain waypoints to establish and improve connectivity. Yet this comes at a cost in terms of battery depletion of the vehicles when moving. For example, the battery of small airplanes (wingspan of 80 cm and battery capacity of 2100 mAh) and quadrocopters (frame of 64×64 cm and battery capacity of 3300 mAh) used in the testbed described in [69] allows flight autonomy in the range of 30 and 20 min, respectively (at speeds of about 10 and 5 m/s, respectively). Thus, moving the vehicle away from its original, mission-driven pathway to improve connectivity likely reduces the lifetime of the vehicle significantly and has to be performed carefully.

These sample use cases show that energy efficiency is and remains an important topic for ad-hoc networks, which establish connectivity when infrastructure networks are not available or not reliable. Mobile devices can further act as clients of infrastructure networks and provide additional device-to-device communication to offload the infrastructure and to enhance the connectivity range of infrastructures. This is done by leveraging technologies providing device-to-device links and device mobility, which creates new "opportunities" for connectivity as we discuss next.

4.6.2   Opportunistic and Delay-Tolerant Networking

Delay-tolerant networks (DTNs) are networks that do not require end-to-end connectivity resulting in nontraditional delays for services. Opportunistic networks are DTNs that make use of mobility to establish connections when devices come into transmission range of one another [70]. Here, mobile devices store data locally, carry them while moving, and forward the data through wireless transmission. Mobile devices are – as in ad-hoc networks – themselves the relays in the network but, different to mobile ad-hoc networks (MANETs), are extremely mobile, and dissemination is more based on flooding than on setting up deterministic routes.

In this setting, the energy consumption of mobile devices, mainly smartphones, is crucial for the operation of an opportunistic network. The wireless networks primarily

TABLE 4.3. Power and Energy Consumption of Wireless Technologies Measured on the Samsung Galaxy Nexus Smartphone [71].

Technology	Operation	Power/Energy Average	Standard Deviation
Bluetooth	Discoverable	2.59 mW	0.56 mW
Bluetooth	Discovery	2027.38 mJ	146.7 mJ
Bluetooth	Connect slave (master)	1998.11 (944.81) mJ	157.77 (77.95) mJ
Bluetooth	Connected slave (master)	58.49 (28.53) mW	3.29 (0.05) mW
Wi-Fi Direct	Turn on	633.31 mJ	115.59 mJ
Wi-Fi Direct	Discovery	340.89 mW	4.02 mW
Wi-Fi Direct	Connect station (AP)	3523.78 (1654.50) mJ	714.44 (395.25) mJ
Wi-Fi Direct	Connected station (AP)	49.75 (231.92) mW	3.9 (9.14) mW
WLAN-Opp	Wi-Fi scan	697.47 mJ	115.07 mJ
WLAN-Opp	Wi-Fi AP turn on	754.03 mJ	257.30 mJ
WLAN-Opp	Wi-Fi AP on	210.97 mW	11.72 mW
WLAN-Opp	Associate station (AP)	3194.32 (2626.86) mJ	722.81 (366.25) mJ
WLAN-Opp	Associated station (AP)	60.79 (210.97) mW	9.74 (11.72) mW

in use are Bluetooth and Wi-Fi – Wi-Fi, not in ad-hoc mode, as this is not available for most off-the-shelf smartphones (unless rooted or jail-broken), but using a kind of soft AP mode. Example technologies are Wi-Fi Direct and WLAN-Opp [66]. Table 4.3 summarizes the energy consumption of a typical smartphone, the Samsung Galaxy Nexus, as measured by the Monsoon Power Monitor [12].

One major observation [71] is that the average power consumption for discovery is least for Bluetooth, and it depends on the duty cycle interval. Bluetooth is 2.5–3 times more efficient than WLAN-Opp, which is twice as efficient as Wi-Fi Direct. The efficiency of Bluetooth originates from its ability to operate while the phone is in sleep mode. Yet, the low energy consumption of Bluetooth comes with the disadvantage of a very short transmission range, which is a major drawback for opportunistic connectivity: Bluetooth supports a transmission range of few meters while Wi-Fi allows a range of up to few hundreds of meters.

An additional important observation is that the different roles of the devices (access point or station, master or slave) result in a different energy consumption for each of the technologies. In a group of devices, thus, static role assignment leads to unequal and unfair energy depletion of some devices. To overcome this phenomenon, a *fair role-switching scheme* has been developed for WLAN-Opp based on estimating the remaining contact duration of peers as a function of the elapsed contact time [71]. In this way, an equal depletion of devices can be achieved without switching too often.

These insights for discovery and solutions for fair connectivity provisioning in opportunistic are generally valid. In the following, we take the specific perspective of opportunistic networking used to connect so far disconnected regions.

4.6.2.1 Use Case Opportunistic Networking to Connect Disconnected Regions. Despite the constantly rising numbers of mobile device usage and the increased mobile Internet access, still only 28% of the households in developing countries can access the Internet (2013 report of the ITU [72]). Here, opportunistic networks can contribute to share access to the Internet by using mobile devices as relays and data carriers. Mobile devices can establish contacts to other mobile devices to forward data until, finally, one device with Internet access (via 3G, e.g.) transfers the data to the Internet. Alternatively, mobile devices may act as carriers from one stationary hub (access point with storage capacity) to another, for example, from a city hub with Internet access to a village hub without. In both cases, mobile devices rely on battery power and if communication modules are always on, this will drain the battery. A way to overcome this problem is to switch communication modules off when not needed and on when contact opportunities exist.

In case of device-to-device communication, this requires an aligning of the wake-up schedules of the devices as proposed in [73]. In this approach, the wake-up cycles depend on predicted future contacts, while energy consumption and communication performance are analytically balanced. The approach is studied and proven successful by applying it to major contact traces. Yet, this is not deterministic and the delivery ratio of information can be significantly impaired by the prediction error. Similarly, in [74], the device discovery duration and interval are configured based on contact characteristics, for example, originating from past observations. The energy efficiency of discovery can be increased as long as the actual contact characteristics correspond to the distributions used for estimation. Once the peers are discovered, the role switching scheme described previously [71] provides fairness and flexibility by adapting role switching depending on the elapsed contact time for device-to-device communication.

In the case of stationary hubs, mobile devices act as ferrying stations and just transmit to hubs, when in range. As devices are data carriers, the mobility flows of humans determine connectivity and transmission options, and the overall capacity of this opportunistic network [75]. It is crucial to switch on communication modules for discovery and connection establishment only when in proximity of a hub (access point). Providing efficient estimation methods for wake-ups is a major concern here.

4.6.3 Summary

In ad-hoc and opportunistic networks, the nodes providing connectivity are often battery powered. Thus, it is of importance to reduce the time the devices stay in power-hungry networking states in order to prolong the devices' lifetime. One option is to switch the communication modules on only for a limited time, apply a batch communication style, and to apply overhearing of communication. Another option arises from the way today's smartphones can be spontaneously connected. As 802.11 ad-hoc is disabled for normal operation mode of smartphones and Bluetooth only provides very limited ranges, Wi-Fi adaptations are in use, such as Wi-Fi Direct and WLAN-Opp. These technologies leverage a soft AP mode that allows clients to connect to. In such a setting, however, the devices are not equal and consume different amounts of energy depending on their role. Consequently, in addition to decreasing the energy consumption of the individual device, fair role-switching strategies may be employed. In a different setting, in case mobility can be controlled to achieve better connectivity as for battery-driven (aerial) robot networks, energy moves even more to the center of investigation as energy required for movement is orders of magnitude higher than energy consumed for networking.

It is worth noting that the research results in this field are often derived from simulations of larger groups of entities, yet based on realistic energy and mobility models. The manifold of devices and embedded computers and modules around requires, so far, ever new calibrations of the energy model along new arising technologies. Thus, there is a need for methodological improvement to overcome this situation by providing sustainable, modular energy models for ad-hoc and opportunistic node classes.

4.7   SUMMARY AND CONCLUSIONS

Wireless networks face particular challenges related to energy consumption, yet, also provide specific options for energy-efficient networking. First, in wireless communications, the signal propagation, as well as the range of a wireless link and its quality depends on the antenna profile and its power characteristics. Then, nodes and devices connect and disconnect frequently and increase network dynamics and, thus, lead to varying needs for connectivity. Finally, mobile nodes and devices are in the focus of energy efficiency research, which are battery powered and the battery is a limited resource. On the one hand, the user device is the final edge of an access network, where the user is exposed to an eventual degradation of the quality of experience because of energy saving for the sake of the battery lifetime. On the other hand, mobile nodes and devices can provide network resources themselves in ad-hoc and opportunistic networks.

In this wide field, we gave an introduction to wireless energy efficiency metrics and discussed measurement methodologies followed in recent wireless networking research with a strong focus on the battery-powered mobile device. The two principal methods, namely, external measurements and internal software-based estimation, can provide valid insights in the energy consumption of wireless network operations. In particular for wider field studies, software-based estimation is a feasible choice. Yet, the variety of devices makes it impractical to refer to a single energy device depletion model leading to inaccurate estimation. Thus, to retrieve accurate energy consumption values, external measurements are preferable.

Concerning energy efficiency, we discussed challenges in access, wireless sensor, and ad-hoc and opportunistic networks. Hereby, we put a focus on the trade-off between quality of experience and energy consumption in access networks and discussed an example mesh network in nature environments that is challenged by varying charging and discharging in the field. Wireless sensor networks require means to adapt to changing situations to operate efficiently, as has been exemplified by an adaptive MAC method. Finally, providing connectivity by battery-powered devices is a major concern in ad-hoc and opportunistic networks. Energy-efficient operation targets the reduction of energy consumption by, for example, introducing duty cycling to communication, and also fairness in resource provisioning. To do so, estimates about future connectivity demands are leveraged.

We conclude that adaptive wireless network solutions outperform static approaches in access, sensor, and ad-hoc and opportunistic networks in terms of energy efficiency.

The smartness of the algorithms described in this chapter stems from a good understanding of the energy consumption of the networking operations and context information, which can be used for optimization.

REFERENCES

[1] Bianzino AP, Raju AK, Rossi D. Apples-to-apples: a framework analysis for energy efficiency in networks. ACM SIGMETRICS Perform Eval Rev 2011;38(3):81–85.

[2] Chen T, Kim H, Yang Y. Energy efficiency metrics for green wireless communications. 2010 International Conference on Wireless Communications and Signal Processing (WCSP); 2010. p 1–6.

[3] Alonso-Rubio J, Fazekas P, Skillermark P, Wajda W, editors. INFSO-ICT-247733 Earth. Most Suitable Efficiency Metrics and Utility Functions. INFSO-ICT-247733 Earth - Delivery D2.4; 2012. p 1–55.

[4] Richter F, Fehske AJ, Fettweis GP. Energy efficiency aspects of base station deployment strategies for cellular networks. 2009 IEEE 70th Vehicular Technology Conference Fall (VTC 2009-Fall); 2009. p 1–5.

[5] Chen Y, Zhang S, Xu S, Li GY. Fundamental trade-offs on green wireless networks. IEEE Commun Mag 2011;49(6):30–37.

[6] Zhang X, Zhang J, Huang Y, Wang W. On the study of fundamental trade-offs between QoE and energy efficiency in wireless networks. Trans Emerg Telecommun Technol 2013;24(3):259–265.

[7] Bernardo V, Curado M, Staub T, Braun T. Towards energy consumption measurement in a cloud computing wireless testbed. 2011 1st International Symposium on Network Cloud Computing and Applications (NCCA); 2011. p 91–98.

[8] Rice A, Hay S. Measuring mobile phone energy consumption for 802.11 wireless networking. Pervasive Mob Comput 2010;6:593–606.

[9] Wang L, Manner J. Energy consumption analysis of WLAN, 2G and 3G interfaces. Green Computing and Communications (GreenCom), 2010 IEEE/ACM Int'l Conference on Int'l Conference on Cyber, Physical and Social Computing (CPSCom); Dec 2010; 2010 p 300–307.

[10] IEC. Standard Digital Interface for Programmable Instrumentation - Part 2: Codes, Formats, Protocols and Common Commands (Adoption of (IEEE Std 488.2-1992). IEC 60488-2 First edition 2004–2005; IEEE 488.2; 2004. p 1–261.

[11] Asplund M, Thomasson A, Vergara EJ, Nadjm-Tehrani S. Software-related energy footprint of a wireless broadband module. 9th ACM International Symposium On Mobility Management And Wireless Access, MobiWac '11. ACM; 2011.

[12] Monsoon Solutions Inc. [Online] Available at http://www.msoon.com/. Accessed 2013 Sep 8.

[13] Qualcomm. Trepn Profiler. [Online] Available at https://developer.qualcomm.com/mobile-development/development-devices/trepn-profiler. Accessed 2013 Dec 5.

[14] Nokia Energy Profiler. Nokia. [Online] Available at http://developer.nokia.com/Resources/Tools_and_downloads/Other/Nokia_Energy_Profiler/Quick_start.xhtml. Accessed 2013 Dec 5.

[15] CurrentWidget. Application for Android. [Online] Available at https://code.google.com/p/currentwidget/. Accessed 2013 Dec 5.

[16] Dong M, Zhong L. Self-constructive high-rate system energy modeling for battery-powered mobile systems. 9th International Conference On Mobile Systems, Applications, And Services, MobiSys '11. ACM; 2011. p 335–348.

[17] Hergenroeder A, Horneber J, Meier D, Armbruster P, Zitterbart M. Distributed energy measurements in wireless sensor networks. ACM Conference on Embedded Networked Sensor Systems (SenSys), Demo Session; November 2009; Berkeley (CA).

[18] Hergenroeder A, Wilke J, Meier D. Distributed energy measurements in WSN testbeds with a sensor node management device (SNMD). International Conference on Architecture of Computing Systems (ARCS); Feb 2010; Hannover. p 341–348.

[19] Yang S-R, Yan S-Y, Hung H-N. Modeling UMTS power saving With bursty packet data traffic. IEEE Trans Mobile Comput 2007;6(12):1398–1409.

[20] Andrea Z, Pellegrini FD. Mathematical analysis of IEEE 802.11 energy efficiency. 7th International Symposium On Wireless Personal Multimedia Communications. IEEE; 2004.

[21] Balasubramanian N, Balasubramanian A, Venkataramani A. Energy consumption in mobile phones: a measurement study and implications for network applications. 9th ACM SIGCOMM Conference on Internet Measurement Conference, IMC '09. ACM; 2009. p 280–293.

[22] Vergara EJ, Nadjm-Tehrani S. EnergyBox: a trace-driven tool for data transmission energy consumption studies. In: Pierson J-M, Da Costa G, Dittmann L, editors. *Energy Efficiency in Large Scale Distributed Systems*, Lecture Notes in Computer Science. Springer Berlin Heidelberg; 2013. p 19–34.

[23] Ye W, Heidemann J, Estrin D. An energy efficient MAC protocol for wireless sensor networks. IEEE International Conference on Computer Communications (INFOCOM); June 2002; New York. p 1567–1576.

[24] Polastre J, Hill J, Culler D. Versatile low power media access for wireless sensor networks. ACM Conference on Embedded Networked Sensor Systems (SenSys); Nov 2004; Baltimore (MD). p 95–107.

[25] Haratcherev I, Halkes G, Parker T, Visser O, Langendoen K. PowerBench: a scalable testbed infrastructure for benchmarking power consumption. International Workshop on Sensor Network Engineering (IWSNE); June 2008; Santorini. p 37–44.

[26] Buettner M, Yee GV, Anderson E, Han R. X-MAC: a short preamble MAC protocol for duty-cycled wireless sensor networks. ACM Conference on Embedded Networked Sensor Systems (SenSys); November 2006; Boulder (CO). p 307–320.

[27] Hurni P, Nyffenegger B, Braun T, Hergenroeder A. On the accuracy of software-based energy estimation techniques. In: Marrón PJ, Whitehouse K, editors. *Wireless Sensor Networks*. Volume 6567, Lecture Notes in Computer Science. Springer Berlin Heidelberg; 2011. p 49–64.

[28] Draper NR, Smith H. *Applied Regression Analysis*, Wiley Series in Probability and Statistics; 1998.

[29] Landsiedel O, Wehrle K, Goetz S. Accurate prediction of power consumption in sensor networks. IEEE Workshop on Embedded Networked Sensors (EmNets); May 2005; Sydney, Australia. p 37–44.

[30] PowerTutor. A Power Monitor for Android-based Mobile Platforms. [Online] http://ziyang.eecs.umich.edu/projects/powertutor. Accessed 2014 Sep 26.

[31] Nacci AA, Trovò F, Maggi F, Ferroni M, Cazzola A, Sciuto D, Santambrogio MD. Adaptive and flexible smartphone power modeling. *Mobile Networks and Applications*. Springer; 2013.

[32] Ickin S, Wac K, Fiedler M, Janowski L, Hong Jin-Hyuk, Dey AK. Factors influencing quality of experience of commonly used mobile applications. IEEE Commun Mag 2012;50(4):48,56.

[33] Ra M, Paek J, Sharma AB, Govindan R, Krieger MH, Neely MJ. Energy-delay tradeoffs in smartphone applications. 8th International Conference On Mobile Systems, Applications, And Services (MobiSys '10). New York: ACM; 2010.

[34] Ickin S, Fiedler M, Wac K. Energy-based anomaly detection in quality of experience. 16th International Symposium On Wireless Personal Multimedia Communications; June 2013; Atlantic City (NJ). p 1,6.

[35] Ickin S, Fiedler M, Wac K. Demonstrating the stalling events with instantaneous total power consumption in smartphone-based live video streaming. Sustainable Internet And ICT For Sustainability (SustainIT); Oct 2012; 2012. p 1,4.

[36] Blume O, Zeller D, Barth U. Approaches to energy efficient wireless access networks. 2010 4th International Symposium on Communications, Control and Signal Processing (ISCCSP). IEEE; 2010. p 1–5.

[37] Boldi M, Petersson S, Fodrini M, Orlando A, Persson P, Nilsson A. Multi antenna techniques to improve energy efficiency in LTE radio access network. Future Network & Mobile Summit (FutureNetw). IEEE; 2011. p 1–8.

[38] Ferling D, Bohn T, Zeller D, Frenger P, Gódor I, Jading Y, Tomaselli W. Energy efficiency approaches for radio nodes. *Future Network and Mobile Summit*. IEEE; 2010. p 1–9.

[39] Auer G, Gódor I, Hévizi L, Imran MA, Malmodin J, Fazekas P, Biczók G, Holtkamp H, Zeller D, Blume O, et al. Enablers for energy efficient wireless networks. 2010 IEEE 72nd Vehicular Technology Conference Fall (VTC 2010-Fall). IEEE; 2010. p 1–5.

[40] Debaillie B, Giry A, Gonzalez MJ, Dussopt L, Li M, Ferling D, Giannini V. Opportunities for energy savings in pico/femto-cell base-stations. *Future Network & Mobile Summit (FutureNetw)*. IEEE; 2011. p 1–8.

[41] Ickin S, Wac K, Fielder M. Quality of Experience-Based Energy Reduction by Controlling the 3G Cellular Data Traffic on the Smartphone. 22nd ITC Specialist Seminar on Energy Efficient and Green Networking; Nov 2013; Christchurch.

[42] Auer G, Giannini V, Desset C, Godor I, Skillermark P, Olsson M, Imran MA, Sabella D, Gonzalez MJ, Blume O, et al. How much energy is needed to run a wireless network? IEEE Wireless Communications 2011;18(5):40–49.

[43] Zeller D, Olsson M, Blume O, Fehske A, Ferling D, Tomaselli W, Gódor I. Sustainable wireless broadband access to the future Internet – sensornet the Earth project. *The Future Internet*. Springer; 2013. p 249–271.

[44] Hock D, Bernardo V, Zinner T, Wamser F, Hummel KA, Curado M, Pries R, Braun T, Tran-Gia P. Evaluating the trade-off between energy efficiency and QoE in wireless mesh networks. 4th International Conference on Communications and Electronics (ICCE 12); August 2012; Hué, Vietnam; 2012.

[45] Hoßfeld T, Fiedler M, Zinner T. The QoE provisioning-delivery-hysteresis and its importance for service provisioning in the future internet. Proceedings of the 7th Conference on Next Generation Internet Networks (NGI), Kaiserslautern, Germany; June 2011.

[46] Nvidia White Paper. The benefits of quad core CPUs in mobile devices. Technical report, 2011.

[47] Blenk A, Wamser F, Zinner T, Kellerer W, Tran-Gia P. Dynamic HTTP download scheduling with respect to energy consumptions. In 24th Tyrrhenian International Workshop On Digital Communications; 2013. p 1–6.

[48] Huang J, Qian F, Gerber A, Mao ZM, Sen S, Spatscheck O. A close examination of performance and power characteristics of 4G LTE networks. In Conference on Mobile Systems, and Services. ACM; 2012.

[49] Ickin S, Fiedler M, Wac K, Arlos P, Temiz C, Mkocha K. VLQoE: video quality of experience instrumentation on the smartphone. Multimedia Tools and Applications Journal. Special Issue on Advances in Tools, Techniques and Practices for Multimedia QoE. Springer; 2013.

[50] Badawy GH, Sayegh AA, Todd TD Energy provisioning in solar-powered wireless mesh networks. IEEE Trans Veh Technol 2010;59(8):3859–3871.

[51] Farbod A, Todd TD. Resource allocation and outage control for solar-powered wlan mesh networks. IEEE Trans Mob Comput 2007;6(8):960–970.

[52] Gladisch A, Daher R, Lehsten P, Tavangarian D. Context-aware energy management for energy-self-sufficient network nodes in wireless mesh networks. 2011 3rd International Congress on Ultra Modern Telecommunications and Control Systems and Workshops (ICUMT). IEEE; 2011. p 1–8.

[53] Ma C, Yang Y. A battery aware scheme for energy efficient coverage and routing in wireless mesh networks. 2007. GLOBECOM'07. IEEE Global Telecommunications Conference. IEEE; 2007. p 1113–1117.

[54] Paramanathan A, Rasmussen UW, Hundeboll M, Rein SA, Fitzek FHP, Ertli G. Energy consumption model and measurement results for network coding-enabled IEEE 802.11 meshed wireless networks. 2012 IEEE 17th International Workshop on Computer Aided Modeling and Design Of Communication Links and Networks (CAMAD). IEEE; 2012. p 286–291.

[55] Feeney LM, Nilsson M. Investigating the energy consumption of a wireless network interface in an Ad Hoc networking environment. INFOCOM 2001. 20th Annual Joint Conference of the IEEE Computer and Communications Societies. Proceedings IEEE, volume 3. IEEE; 2001. p 1548–1557.

[56] A^4-Mesh Consortium. A^4-Mesh - Project Overview. [Online]. Available at https://a4-mesh .unibe.ch/. Accessed 2013 Dec 13.

[57] Jamakovic A, Dimitrova DC, Anwander M, Macicas T, Braun T, Schwanbeck J, Staub T, Nyffenegger B. Real-world energy measurements of a wireless mesh network. Energy Efficiency in Large Scale Distributed Systems Conference; 2013. p 218–233.

[58] Vallina-Rodriguez N, Crowcroft J. Energy management techniques in modern mobile handsets. IEEE Commun Surv Tutorials 2013;15(1):179–198.

[59] El-Hoiydi A, Decotignie JD. WiseMAC: an ultra low power MAC protocol for multihop wireless sensor networks. International Workshop on Algorithmic Aspects of Wireless Sensor Networks (ALGOSENSORS), Turku, Finland; July 2004. P 18–31.

[60] Dunkels A, Mottola L, Tsiftes N, Osterlind F, Eriksson J, Finne N. The announcement layer: beacon coordination for the sensornet stack. European Conference on Wireless Sensor Networks (EWSN); Feb 2011; Bonn, Germany. p 211–226.

[61] Wälchli M, Skoczylas P, Meer M, Braun T. Building intrusion detection with a wireless sensor network. ICST International Conference on Ad Hoc Networks (AdHocNets); Sep 2009; Niagara Falls, Canada. p 607–622.

[62] Asplund M, Nadjm-Tehrani S. A partition-tolerant manycast algorithm for disaster area networks. 2009 28th IEEE International Symposium On Reliable Distributed Systems, SRDS '09. IEEE Computer Society; 2009. p 156–165.

[63] Asplund M, de Lanerolle T, Fei C, Gautam P, Morelli R, Nadjm-Tehrani S, Nykvist G. Wireless Ad Hoc Dissemination for Search and Rescue. 7th International ISCRAM Conference; 2010.

[64] Anzaldi D. ORWAR: A Delay-Tolerant Protocol Implemented on the Android Platform; 2010.

[65] Vergara EJ, Nadjm-Tehrani S, Asplund M, Zurutuza U. Resource footprint of a manycast protocol implementation on multiple mobile platforms. 2011 5th International Conference on Next Generation Mobile Applications, Services and Technologies (NGMAST); 2011. p 154–160.

[66] Trifunovic S, Distl B, Schatzmann D, Legendre F. WiFi-Opp: Ad-Hoc-Less opportunistic networking. CHANTS'11: 6th ACM Workshop on Challenged Networks; 2011. p 37–42.

[67] Raciti M, Cucurull J, Nadjm-Tehrani S. Energy-based adaptation in simulations of survivability of Ad Hoc communication. 2011 IFIP Wireless Days (WD); 2011. p 1–7.

[68] Cucurull J, Nadjm-Tehrani S, Raciti M. Modular anomaly detection for smartphone Ad Hoc communication. In: Laud P, editor. *Information Security Technology for Applications.* Volume 7161, Lecture Notes in Computer Science. Springer Berlin Heidelberg; 2012. p 65–81.

[69] Asadpour M, Giustiniano D, Hummel KA, Heimlicher S, Egli S. Now or later? – Delaying data transfer in time-critical aerial communication. CONEXT 2013. ACM; 2013. Accepted.

[70] Conti M, Kumar M. Opportunities in opportunistic computing. Computer 2010;43(1):42–50.

[71] Trifunovic S, Picu A, Hossmann T, Hummel KA. Slicing the battery pie: fair and efficient energy usage in device-to-device communication via role switching. CHANTS'13: 8th ACM MobiCom Workshop On Challenged Networks. New York: ACM; 2013. p 31–36.

[72] The World in 2013. ICT Facts and Figures. [Online]. Available at http://www.itu.int/en/ITU-D/Statistics/Documents/facts/ICTFactsFigures2013-e.pdf. Accessed 2013 Dec 12.

[73] Gao W, Li Q. Wakeup scheduling for energy-efficient communication in opportunistic mobile networks. IEEE INFOCOM 2013; 2013. p 2058–2066.

[74] Bo H, Srinivasan A. eDiscovery: energy-efficient device discovery for mobile opportunistic communications. ICNP 2012: 20th IEEE International Conference on Network Protocols. IEEE Computer Society; 2012. p 1–10.

[75] Alhussainy A, Hummel KA, Antoniadis P. How much can we carry? A capacity analysis of delay tolerant networking in developing countries. MobiCom - LCDNET Workshop 2013. ACM; 2013.

5

POWER MODELING

Jason Mair,[1] Zhiyi Huang,[1] David Eyers,[1] Leandro Cupertino,[2]
Georges Da Costa,[2] Jean-Marc Pierson,[2] and Helmut Hlavacs[3]

[1]*Department of Computer Science, University of Otago, Dunedin, New Zealand*
[2]*Institute for Research in Informatics of Toulouse (IRIT),*
University of Toulouse III, Toulouse, France
[3]*Faculty of Computer Science, University of Vienna, Vienna, Austria*

5.1 INTRODUCTION

Power consumption has long been a concern for portable consumer electronics, with many manufacturers explicitly seeking to maximize battery life in order to improve the usability of devices such as laptops and smart phones. However, it has recently become a concern in the domain of much larger, more power hungry systems such as servers, clusters, and data centers. This new drive to improve energy efficiency is in part due to the increasing deployment of large-scale systems in more businesses and industries, which have two primary motives for saving energy. Firstly, there is the traditional economic incentive for a business to reduce their operating costs, where the cost of powering and cooling a large data center can be on the order of millions of dollars [1]. Reducing the total cost of ownership for servers could help to stimulate further deployments. As servers become more affordable, deployments will increase in businesses where concerns over lifetime costs previously prevented adoption. The second motivating factor is the increasing awareness of the environmental impact – greenhouse gas emissions –

Large-Scale Distributed Systems and Energy Efficiency: A Holistic View, First Edition.
Edited by Jean-Marc Pierson.
© 2015 John Wiley & Sons, Inc. Published 2015 by John Wiley & Sons, Inc.

caused by power production. Reducing energy consumption can help a business indirectly to reduce their environmental impact, making them more clean and green.

The most commonly adopted solution for reducing power consumption is a hardware-based approach, where old, inefficient hardware is replaced with newer, more energy-efficient alternatives. Hardware upgrades provide a means of improvement that is transparent to end users, requiring no changes in user behavior. Despite this convenience, there are several key drawbacks to such a hardware deployment. The foremost problem is the significant financial cost associated with upgrading hardware, which will be substantial for any large deployment. Moreover, such upgrades challenge sustainability, creating significant amounts of material waste that is hard to handle. Furthermore, efficiency improvements are often mistakenly equated with a corresponding reduction in total power consumption [2]. This is commonly not the case, as efficiency improvements have a tendency to increase the scale of system deployments, resulting in greater energy consumption [3]. Previously, such impacts were exacerbated by data center overprovisioning, which resulted in a substantial amount of idle resources [4].

Alternatively, a software-based approach can be used, which adapts runtime utilization characteristics to leverage many of the existing power-saving mechanisms incorporated into modern hardware. It is currently not possible to directly measure the power of individual applications, requiring the development of power models capable of providing power values at a significantly finer granularity than hardware power metering allows, that is, application- or component-specific power consumption statistics. By incorporating power measurements, software policies will be capable of quantitatively evaluating the runtime trade-offs made between power and performance for a given configuration selection.

In addition to improving the effectiveness of many existing power-saving policies, such as workload consolidation within a data center, power models allow new policies to be developed, which were not possible previously. One such policy is the implementation of software-based power caps, where tasks are free to execute on a system as long as total power consumption remains below a set threshold. When exceeded, applications will be progressively throttled or stalled until power consumption decreases. Such a policy can be applied at a finer granularity, enforcing caps specific to applications, potentially reining in rogue applications that are prone to excessive power consumption. A further policy, proposed by Narayan and Rao [5], is to charge data center users for power use, similar to how other resources would be charged. These are but two of the possible use-cases, with more discussed later in the chapter, none of which could be realized without the inclusion of accurate, fine-grained power estimation models.

Advanced power-saving policies commonly require application-specific power values for determining optimal configurations at runtime. Power meters have traditionally been used to provide application-specific power measurements in single processor systems, as only one task was able to execute at any given time. However, modern multi-core processors present a more significant challenge, where system resources can be shared between a large number of concurrently executing tasks. As will be discussed in the next section, hardware power metering has not kept pace with the new processor developments as these meters are not capable of providing the fine-grained power measurements required to isolate individual applications. Therefore, techniques for power estimation models that seek to quantify the relationship between application performance, hardware utilization, and the resulting power consumption have been proposed.

It has long been understood that a close, fine-grained relationship exists between modest changes in application performance and power use. This is intuitive as the power use of a system is strictly dependent on the utilization levels of each component. This relationship is often leveraged by power-saving policies, designed to lower utilization levels of key components in response to changes in execution workloads. The most prominent policies to enact these responses are processor governors, which utilize hardware-based dynamic voltage and frequency scaling (DVFS). Power estimation models attempt to quantify such changes, that is, determine the change in power consumption for a corresponding variation in component utilization (performance).

For example, if the running software is central processing unit (CPU) intensive, the processor will have a high-utilization level and a correspondingly high power level. Alternatively, if a large number of cache-misses are observed, memory accesses will be high, causing processor stalls and low utilization, resulting in a lower overall power draw. In quantifying the strength of the relationships between key performance events and power, an analytical model can be derived, enabling accurate runtime power estimation.

This chapter presents the motivation, fundamental concepts, and implementation methodologies for power modeling. The remainder of the chapter is organized as follows. The limitations of hardware-based power metering is discussed in Section 5.2, providing the primary motives for modeling power. Section 5.3 presents various performance monitoring techniques that are commonly used for collecting application and component performance values. Following this, Section 5.4 discusses the relationship between power and performance that needs to be quantified in the analytical power model. An overarching view of model construction is given in Section 5.4, before a detailed description of the steps involved in model construction, such as event selection, model training, and model evaluation. Experimental results for a number of use-cases are presented in Section 5.6, along with information about existing software that can be used for power modeling in Section 5.7. Finally, Section 5.8 concludes the chapter.

5.2 MEASURING POWER

Despite hardware power meters providing the most accurate source for system power measurements, they are incapable of providing the fine-grained, application-specific values required by some power-aware policies. The measurement granularity is dependent on the type of power meter used. They are either external meters, placed between the wall socket and system power supply, or internal meters, placed within a system. Power measurements are used as the target variable while creating a power estimation model.

5.2.1 External Power Meters

The most commonly used method for monitoring runtime system power is through the use of an external, hardware power meter. For small-scale, standalone system deployments, commodity-wall-connected power meters, such as the Watts Up? Pro[1] and iSocket[2] (InSnergy Socket) are used. Alternatively, large-scale, data center deployments can use intelligent power distribution units (PDUs), which are standard rack PDUs with the additional capability of independently monitoring power for each connected machine. Despite incurring an additional purchase/upgrade cost for hardware, power meters have the significant advantage of easy deployment, requiring no alterations to be made to existing equipment or infrastructure.

However, power meters have two drawbacks regarding the granularity of results. First, the sample rate of power, typically once a second, is insufficient for detailed, fine-grained power analysis of application characteristics [6]. Second, power meters only return coarse-grained power values, for the entire system, making it impractical to determine relative power use of individual applications or system components. Without this capability, power management policies can only be acted upon the entire system, rather than individual applications. This becomes a more significant restriction as processor core counts increase, allowing for more concurrently executing applications. Therefore, another solution is required for fine-grained power-saving policies.

5.2.2   Internal Power Meters

A solution to the problem of coarse-grained power measurements is to embed lower level power sensors inside a system, enabling the isolation of component-specific power use. Fine-grained measurements are possible by independently monitoring the direct current (DC) power rails supplying power to each system component at the required voltage. Two of the most commonly used metering techniques are shunt resistors and clamp meters. Shunt resistors are placed in line for each power rail and measure the voltage drop across the resistor, allowing the current and power to be calculated. For easier deployment, clamp meters can be placed around each power rail, using Hall effect sensors to measure power. Despite such techniques being used during product development and testing of system components, manufacturers rarely incorporate internal meters into commodity products, partly due to additional cost [7].

However, since the Sandy Bridge microarchitecture, Intel has begun to embed power sensors in new processor designs, making predicted power values available through hardware registers. Currently, power measurements are restricted to a selection of three granularities: the entire processor package, power for all cores, or integrated graphics power [8]. System-wide measurements can be made using third party solutions, such as PowerMon2[3], which uses inline metering to monitor all system components using the 3.3-, 5-, and 12-V power rails. More specific monitoring is available through the NI[4] and DCM[5] meters, which only meter the 12-V rail powering the processor. This highlights one of the key limitations of internal metering, that is, not all system components are able to be monitored. Components such as the power supply unit are outside the

---

[1]http://www.wattsupmeters.com.

[2]http://web.iii.org.tw.

[3]http://github.com/beppodb/PowerMon.

[4]http://www.ni.com.

[5]A noncommercial power meter by Universitat Jaume I.

scope of metering, while not all solutions provide enough sensors to build a full system power model.

Despite the significantly finer granularity of power measurements, internal meters are incapable of isolating application-specific power for shared resources. For example, multi-core processors are powered by a single power rail, meaning individual core consumption is indistinguishable. Furthermore, placing additional equipment within a system can disrupt the airflow, causing increases in system temperature and a corresponding increase in power use [9]. This is not to mention the added inconvenience and potential cost of a manual deployment of metering equipment inside existing system deployments.

5.3 PERFORMANCE INDICATORS

Performance values are the second key input parameter for power modeling, which are used as a proxy for hardware utilization levels. During training, performance events provide the independent variables to be correlated with power observations. For the derived model, performance events are the only source of input used for power estimation, requiring sample rates to match runtime power values. Therefore, performance event selection is not only dependent on correlation strength but additionally on potential restrictions imposed by the expected execution environment. Fortunately, many alternative methods exist for monitoring application performance, where each has been designed to serve a different purpose. Techniques range from instrumenting applications and the corresponding execution, to monitoring low-level hardware events to unobtrusively glean performance insights at runtime. A range of such monitoring methods are presented in this section, enabling power model deployment across varied environments.

5.3.1 Source Instrumentation

The most commonly used technique for performance analysis is source code instrumentation, where additional instructions are inserted into the source code at key points of interest in order to provide detailed information during execution. Typical performance information can include data values or the execution time of code segments or functions. This performance data is mainly used during application development and testing in order to determine any points of execution bottleneck, isolating where a developer's efforts should be focused to improve an application's overall performance.

Source code instrumentation can be achieved either by manual code instrumentation, where instructions are selectively placed by the developer in a few key points of interest, or more extensively through the use of compiler tools. Gprof [10] is one such tool, capable of generating function call graphs and determining the execution time for each function and its corresponding children.

Unfortunately, this dependence on the availability of application source code imposes some significant limitations on the usability of the approach. First, the instrumentation of code can alter the execution characteristics of an application [11], adding overhead that increases execution effort, and thus cause more energy to be used. Second, the performance statistics themselves are not sufficient to isolate component utilization levels. For this technique to be usable in power estimation, it would need to be supplemented with additional sources of performance data, such as hardware performance counters, which will be discussed shortly.

5.3.2 Binary Instrumentation

Binary instrumentation allows for analysis functions to be inserted into an application binary, providing instrumentation of applications whose source code is not available. The Pin tool from Intel [12] is able to achieve this by using JIT (just in time) recompilation of the executable, whereby a user's predefined analysis routine is executed within the source binary. Instrumentation routines can be triggered when predetermined conditions are met. For instance, these can occur when a specific function is called, a new function is called, or on memory writes. Pin has been written such that it can be used with architecture-independent profiling tools.

However, binary instrumentation suffers from similar limitations to source code instrumentation, with the primary concern being runtime overhead. For binary instrumentation, this can be even more significant, as a persistent overhead is incurred because of recompilation, which has been measured to be 30% before the execution of any analysis routes. While it has been proposed that such overheads can be reduced by limiting the profiling time by dynamically attaching and detaching Pin, this is not sufficient for the use case of requiring runtime performance analysis to allow for persistent power estimation.

5.3.3 Performance Monitoring Counters

Performance monitoring counters (PMCs) are a set of special-purpose hardware registers designed to monitor and record low-level performance events occurring at runtime in the processor. Such low-level performance events can include cache misses, processor stalls, instruction counts, and retired operations. This allows for detailed insights into the utilization of different regions within a processor's hardware that are not possible with other monitoring techniques. Furthermore, the hardware-specific nature requires PMC registers to be placed on a per-core basis, enabling fine-grained performance monitoring within shared resources, i.e. multi-core processors.

However, the use of hardware-specific performance monitoring can give rise to some additional challenges, where different manufacturers, or even microarchitecture versions, will support a different number of events and hardware registers, for example, both AMD and Intel have their own model-specific PMC specifications [13, 14]. The AMD 10h microarchitecture supports four performance registers whose value can be selected from the 120 available performance events, where the Intel Sandy Bridge microarchitecture supports eight general-purpose performance counters per core, or four per-thread if hyperthreading is used.

Tools such as *perf*[6] and *PAPI*[7] have been developed to help with some of these hardware dependence issues by providing a standard interface to the user regardless of

---

[6]https://perf.wiki.kernel.org/index.php/Main_Page.
[7]http://icl.cs.utk.edu/papi/.

TABLE 5.1. A Selection of Hardware Performance Counters Available in *perf*

Name	Description
cpu-cycles	Total cycles (affected by CPU frequency scaling)
instructions	Retired instructions
branch-instructions	Retired branch instructions
branch-misses	Mispredicted branch instructions
bus-cycles	Bus cycles, which can be different from total cycles
idle-cycles-frontend	Stalled cycles during issue
idle-cycles-backend	Stalled cycles during retirement
ref-cycles	Total cycles (not affected by CPU frequency scaling)
L1-dcache-(loads/stores/prefetches)	Level 1 data cache read/write/prefetch accesses
L1-dcache-(loads/stores/prefetches)-misses	Level 1 data cache read/write/prefetch misses
LLC-(loads/stores/prefetches)	Last-level cache read/write/prefetch accesses
LLC-(loads/stores/prefetches)-misses	Last-level cache read/write/prefetch misses
iTLB-loads	Instruction TLB read accesses
iTLB-load-misses	Instruction TLB read misses
node-(loads/stores)	Local memory read/write accesses
node-loads-misses	Local memory read misses

the underlying microarchitecture. While microarchitecture support may vary, many of the main performance events are supported across architectures, regardless of how they are implemented. A selection of the PMCs supported by *perf* is given in Table 5.1.

5.3.4 Operating System Events

The operating system (OS) is in a unique position to oversee all of the component interactions within a system, placing it in the best position to provide a broad picture of system performance. While the PMCs are able to provide fine-grained, low-level performance events for the processor during execution, these details do not allow for insights into the performance of other components, such as the hard drive or network card. Much of the interaction between components is handled by the OS kernel, which is outside the scope of user-space monitoring tools. However, some of the OS events require kernel patches/modules to be accessible from the user perspective.

Therefore, tools, such as *Oprofile*[8] and *netatop*[9], that are capable of monitoring OS kernel events during runtime have been developed. These tools enable the monitoring of events, such as system calls, interrupts, bus, and network utilization. Such features are crucial for modeling system components other than the processor and memory, which have traditionally not been the focus of detailed performance analysis.

---

[8]http://oprofile.sourceforge.net.
[9]http://www.atoptool.nl/downloadnetatop.php.

5.3.5   Virtual Machine Performance

Virtualized environments present a challenging problem for performance monitoring. Even though some PMCs can be accessed from the host (physical) machine within some virtualization software, such as VMware and KVM; the guest virtual machines (VMs) do not have direct access to the underlying hardware. This may prevent the use of some previously discussed profiling techniques. For instance, Xen does not virtualize the PMC registers because of the significant performance cost that would be incurred, preventing the use of tools such as *perf* and *Oprofile* in the guest machine.

Tools such as *Xenoprof*[10] instrument the hypervisor and the guest OS to enable the monitoring of PMCs within the hypervisor, which are then matched to the guests' operations. As *Xenoprof* is an extension of *Oprofile*, it is capable of providing similar performance analysis functionality. Recent versions of other virtualization environments, such as KVM and Qemu, have begun to include guest OS support for PMCs.

5.4   INTERACTION BETWEEN POWER AND PERFORMANCE

While the performance characteristics of key system components are generally well understood, the corresponding power characteristics remain less so. This can largely be attributed to differences in component interactions, where performance is often considered independent, and power has many flow-on effects, creating interdependencies between components. It is only with careful consideration of these effects that the relationship between power and performance can be understood for each individual component. Therefore, this section presents an overview of some of these component-based relationships, along with the corresponding execution states relevant to power modeling.

5.4.1   Central Processing Unit (CPU)

The processor is one of the components that consume the largest amount of power within a system, having a sizable idle value and a broad range of dynamic operating power values. The industry standard for processors' power dissipation comparison is its thermal design power (TDP). This metric defines the maximum power a cooling system is expected to dissipate and may significantly vary between processors' models, ranging from 5 to 220 W, as can be seen in Table 5.2. For example, the AMD Opteron 8380 is documented as having an average CPU power of 75 W, measured as the expected power use while executing a standard set of benchmarks and a TDP of 115 W. However, power is capable of going even higher than the TDP, except a hardware shutoff will be triggered to prevent hardware damage. This illustrates the significant, dynamic range of operating power use that can be experienced by a processor.

Much of the runtime variation is attributed to the diverse utilization levels experienced by running applications of different workload types. All applications lie somewhere on a spectrum between memory-bound and CPU-bound operation. A CPU-bound application performs a large number of calculations during execution, requiring a very small working set of data. This results in high processor utilization, where execution

---

[10]http://xenoprof.sourceforge.net/.

TABLE 5.2. Thermal Design Power (TDP) Specifications for a Range of Servers and Desktop Processors

Processor	Cores	Maximum Frequency, MHz	TDP, W
Intel® Atom™ E3815	1	1460	5
AMD Opteron™ X1150	4	2000	9
Intel® Atom™ E3845	4	1910	10
Intel® Core™ i7-4600U	2	2100	15
AMD Athlon™ II X2 260u	2	2000	25
Intel® Core™ i7-3615QE	4	2300	45
Intel® Core™ i7-4960HQ	4	2600	47
Intel® Xeon® E7-4807	6	1860	95
AMD Opteron™ 8380	4	2500	115
Intel® Xeon® E7-4860	10	2266	130
Intel® Core™ i7-4960X Extreme Ed.	6	4000	130
AMD Opteron™ 6386 SE	16	2800	140
AMD FX-9590 Black Edition	8	4700	220

time is dominated by processor operations. Alternatively, a memory-bound application is almost the complete opposite, where execution time is dominated by the time delay of fetching data from main memory or disk. Memory fetches stall processor execution, which remains idle while the data is retrieved. This results in few calculations been performed and a correspondingly low processor utilization.

This variation in workload utilization characteristics has been leveraged by the most prevalent power-saving policies in modern OSs. Power is saved by adjusting the processors' operating frequency at runtime using DVFS, so that it is ideally set proportionally to the memory boundedness of an application. Using a low operating frequency will slow the rate of processor operations, increasing execution time for compute tasks while saving power. As only processor operations are impacted, a memory-bound workload will experience minimal performance degradation as the memory access latency is not affected. However, running a CPU-bound workload at a low frequency will sacrifice a great deal of performance. Many alternate policies have been implemented to evaluate the trade-off between power and performance, attempting to maximize savings without impacting performance. Figure 5.1 illustrates the variations in power dissipation for different operating frequencies of an Intel Core i7-3615QE running Linux's CPU stress benchmark.

Unfortunately, such policies do not allow for any power savings while executing CPU-bound applications, resulting in high power consumption. To achieve such savings, manufacturers have implemented fine-grained, low-level power-saving techniques in hardware, namely, C-states. Aggressive clock gating is used to switch off parts of the microprocessor's circuit, temporarily suspending functional units, where state is maintained by stopping flip-flops. Reasonable power savings may be made with the ever increasing density of processors and number of functional units. However, this essentially creates a hidden power state, strictly controlled in hardware, which the OS is

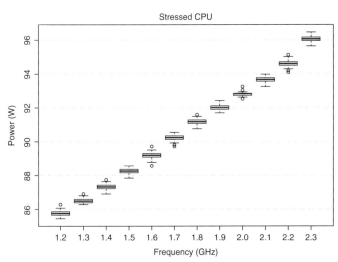

Figure 5.1. Power dissipation for the Linux CPU stress benchmark running on an Intel® core™ i7-3615QE at various operating frequencies.

not able to observe. This raises new challenges for modeling power; although if enough fine-grained details are known about the current application workload, the processor's functional unit state could potentially be inferred by the expected unit utilization.

While the processor consumes a large amount of power, it is worth remembering that some of the observed consumption may be due to flow-on effects from other system components. The most straightforward illustration of this is the power use of system fans. As the processor's utilization increases, the temperatures generated increase, causing the cooling system to use more power. However, this relationship is complicated by the thermal changes occurring at a slower rate than the corresponding changes in utilization, as was observed in [15]. Such cross-component power dependencies are more significant for the processor than any other system component, given the central role played in all system operations.

5.4.2 Memory

The interdependence of processor and memory power consumption was indirectly shown in the previous section, where memory-bound workloads stall execution, lowering utilization and power consumption of the processor. However, the power reduction in the processor cannot be easily isolated from any potential increase in power use from the memory modules because of the changes occurring simultaneously.

This can lead to the actual power use of memory modules been obscured, causing erroneous conclusions to be drawn as to the significance of power use. For instance, memory is sometimes thought to consume a sizable amount of power, but the specifications for Kingston hyperx memory shows a power draw of only 0.795 W[11]

---

[11] http://www.valueram.com/datasheets/khx1600c8d3t1k2_4gx.pdf,

TABLE 5.3. Power States for Two Western Digital Hard Drives

	WD VelociRaptor Workstation Hard Drive, W	WD SiliconDrive, W
Random Read/Write	5.1	1.0
Sequential Read/Write	5.8	1.0
Idle	4.2	0.4
Standby and Sleep	1.1	

while operating. A typical system may contain about eight memory modules, giving a total of 6.36 W, which is almost insignificant in the context of other system components.

Observed changes in power consumption for a memory-dominant workload can most likely be attributed to cross-component power dependencies, where the memory modules themselves have minimal impact. Instead, power reduction comes from lower processor utilization, given that a new task is not switched onto the processor, which will have the further flow-on effect of reducing temperatures.

5.4.3 Input/Output (I/O)

A certain percentage of memory accesses will result in pages being fetched from the hard disk, incurring additional processor latency as data transfers are significantly slower than the processor's operating speed. However, any large data transfers will be handled by a direct memory access (DMA) operation, allowing the processor to continue execution while transfers proceed independently.

As a result, the processor will not be aware of the hard disk's operating state at any given time. Therefore, hard disk utilization levels can only be monitored from the OS, which is able to track the interrupts used to handle the transfer, in addition to bus utilization levels.

Despite the availability of utilization values, workload-specific power is not always modeled if only a small number of hard disks are used in a given system. This is due to the relatively narrow range of power use while running. For instance, the WD Veloci-Raptor,[12] shown in Table 5.3, has a maximum read/write power of 5.8 W and an idle of 4.2 W, providing a maximum variation of 1.6 W. This is a sizable power saving as a percentage of hard disk power but in the broader context of a server using upwards of 400 W is an insignificant value. A constant value, providing a small estimation error, could be considered an acceptable trade-off in certain circumstances. A similar case can also be made for the WD SiliconDrive[13] solid-state disk, also shown in Table 5.3. However, as the number of hard disks used increases, this error becomes much less acceptable, requiring modeling.

5.4.4 Network

A further source of system power consumption is the network interface card (NIC), which acts like an input/output (I/O) device in data centers using network storage,

[12] http://www.wdc.com/wdproducts/library/SpecSheet/ENG/2879-701284.pdf,
[13] http://www.wdc.com/global/products/specs/?driveID=1120&language=1.

requiring data to periodically be transferred from remote servers. Much similar to the hard disk, the NIC can use nearly as much power in idle as when active. This is largely due to the requirement for network state to be maintained, ensuring availability and responsiveness. For example, the two 10-Gbps Ethernet NICs used in [16] consume 21.2 and 18.0 W while idle. When active, the power for each card increases by only 0.2 W. Surprisingly, the network activity does not seem to affect power consumption as much as might be expected.

Similar results were also observed in the fiber protocol network card that had an offload processor, where no other NIC did. The offload processor caused the idle power to be just over double that of a similar network card that did not have an offload processor. Switching from idle to active showed negligible power difference, indicating the offload processor is not likely to be using any power-saving features, such as sleep states.

For the given network card details, the power draw can be modeled as a constant value, as the estimation error will be very small. The maximum estimation improvement will be less than 1%, meaning it is not worth the performance overhead that would potentially be incurred by monitoring network utilization.

5.4.5   Idle States

Power models seek to model the power response in components for various utilization levels. However, one utilization level that is often not explicitly modeled [17] is the base power while the system is idle. This is important because in many large-scale server deployments, a significant proportion of time is spent idle [4]. If a model does not incorporate these workload phases, then the model will begin to diverge from real-world power use over long periods of operation.

Power models essentially estimate the dynamic response in power for a corresponding change in utilization, specifically the dynamic power of a system. Therefore, the system power, which does not change with utilization, is considered static power, representing the base power for the system. The static power includes many unmodeled system components, such as the power supply unit or motherboard chipset. At a finer granularity, it can also be thought of including the base power for many of the "dynamic" components. For instance, the processor consists of both static and dynamic power, where dynamic power is the utilization response and static power is the persistent base power for the component.

To compute the impact of power states (C-states) over its available operational frequencies (P-states), one can measure its deeper idle state power savings as follows:

$$\text{Power Savings} = P_{C0} - P_{CX}, \qquad (5.1)$$

where P_{CX} is the power dissipated while the system is on its deepest idle state (CX) and P_{C0} is the power measured when the system is idle but on its active C-state (C0). All values should be collected at the same frequency given by a P-state. Figure 5.2 shows the boxplot of these idle power savings for each available frequency on a Intel Core i7-3615QE. Considering that this CPU has a TDP of 45 W (Table 5.2), the idle power-saving technique can reduce the power consumption up to 33% of the processors' TDP. Furthermore, it will be shown in the model evaluation section that not making this

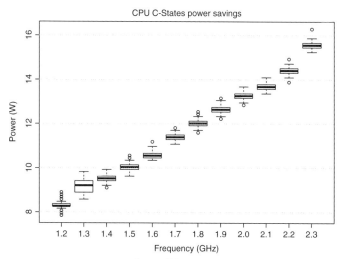

Figure 5.2. Power savings of an Intel® Core™ i7-3615QE CPU due to processors' idle states (C-states) in various P-states.

distinction between what is modeled and not modeled has the potential to misrepresent the accuracy of estimations.

In summary, different workload types will keep different components busy in the system and, therefore, incur different power usage patterns. This observation is crucial for building power estimation models based on system events.

5.5 POWER MODELING PROCEDURE

The process of deriving a power model, capable of providing accurate runtime power estimates without the need for special-purpose hardware metering, can be broken down to four steps: (i) variable selection, (ii) training data acquisition, (iii) model construction, and (iv) model evaluation. The process followed during each stage of development will ultimately determine the generality and accuracy of the resulting model. In this section, each step is independently discussed, providing general guidance, which can be used to create implementations in a variety of system environments.

5.5.1 Variable Selection

The first step in deriving a power estimation model is the selection of performance events that strongly correlate with power, namely, key performance indicators (KPI), for a diverse set of workloads. The available performance events are largely dictated by the chosen modeling methodology and systems execution environment.

For instance, many modeling methodologies restrict performance monitoring to the processor and memory modules, given their dominance of both execution performance and power consumption. In such cases, fine-grained performance events are desired, resulting in the selection of PMCs for their ability to monitor low-level events. This in turn imposes a limit on the number of events that can be monitored simultaneously, because of the microarchitecture dependence of the chosen approach. Alternatively, including network and I/O components in the modeling methodology requires the use of kernel performance events, possibly in addition to PMCs. Therefore, the initial specification of modeling methodology will determine the type of performance event best suited to the desired modeling objectives.

Once the performance monitoring method is selected, an initial dataset is required for determining the strength of correlation for each performance event. The intention of this dataset is to collect a representative sample of performance and power values for each performance event, across a variety of workload types, ensuring a generalized estimation model. The most commonly adopted approach is to periodically collect performance and power values during the execution of an entire benchmark suite, such as SPEC or NAS Parallel Benchmarks (NPB). By executing the entire suite, the resulting dataset should incorporate different execution characteristics. A more comprehensive approach is sometimes adopted, where a suite of microbenchmarks is used in place of a benchmark suite. Bertran et al. [18] used a suite of 97 microbenchmarks to stress every possible power component in turn. Regardless of the approach taken, this training phase can be time consuming for a large number of performance events as the ability to simultaneously monitor counters is limited, requiring multiple iterations of each benchmark to collect all performance events.

Finally, the dataset is used to determine the correlation of each event to power, allowing the top events to be selected. For a large set of performance events, principle component analysis is the best statistical method for finding the principal events. However, a common compromise is to use domain-specific knowledge to restrict the scope of performance events to key units of interest. For example, Singh et al. [17] decomposed the processor and memory into four categories, considered the most significant functional units: floating-point unit (FPU), memory accesses, processor stalls, and instructions retired. Consequently, only 13 PMCs needed to be collected for the dataset, with a single, strongly correlated event being selected to represent each category. Such a small dataset facilitated simpler, manual correlation methods.

5.5.2   Training Data Collection

While the benchmarks used for event selection provide a representative sample of workload types and utilization levels, they are not guaranteed to represent an exhaustive set of possible values. For a power model to be widely deployable, it needs to be capable of accurately estimating the power of previously unseen workloads, requiring benchmark independence. Therefore, microbenchmarks are exclusively used for collecting model training data.

A specific microbenchmark is created for each of the selected performance events, with each being configured to explore a diverse spread of performance values. If microbenchmarks were used for event selection, those corresponding to the selected events can be reconfigured and reused for collecting the model training data. By replicating performance events beyond typical ranges, the resulting model will be more capable of accurately estimating power for less commonly seen applications. However, this requires a trade-off to be made between accuracy and training time, as a significant number of execution configurations exist. A commonly used compromise is to explore a selected sample of boundary cases, while spending the majority of training time within typical ranges.

5.5.3 Learning from Data

The most commonly used approach for modeling power is to derive a linear regression model from a training set of key performance indicators (KPI)/power observations. Training data is periodically collected as a series of tuples, $\langle power, KPI_1, \ldots, KPI_n \rangle$, where the resulting accuracy of the model will depend on how well the training data represents the expected workload type for power estimation. For the regression model, power is the dependent variable estimated by the explanatory performance values.

Let $\mathbf{y}$ be a vector of n power measurements (observations) from the training dataset

$$\mathbf{y} = [y_1, y_2, \ldots, y_n], \tag{5.2}$$

where n is the total number of tuples in the dataset. The performance events are the independent variables used for predicting power, defining a $X_{n \times m}$ matrix, where each row of the matrix is described as

$$\mathbf{x}_i = [x_{i,1}, x_{i,2}, \ldots, x_{i,m}] \quad i \in \{1, \ldots, n\}, \tag{5.3}$$

where $\mathbf{x}_i$ is a vector of m key performance event measurements taken at time t_i. This forms the linear regression model:

$$y_i = \beta_0 + \sum_{j=1}^{m} \beta_j \phi_j x_{i,j} + \xi_i, \tag{5.4}$$

where ξ_i is the measurement error and $\phi_1, \ldots, \phi_m$ are nonlinear functions. The β coefficient parameters can be estimated by calculating the least squares

$$S = \sum_{i=1}^{n} \left(y_i - \beta_0 - \sum_{j=1}^{m} \beta_j \phi_j x_{i,j} \right)^2, \tag{5.5}$$

which minimizes the sum of the squared errors for all of the coefficients.

The resulting regression coefficients, $\beta_0, \ldots, \beta_m$, are used to form the power estimation model, where the runtime measurements of performance events are used as input parameters to the model to estimate the dependent power value. This determines the analytical relationship between a set of key performance events and power. The accuracy of the resulting model will depend on many factors, including the selection of performance events, which is discussed in more detail throughout this section.

5.5.4 Event Correlation

The power model is constructed by quantifying the relationship between the selected performance events and power for an extensive model training dataset. In the model, performance events provide the explanatory variables used to predict the dependent power variable. This arrangement lends itself well to the use of regression techniques to form an estimation model. One of the simplest and most readily applied regression techniques is to derive a series of per-component regression models, combined into a single model:

$$Power = X_{CPU} + X_{memory} + X_{I/O} + \xi \qquad (5.6)$$

While such a model is easily understood, given the prevalence of component-specific performance events, the previously discussed impact of cross-component effects is largely neglected. The use of an error term may mitigate some of the impact but does not resolve the underlying problem, with the model's simplicity sacrificing accuracy. Support vector regression provides a more robust regression method by fitting a single, nonlinear function to a small training dataset. This approach was used in [19].

The accuracy of simple regression models is limited by the use of a single fitting function, required to adequately represent the execution characteristics of widely varying utilization levels and workload types. The resulting estimation model may become overly general, where a more accurate fit could be achieved by characterizing utilization. The variation in high- and low-utilization behaviors was noted by Singh et al. [17]. To rectify these differences, a piecewise regression model was proposed, enabling different estimation functions to be used at each of the utilization levels.

The improvements provided by workload characterization can be further extended by using a workload classification scheme. By classifying execution workloads, a separate regression model can be derived for each source of a dominant workload. For instance, most derived models are processor centric, achieving good estimation accuracy for processor-dominated workloads. However, the accuracy can be significantly worse for other workloads, such as memory-bound applications, because of the model's bias toward processor power. Enabling the model to tailor power estimates to a given workload helps to remove much of this bias by using the most appropriate estimation function at the appropriate time. Such an approach was taken in Dhiman et al. [20], where it was observed that similar utilization levels often resulted in different power consumption for various workload types. Classification allowed each workload to be treated separately, improving the overall estimation accuracy.

5.5.5   Model Evaluation Concepts

Power models are evaluated by assessing the effectiveness of power estimates for a suite of benchmarks. For a fair evaluation, the chosen benchmark suite should not be the same as was used during event selection, but should similarly consist of a diverse set of workload types. This helps to determine how well a given model will generalize across various utilization levels, as a poorly selected set of performance events and training dataset may contain bias toward a specific workload.

5.5.5.1   Statistical Metrics.   Summary statistics such as the median error are commonly used to present the evaluation error of the estimation model, but this has the potential to misrepresent the accuracy of the model. This is primarily due to the selection of evaluation benchmarks, which are typically scientific workloads, and their dominance of a single execution phase. For example, a compute-intensive benchmark will spend much of its execution time in high-utilization phases, with a significantly smaller portion

of execution time spent executing memory-bound tasks, such as reading/writing log files. As a result, a power estimation model will achieve a low median error overall if it is able to closely estimate the dominant execution phase – compute-intensive work – given its dominance. Therefore, the median error is not affected by the other execution phases, making it a poor metric to gauge the quality of fit for all execution phases.

Alternatively, the mean absolute error (MAE) provides the mean estimation error for all execution phases and will thus be negatively impacted by any significant outliers caused by poor estimation during nondominant phases. However, this only solves part of the problem, as a single metric, such as the MAE or median error, is not capable of providing a meaningful description of total execution accuracy. They can only provide cursory insights. More details can easily be provided by additionally including the standard deviation, which describes the spread of estimation values from the mean over the entire execution.

5.5.5.2 *Static versus Dynamic Power.*
The importance of the distinction between static and dynamic power, as was previously discussed, is an important consideration to be made when evaluating power estimation. The most important takeaway is that a power model is essentially only estimating the dynamic power of a system. That is the response in power consumption to a corresponding change in performance events or utilization. Presenting the estimation error as a percentage of the system's dynamic power – that is actually being estimated – allows for fairer comparisons to be made between different models, developed on different systems. An example of this was given in [15].

> For example, suppose there are two different power models with identical mean estimation errors of 5%, but for different machines with an equal total power consumption of 200 W. Without further information, the initial conclusion that can be drawn by the reader is both power models are equally accurate. However, a different conclusion can be drawn if it was additionally known that machine "A" has a dynamic power (also known as workload-dependent power) of 30%, while machine "B" has a larger dynamic power of 60%. Given a total error of 10 W (5% of total 200 W) and the constant static power (also known as base power), it is now clear that the model based on machine "A" has a 16.6% error for dynamic power while the model based on machine "B" has a much lower error of 8.3% for dynamic power. The extra information on the proportion of static power and dynamic power enables a fair comparison to be made between the two, otherwise apparently identical power estimation models.

Results can appear misleading or lead to erroneous conclusions if they are not presented in the fairest way possible. Furthermore, the actual accuracy of an estimation model can potentially be obscured by the relative static and dynamic power values on systems with a relatively small dynamic power range as a proportion of total power. Such cases are more likely on systems that use low-power components, which can have minimal operating ranges.

5.5.6 Power Estimation Errors

While it is desirable to achieve perfect power estimation, such an objective may be unobtainable in practice. Such attempts may incur significant runtime overhead, where a less accurate, but more efficient power model, may prove to be sufficient for most use-cases.

5.5.6.1 *Estimation Errors.* In modeling hardware component power consumption, a trade-off between model complexity and accuracy is required. This problem is exacerbated by the increasing complexity of newer microarchitectures, which can be attributed to the incorporation of hardware threading, fine-grained power-saving modes, and increasing component densities. Therefore, estimation models must approximate many of these power factors, balancing runtime performance monitoring, and model complexity with estimation accuracy. Collecting a large number of performance events and modeling all of the corresponding interactions may reach a point where it becomes more akin to simulation, with gains in accuracy being outweighed by the runtime overhead.

Fortunately, if appropriate care is taken while deriving the model, many sources of approximation can be controlled for, or incorporated into, the model. For instance, Mair et al. [21] noted that the version of compiler used or the compiler optimization level impacts a benchmarks power characteristics. Such variations could be incorporated into the model by treating alternative compiler/benchmark configurations as separate benchmarks used during training, instead of a single benchmark run multiple times. Temperature is another commonly considered factor influencing power consumption, which can be difficult to reliably measure. This is primarily due to the poor quality of standard measurement equipment and significant latencies in observable thermal effects within a system. A simple, but apparently rarely considered, approach to mitigating some of the impact is to ensure that execution times are sufficiently long so that a stable operating temperature is reached before data collection. Short periodic executions can lead to below-average power use for a given workload, as the temperature will be below the typical operating point given insufficient time for processor warm-up. These two factors, among others, illustrate the importance of taking care in setting up a model's experimental configuration.

However, some sources of estimation error are beyond measurement and are unable to be incorporated into the model. The most common source of these errors is hardware power-saving features that operate independently of the OS and are, therefore, transparent to the system. The best example of this, which was previously mentioned, is the anecdotal evidence of aggressive clock gating in modern processors [7], where functional units within the processor are shut off while inactive, in order to save power. Given the lack of understanding as to how this feature operates, it is even difficult to trigger the occurrence of certain actions during model training in an attempt to incorporate the respective power variations. A further source of inconsistent hardware power measurements may be due to manufacturing variability. An experiment in [7] observed an 11% difference in power between two Intel Core i5-540M processors, in the same experimental configuration. This can exacerbate estimation errors where a model is trained on one processor and is used on other processors, thought to be identical. This illustrates the unlikely nature of eliminating all sources of estimation error. Therefore, the question should be what is an acceptable estimation error?

5.5.6.2 An Acceptable Error. There is no single criterion for determining if a given power estimation model is accurate enough, as each use-case will have different tolerances of estimation errors. For instance, using the power model to evaluate how best to consolidate workloads in a data center has a rather high tolerance, suggested to be 5–10% by McCullough et al. [7], because of the coarse-grained nature of per-server power estimation. Alternatively, if the same data center were to use this model to charge clients for the power each submitted job uses during execution, an error that is high for the entire system would not be tolerated. Such a high error would possibly lead to charging clients for resources not actually used.

The most commonly proposed use for power models is in making power-aware task schedulers. Power-aware task scheduling is a rather generic term, giving rise to many different scheduling policies. For the discussion here, we define "power-aware task scheduling" as using a scheduler that prioritizes resource allocation to the most power efficient uses, while maintaining all strict resource requirements and workload deadlines. For instance, to determine which task should be allocated additional processor cores, the power model can be used to determine the change in power in response to a given allocation. The power efficiency for each task is then evaluated as the size of the relative power change, thereby indicating which task will use the least additional power. A fair evaluation has two accuracy requirements. First, the estimation error needs to remain stable across workloads to prevent any bias in evaluation. Second, the estimation error needs to be less than the power difference of any two cores; otherwise the error may hide the real change in power. These requirements mean the allowable estimation error will be system specific, as different architectures will have processors with significantly varying operating ranges for power use. Unfortunately, this means that no single rule exists for determining a specific threshold for modeling accuracy. However, the simple fact remains, the greater the estimation accuracy, the better.

5.5.7 Related Work

A variety of power estimation models have previously been proposed, varying in the selection of performance events and the correlation methods. Many of the early models were derived from the observed relationship between system utilization, typically measured as instructions per cycle (IPC), and power [22]. Essentially, only the processor power is modeled, but a reasonable estimation accuracy was able to be reached. This was due in a large part to the dominance of processor power in the simple, single-core system.

Mantis [23] extended the relationship between utilization and power to other system components, deriving a power model for the entire system by incorporating memory, hard disk, and network performance in addition to processor utilization. The selected performance events come from hardware PMCs and OS performance events: CPU utilization, off-chip memory access counters, hard disk I/O rate, and network I/O rate. The power model is derived from an initial, one-time calibration phase in which benchmarks are run to stress each of these system components in turn, while recording the power from each alternating current (AC) line. A linear program is then used to derive the power model by minimizing the estimation error across all performance events with a linear function. However, the model's accuracy relies on the calibration phase providing a range of utilization levels that are representative of realistic workloads and not merely the scientific workloads used for model evaluation.

More refined power models are possible by modeling subcomponents instead of aggregate component utilization levels. Bellosa [24] noted a strong linear relationship between four synthetic workloads designed to stress individual processor functional units, four logically correlated low-level performance events and power. The four performance events were processor μops, FLOPS, l2-cache misses, and memory transactions. By isolating the power draw of each low-level function, the linear models were able to be combined into a single power model, Joule Watcher.

A similarly fine-grained, processor-based, power model was proposed by Singh et al. in [17], which used domain-specific knowledge to decompose the processor into four key functional units. A single, strongly correlated PMC was found for each functional unit. Event-specific microbenchmarks were designed to stress the breadth of potential operating values, taking care to include some extreme outliers. Through this exploration of a large utilization space, it was observed that some performance events experienced different power characteristics at low levels than at high levels, which can only be modeled with a nonlinear function. The model was further improved through the use of a piecewise linear function, separating the low event values from high, allowing subtly more complex event characteristics to be modeled. However, the improvements provided were not explicitly evaluated, merely the accuracy of the resulting model.

The increasing complexity of processor hardware has raised some concerns that linear models may not be sufficiently complex to accurately model power anymore. In fact, these concerns are not new but merely an extension of the ongoing debate regarding the required trade-off between model complexity and accuracy. A marginally more complex model was proposed by Bircher and John [25] where the key subsystems are modeled independently using a quadratic function. The five key subsystems modeled are CPU, memory, chipset, I/O, and disk. The power for each subsystem is determined during an initial training period by placing resistors in series with the power supply, making it a significantly more complicated procedure than the other approaches discussed so far. After the power for each component is isolated, a series of benchmarks are run, stressing each subsystems in turn. The resulting model uses processor-centric performance events, all PMCs with the exception of interrupt counters, to model all of the components. This is a rather unique approach, as many of the previous systems rely on OS events to monitor utilization levels for components such as the hard disk. Instead, the processor PMCs are used to analyze the "trickle-down" effect of processor events through other system components. For instance, a last-level cache miss will cause a memory access, which may in turn cause a disk access. Monitoring these effects allowed the subsystem components to be modeled using only six performance events, with an average error of less than 9% per subsystem.

A potential problem with using general utilization metrics, such as IPC, is that they provide insufficient detail to adequately distinguish between various workload types. This was observed by Dhiman et al. [20] when executing a series of benchmarks in a range of alternate configurations, which resulted in different levels of power use for similar utilization levels. Therefore, the authors proposed a modeling technique based on a rudimentary clustering of workload types using a Gaussian mixture model (GMM), with four input performance counters: IPC, memory accesses per cycle (MPC), cache transactions per cycle (CTPC), and CPU utilization. The resulting power model was able to outperform two simple, alternative regression-based models during evaluation.

These are but a selected few of the wide variety of power models that have previously been proposed. They differ in the approach taken for performance event selection, collection of training data, modeled system components, and the regression method used to derive the power model. Nevertheless, they were mostly constructed following the four general steps discussed previously in this section.

5.6 USE-CASES

Power models have proved useful in a variety of use-cases for different user groups. This section presents some of these applications, focusing on three types of users: end users, software developers, and system managers. Each of these alternative uses provides background motivation for the creation of power models that differ according to architectural requirements. Here we divide the power modeling methodology based on single-core, multi-core, and distributed systems, summarizing how some implementations work and discussing their level of accuracy.

5.6.1 Applications

Depending on the interest/knowledge of the user, the power dissipated by an application/ machine may be differently exploited. If we consider the end user, that is, a person who interacts with the system without bothering about implementation details, such estimators may provide a user with feedback on how much power is dissipated by the system while executing some programs, increasing the awareness of the potential impacts. This can be achieved either a priori, using energy efficiency labels, or at execution time, providing an energy per process monitoring solution. While the former faces some disagreement on how the labels should be created, the latter method is already used, mainly by the OSs of portable devices.

For software developers, hardware's usage deeply depends on how the application is implemented. The impact of an application over its dissipated power includes the libraries that it uses, its coding patterns, and the compilers employed. In [26], the authors compare the impact of compiling a similar code using different compilers and programming languages on its overall energy consumption. They used different implementations of the Tower of Hanoi solver and compared their energy spent to solve the same problem size. The codes were written by different authors and their expertise on the programming languages are not taken into account in the evaluation. A similar approach can be done to select which compilation flags and libraries given software may use.

Possibly, because of its highest energy consumption, the system manager will receive the greatest benefit. The possibility of monitoring applications' power usage may lead to new resource management policies. In [27], the authors exploit the energy as a resource on Linux systems, proposing kernel-level allocation policies. Some portable OS, such as Google's Android and Apple's iOS monitor application power consumption to manage system resource use. At the data center level, the resource allocation and job scheduler can use such information to turn nodes on or off.

5.6.2   Single-Core Systems

Single core systems provide the most convenient environment for implementing the previously discussed power models. On such systems, as there is only a single flow of execution, it is simpler to take the necessary measurements. Indeed, there is only one subject, as the core is the same as the processor and as the node. It is then possible to correlate measurements from the network (node level) to measurement from the performance counters. In [28], the authors demonstrate the following three-step implementation:

1. monitoring of 165 sensors (system, performance counters);
2. selection of relevant sensors to model power consumption of a host;
3. linear regression fitting to obtain the final model.

The second step in this study is present in order to reduce the time needed for the fitting. The detailed algorithm is simple: first, find the sensor that has the most correlation with power (see Figure 5.3), then find the one that has the most correlation with the residual, and so on. The study shows the model error as a function of the number of variables used. It has to be noted that models for mono-core systems can be quite precise and can reach a precision of a few percentage points using only three well-chosen sensors and can reach a 1% precision using five variables. For this study, the workload was created using several synthetic benchmarks: CPU, memory, disk, and network.

5.6.3   Multi-core and Multiprocessor

Modeling multi-core architectures is not as simple as it may seem. Owing to resource sharing, the power dissipated by several cores is not simply the sum of each core. Weaver et al. [29] use RAPL sensors to surpass this issue, evaluating the power of each CPU component with no power model. The authors profile the power of high-performance computing (HPC) applications by running some benchmarks, for example, the Cholesky decomposition, while monitoring the Running Average Power Limit (RAPL) register. Although this can be a good approach for HPC environment, where the nodes are fully dedicated to execute one application at a time, it can only be used on some generations of Intel processors.

Basmadjian and De Meer [30] address this issue by modeling each CPU component, where each of them is stressed at different levels through the execution of microbenchmarks. Hence, the authors propose a power model based on the collected measurements, including the power-saving techniques. The power models are validated using

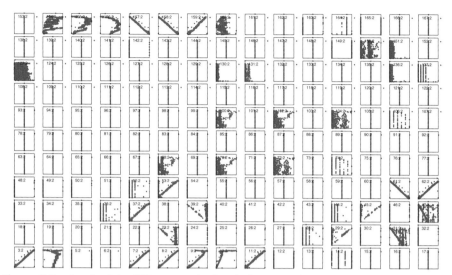

Figure 5.3. Graph of the 165 measured values in function of energy consumption for a synthetic disk benchmark.

two benchmarks: while-loop and lookbusy. The reported errors are usually less than 5% and always under 9% (3 W). The authors also claim that the additive approach (considering the power of a multi-core as the sum of several single core CPU) can overestimate the power consumption of the CPU by up to 50%.

5.6.4 Distributed Systems

Recent efforts aim to create/adapt existing data centers to be more energy efficient by modeling the power consumption. In [31], the authors propose a hierarchical model to estimate the energy consumption of the entire data center, including PSUs, and rack/tower servers at the node level. Even though the authors propose a fine-grained power estimation, there is a lack of validation: the total estimated power of a data center is not compared with its actual consumption. In [32], the authors propose new heuristics to provide an energy-aware service allocation; these heuristics consider not only the energy but also the performance of servers.

CoolEmAll is a European project that addresses the energy efficiency of data centers [33]. Its main goals are to propose new energy-efficient metrics and provide complete data center monitoring, simulation, and visualization software to help to aid the design and optimization of new and/or existing data centers. Owing to the high cost of data center's cooling system, the heat generation is also considered in job scheduling. CoolEmAll measures hotspots on a data center through computational fluid dynamics (CFD) simulations, providing results that are more accurate than heat matrix simulations. These simulations include a high granularity of information that encloses the estimation of power use of each application, the impact of fans on the airflow, the distribution of nodes in a rack, and the distribution of racks in a room.

5.7 AVAILABLE SOFTWARE

Tools for estimating the power consumption of computing devices are widely available as both commercial and open source software systems. These tools vary according to the level (system wide, application, or thread) and accuracy of their estimations. All of the software described here is open source, but the accuracy of these software systems is not evaluated.

Powerstat [34] is an Ubuntu package that fetches the power drained by the battery and logs it along with the resource utilization of the machine. The software does not have a power model and thus can only provide system-wide power consumption information. This is the simplest approach to allow users to have an overall impression of the impact of applications on power consumption, but it requires the use of portable devices and does not work while the devices are plugged into main power.

PowerTOP [35] is a power estimation tool that monitors not only applications but also devices such as the display and Universal Serial Bus (USB) devices (e.g., keyboard, mouse). It identifies the most power consuming applications/devices and proposes some tuning guidelines. PowerTOP uses information gained by interrupting each process in order to estimate its power consumption, that is, it needs the total power consumption of the machine provided by a power meter. For portable devices, this power is retrieved from the battery discharging data, while for other devices, it supports using the Extech Power Analyzer/Datalogger (model number 380803). The use of a power meter also allows it to calibrate the power model, providing a more accurate estimation. PowerTOP is written in C++ and requires some kernel configuration options enabled in order to function properly, so depending on the system in use, the kernel may need to be recompiled. It is being ported to Android devices as well.

pTop [36] is a kernel-level tool that is software-based (i.e., there is no need to run on battery power or use external power meters). To use pTop, the target system needs to be running at least Linux kernel version 2.6.31, with a kernel patch applied. Energy is composed as the sum of energy used by a set of different components: CPU, memory, disk, and the wireless network. For the CPU model, it uses a load-proportional model based on its minimum and maximum power consumption. For the other devices, power-per-event (e.g., memory read, disk access, network upload) data needs to be provided and the device consumption is based on the number of times the event occurred by the energy spent to realize each event. It was originally conceived for laptops. All devices' specifications must be provided by the user (no preexisting calibration data is included).

A similar tool is provided by PowerAPI [37], a Scala-based library that estimates the power at the process level. In contrast to pTop, it contains a complementary metal-oxide semiconductor (CMOS) CPU power formula that depends on the CPU's TDP allowed frequencies, and their respective operating voltages. It also contains a graphical interface to plot runtime graphs instead of a top-like interface. As for pTop, PowerAPI requires that the user provides the hardware specifications.

The Intel Energy Checker software development kit (SDK) [38] proposes to measure the "greenness" of systems by comparing the dissipated power with the productivity of a system, facilitating energy efficiency analysis and optimizations. It was originally conceived to run in data center or telecom environments, but nowadays, the SDK can be used on client or mobile platforms as well. Energy Checker supports a variety of programming languages (e.g., C/C++, C#, Objective-C, Java, PHP, Perl, and other scripting languages) enabling source code instrumentation. It uses different metrics for each type of application. These metrics need to have at least two counters: one to provide the amount of useful work and the other to give the energy consumed while performing this work. This SDK can operate with or without a power meter. If the user does not have a power meter, a CPU proportional power estimator is used. This estimator only considers the variable power drawn by the computing node. Otherwise, it supports a wide variety of power meters.

Ectools [39] aims to aid the research of new power models. It is a set of tools conceived not only to profile and monitor the power dissipated by applications but also to develop and compare new estimators. Its core library (libec) provides a set of power sensors/estimators. The sensors can be either used as variables for the power models or extended into new sensors. The library provides a CPU proportional power estimator that can be calibrated in the presence of a power meter. Interfaces for accessing ACPI, Plogg, and WattsUp Pro power meters data are available, allowing an easy way to access the system-wide dissipated power. Ectools contains three auxiliary tools: (i) a data acquisition application (ecdaq) that logs all available system-wide sensors while running a given benchmark to allow further data analysis; (ii) a processes' top list (ectop) that can be configured to show specific sensors or estimators, enabling the user to compare different power models at runtime and order the list by a specific sensor/estimator; and (iii) an application energy profiler (valgreen) that provides the total energy spent during the execution of an application. Ectools is written in C++ and can be used to monitor the power dissipated by VMs.

5.8 CONCLUSION

By quantifying the observed relationship between key execution performance events and system power consumption, an analytical power model can be derived. Such power models are capable of providing power values at a significantly finer granularity than hardware power metering allows, providing application- or component-specific power consumption statistics. The availability of application-specific power values allows for significantly improved runtime power analysis over what has previously been possible.

This chapter presented and discussed the concepts behind, and steps involved in, deriving an analytical power estimation model. These steps included performance event selection, training data collection, model derivation, and model evaluation. The discussion accompanying each step was purposely kept general in order to avoid details that would make the material too implementation or architecture specific. This in turn enables the high-level concepts presented in the chapter to be broadly applied to power modeling across a diverse set of system configurations and execution environments. However, more specific details were presented regarding previously published experimental results, with implementations achieving average estimation errors below 5%. Furthermore, power modeling techniques are increasingly being utilized within widely available software packages, which is likely to stimulate more general uses of detailed power analysis. In the future, power models are set to become an integral feature in the development of advanced software-based power-saving policies.

REFERENCES

[1] Greenberg A, Hamilton J, Maltz DA, Patel P. The cost of a cloud: research problems in data center networks. SIGCOMM *Comput Commun Rev* 2008;39(1):68–73.

[2] Larrick RP, Cameron KW. Consumption-based metrics: from autos to IT. Computer 2011;44(7):97–99.

[3] Tomlinson B, Silberman MS, White J. Can more efficient IT be worse for the environment? Computer 2011;44(1):87–89.

[4] Barroso LA, Holzle U. The case for energy-proportional computing. Computer 2007;40(12):33–37.

[5] Narayan A, Rao S. Power-aware cloud metering. IEEE Transactions on Services Computing, 99(PrePrints); 2013. p 1.

[6] Diouri M, Dolz MF, Glück O, Lefèvre L, Alonso P, Catalán S, Mayo R, Quintana-Ortí ES. Solving some mysteries in power monitoring of servers: take care of your wattmeters! In Energy Efficiency in Large Scale Distributed Systems; 2013. p 3–18.

[7] McCullough JC, Agarwal Y, Chandrashekar J, Kuppuswamy S, Snoeren AC, Gupta RK. Evaluating the effectiveness of model-based power characterization. Proceedings of the 2011 USENIX Conference on USENIX Annual Technical Conference, USENIXATC'11; Berkeley (CA); 2011. USENIX Association. p 12–12.

[8] Rotem E, Naveh A, Rajwan D, Ananthakrishnan A, Weissmann E. Power-management architecture of the Intel microarchitecture code-named sandy bridge. IEEE Micro 2012;32(2):20–27.

[9] Milenkovic A, Milenkovic M, Jovanov E, Hite D, Raskovic D. An environment for runtime power monitoring of wireless sensor network platforms. Proceedings of the 37th Southeastern Symposium on System Theory, 2005. SSST '05; 2005. p 406–410.

[10] Graham SL, Kessler PB, Mckusick MK. Gprof: a call graph execution profiler. SIGPLAN Not 1982;17(6):120–126.

[11] Hsu CH, Kremer U. The design, implementation, and evaluation of a compiler algorithm for CPU energy reduction. SIGPLAN Not 2003;38(5):38–48.

[12] Luk CK, Cohn R, Muth R, Patil H, Klauser A, Lowney G, Wallace S, Reddi VJ, Hazelwood K. Pin: building customized program analysis tools with dynamic instrumentation. SIGPLAN Not 2005;40(6):190–200.

[13] AMD. BIOS and Kernel Developer's Guide (BKDG) For AMD Family 10h Processors; 2013.

[14] Intel Corporation. Intel 64 and IA-32 Architectures Software Developer's Manual Volume 3B: System Programming Guide, Part 2; 2013.

[15] Mair J, Huang Z, Eyers D, Zhang H. Myths in PMC-based power estimation. Energy Efficiency in Large Scale Distributed Systems; 2013. p 35–50.

[16] Sohan R, Rice A, Moore AW, Mansley K. Characterizing 10 GBPS network interface energy consumption. 2010 IEEE 35th Conference on Local Computer Networks (LCN); 2010. p 268–271.

[17] Singh K, Bhadauria M, McKee SA. Real time power estimation and thread scheduling via performance counters. SIGARCH Comput Archit News 2009;37(2):46–55.

[18] Bertran R, Gonzalez M, Martorell X, Navarro N, Ayguade E. Decomposable and responsive power models for multicore processors using performance counters. Proceedings of the

24th ACM International Conference on Supercomputing, ICS '10. New York: ACM; 2010. p 147–158.

[19] Yang H, Zhao Q, Luan Z, Qian D. iMeter: an integrated VM power model based on performance profiling. Future Generation Computer Systems 36. 2014. p 267–286.

[20] Dhiman G, Mihic K, Rosing T. A system for online power prediction in virtualized environments using Gaussian mixture models. 2010 47th ACM/IEEE Design Automation Conference (DAC); 2010. p 807–812.

[21] Mair J, Eyers D, Huang Z, Zhang H. Myths in PMC-based Power Estimation. Under review; 2013.

[22] Li T, John LK. Run-time modeling and estimation of operating system power consumption. ACM SIGMETRICS Perform Eval Rev 2003;31(1):160–171, ACM.

[23] Economou D, Rivoire S, Kozyrakis C, Ranganathan P. Full-system power analysis and modeling for server environments. Workshop on Modeling Benchmarking and Simulation (MOBS); 2006.

[24] Bellosa F. The benefits of event: driven energy accounting in power-sensitive systems. Proceedings of the 9th Workshop on ACM SIGOPS European Workshop: Beyond the PC: New Challenges for the Operating System, EW 9. New York: ACM; 2000. p 37–42.

[25] Bircher WL, John LK. Complete system power estimation: a trickle-down approach based on performance events. IEEE International Symposium on Performance Analysis of Systems Software, 2007. ISPASS 2007; 2007. p 158–168.

[26] Noureddine A, Bourdon A, Rouvoy R, Seinturier L. A preliminary study of the impact of software engineering on GreenIT. 1st International Workshop on Green and Sustainable Software; Zurich, Suisse; June 2012. p 21–27.

[27] Zeng H, Ellis CS, Lebeck AR, Vahdat A. ECOSystem: managing energy as a first class operating system resource. SIGOPS Oper Syst Rev 2002;36(5):123–132.

[28] Da Costa G, Hlavacs H. Methodology of measurement for energy consumption of applications. 2010 11th IEEE/ACM International Conference on Grid Computing (GRID); 2010. p 290–297.

[29] Weaver VM, Johnson M, Kasichayanula K, Ralph J, Luszczek P, Terpstra D, Moore S. Measuring energy and power with papi. 2012 41st International Conference on Parallel Processing Workshops (ICPPW); 2012. p 262–268.

[30] Basmadjian R, De Meer H. Evaluating and modeling power consumption of multi-core processors. 2012 3rd International Conference on Future Energy Systems: Where Energy, Computing and Communication Meet (e-Energy); 2012. p 1–10.

[31] Basmadjian R, Ali N, Niedermeier F, de Meer H, Giuliani G. A methodology to predict the power consumption of servers in data centres. Proceedings of the 2nd International Conference on Energy-Efficient Computing and Networking, e-Energy '11. New York: ACM; 2011. p 1–10.

[32] Borgetto D, Casanova H, Da Costa G, Pierson JM. Energy-aware service allocation. Future Gener Comput Syst 2012;28(5):769–779.

[33] Berge M, Da Costa G, Kopecki A, Oleksiak A, Pierson JM, Piontek T, Volk E, Wesner S. Modeling and simulation of data center energy-efficiency in CoolEmAll. In Energy Efficient Data Centers; 2012. p 25–36.

[34] Canonical Ltd. Powerstat; 2012.

[35] Intel Corporation. PowerTop; 2013.

[36] Do T, Rawshdeh S, Shi W. pTop: a process-level power profiling tool. HotPower '09: Proceedings of the Workshop on Power Aware Computing and Systems. New York: ACM; 2009.

[37] INRIA. PowerAPI; 2013.

[38] Intel Corporation. Intel Energy Checker Software Developer Kit User Guide; 2010.

[39] Cupertino LF, Costa G, Sayah A, Pierson JM. Energy consumption library. In: Pierson J-M, Da Costa G, Dittmann L, editors. *Energy Efficiency in Large Scale Distributed Systems*, Lecture Notes in Computer Science, Springer Berlin Heidelberg; 2013. p 51–57.

6

GREEN DATA CENTERS

Robert Basmadjian,[1] Pascal Bouvry,[2] Georges Da Costa,[3]
László Gyarmati,[4] Dzmitry Kliazovich,[2] Sébastien Lafond,[5]
Laurent Lefèvre,[6] Hermann De Meer,[7] Jean-Marc Pierson,[3]
Rastin Pries,[8] Jordi Torres,[9] Tuan Anh Trinh,[10] and
Samee Ullah Khan[11]

[1] *ONE LOGIC GmbH, Passau, Germany*
[2] *Faculty of Science, Technology and Communication,*
University of Luxembourg, Walferdange, Luxembourg
[3] *IRIT, University of Toulouse, Toulouse, France*
[4] *Telefonica Research, Madrid, Spain*
[5] *Department of Information Technologies, Åbo Akademi University, Åbo, Finland*
[6] *Inria, LIP Laboratory, Ecole Normale Superieure of Lyon,*
University of Lyon, Lyon, France
[7] *Faculty of Computer Science and Mathematics, University of Passau,*
Passau, Germany
[8] *Department of Industrial Research and Innovation, VDI/VDE-IT, Germany*
[9] *Computer Architecture department, Barcelona Supercomputing Center – UPC*
Barcelona Tech, Barcelona, Spain
[10] *Department of Telecommunications and Media Informatics, Budapest University*
of Technology and Economics, Budapest, Hungary
[11] *Department of Electrical and Computer Engineering,*
North Dakota State University, Fargo, USA

Large-Scale Distributed Systems and Energy Efficiency: A Holistic View, First Edition.
Edited by Jean-Marc Pierson.
© 2015 John Wiley & Sons, Inc. Published 2015 by John Wiley & Sons, Inc.

6.1 INTRODUCTION

The wide adoption of the novel Internet services of the past decade, for example, Web 2.0 services, cloud services, and cloud computing, modified the structure of the whole Internet ecosystem. Contrary to the earlier disperse structure, where each service had its own server to be operated on, the infrastructures of the current cloud services are highly centralized; numerous services are run by a single infrastructure. These facilities are commonly known as *data centers*.

The operators' profit-awareness causes the recent golden age of the data centers. Owing to the economies of scale principle, the expenditures (both capital and operational) can be reduced with these highly concentrated architectures. The energy consumption of the data centers is accounted for 15% of the total expenditures of a data center [1] while data centers have a nonnegligible share of the total energy consumption of the society. On the basis of the study of Koomey [2], the average power dissipated by data centers was 6.4, 4.7, and 1.8 GW in the United States, Western Europe, and Japan, respectively, in 2005. The energy consumption of data centers was as high as 1.5% of the total energy consumption in the United States in 2006. Moreover, these ratios are increasing as a result of the recent data center deployments. In addition, the *Efficient Servers* project evaluated the increase of electric energy consumption of servers in Western Europe at 37% between 2003 and 2006 [3]. In 2007, the energy consumed in data centers in Western Europe was 56 TWh and is projected to increase to over 100 TWh per year by 2020 [4]. This will represent about seven times the capacity of the new EPR nuclear reactor in Olkiluoto, Finland, which is currently under construction.

As the price of electricity is continuously augmenting [1] and the environment-aware operation of the companies is becoming more and more desirable by the customers, the energy-efficient operation of data centers is required from both a financial and a social viewpoint. Therefore, the operators of the data centers are interested in more energy-efficient data center infrastructures and operations. This is justified by the press releases of leading information technology (IT) companies; there is a new statement almost every week.

Data centers have become prevalent in the literature in the recent years; tremendous work has been made toward reducing the energy consumption of the data centers. Albeit this fact, a comprehensive survey of the energy efficiency of the data centers has not been published yet. Therefore, in this chapter, we summarize the proposals dealing with the energy consumption and its reduction possibilities. The achievements are presented by the following areas. The energy consumption of data centers' hardware infrastructure is reviewed in Section 6.2. Section 6.3 discusses middleware proposals, which optimize the energy consumption of data centers. Cooling and heat control play a crucial role in the data center facilities: they are necessary to precede hardware failures; however, significant amount of energy is utilized by these equipments. Thus, energy-efficient cooling solutions are summarized in Section 6.5. Finally, the properties of data centers' network infrastructures are overviewed because the energy consumption of the switches and routers is not negligible (Section 6.4). The relation of the areas reviewed in this paper is illustrated in Figure 6.1. We hope this survey will serve as a ground that will

---

[1] http://www.eia.doe.gov/cneaf/electricity/epa/epat7p4.html.

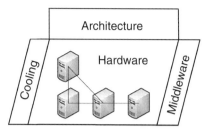

Figure 6.1. Areas where the energy consumption of data centers can be reduced.

help the research community to address the open issues of the topic of data centers' energy efficiency.

6.2 OVERVIEW OF ENERGY CONSUMPTION OF HARDWARE INFRASTRUCTURE IN DATA CENTER

6.2.1 Energy Consumption Rankings and Metrics

Data centers are composed of several distributed equipment and infrastructures that contribute to their energy consumption [5]. In most of the papers, we can figure out a portion for chillers, AC-DC converters, power supply, fans, and servers. Servers' consumption depends on embedded devices and components [6] such as the central processing unit (CPU) (37% of power dissipation), memory (17%), Peripheral Component Interconnect PCI slots (23%), motherboard (12%), disk (6%), and fans (5%).

While European Commission has launched the EU code of conduct for data centers;[2] several initiatives propose to evaluate and rank data centers depending on their performance and power usage:

- The TOP500 list that lists the 500 biggest supercomputers in the world. The power used for an entire system is also listed in kilowatts. On the June 2010 TOP500 list, the first rank occupied by the Jaguar center from Oakridge National Laboratory uses a power of 6950 kW. [3]
- The Green500 [7] ranks supercomputers and also provides the whole consumption of the entire system in kilowatt. The centers are ranked by a metric based on Mflops per watt. Additional lists such as the Little List and the HPCC list have recently been added. On the June 2010 Green500 list, the first rank is occupied by the machines from Forschungszentrum Juelich, which uses 57.54 kW of power and has an energy efficiency of 773 MFlops/W. [4]
- Through ENERGY STAR Data Center Energy Efficiency Initiatives, the US Environmental Protection Agency (EPA) proposes to rank data centers depending on their energy efficiency.[5] EPA selected the power usage effectiveness

---

[2]http://re.jrc.ec.europa.eu/energyefficiency/html/standby_initiative_data_centers.htm.
[3]http://top500.org.
[4]http://www.green500.org.
[5]http://www.energystar.gov/index.cfm?fuseaction=labeled_buildings.locator.

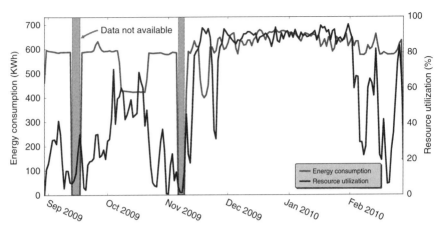

Figure 6.2. Grid5000 Lyon site energy consumption and usage of nodes over 6 months.

(PUE) as the metric to evaluate data center energy performance. The PUE is a standard industry metric, equal to the total energy consumption of a data center (for all fuels) divided by the energy consumption used for the IT equipment. The PUE generally ranges from 1.25 to 3.0 for most data centers.

- The Green Grid consortium proposes some metrics [8] and tools to evaluate the power efficiency of data centers. Rawson et al. [8] reaffirms the use of PUE but redefines its reciprocal as data center infrastructure efficiency (DCiE).

Even when not performing any application or services, a data center consumes energy. By correlating usage and energy consumption, we can observe the impact of applications of electrical consumption. As an example, Figure 6.2 presents the energy usage of the Grid5000 [6] [9] site of Lyon (135 computing nodes) on a 6-month period [10]. This figure also presents the resource utilization according to the reservation log obtained from the Resource Management System; the utilization indicates the percentage of reserved nodes and, hence, does not imply that CPUs, storage, or network resources were used by reservations at the same rate.

Next sections will focus on three main components of the servers: processing, storage, and communicating elements.

6.2.2 Processing: CPU, GPU, and memory

As seen in Section 6.2.1, the processing elements are the main consumers in data centers. Processors (CPU) and memory account together for about 54% of the total consumption, with a rough 37% share for CPU and 17% for memory. When graphics processing units (GPUs) are present, they can represent up to a tremendous 50% share of the total consumption.

---

[6]Some experiments of this paper were performed on the Grid5000 platform, an initiative from the French Ministry of Research through the ACI GRID incentive action, INRIA, CNRS, and RENATER and other contributing partners (http://www.grid5000.fr).

Processors are nowadays all multi-cores, and many-cores are becoming more and more present in data centers. The next generation of powerful machines will embark up to 256 cores in one CPU. Nowadays, most of the data centers rely on four to eight cores per processors. The actual power dissipation processors range from 80–100 W when idle to 200–250 W when loaded, where the consumption of each core is more or less the total divided by the number of cores (but no mechanisms exist for actually measuring it in the processors).

The range of energy consumption of processors can be estimated in two manners: by actual measurements under different circumstances (different loads) – sometimes directly on the main board like in [11] – or indirectly by measuring the total consumption of a node at the plug and deriving from these observations the individual consumptions (see [12] for a model comparison). In the upcoming norm ACPI 4.0 [13], it is possible to get the current power consumptions of individual elements, such as CPU, for instance. But no data center is today functioning with such ACPI 4.0 compliant components.

The current ACPI norm embedded in processors found in data centers allows for turning the processor in different operating C-states (C0, C1, C3) from normal operating state to deep sleep as seen in Chapter 2. Additionally, P-states indicate at what speed the processor should run from the maximum frequency (P0) to the lowest one. DVFS (Dynamic Voltage Frequency Scaling), the mechanism by which the operating system controls these P-states is the most used one in current data centers middleware, as it will be denoted in Section 6.3.

While traditional data centers are not using GPU or Cells, a current trend for the most powerful computers is to use such alternative hybrid architectures (combining CPU with Cells/GPU) to deliver even more processing power. In the Top500 list, the Chinese Nebulae ranks second (June 2010); it is composed of Intel CPU and Nvidia GPU. In the Green500 list [7], we can find such data centers in the first eight positions. Indeed, from an energy point of view, it can be competitive, because the scheduled jobs finish earlier, energy (which is power × time) is spent for a shorter time and the Flops per watt metric reaches 773 MFlops/W. Nvidia ships the Tesla GPU Computing Systems, consisting of 1U servers embedding four GPUs (for instance, the S2050 is delivering 2 TFlops in double precision at the cost of 900 W). Each GPU individually can consume as much as 250 W, for instance, the Tesla C2050. The main problem with such infrastructure is when it is idle, because it is not possible to deactivate a GPU card: when installed, it will anyway consume an important minimal amount of power (not less than 50–60 W), and there is no such mechanism to completely switch off GPU elements.

In previous generation multi-core processors – still in use in many data centers – it was not possible to manage the cores individually. All cores had to be in the same C- and P-states. Recently, AMD and Intel are producing multi-cores that allow for a differentiated policy for the different cores (AMD Turbo Core and Intel Throttling in I7 family). Hence, a core can be switched off completely if not needed. New processors even allow a core to increase its frequency above the official maximal frequency (the P0-state) when the overall temperature and power envelop is not exceeded (Turbo Boost Technology from Intel, for instance). To the best of our knowledge, no energy consumption comparison has been done with these innovative operating modes.

As already stated, memory banks consume about 17% of the node's consumption. Most of the nodes in a data center have nowadays DRAM DDR3 memory units, composed of memory cells. A memory unit consumes the power of basically two different types. First, it always consumes a background power to enable receiving commands (such as input/output) and to refresh the data by recharging the capacitors that lose charge over time. Second, it consumes more power when it has to go to the active state (so that it can actually perform data retrieval and communication with outward drivers). On an energy saving point of view, the DVFS and the operating states that we mentioned for the CPU also hold true; hence, a memory can be in different states, each one differentiates with others with the time to come back to operation and the power consumed. Common DDR3 runs at 1.5 V while Kingston manufacturer has a DDR3 that operates at 1.25 V for 1600 MHz, until DDR4 is actually produced in mass, requiring less power (1 V) and up to 3200 MHz.

6.2.2.1 Cost and Energy Reduction Evaluation for ARM-Based Data Centers.
Because the processor architectures used in embedded systems have been designed with strong energy efficiency requirements from the beginning, the possibility to use mobile device processors in servers and data centers has lately sparked interest among researchers and the industry. In particular, the feasibility to use ARM-based processors has been recently analyzed [14–17] and few commercial solutions were pushed on the market.

ARM processors are based on Restricted Instruction Set Computer (RISC) CPUs and are, therefore, designed to operate based on a simplified, highly optimized and fixed-length set of instructions. Because of the main characteristics of the set of instructions used by ARM CPUs that are (i) one instruction per cycle, (ii) register to register operations, (iii) simple address mode, and (iv) simple instruction formats [18], the design of the CPU control unit is considerably simplified and dissipates less power compared to other types of architectures. On the other hand, an x86 processor, the overleading architecture currently found in data centers, is based on Complex Instruction Set Computer (CISC) CPUs using a set of complex instructions of variable length and features multiple addressing modes and multiple instruction formats [19].

In order to evaluate the potential cost savings when using ARM-based CPUs in a data center, the overall cost of data centers must be taken into account. Hamilton presents in [20, 21] a cost model for a hypothetical data center and gives a cost comparison between different elements such as infrastructure, networking equipment, servers, and power. The model assumes a data center with around 50,000 servers, an overall 10-year infrastructure amortization time, a 4-year amortization time for the networking equipment, and a 3-year amortization time for the servers. The model takes into account a 5% yearly interest for the capital used to fund the data center and assumes an energy cost of $0.07/kWh. An 80% average critical load usage is assumed, and a server is assumed to dissipate 165 W. The resulting monthly cost of the different cost elements in the data center is shown in Figure 6.3.

Figure 6.3 shows that the direct cost contribution of power accounts for 13% of the total data center cost. However, the power has also an indirect impact on the infrastructure cost as the cooling and power distribution infrastructures are based on the maximal

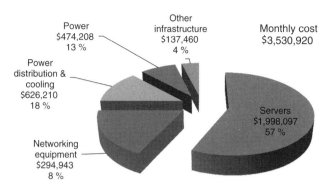

Figure 6.3. Monthly costs for a data center [20, 21].

TABLE 6.1. Ability of Apache 2.2 to Serve a 10-Byte Static Files Using Different Hardware

Machine	Request/s	Requests/J
Quad-Core Intel Xeon E5430 (2.66 GHz)	33,000	413
Pentium 4 (2.8 GHz)	7,100	80
Dual-Core Cortex-A9 MPCore (1 GHz)	4,600	4,600
Quad-Core Cortex-A9 MPCore (400 MHz)	3,400	2,833
Cortex-A8 (600 MHz)	760	760

power dissipated by the servers. Therefore, improving the energy consumption of the servers will overall affect 31% of the total data center cost.

Using Hamilton's model, the evaluation of the potential cost reduction when using ARMv7-based CPUs is presented in [14]. In this work, a quad-core ARM cortex A9 processor, using a Versatile Express development platform, and a dual-core ARM cortex A9 processor, using a Tegra 200 series developer kit, are evaluated. The versatile express consists of a V2M-P1 motherboard and a CoreTile V2P-CA9 Express A9 MPCore daughter board. The daughter board has 1 GB of DDR2 memory and a Cortex A9 NEC CPU clocked at 400 MHz. The Tegra 200 series developer kit has a Tegra 250 processor with 1 GB DDR2 memory and is clocked at 1 GHz. Three benchmarks representing typical applications found in data centers and server farms were evaluated on these two platforms: (i) Autobench to evaluate the performance of the Apache 2.2 HTTP server, (ii) SPECweb2005, and (iii) Erlang runtime system.

Table 6.1 shows the performance and energy efficiency of the Cortex-A9-based platforms for traditional server tasks compared to x86 machines. These results are obtained for Apache 2.2 serving a 10-byte static file. From Table 6.1, although the quad-core Intel Xeon platform can handle seven times more request per second than the dual-core Cortex A9, we notice that the ARM-based processor provides a 10-fold better energy efficiency. The SPECweb2005 benchmark was used to evaluate the performance of the Tegra 250 processor with more demanding Web services. SPECweb2005 consists of a

TABLE 6.2. Number of Simultaneous Sessions Using Different Hardware

Machine	e-commerce	Banking	Support
Quad-Core Intel Xeon X3360 (1)	3600	2700	4200
Quad-Core Intel Xeon X3360 (2)	7360	6240	7840
Dual-Core Cortex-A9 MPCore (1 GHz)	230	180	220

TABLE 6.3. Number of Simultaneous Sessions per Dissipated Watt

Machine	e-commerce	Banking	Support
Quad-Core Intel Xeon X3360 (1)	38	28	44
Quad-Core Intel Xeon X3360 (2)	77	66	83
Dual-Core Cortex-A9 MPCore	230	180	220

TABLE 6.4. Maximum Number of Calls per Second Handled by the Erland SIP Proxy

SMP	Intel Xeon L5430 (2.66 GHz)	Quad-Core Cortex-A9 (400 MHz)	Dual-Core Cortex-A9 (1 GHz)
1	130	5	5
2	240	12	13
4	350	30	13
8	400	30	13

set of three different workloads: support, e-commerce, and banking. The support simulates the workload of a hypothetical customer support Web service, the e-commerce workload emulates a Web-based shopping system, and the banking an online banking system. Table 6.2 presents the performance of SPECweb2005 on two x86 machines and the Tegra 250 while Table 6.3 gives the corresponding energy efficiency of the platforms. Two Xeon X3360 machines are used as references in this comparison, the second one having an optimized disk architecture to serve the data requested by the benchmarks. The optimized Xeon X3360 machine can sustain around 33 times more sessions compared to the Tegra 250 platform, but provides 3 times lower power efficiency.

Finally, an Erlang-based SIP proxy is used as benchmark to evaluate the performance and energy efficiency of the studied processors on a typical telecom application found in data centers. The performance of the proxy was measured based on the maximal number of calls per second the platforms were able to handle, and the corresponding energy efficiency is expressed in number of calls per consumed joule. The reference x86 machine has two quad-core Intel Xeon L5430 processors clocked at 2.66 GHz. The performance results are presented in Table 6.4, and the corresponding energy efficiencies are given by Table 6.5. The reference x86 machine was able to handle 400 calls/s while

TABLE 6.5. Energy Efficiency in Number of Calls per Joule

SMP	Intel Xeon L5430 (2.66 GHz)	Quad-Core Cortex-A9 (400 MHz)	Dual-Core Cortex-A9 (1 GHz)
1	2.6	4	5
2	4.8	10	13
4	7	25	13
8	8	25	13

the quad-core cortex A9 was able to handle 30 calls/s with eight schedulers (SMP) as using more schedulers than the number of available physical CPUs does not bring any performance increase. This leads to an energy efficiency of 25 calls/J for the quad-core Cortex A9 versus 8 calls/J for the Xeon machine.

Using the energy efficiency results of Tables 6.3 and 6.5 in the cost model proposed by Hamilton, we can evaluate the cost saving potential of using ARM cortex A9 processors over the overall data center cost at around 10% for the Erlang SIP proxy and 12.7% for Web services represented by the SPECweb2005 benchmarks. In terms of financial cost benefits, this leads to, respectively, a $ 350,000 and $ 448,000 monthly cost reduction or a $12.6M and $16.1M cost reduction over the 3-year amortization time for the servers.

Following the demonstration of the cost and energy reduction potential of ARM-based data centers, a set of commercial solutions appeared on the market. In 2011, Sandia National Laboratories demonstrated a mini supercomputer based on 196 Cortex-A8 CPUs using the Texas Instrument OMAP3530 chip. The company Calxeda is currently shipping the EnergyCore ECX-1000 chip containing a quad-core Cortex A9 processor as well as a Quad-Node EnergyCard embedding four EnergyCore ECX-1000 chips. The EnergyCore and EnergyCard from Calxeda are directly targeting the data center market.

Recently, a joint initiative in the Europe-funded project EuroCloud pushes ARM Cortex A9 processors, linked with 3D DRAM to create 3D server on chip, serving as a basis for compact and energy-efficient data centers [22]. Also within the Europe-funded Mont-Blanc project [23], the Barcelona Supercomputer Center is currently evaluating ARM-based supercomputers consisting of prototype boards using Nvidia's Tegra 3 (quad-core Cortex-A9 CPUs) and Samsung Exynos 5 (dual-core ARM Cortex-A15 CPUs) processors. The Mont-Blanc project aims at designing a new type of computer architecture capable of setting future global high-performance computing (HPC) standards that will deliver Exascale performance while using 15–30 time less energy.

Although a few ARM-based commercial solutions targeting data centers and server farms were lately pushed on the market, much expectation is put on the future ARMv8 architectures. The industry is already working on the design of 64-bit 3D many-core processors based on the ARMv8 architectures and predicts energy-efficient cloud data centers of several hundreds of server-in-a-single chip achieving thousands of cores on a single board [16].

6.2.3   Storage

Storage is an important feature of a data center. With estimates foreseeing a growth of 50% of data centers requirements in terms of storage in the next years, it shall continue to draw attention.

Different technologies coexist for storing data in data centers. Most of the time, an NAS (network-attached storage) is present, in order to concentrate the data outside the working nodes, while these nodes keep temporary data and their operating systems. Another possibility is to use an SAN (storage area network) that allows to share and coordinate distributed disks. The difference lies in the access pattern: in an SAN, the devices are directly addressed by blocks by the file system of the nodes, acting as if the distant disk is present locally, while in an NAS, an explicit communication protocol has to be set up over Internet Protocol (IP), like Network File System (NFS), for instance. As NAS and SAN involve technologies related to networks, we let the communication part to the next section and focus here on the storage devices themselves.

Traditional hard disk drives (HDDs) constitute the most prominent technologies, while solid-state drive (SSD) based on flash memory is becoming more and more attractive, together with hybrid HDDs technologies (magnetic rotating drives like HDD combined with SSD for a part of application/data often used). This latter technology is not yet applied in data centers; thus, we will not detail it here.

Despite its 50 years of existence, HDDs are still widely in use in businesses today. This technology is based on continuous rotating disk platters and a disk head that is positioned dynamically beneath the disk at the right location to read the bytes of data. Owing to the mechanical parts, HDDs still have a high power consumption: typical HDDs consume (numbers for a 2-TB Seagate Constellation ES at 7200 RPM, SATA, 140 MB/s transfer rate, $3''5$) about 7 W when idle and 10—11 W when busy (read operations being more power consuming). As seen in Chapter 2, several techniques are used to reduce power consumption of HDDs such as reducing their speed or smart head control.

SSDs are garnering much interests in the past years. Their most important feature is the improved access time. A multilevel cell (MLC) SSD has an access time of 0.5 ms compared to an access time of 15.7 ms for a 7200 RPM HDD. Please note that the highest performances coming for SDD access rate can be limited from an application point of view in some cases (see study on the comparison metrics [24]). As no mechanics exist in an SSD drive, the power consumption is only a fraction of the one of an HDD. A typical Seagate SSD drive (Pulsar, 200 GB, SATA, 300 MB/s) consumes only 0.75 W when idle and 1.3 W in operation. This improved energy performance comes with a higher price and limited capacities, making them not really sustainable in big data centers that host Tera or Peta Bytes of data.

6.2.4   Communicating Elements

While Section 6.4 presents data center network architectures and their relevant costs; this section focuses on associated network equipment costs in terms of energy. While networks are not mainly energy consumer equipment in data centers [6], this infrastructure is part of the whole consumption of the system (Network Interface cards, switches, routers, wired links).

Data centers mainly use Ethernet technology as the basic block for communicating equipment. Through the IEEE P802.3az Energy Efficient Ethernet Task Force,[7] a consortium mixing academic and industries is proposing new solutions for obtaining Energy-Efficient Ethernet solutions. Today, energy consumption of Ethernet networks is not greatly linked with bandwidth utilization. So even in low or no usage context, networks equipment consumes energy at high level. As a first approach, by proposing Adaptive Link Rate solutions, energy savings can be obtained by quickly changing the speed of network links in response to the amount of data that is being transmitted. Now, for high-speed Ethernet networks (1 and 10 Gbits) used in data centers, the Energy Efficient Ethernet Task Force is proposing low-power idle modes, which should allow to power down and quickly wake up specific components of Ethernet products.

6.3 MIDDLEWARE SOLUTIONS THAT REGULATE AND OPTIMIZE THE ENERGY CONSUMPTION IN DATA CENTERS

6.3.1 An Overview of the Middleware

For many years, research in middleware mainly focused on performance management [25]. However, middlewares are currently challenged to rethink the resource/service management strategies to add energy efficiency to the list of critical operating parameters to control, already including availability, reliability, and performance. The energy parameter has been included in a decisive way shifting the paradigm from "time to solution" to "kilowatt hours to solution."

However, considering power management at middleware level is not a new issue in the resource management arena. There are several works from some years ago proposing energy management for servers that focus on applying energy optimization techniques in multiprocessor environments [26, 27]. The proposals range from load balancing for power and performance optimization [28] to economical approaches for managing shared server resources, for example, [29], where Chase et al. use a greedy resource allocation distributing a Web workload among different servers assigned to each service.

Trying to tidy up the research work done until now in this area, we could consider two important aspects in order to classify the existing literature: (i) the system modeling used for making decisions and (ii) the set of control mechanisms required to make decisions effective. Figure 6.4 shows the relation of the physical system, the models, and the controlling mechanisms.

A number of companies, such as Symantec [30], Aperture [31], RackWise [32], iTracs [33], CISCO [34], nlyte [35], Intel [36], HP [36], BMC [37], egenera [36], and Specorp [30], offer commercial software to manage and optimize data centers. Because none of the aforementioned companies have made their solutions transparently available, it is an extremely difficult and perhaps impossible exercise to quantitatively compare middleware systems. The fact that current data centers (and data center middleware) are always designed to and operated at peak performance, such a practice entails promising

---

[7]http://www.ieee802.org/3/az/.

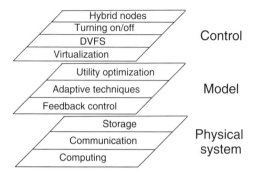

Figure 6.4. Areas where the power consumption of data centers can be reduced.

extensions and exploitation of fundamental interdisciplinary concepts that would further reduce the overall energy consumption of a data center. From scientific literature, we find an isolated problem solving approach, that is, energy, power, or thermal aspects related to a data center (or a large-scale computing system) are tackled separately in the context of computing, storage, and communications. Therefore, in the following, we give an overview of the state of the art in the three aforementioned categories.

6.3.1.1 Computing. Both independent [38] and precedence [39] task models have been considered on uniprocessor [40] or multiprocessor [41] systems using static [42] and dynamic scheduling [32]. The aforementioned models have been treated to present works in the domain of energy-efficient HPC [43], Web servers [44], computational grids [45], data centers [46], cluster computing [41], and cloud computing [47]. Mapping methodologies [48] based on a given application [49] and machine [50] load have been considered. Energy efficiency has also been the focus for application placement [51], task duplication [30], and task migration [52] models. A majority of the aforementioned works have either used dynamic voltage (or frequency) scaling (DV/FS) [32] as a medium to exploit the complex relationship between processor speed, power dissipation, and energy consumption or dynamic power management (DPM) [53] to completely shutdown processing units.

6.3.1.2 Communications. Achieving energy or power efficiency in communication medium is difficult because accurate knowledge [47] about the communications or prediction mechanisms [35] to project communications must be in place [30]. Earlier works opted to treat the entire communication fabric as a uniform medium [43]. Thereafter, DV/FS [54] and dynamic network shutdown (DNS) [55] that is analogous to the DPM technique were introduced to effectively regulate power consumptions [56]. The critical drawback of the aforementioned methodologies is the required additional complex hardware modifications. In contrast, on–off links require much simpler hardware [57] and have been reported to have comparable performance with previous counterparts but reduced switching overhead. The major challenges in energy- or power-efficient communication fabric include (but not limited to) connectivity, potential network deadlocks, and rerouting when links are asleep [36]. More recently, inspired by the work in fault-tolerant routing protocols, incurious researchers have focused on steering network traffic and providing network connectivity as links shut down to save power [49, 58, 59]. However, fault-tolerant approaches are reactive and merely performance oriented. The aforementioned methodologies have thus far not been utilized in the context of large-scale distributed computing systems and in particular data centers.

6.3.1.3 Storage. The DPM scheme, being the only applicable mechanism in the storage domain [60], covers three levels – cache, memory, and disk, which use hardware power management features, such as multiple power states, DRAMs [46], and multiple spin speed hard disks [61]. Moreover, Rambus Dynamic Random Access Memory (RDRAM) chip [62] (if used) in a memory system can be set to an appropriate power state independently, thereby, enabling dynamic switching of RDRAM with power-aware page allocation in the operating system [63] becomes a feasible solution. However, page misses may hamper the ability to successfully make the system energy efficient [33]. It has been noted that a large portion of the power budget goes into disk assessing [59, 63, 64].

6.3.2 System Modeling

Middleware requires models that capture the most important factors of the systems while allowing abstract reasoning. The models will allow formalizing behaviors and interactions that help the use of optimization techniques (from simple heuristics to complex techniques) based on what-if predicting techniques. It is important to remark that optimizations at different system levels interfere between each other. This makes the behavior of the current systems unmanageable at execution time. This requires novel optimization techniques that implements self-acquired properties at runtime. These autonomic techniques have been developed to manage workload fluctuations and determine optimal trade-offs between performance and energy costs.

Taking into account the techniques involved in decision making, we can group the relevant related work in three main groups (although there can be orthogonalities among them): feedback control theory, adaptive techniques, and utility-based optimization techniques.

6.3.2.1 Feedback Control Theory. Feedback control theory, where a controller manipulates the inputs of a system to obtain the desired effect on the output of the system. The main advantage of this approach is that it guarantees system stability. Furthermore, upon a change in workloads, these mechanisms can accurately model transient behavior and can adjust the system configuration within the time frame of a transitory. Most control theoretic approaches adopt system identification techniques to build linear time-invariant models and then apply classical proportional integral differential control. Kusic et al. [65] implement a limited lookahead controller to determine the servers in active state, the operating frequency, and the placement of virtual machines (VMs) on physical servers. Kalyvianaki et al. [66] propose the use of Kalman filters to track and control the CPU utilization in virtualized environments to guide capacity allocation. Analogously, Raghavendra et al. [67] propose a control-oriented framework to coordinate different kinds of power managers.

6.3.2.2   Adaptive Techniques. Adaptive techniques, where the learning process is based on live systems, do not require an analytical model of the system. For example, Tesauro et al. [68] present a capacity allocation technique that determines the assignment of physical servers to applications that maximizes the fulfillment of SLAs. Kephart et al. [69] apply machine learning to coordinate multiple autonomic managers with different goals. A recognized advantage of machine learning techniques is that they accurately capture system behavior with little built-in system-specific knowledge. Reinforcement learning approaches have also been used to reduce power consumption in clusters. Tesauro et al. [69] and Kephart et al. [70] present a reinforcement learning approach to simultaneous online management of both performance and power consumption. These approaches look at learning what policies should be applied, given a system status.

6.3.2.3   Utility-Based Optimization Techniques. Utility-based optimization techniques are introduced to optimize users' satisfaction by expressing their goals in terms of user-level performance metrics. For example, a server consolidation project on blade servers based on a power budget mechanism is presented by Ranganathan et al. [71], while Choi et al. [72] provided power budget policies for virtualized environments and an accurate model to predict the average power consumption of server system. Yiyu et al. [73] integrated utility-based and control-oriented techniques for energy management in hosting centers.

6.3.3   Control Mechanisms

Middleware requires new advanced management mechanisms to provide the necessary control knobs to successfully manage the resources in order to add energy efficiency as an operating parameter. Today, most common techniques used in the research literature of the area can be summarized as virtualization, turning on/off servers, dynamic voltage, frequency scaling, and hybrid nodes/hybrid direct current (DC).

6.3.3.1   Virtualization. Virtualization is a key strategy to reduce power consumption. With virtualization, multiple virtual servers can be hosted on a smaller number of more powerful physical servers, using less electricity.

Virtualization is a mechanism currently used for consolidation. Petrucci et al. [74] proposed a dynamic configuration approach for power optimization in virtualized server clusters and outlined an algorithm to dynamically manage the virtualized server cluster. Following the same idea, Liu et al. [75] aimed to reduce virtualized data center power consumption by supporting VM migration and VM placement optimization while reducing the human intervention, but no evaluation is provided. Other work of Verma et al. [76] also proposed a virtualization-aware adaptive consolidation approach, measuring energy costs executing a given set of applications.

6.3.3.2   Dynamic Voltage and Frequency Scaling. Dynamic voltage and frequency scaling (DVFS) allows the reduction of voltage and frequency providing substantial saving in power at the cost of slower program execution. Current microprocessors allow power management by DVFS. DVFS offers dynamic adjustment of supply voltage to the minimum level required for processing elements to operate at a desired clock frequency. Voltage scaling has been widely acknowledged as a very powerful, flexible, and feasible technique for trading off power consumption for execution time.

Depending on the type of tasks executed, DVFS approach can be classified into different categories.

The work reported in [77] was the first to characterize a convex function that optimized energy consumption of a set of independent tasks. The work was further extended by Hong et al. [78] that provided a heuristic (for a similar problem) for a fixed-priority static scheduling. In continuum, an energy-aware resource allocation heuristic for nonpreemptive scheduling was proposed by Quan and Hu [79]. Manzak and Chakrabarti [80] pointed out that extreme variations in power consumption and tasks invalidate the conclusion provided in [32] that uniform voltage scaling was the optimal procedure. To circumvent such an anomaly, the work in [81] reported an iterative slack allocation algorithm based on the Lagrange multiplier method. It is worth addressing the dynamic voltage scaling (DVS)-based techniques for soft real-time systems. In such systems, it is not required to fulfill deadlines; therefore, negating the purpose of using deadlines as a criterion for optimization. The DVS techniques for soft real-time systems need to trade-off power savings for average response times for tasks. Therefore, one possible application of such an academic problem could be the conception of energy-efficient Web services.

For scheduling tasks with precedence relationships, Bambha et al. [82] used a combined global/local search strategy. It uses a genetic algorithm combined with simulated annealing for global search and hill-climbing coupled with Monte Carlo techniques for local search. Zhang et al. [83] formulated the problem as a linear programming (LP) for continuous voltage levels, which can be solved in polynomial time. The work of Gruian and Kuchcinski [84] proposes a scheduling heuristic with a special priority function to trade-off energy reduction for processing delay. The schedule is constructed step by step. At each step, a ready task is selected based on an assigned priority and scheduled in the timestamp at which the partial schedule can achieve a maximal probabilistic energy reduction. The complexity of this approach is high because of the number of discrete time steps that must be evaluated in scheduling a task. Moreover, probabilistic evaluation of energy reduction of a partial schedule does not necessarily yield the best decision for the final schedule. Seredynski et al. [85] use a genetic algorithm to optimize task assignment, scheduling the task execution order, and infatuated slack allocation scheme that advocates a small time unit to the task that leads to the most energy reduction in each step. The work reported in [86] alters communication speed selection for communication paths and DVS on processors to achieve a trade-off between communication and computation power. This is the only work that tries to combine the two necessary computing elements (processing elements and communication paths).

The general facility to reduce energy consumption using hardware supporting multiple operating states is introduced in [87]. Ge et al. [88] classified the impact of using DVFS for different application types. This feature could be used by the middleware, for example, [69], where the authors use frequency scaling in a scheme that trades off Web application performance and power usage while coordinating multiple autonomic managers.

6.3.3.3 *Turning On/Off.* Turning on/off servers allows that the overall consumption can be reduced through consolidation. Khargharia et al. [89] introduced a theoretical methodology for autonomic power and performance management in e-business data centers. They optimize the performance per watt at each level of the hierarchy while maintaining scalability. The authors opt for a mathematically rigorous optimization approach that minimizes wasted power while meeting performance constraints. Petrucci et al. [90] developed a mixed integer programming formulation to dynamically configure the consolidation of multiple services/applications in a virtualized server cluster focused on Web workloads. The approach is power efficiency centered and takes into account the cost of turning on/off the servers. Berral et al. [91] proposed a framework that provides an intelligent consolidation methodology using different techniques such as turning on/off machines, power-aware consolidation algorithms, and machine learning techniques to deal with uncertain information while maximizing performance. Other approaches dealing with uncertainty are [92], where statistic methods based on correlation are used to predict usage and so to consolidate works.

6.3.3.4 *Hybrid Nodes/Hybrid Data Centers.* The hybrid nodes/hybrid data centers mix low-power systems and high-performance ones in the same node/data center, offering more control to the management middleware. Today, a good approach for energy saving is to have a middleware that can manage a hybrid data center architecture that mixes low-power systems and high-performance ones in the same data center [93, 94]. Filani et al. [95] offered a solution that includes a platform resident Policy Manager (PM), which monitors power and thermal sensors and enforces platform power and thermal policies. They explained and proposed how the PM can be used as the basis of a data center power management solution.

6.3.4   A Use Case of Leveraging Energy Efficiency in Data Centers

In this section, we present a middleware solution that takes into account the aforementioned modeling techniques as well as controlling mechanisms. More precisely, the corresponding middleware was realized within the context of EU FP7 FIT4Green[8] project. It has as an aim of reducing the CO_2 emissions as well as the energy consumption of data centers' information and communication technology (ICT) resources by 20%, which will have an indirect impact on the energy use of cooling systems.

6.3.4.1 *Concept.* As mentioned earlier, the proposed approach tackles the problem by reducing the carbon footprint of data centers through the deployment of ICT. There are various approaches of increasing the energy efficiency in data centers. Most of them are hardware oriented through investing in energy-efficient IT equipment or HVAC (heat, ventilation, air condition). Success in these areas, however, can only be incremental, as the capital cost of replacing old equipment is high. Therefore, the proposed solution is based on a different perspective: independently of the current IT and HVAC infrastructure, an energy-aware middleware that rearranges the workload in

---

[8]http://www.fit4green.eu/.

a data center and among a federation of data centers according to the optimal energy and/or CO_2 emissions efficiency is proposed. The middleware is designed agnostic of the existing data center automation and management frameworks and takes into account not only transferring workload to the most efficient clusters in a data center but also reallocating workload within a federation of data centers with the ultimate objective of reducing the global energy and/or CO_2 emissions. It is worth pointing out that the devised plug-in is suitable for any computing style being traditional, supercomputing, or cloud computing.

6.3.4.2   *Implementation.*   The cornerstone of the proposed approach is a set of energy optimization algorithms (e.g., policies) that reallocates the workload (e.g., VMs, and jobs) by taking into account technical service-level agreements (SLAs) and other restrictions, to optimize energy and/or CO_2 emissions through two basic procedures: With the so-called "global optimization," the algorithms check in regular intervals (e.g., every 5 min) the state of the system from energy and ICT load point of view and reorganize the workload in case they calculate a potential energy reduction. Additionally, an optimization is carried through every time a new workload enters the system, be it the execution of a batch job in the case of supercomputing data center or the creation of a new VM in the case of a cloud computing data center. Those optimization algorithms are based on constraint programming (CP) paradigm. To this end, an innovative architecture was designed, in order to cope with the complexity of the various SLAs and data center requirements, as well as the different algorithms available.

However, in order that these optimization algorithms can take the most suitable energy- and/or CO_2-saving decisions, the existence of accurate power prediction models becomes primordial. To this end, power consumption estimation models for ICT resources such as servers, storage devices, and networking equipment were devised.

As both the optimization algorithms and the power estimation models periodically check the state of the data center, a detailed description of data centers' ICT resources is provided with their relevant energy-related attributes and interconnections. The identified energy-related attributes is classified into two classes: dynamic and static. The former denotes the fact that the value of the attribute changes dynamically and it needs to be kept up-to-date through the data centers' monitoring framework. On the other hand, static attributes are those whose value remains constant; most of the times, the values of static attributes can be obtained from the manufacturers data sheet.

6.3.4.3   *Obtained Results.*   In order to evaluate the impact of the proposed energy-aware middleware and demonstrate that it works agnostic of the existing data center framework, the choice of three testbeds representing three different computing styles are suggested. One testbed is a traditional data center that provides business services to internal customers, the other is a scientific supercomputing center, and the final one is a cloud computing data center offering infrastructure as a service (IaaS) platform. For each testbed, different scenarios were created by taking into account two cases: single-site data center and federation of data centers. In the traditional data center, which is provided by ENI in Italy, the workload is characterized by two peaks occurring at the beginning (between 8 and 10 AM) of the simulated working day and at the end (between

4 and 6 PM), with a dip at lunchtime. Even in the single-site case, the proposed middleware managed to reduce by 30% the average consumption by semiautomatically shutting down servers during the times of low utilization. In the federation case, more savings were achieved in terms of energy consumption than in the single-site case that ranged between 28% and 50%. In the supercomputing testbed – the Forschungszentrum Jülich in Germany – the utilization rate of the resources is regularly much higher than in the traditional data center. Thus the potential for shutting down servers and consolidating workload on fewer servers is much reduced. Therefore, savings were 4–27% in single site depending on the utilization of the data center and 30–42%, even 52% in the federated site. These savings were based on setting the unused servers to low-power standby mode and by allocating the new jobs to the different data centers in an energy-efficient manner. The cloud computing scenario is represented by HPIS, a laboratory for cloud computing in Milan. As the laboratory does not offer real services, the workload for the IaaS platform was generated synthetically, through the monitoring of real customer activities. The major load generator of this testbed was the allocation of VMs, which was done based on the identified workload profile. Through the deployment of the proposed middleware, the energy consumption of the testbed was reduced by 10–24% in the single-site case – with the middleware itself consuming not more than an additional 3.5% of energy. The ability to exploit the federation as a unique pool of resources at allocation time allows achieved saving to range from 17% to 22%. These energy savings were achieved by allocating the new VMs in an energy-efficient manner and by turning off the unused servers. The number of servers was also optimized by using live migration of VMs from server to another energy-efficient one.

6.3.4.4 Conclusion and Future Perspective. In the end, it was shown that through optimization algorithms it is possible to reduce energy consumption of ICT sector. Hence, the proposed approach has the following three-dimensional benefits:

1. For the environment: reduction of CO_2 emissions.
2. For the data center businesses:
   - Reduction of costs and, therefore, prices.
   - Marketing options for green services.
   - Provision of potential energy legislation.
3. For the data center end users: reduction of cost for services.

In order to go one step further from what was achieved by the proposed middleware solution for data centers, the EU FP7 All4Green project takes into account the ecosystem comprising of the following three entities: Energy provider, data centers, and IT customers. More precisely, during power shortage/surplus situations, the energy provider asks for power adaption collaboration (e.g., decrease/increase) from data centers. This can be achieved either through

- Local flexibilities such as heating up/cooling down the data center (e.g., air conditioner) or discharging/charging the battery (e.g., UPS).

- External flexibilities involving IT customers who willingly cooperate with data centers by accepting reduced quality of service (QoS)-related metrics of their services (e.g., workload shedding or shifting).

All these are realized by means of introducing three novel contracts:

1. GreenSupplyDemandAgreement (GreenSDA): It consists of contractual terms between an energy provider and data centers. For instance, such terms specify the following:
   - The minimum and maximum power (in kW) to increase and decrease. Also for each power adaption capability, the minimum and maximum duration (in min) is defined.
   - The number of requests an energy provider can send to a data center per month. Also, the number of rejects a data center can send to energy provider per month.
2. GreenServiceLevelAgreement (GreenSLA): It consists of contractual terms between a data center and its IT customers. For instance, such terms specify the flexibilities based on a time period such as "High availability and performance in working days" and "low availability and performance during nights and weekends."
3. GreenWorkloadServicesOutsourcingAgreement (GreenWSOA): It consists of agreements between two data centers that intend to collaborate in improving each other's (green) performance/efficiency by exchanging workload. By committing to a GreenWSOA, the collaborating data centers thus become a federation.

The obtained preliminary results were encouraging that show high potential of data centers to participate in demand response programs, such that the data centers can reduce their energy consumption by means of energy-aware middlewares as the one presented in this section.

6.4 DATA CENTER NETWORK ARCHITECTURES

Although the main power consumers in a data center are the servers, the network, including network interface cards and layer 2/3 switches, consumes about 15% of the total power consumption [1]. Therefore, we take a closer look at the impact of different data center network architectures on the power consumption.

6.4.1 Architectures

Several different network architectures have been proposed for data centers ranging from switch-centric approaches such as butterfly, Clos network, and VL2 to server-centric approaches such as mesh, torus, ring, Hypercube, DCell, and BCube. In this section, we

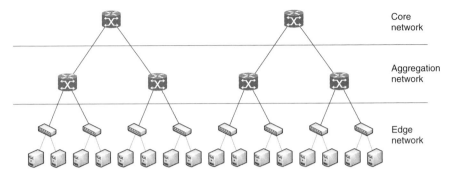

Figure 6.5. Hierarchical data center architecture (three-tier topology).

only highlight the most promising and well-known approaches and evaluate their impact on the total power consumption.

6.4.1.1 Hierarchical Network Architecture. Several small and medium data centers today consists of a two-tier or a three-tier network tree topology. An example of a three-tier topology is shown in Figure 6.5. According to [96, 97], a two-tier design supports up to 5000 hosts and a three-tier topology scales up to several ten thousands hosts. A two-tier data center architecture consists of a core tier as root and an access tier with the servers. A three-tier architecture has an additional middle tier, the aggregation tier. The servers itself are connected via gigabit Ethernet while 10-GB Ethernet is used for the core and aggregation network. Within the next few years, the 10-GB Ethernet connections will be exchanged by 40 or 100 Gbps links. This reduces the number of core switches or helps to reduce the oversubscription factor. According to [98], paths through the highest levels of the tree are oversubscribed by factors of 1:80 to 1:240. This high oversubscription rate is used to reduce the number of switches in the core and aggregation layer whose costs are about $700,000 for a 128-port 10-GB Ethernet switch.

6.4.1.2 Clos Networks (Fat-Tree and VL2). In contrast to the general three-tier topology, a fat-tree topology uses commodity Ethernet switches. The fat-tree architecture was developed to reduce the oversubscription ratio and to remove the single point of failure of the hierarchical architecture. An example of a fat-tree data center architecture is shown in Figure 6.6. Thereby, hosts connected to the same edge switch form their own subnet. Thus, all traffic to the same lower layer switch is switched, whereas all other traffic is routed.

The example in Figure 6.6 shows that fat-tree is a switch-centric structure where the switches are concatenated. The VL2 architecture is quite similar to fat-tree except that fewer cabling is needed. Greenberg et al. [98] claimed that switch-to-switch links are faster than server-to-switch links and, therefore, used 1-Gbps links between server and switch and 10-Gbps links between the switches. By this, they reduce the number of cables required to implement the Clos topology. However, high-end intermediate switches are needed and thus, the trade-off made is the cost of those high-end switches.

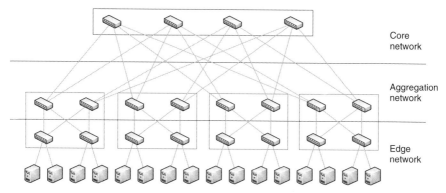

Figure 6.6. Fat-tree data center architecture.

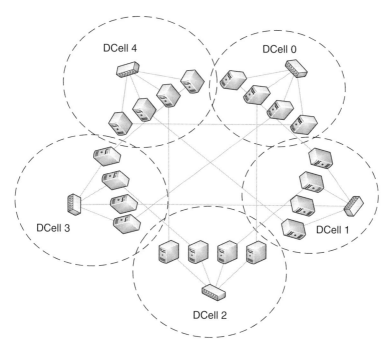

Figure 6.7. DCell data center architecture.

6.4.1.3 DCell. The DCell data center architecture was developed to provide a scalable infrastructure and to be robust against server failures, link outages, or server-rack failures [99]. A DCell physical structure is a recursively defined architecture whose servers have to be equipped with multiple network ports. Each server is connected to other servers and to a mini switch, cf. Figure 6.7. In the example, $n = 4$ servers are connected to a switch, forming a level-0 DCell. According to [99], n should be chosen ≤ 8 to be able to use commodity eight-port switches with 1 or 10 Gbps per port. A level-1 DCell is constructed using $n + 1$ level-0 DCells; in our example, five

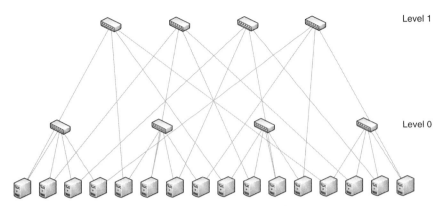

Figure 6.8. BCube data center architecture.

level-0 DCell form the level-1 DCell. In order to connect the level-0 DCells, each DCell is connected to all other DCells with one link. A level-2 DCell and the level-k DCell are constructed the same way.

Thus, the DCell architecture is a server-centric structure that uses commodity switches and the fewest number of switches of all presented data center architectures. However, the cabling complexity might prevent large deployments.

6.4.1.4 BCube. BCube is similar to the DCell structure, just that the server-to-server connections are replaced by server-to-switch connections for faster processing [100]. Figure 6.8 shows a BCube$_k$ $(k = 1)$ architecture with $n = 4$ servers per switch. From the figure, we can see that the total number of servers is $N = n^{k+1}$ and each server has to be equipped with $k + 1$ ports. Each level has n^k switches and the total number of levels is $k + 1$.

Similar to DCell and in contrast to the fat-tree architecture, BCube is server oriented and can use existing commodity Ethernet switches.

6.4.1.5 MDCube. BCube was designed for intracontainer networking with about 2500 servers. In order to connect several containers together, Wu et al. [101] proposed the Modularized Data Center Cube (MDCube). MDCube connects all containers using optical fibers without extra high-end switches or routers. Compared to DCell, it reduces the cabling complexity, and in comparison to fat-tree, the approach can be built directly with commodity switches without needing any switch upgrades. More details about the construction of an MDCube can be found in [101].

6.4.1.6 High-Level Properties of the Topologies. Table 6.6 shows a comparison of the last four presented architectures in terms of performance and costs. Looking at the server-to-server communication, fat-tree achieves the lowest throughput, because each server is only equipped with one port. However, for all-to-all communication, fat-tree performs best. Considering the costs in terms of intra- and intercontainer cabling and number of switches, DCell uses the lowest number of switches, while

TABLE 6.6. Performance and Cost Comparison of Different Data Center Architectures[a]

	Fat-Tree	DCell	BCube	MDCube
Server-to-server	1	$k' + 1$	$k + 1$	$\log_n t$
All-to-all	N	$\dfrac{N}{2^{k'}}$	$\dfrac{n(N-1)}{n-1}$	$\dfrac{N}{1.5 + 0.75D}$
Traffic balance	Yes	No	Yes	Yes
Graceful degradation	Fair	Good	Good	Good[b]
Switch upgrade	Yes	No	No	No
Inner- cable NO.	$N \log_{\frac{n}{2}} \dfrac{t}{2}$	$N\left(\dfrac{k''}{2} + 1\right)$	$N \log_n t$	$N \log_n t$
Inter- cable NO.	$N \log_{\frac{n}{2}} \dfrac{N}{t}$	$N\left(\dfrac{k' - k''}{2}\right)$	$N \log_n \dfrac{N}{t}$	$\dfrac{N}{2n} \log_n t$
Switches NO.	$\dfrac{N}{n} \log_{\frac{n}{2}} \dfrac{N}{2}$	$\dfrac{N}{n}$	$\dfrac{N}{n} \log_n N$	$\dfrac{N}{n} \log_n t$

[a]Ref. [101]

[b] n is port number of switches. t is the number of servers in a container, while N is the number of all. DCell has $k' = \log_2 \log_n N$ and $k'' = \log_2 \log_n t$. MDCube has $\log_n t = k + 1$.

TABLE 6.7. Power Consumption and Diameter of Data Center Architectures[a]

Architecture	Power Consumption	Diameter
Tree	$En^k + E_{sw} \sum_{i=0}^{k-1} n^i$	$2k$
Fat-tree	$En^3/4 + E_{sw}[(n/2)^2 + n^2]$	6
DCell	$\approx (E + E_{sw}/n)(n + 1)^{2k}$	$s^{k+1} - 1$
BCube	$En^{k+1} + E_{sw} \sum_{i=1}^{k+1} n^i$	$k + 1$

[a]Ref. [102]

fat-tree uses the largest number. While the cabling costs inside a container are quite similar, MDCube uses the lowest number of cables for intercontainer connections.

6.4.2 Power Consumption of Data Center Architectures

Gyarmati and Trinh [102] analyzed four different data center architectures in terms of power consumption. The total power consumption consists of the power requirements of the switches, and the power consumed at the servers that have multiple ports. Thereby, the power consumption of the servers as well as the power consumption of additional devices such as cooling is not taken into account. Table 6.7 shows the power consumption and the diameter of four different architectures. The power consumption of a single server and a switch is denoted as E and E_{sw}. It is obvious that the power consumption strongly depends on the number of used ports, denoted by n, and the number of structural levels, denoted by k.

Using these equations from [102], we can see that in small-size data centers, BCell and DCell have roughly the same energy requirements. However, when increasing the

TABLE 6.8. Switch Power Consumption[a]

Configuration	Rack Switch, W	Tier-2 Switch, W
Power$_{chassis}$	146	54
Power$_{linecard}$	0 (included in chassis power)	39
Power$_{10Mbps}$ (per port)	0.12	0.42
Power$_{100Mbps}$ (per port)	0.18	0.48
Power$_{1Gbps}$ (per port)	0.87	0.9

[a]Ref. [103]

number of servers, DCell consumes less power than BCube. The power consumption of the fat-tree architectures is between DCell and BCube. The tree structure of course consumes the fewest power but is also not robust against link, switch, or port failures.

According to Mahadevan et al. [103], the power consumption of a switch can be further subclassified. The power consumed by a switch depends on the power of the chassis, the power consumption of the line card, as well as the power consumption of different link rates. Looking at Table 6.8, we can see that a 1-Gbps port rack switch consumes almost five times more power than a 100-Mbps port.

In the paper, three schemes are presented to reduce the power consumption in a data center. The first scheme is called link state adaptation (LSA). In this scheme, the power controller monitors the links and dynamically adapts the line speed to the states *disabled*, 10 Mbps, 100 Mbps, or 1 Gbps. However, this line speed adaptation cannot be performed immediately, and thus the delay of the switching has to be taken into account. The second scheme is called network traffic consolidation (NTC). This scheme is also known as traffic aggregation scheme (TAS). Thereby, the traffic in a low-loaded data center is aggregated on a few links while the other links and switches are disabled. Considering a fat-tree, BCube, or DCell architecture, redundant links can also be disabled when not needed. This scheme can reduce the power consumption significantly, while taking into account the trade-off between power savings and availability. The last scheme presented in [103] is the server load consolidation (SLC). Here, server jobs are migrated to fewer servers using virtualization techniques. This is also an indirect way to consolidate network traffic on fewer links and allows a controller to turn off nonutilized ports or switches. However, the energy savings achieved with these three schemes always come along with lower availability and less reliability.

6.4.3 Additional Proposals for Energy-Efficient Data Centers

Finally, we review three proposals dealing with the architecture of the data centers. Albeit these methods are diverse; they all intend to reduce the power consumption of the data center networks. To be more energy efficient, the first one powers off unutilized switches, the second applies residential access gateways to form a data center, while the third introduces a highly scalable and flexible network topology generation method.

6.4.3.1 Elastic Tree. All the abovementioned mesh-like approaches (fat-tree, BCube, DCell) except the hierarchical network architecture help to be robust against

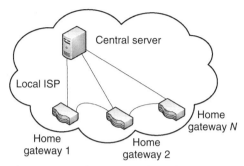

Figure 6.9. The nano data center architecture utilizes the resources of the home gateways of end users.

failures by using more components and more paths. However, as shown in [102], this also increases the power consumption, with the BCube architecture as the largest power consumer. However, although the number of traffic fluctuates during the day, the power consumption is fixed, see, for example, Google production data center [104]. Thus, Heller et al. [104] propose to reduce the power consumption by dynamically turning off switches and links that are not needed. The approach is called *Elastic Tree* whose underlying topology is a fat-tree. Using a testbed based on OpenFlow, it is shown that in the data center network, up to 60% power can be saved, depending on the traffic matrices. Safety margins are used to become robust against highly varying traffic fluctuations.

6.4.3.2 Nano Data Centers. Nano data centers can be made out of Internet service provider (ISP)-controlled home gateways to form a distributed, peer-to-peer data center structure [105]. The first order goal of nano data centers is to form an energy-efficient content delivering data center. To exploit the advantage of the peer-to-peer structure, the users' requests are served from home gateways whenever it is possible; thus, the load of the content servers, located in the facilities of the operator, is decreased. Figure 6.9 illustrates the architecture of the nano data centers.

The architecture shares storage and computational resources among the participants; the solution uses the underutilized resources and the already committed power consumption of the equipment. The energy efficiency of the structure arises from two properties: as the gateways are located in the residence of the subscribers, the heat dissipation is solved without extra cooling facilities; the demand and the services are colocated that reduces the intranetwork traffic. Valancius et al. claim that the power consumption can be decreased by at least 20% compared to traditional data center architectures.

6.4.3.3 Scafida. A recently proposed data center network generation method [106], called *Scafida*, offers a highly scalable and flexible design. Scafida is inspired by biological networks, namely, scale-free networks, which are energy efficient as they survived the evolutionary competition. The Scafida algorithm generates the data center topology iteratively, that is, the nodes are added one by one to the network. The algorithm's input parameters are the number of servers, the number and type of the switches,

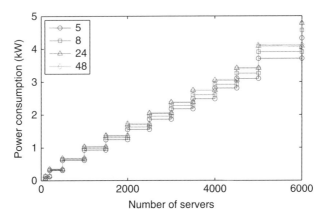

Figure 6.10.   Energy proportionality of the Scafida data center networks.

and the number of servers' ports; these parameters cause the high scalability and flexibility of Scafida. Owing to this, the Scafida algorithm is capable to create data centers out of any set of network switches; accordingly, the operator of the system is able to specify in advance the consumable power of the Scafida data center.

The power consumption of several Scafida topologies is shown in Figure 6.10 by scaling the number of servers within the structure. Topologies are generated with the 5-, 8-, 24-, and 48-port commodity switches; the servers are attached to the network with only one link. The power consumption of Scafida data centers is proportional to the size of the system regardless of the type of the switches; the steps of the plots are only due to the scaling of the simulation parameters. Thus, if Scafida topologies would be generated for all the possible number of servers, the curves of Figure 6.10 would be linear without any significant jumps. This implies that the Scafida data center structure is energy proportional design.

6.5   SOLUTIONS FOR COOLING AND HEAT CONTROL IN DATA CENTER

Computing equipment dissipate a large amount of heat that is exhausted in the facility. The facility must be maintained to an acceptable level of temperature and humidity. The facility also must be ridiculed of airborne particles and contaminants. We find a rich literature related to climate control dating back to 1970s. However, in this section, we only survey the latest state of the art. Before 1980, data centers had many of the same characteristics as those of the modern day facilities with the exception that heat loads were much less. The design considerations have since then not changed drastically as reliability [46], redundancy, maintenance [54], cost, and space remain the primary concerns. Constantly increasing costs and energy consumption of modern cooling systems urge the need for energy-efficient cooling solutions. On the other side, overheating of data center components reduces their reliability considerably [46]. Air flow direction has a major effect on the cooling of facilities; therefore, in [107], Obler illustrated various cooling concepts with a few different air flow directions. Air delivery also has been the focus of several works. These works consider whether air should be delivered from overhead or from underneath a raised (false) floor [49] ceiling height requirements that may reduce air stratification [56] raised floor height [107], and proper layout of computing equipment that would reduce hot spots [108].

Data center thermal control solutions can be broadly divided into mechanical- and software-based according to the approach they adapt. Mechanical-based approaches focus on the air flow dynamics for efficient cooling while software-based approaches, being aware of the thermal properties of the data center infrastructure, optimize the process of the workload scheduling.

6.5.1   Mechanical-Based Approaches

Mechanical-based approaches can be further divided into (i) nonraised floor facilities and (ii) raised floor facilities. The nonraised floors were the offshoot of the earlier computer room design. However, quickly it was realized that such a design was not economically feasible for large-scale data centers. Some of the notable works in nonraised floorings include a thorough computational fluid dynamic analysis to determine optimal air flow and air flow distribution [54]. The raised floors maintain a near layout to all interconnection cabling. Owing to the squared dependency between the air flow pressure and its velocity, the airflow patterns remain independent of the flow rate. Air supply through the raised floor along the walls and under the computer equipment with exhaust through a false ceiling is considered by Grande [109].

The effect of air flow, volume, and tile openings on heat load was considered by Khoshhala et al. [110]. Innovative self-contained air conditioning systems, liquid cooled systems, and chillers with integral air handling and refrigeration mechanisms installed within the facility are discussed in [39, 46, 49, 110]. Femal and Freeh [46] proposed a framework for the throughput optimization and load balancing of the available power with a focus on systems constrained by the number of power circuits available or having nonuniform power footprint because of the heterogeneous nature of user workloads. Khoshhala et al. [110] proposed a system for local cooling demonstrating that because of the high heat transfer rate, the inlet air temperature has no significant effect on cooling in certain setups. Wireless sensor networks initially considered for the greenhouse monitoring scenarios can be easily adapted to operate in a data center facility delivering temperature measurements to the main coordination module. Their indoor characteristics are addressed in [39].

In all of the aforementioned methodologies, the key drawbacks are (i) "bulk cooling," which is wasteful; (ii) "threshold cooling," which is an untimely cooling; and (iii) "single-methodology cooling," which does not allow embarrassing state-of-the-art cooling mechanisms.

The efficiency of the heat removal process in a facility is proportional to the available climatic information. Therefore, a low-cost, nondestructive, and readily deployable climatic information gathering wireless sensor network should be developed. The core idea being that in lieu of a central thermostat, distributed temperature sensors are utilized to accurately measure temperature at different locations of the data center that can be as fine grained as possible. The prior work on wireless sensor network deployment in greenhouses uses IEEE 802.15.4/ZigBee for (i) measuring substrate water, electrical conductivity, photosynthetic radiation, and leaf wetness [111]; (ii) regulating climate for rapid melon and cabbage growth [112]; (iii) measuring soil moisture [39]; (iv) multispectral imaging for cabbages [113]; and (v) affect of lighting conditions on ambient temperature [114].

Next-generation systems will include a combination of a wireless sensor network and an event-based control system that can effectively and efficiently offer a fine-grained control of the data center atmosphere. For the above, the following issues must be addressed: (i) issues posed to a multivariable, interacting control system by possibly faulty communications; (ii) location of sensors to correctly represent, for the purpose of control and spatially distributed quantities; (iii) efficient use of actuators to minimize wear; and (iv) effects of event-based sampling. The climatic information acquisition coupled with event-based sampling is typically subjected to machine-learning-based techniques that can proactively control the data center environment. Thermal management of data centers includes (i) air movement or ventilation, (ii) heat rejection, and (iii) humidity control. Because computational fluid dynamics (CFD) addresses heat transfer, air movement, and humidification in a unified approach, CFD is excellently suited to address the aforementioned outstanding issues. Thus, applying CFD tools, such as StarCD [115], Fluent [116], or OpenFoam [117], can predict both flow of hot and cold air and heat transfer in data centers. For the air movement or ventilation, the approach is to predict the distribution of the air velocity in terms of magnitude and direction within a data center. Because cooling is largely achieved by convection, a sufficient velocity of the air affects the cooling rate to a large extent. The predicted velocity field has to be also analyzed to identify (i) recirculation zones where no exchange of hot and cold air takes place; (ii) dead corners where effectively no or only little air movement occurs and thus leads to very reduced cooling rates; (iii) bypass air that streams without contact to the equipment, and therefore, does not contribute to cooling, and (iv) cold air contamination of coolers takes place if a cooler does not receive the warmest possible air, and thus, operates less efficiently. On the basis of the aforementioned analysis, measures such as ideal placement of perforated tiles throughout the room can be derived, which provide ventilation complying with the requirements of the data centers. This procedure may lead to a scenario of different measures of which all of them are to be evaluated by CFD. Within this process, CFD offers an additional advantage because predicting the effect of a proposal involves only a fraction of costs than changing the hardware [111].

Heat rejection is proportional to the temperature difference between the cold air stream and the surface temperature of the equipment. Therefore, the heat rejected can only be assessed by a spatial temperature distribution of the cooling air [107]. Expanding CFD predictions by a prediction of the spatial temperature distribution in conjunction with the spatial distribution of the air velocity will provide a detailed view of local heat transfer rates of the equipment, thereby, identifying hotspots. Once identified, these hotspots can be avoided by (i) reducing the cooling temperature of the air stream that increases the temperature difference and thus improves the cooling efficiency and (ii) increasing the air velocity in the region of the hot spot that leads also to an improved cooling efficiency. Either measure or a combination of both may be evaluated by a simultaneous prediction of the spatial distribution of both air velocity and temperature by CFD for a better cooling of the equipment [110]. Such a methodology is cost effective because by rating the predicted results of different measures in terms of cooling efficiency allows identifying a solution that perhaps requires minor changes in operation or setup only or at least involves minimal costs. For humidity control, similar to a CFD prediction that includes air velocity and temperature, the spatial distribution of humidity can be obtained. These results will indicate whether the humidity levels fall within a given recommended range for a data center or otherwise.

6.5.2 Software-Based Approaches

Software-based approaches aim at minimizing costs associated with data center cooling expenses by intelligent scheduling of incoming jobs. Typically, the policy of the software-based approaches focuses on (i) preventing a server temperature crossing a predefined threshold and (ii) increasing efficiency of computer room air conditioning (CRAC) units by maximizing their temperature [118]. Raising the temperature coming from CRAC units will minimize the energy consumed by a CRAC unit used to remove a unit of heat contributing into CRAC efficiency. However, the temperature increase should be performed only when inlet server temperatures are within a "safe" range. In [118], task scheduling is performed according to the power budget of each server, which is defined as the product of server power and the deviation of its outlet energy from the reference desired value. Such cooling optimization approaches may be nearly half the costs associated with cooling. Thermal-aware scheduling algorithms presented by Tang et al. [119] distribute the jobs spatially, preventing excessive heat conditions. Such method will trade the reduction in energy consumption of cooling equipment with a moderate increase in servers' consumption, as idle or under-loaded servers consume more energy per executed task than those highly loaded. Mukherjee et al. [120] took a step further and extended spatial distribution of jobs, adding a temporal dimension. Temporal thermal-aware job scheduling tries to allocate the jobs at energy-efficient equipment, extending the task execution time up to the allowed threshold. In a scenario with heterogeneous nature of jobs and data center infrastructure, it becomes useful to track thermal footprint of the executed jobs [121]. The availability of such thermal profiles allows distribution on jobs favoring computing resources with minimum levels of heat emission for a certain type of jobs. Current approaches for data center thermal management adapt either mechanical-based or software-based techniques independently. Mechanical-based approaches are simple and can be implemented in a distributed manner. But, the software-based approaches, being centralized, can deliver better level of optimization in terms of individual jobs and system performance. It is obvious that future thermal management systems for data centers will be complex and include both mechanical-based and software-based techniques.

ACKNOWLEDGMENTS

This work was partially supported by the COST (European Cooperation in Science and Technology) framework, under Action IC0804. The authors would like to thank particularly G. Da Costa and D. Careglio for their valuable coordination of the Working Group 1 deliverable of the Action, entitled "Hardware Leverages to Reduce Energy Consumption in Large Scale Distributed Systems" and available for download at www.cost804.org. The authors want to thank A.-C. Orgerie and M. Dias de Assuncao for their contributions to this paper.

REFERENCES

[1] Greenberg A, Hamilton J, Maltz DA, Patel P. The cost of a cloud: research problems in data center networks. SIGCOMM Comput Commun Rev 2009;39(1):89–73.

[2] Koomey J. Worldwide electricity used in data centers. Environ Res Lett 2008;3:034008.

[3] Schäppi B, Bellosa F, Przywara B, Bogner T, Weeren S, Anglade A. Energy efficient servers in Europe. Energy consumption, saving potentials, market barriers and measures. Part 1: Energy consumption and saving potentials. Tech. Rep. The Efficient Servers Consortium November 2007, by Intelligent Energy Europe. http://www.ing.unitn.it/ fontana/GreenInternet/Europe%20scenario/EServer_PartI_Saving Potentials_and_Scenarios_28112007.pdf

[4] Code of conduct on data centres energy efficiency, version 2.0. Tech. rep. European Commission, Directorate-General JRC, Joint research centre, Institute for Energy, Renewable Energies Unit; 2009. http://iet.jrc.ec.europa.eu/energyefficiency/ict-codes-conduct/data-centres-energy-efficiency

[5] Jean-Marc P, Hlavacs H, editors. Proceedings of the COST Action IC804 on Energy Efficiency in Large Scale Distributed Systems—1st Year. IRIT; 2010.

[6] Fan X, Weber W-D, Barroso LA. Power provisioning for a warehouse-sized computer. ISCA '07: Proceedings of the 34th Annual International Symposium on Computer Architecture. New York: ACM; 2007. p 13–23. DOI: http://doi.acm.org/10.1145/1250662 .1250665.

[7] Feng WC, Scogland T. The green500 list: Year one. 23rd IEEE International Parallel and Distributed Processing Symposium (IPDPS)—Workshop on High-Performance, Power-Aware Computing (HP-PAC); Rome; 2009.

[8] Rawson A, Pfleuger J, Cader T. Green grid data center power efficiency metrics: PUE and DCiE. The Green Grid; 2008.

[9] Grid'5000: A Large Scale And Highly Reconfigurable Experimental Grid Testbed Raphaël Bolze, Franck Cappello, Eddy Caron, Michel Dayde, Frédéric Desprez, Emmanuel Jeannot, Yvon Jégou, Stephane Lanteri, Julien Leduc, Nouredine Melab, Guillaume Mornet, Raymond Namyst, Pascale Primet, Benjamin Quétier, Olivier Richard, Talbi El-Ghazali, Iréa Touche.

[10] de Assuncao MD, Gelas J-P, Lefèvre L, Orgerie A-C. The green grid5000: instrumenting a grid with energy sensors. 5th International Workshop on Distributed Cooperative Laboratories: Instrumenting the Grid (INGRID 2010); Poznan, Poland; 2010.

[11] Joseph R, Martonosi M. Run-time power estimation in high performance microprocessors. ISLPED '01: Proceedings of the 2001 International Symposium on Low Power Electronics and Design. New York: ACM; 2001. p 135–140. DOI: http://doi.acm.org/ 10.1145/383082.383119.

[12] Rivoire S, Ranganathan P, Kozyrakis C. In: Zhao F, editor. *A Comparison of High-Level Full-System Power Models*. HotPower, USENIX Association; 2008. Available at: http:// dblp.uni-trier.de/db/conf/osdi/hotpower2008.html#RivoireRK08. Accessed 2014 Sep 29.

[13] ACPI. Advanced Configuration and Power Interface Specification; 2010. Available at: www.acpi.info/spec.htm. Accessed 2014 Sep 29.

[14] Svanfeldt-Winter O, Lafond S, Lilius J. Cost and energy reduction evaluation for ARM based web servers. 2011 IEEE 9th International Conference on Dependable, Autonomic and Secure Computing (DASC); 2011. p 480–487. DOI: 10.1109/DASC.2011.93.

[15] Aroca RV, Gonçalves LMG. Towards green data centers: a comparison of x86 and ARM architectures power efficiency. J Parallel Distrib Comput 2012;72(12):1770–1780. DOI: http://dx.doi.org/10.1016/j.jpdc.2012.08.005.

[16] Saponara S, Fanucci L, Coppola M. Many-core platform with NOC interconnect for low cost and energy sustainable cloud server-on-chip. Sustainable Internet and ICT for Sustainability (SustainIT); 2012. p 1–5.

[17] Fürlinger K, Klausecker C, Kranzlmüller D. Towards energy efficient parallel computing on consumer electronic devices. Proceedings of the 1st International Conference on Information and Communication on Technology for the Fight Against Global Warming, ICT-GLOW'11. Berlin, Heidelberg: Springer-Verlag; 2011. p 1–9. Available at: http://dl.acm.org/citation.cfm?id=2035539.2035541. Accessed 2014 Sep 29.

[18] Stallings W. Reduced instruction set computer architecture. Proc IEEE 1988;76(1):38–55. DOI: 10.1109/5.3287.

[19] Jamil T. Risc versus CISC, Potentials. IEEE 1995;14(3):13–16. DOI: 10.1109/45.464688.

[20] Hamilton J. Cooperative expendable micro-slice servers (CEMS): low cost, low power servers for Internet-scale services. 4th Biennial Conference on Innovative Data Systems Research (CIDR); 2009.

[21] Hamilton J. Overall data center costs. Available at: http://perspectives.mvdirona.com/2010/09/18/OverallDataCenterCosts.aspx. Accessed 2013 June 19.

[22] The Energy-conscious 3D Server-on-Chip for Green Cloud Services Project (Project No: 247779 "EuroCloud") of the European Commission's FP7 ICT Initiative. url-http://www.eurocloudserver.com

[23] Mont-Blanc. European Approach Towards Energy Efficient High Performance. http://www.montblanc-project.eu. Accessed 2014 Sep 29.

[24] Rydning J, Reinsel D, Janukowicz J. White paper: the need to standardize storage device performance metrics; Sep 2008.

[25] Guitart J, Torres J, Ayguadé E. A survey on performance management for internet applications. Concurr Comput Pract Exp 2010;22(1):68–106.

[26] Lefurgy C, Rajamani K, Rawson F, Felter W, Kistler M, Keller T. Energy management for commercial servers. Computer 2003;36(12):39–48. DOI: 10.1109/MC.2003.1250880.

[27] Bianchini R, Rajamony R. Power and energy management for server systems. Computer 2004;37(11):68–76. DOI: 10.1109/MC.2004.217.

[28] Pinheiro E, Bianchini R, Carrera E, Heath T. Load balancing and unbalancing for power and performance in cluster-based systems. Workshop on Compilers and Operating Systems for Low Power, Volume 180; Citeseer; 2001. p 182–195.

[29] Chase JS, Anderson DC, Thakar PN, Vahdat AM, Doyle RP. Managing energy and server resources in hosting centers. SOSP '01: 18th ACM Symposium on Operating Systems Principles. New York: ACM; 2001. p 103–116. DOI: http://doi.acm.org/10.1145/502034.502045.

[30] R. C, Humidity control: Systems meet varied demands. Consulting Specifying Engineering 11 1992. p 50–60.

[31] Emerson. Aperture Data Management. Available at: http://www.aperture.com/. Accessed 2014 Sep 29.

[32] Pouwelse J, Langendoen K, Sips H. Energy priority scheduling for variable voltage processors. Proceedings of the 2001 International Symposium on Low Power Electronics and Design, ISLPED '01. New York: ACM; 2001. p 28–33. DOI: http://doi.acm.org/10.1145/383082.383089.

[33] Banginwar R, Gorbatov E. Gibraltar: application and network aware adaptive power management for IEEE 802.11. 2nd Annual Conference on Wireless On-demand Network Systems and Services, 2005. WONS 2005; 2005. p 98–108. DOI: 10.1109/WONS.2005.20.

[34] Cisco. Data center management software. Available at: http://www.cisco.com/go/spdatacenter. Accessed 2014 Sep 29.

[35] Microsoft. Top 10 business practices for environmentally sustainable data centers. Available at: http://www.microsoft.com/environment/our_commitment/articles/datacenter_bp.aspx. Accessed 2014 Sep 29.

[36] Cisco. Data center networking best practices. Available at: http://www.cisco.com/en/US/solutions/collateral/ns340/ns414/ns742/ns743/. Accessed 2014 Sep 29

[37] Bell D. *Distributed Database Systems*. Boston (MA): Addison-Wesley Longman Publishing Co., Inc.; 1992.

[38] L. B. N. Laboratory. Data Center Energy Management Best Practices. Available at: http://hightech.lbl.gov/dctraining/best-practices.html. Accessed 2014 Sep 29.

[39] Liu H, Meng Z, Cui S. A wireless sensor network prototype for environmental monitoring in greenhouses. International Conference on Wireless Communications, Networking and Mobile Computing, 2007. WiCom 2007; 2007. p 2344–2347. DOI: 10.1109/WICOM.2007.584.

[40] Lefurgy C, Wang X, Ware M. Server-level power control. 4th International Conference on Autonomic Computing, 2007. ICAC '07; 2007. p 4–4. DOI: 10.1109/ICAC.2007.35.

[41] Wang X, Chen M. Cluster-level feedback power control for performance optimization. IEEE 14th International Symposium on High Performance Computer Architecture, 2008. HPCA 2008; 2008. p 101–110. DOI: 10.1109/HPCA.2008.4658631.

[42] Pinheiro E, Bianchini R, Carrera E, Heath T. Dynamic cluster reconfiguration for power and performance. Compilers and Operating Systems for Low Power; 2001. p 75–93.

[43] Boden N, Cohen D, Felderman R, Kulawik A, Seitz C, Seizovic J, Su W-K. Myrinet: a gigabit-per-second local area network. IEEE Micro 1995;15(1):29–36. DOI: 10.1109/40.342015.

[44] Elnozahy M, Kistler M, Rajamony R. Energy conservation policies for web servers. Proceedings of the 4th Conference on USENIX Symposium on Internet Technologies and Systems—Volume 4, USITS'03, USENIX Association; Berkeley (CA); 2003. p 8–8. Available at: http://portal.acm.org/citation.cfm?id=1251460.1251468. Accessed 2014 Sep 29.

[45] Vasic M, Garcia O, Oliver J, Alou P, Cobos J. A DVS system based on the trade-off between energy savings and execution time. 11th Workshop on Control and Modeling for Power Electronics, 2008. COMPEL 2008; 2008. p 1–6. DOI: 10.1109/COMPEL.2008.4634665.

[46] Femal ME, Freeh VW. Boosting data center performance through non-uniform power allocation. International Conference on Autonomic Computing; 2005. p 250–261. DOI: http://doi.ieeecomputersociety.org/10.1109/ICAC.2005.17.

[47] Jones WP. Computer rooms. Air Cond Appl Des 1977;18:181–185.

[48] Ceri S, Pelagatti G. *Distributed Databases: Principles and Systems*. New York: McGraw-Hill; 1984.

[49] Watford EL. One engineering solution for temperature and humidity control when computers are added. Air Cond Heat Vent 1959;56:89–90.

[50] Chen G, He W, Liu J, Nath S, Rigas L, Xiao L, Zhao F. Energy-aware server provisioning and load dispatching for connection-intensive internet services. Proceedings of the 5th USENIX Symposium on Networked Systems Design and Implementation, NSDI'08; USENIX Association; Berkeley (CA); 2008. p 337–350. Available at: http://portal.acm.org/citation.cfm?id=1387589.1387613. Accessed 2014 Sep 29.

[51] Wu Q, Juang P, Martonosi M, Peh L-S, Clark D. Formal control techniques for power-performance management. IEEE Micro 2005;25(5):52–62. DOI: 10.1109/MM.2005.87.

[52] Zhou X, Cai Y, Godavari G, Chow C. An adaptive process allocation strategy for proportional responsiveness differentiation on web servers. Proceedings. IEEE International Conference on Web Services; 2004. p 142–149. DOI: 10.1109/ICWS.2004.1314733.

[53] Energy Star. EPA report on server and data center energy efficiency. Available at: http://www.energystar.gov/index.cfm?c=prod_development.server_efficiency_study. Accessed 2014 Sep 29.

[54] Schmidt R. Thermal management of office data processing centers. Advances in Electronic Packaging—Proceedings of the Pacific Rim/ASME International Electronic Packaging Technical Conference (INTERpack'97); 1997. p 15–19.

[55] Arularasan R, Velraj R. CFD analysis in a heat sink for cooling of electronic devices. Int J Comput Internet Manage 2008;16(3):1–11.

[56] Murugesan S. Harnessing green it: principles and practices. IT Prof 2008;10(1):24–33. DOI: 10.1109/MITP.2008.10.

[57] Solly PJ. Air-conditioning for a computer department. Consult Eng 1966;20(5):72–76.

[58] Zhu H, Tang H, Yang T. Demand-driven service differentiation in cluster-based network servers. INFOCOM 2001. 20th Annual Joint Conference of the IEEE Computer and Communications Societies. Proceedings, Volume 2. IEEE; 2001. p 679–688. DOI: 10.1109/INFCOM.2001.916256.

[59] Zhou X, Xu C-Z. Harmonic proportional bandwidth allocation and scheduling for service differentiation on streaming servers. IEEE Trans Parallel Distrib Syst 2004;15(9):835–848. DOI: 10.1109/TPDS.2004.43.

[60] Hutchins P, Wade J, Sparts G. Energy savings in computer/data centers. Energy and Pollution Control Opportunities to the Year 2000; 1994. p 339–342.

[61] Song M. Energy-aware data prefetching for multi-speed disks in video servers. Proceedings of the 15th international conference on Multimedia, MULTIMEDIA '07. New York: ACM; 2007. p 755–758. DOI: http://doi.acm.org/10.1145/1291233.1291403.

[62] Newhall T, Amato D, Pshenichkin A. Reliable adaptable network RAM. 2008 IEEE International Conference on Cluster Computing; 2008. p 2–12. DOI: 10.1109/CLUSTR.2008.4663750.

[63] Brown WG. Equipment cooling for modernization. Br Telecommun Eng 1984;2:246–250.

[64] Haines RW. Keeping cool. Datamation 1986;32:83–84. Available at: http://portal.acm.org/citation.cfm?id=12273.13307. Accessed 2014 Sep 29.

[65] Kusic D, Kephart J, Hanson J, Kandasamy N, Jiang G. Power and performance management of virtualized computing environments via lookahead control. International Conference on Autonomic Computing, 2008. ICAC '08; 2008. p 3–12. DOI: 10.1109/ICAC.2008.31.

[66] Kalyvianaki E, Charalambous T, Hand S. Self-adaptive and self-configured CPU resource provisioning for virtualized servers using Kalman filters. Proceedings of the 6th International Conference on Autonomic Computing, ICAC '09; New York; ACM; 2009. p 117–126. DOI: http://doi.acm.org/10.1145/1555228.1555261.

[67] Raghavendra R, Ranganathan P, Talwar V, Wang Z, Zhu X. No "power" struggles: coordinated multi-level power management for the data center. SIGARCH Comput Archit News 2008;36:48–59. DOI: http://doi.acm.org/10.1145/1353534.1346289.

[68] Tesauro G, Jong N, Das R, Bennani M. A hybrid reinforcement learning approach to autonomic resource allocation. International Conference on Autonomic Computing; 2006. p 65–73. DOI: http://doi.ieeecomputersociety.org/10.1109/ICAC.2006.1662383.

[69] Kephart J, Chan H, Das R, Levine D, Tesauro G, Rawson F, Lefurgy C. Coordinating multiple autonomic managers to achieve specified power-performance tradeoffs. 4th International Conference on Autonomic Computing, 2007. ICAC '07; 2007. p 24–24. DOI: 10.1109/ICAC.2007.12.

[70] Tesauro G, Das R, Chan H, Kephart J, Levine D, Rawson F, Lefurgy C. Managing power consumption and performance of computing systems using reinforcement learning. Adv Neural Inf Process Syst 2007;20:1–8.

[71] Ranganathan P, Leech P, Irwin D, Chase J. Ensemble-level power management for dense blade servers. SIGARCH Comput Archit News 2006;34:66–77. DOI: http://doi.acm.org/10.1145/1150019.1136492.

[72] Choi J, Govindan S, Urgaonkar B, Sivasubramaniam A. Profiling, prediction, and capping of power consumption in consolidated environments. IEEE International Symposium on Modeling, Analysis and Simulation of Computers and Telecommunication Systems, 2008. MASCOTS 2008; 2008. p 1–10. DOI: 10.1109/MASCOT.2008.4770558.

[73] Chen Y, Das A, Qin W, Sivasubramaniam A, Wang Q, Gautam N. Managing server energy and operational costs in hosting centers. Proceedings of the 2005 ACM SIGMETRICS International Conference on Measurement and Modeling of Computer Systems, SIGMETRICS '05. New York: ACM; 2005. p 303–314. DOI: http://doi.acm.org/10.1145/1064212.1064253.

[74] Petrucci V, Loques O, Niteroi B, Mossé D. Dynamic configuration support for power-aware virtualized server clusters. WiP Session of the 21th Euromicro Conference on Real-Time Systems; Dublin, Ireland, Citeseer; 2009. p 1–4.

[75] Liu L, Wang H, Liu X, Jin X, He WB, Wang QB, Chen Y. Greencloud: a new architecture for green data center. Proceedings of the 6th International Conference Industry Session on Autonomic Computing and Communications Industry Session, ICAC-INDST '09. New York; ACM; 2009, pp. 29–38. DOI: http://doi.acm.org/10.1145/1555312.1555319.

[76] Verma A, Ahuja P, Neogi A. Power-aware dynamic placement of HPC applications. Proceedings of the 22nd Annual International Conference on Supercomputing, ICS '08. New York: ACM; 2008. p 175–184. DOI: http://doi.acm.org/10.1145/1375527.1375555.

[77] Yao F, Demers A, Shenker F. A scheduling model for reduced CPU energy. Proceedings of the 36th Annual Symposium on Foundations of Computer Science, Citeseer; 1995. p 374–382.

[78] Hong I, Kirovski D, Qu G, Potkonjak M, Srivastava M. Power optimization of variable-voltage core-based systems. IEEE Trans Comput-Aided Des Integr Circuits Syst 1999;18(12):1702–1714. DOI: 10.1109/43.811318.

[79] Quan G, Hu X. Energy efficient fixed-priority scheduling for real-time systems on variable voltage processors. Design Automation Conference, 2001. Proceedings; 2001. p 828–833. DOI: 10.1109/DAC.2001.156251.

[80] Manzak A, Chakrabarti C. Variable voltage task scheduling algorithms for minimizing energy. Proceedings of the 2001 International Symposium on Low Power Electronics and Design, ISLPED '01. New York: ACM; 2001. p 279–282. DOI: http://doi.acm.org/10.1145/383082.383168.

[81] Jha NK. Low power system scheduling and synthesis. Proceedings of the 2001 IEEE/ACM international conference on Computer-aided design, ICCAD '01. Piscataway (NJ): IEEE Press; 2001. p 259–263. Available at: http://portal.acm.org/citation.cfm?id=603095.603147. Accessed 2014 Sep 29.

[82] Bambha N, Bhattacharyya S, Teich J, Zitzler E. Hybrid global/local search strategies for dynamic voltage scaling in embedded multiprocessors. Proceedings of the 9th International Symposium on Hardware/Software Codesign, 2001. CODES 2001; 2001. p 243–248. DOI: 10.1109/HSC.2001.924683.

[83] Zhang Y, Hu XS, Chen DZ. Task scheduling and voltage selection for energy minimization. Proceedings of the 39th Annual Design Automation Conference, DAC '02. New York: ACM; 2002. p 183–188. http://doi.acm.org/10.1145/513918.513966.

[84] Gruian F, Kuchcinski K. Lenes: task scheduling for low-energy systems using variable supply voltage processors. Proceedings of the 2001 Asia and South Pacific Design Automation Conference, ASP-DAC '01. New York: ACM; 2001. p 449–455. http://doi.acm.org/10.1145/370155.370511.

[85] Seredynski M, Bouvry P, Klopotek M. Performance of a strategy based packets forwarding in Ad HOC networks. 3rd International Conference on Availability, Reliability and Security, 2008. ARES 08; 2008. p 1036–1043. DOI: 10.1109/ARES.2008.181.

[86] Liu J, Chou PH, Bagherzadeh N. Communication speed selection for embedded systems with networked voltage-scalable processors. Proceedings of the 10th International Symposium on Hardware/Software Codesign, CODES '02. New York: ACM; 2002. p 169–174. DOI: http://doi.acm.org/10.1145/774789.774824.

[87] Lu Y-H, Benini L, De Micheli GD. Operating-system directed power reduction. Proceedings of the 2000 International Symposium on Low Power Electronics and Design, ISLPED '00. New York: ACM; 2000. p 37–42. DOI: http://doi.acm.org/10.1145/344166.344189.

[88] Ge R, Feng X, Cameron KW. Performance-constrained distributed DVS scheduling for scientific applications on power-aware clusters. Proceedings of the 2005 ACM/IEEE Conference on Supercomputing, SC '05. Washington (DC): IEEE Computer Society; 2005. p 34–3–. DOI: http://dx.doi.org/10.1109/SC.2005.57.

[89] Khargharia B, Hariri S, Yousif M. Autonomic power and performance management for computing systems. Cluster Comput 2008;11:167–181, DOI: 10.1007/s10586-007-0043-6.

[90] Petrucci V, Loques O, Mossé D. A dynamic configuration model for power-efficient virtualized server clusters. 11th Brazillian Workshop on Real-Time and Embedded Systems (WTR), Volume 2, Citeseer; 2009. p 35–44.

[91] Berral JL, Goiri IN, Nou R, Julià F, Guitart J, Gavaldà R, Torres J. Towards energy-aware scheduling in data centers using machine learning. Proceedings of the 1st International Conference on Energy-Efficient Computing and Networking, e-Energy '10. New York: ACM; 2010. p 215–224. DOI: http://doi.acm.org/10.1145/1791314.1791349.

[92] Verma A, Dasgupta G, Nayak TK, De P, Kothari R. Server workload analysis for power minimization using consolidation. Proceedings of the 2009 Conference on USENIX Annual Technical Conference, USENIX'09, USENIX Association; Berkeley (CA); 2009. p 28–28. Available at: http://portal.acm.org/citation.cfm?id=1855807.1855835. Accessed 2014 Sep 29.

[93] Chun B-G, Iannaccone G, Iannaccone G, Katz R, Lee G, Niccolini L. An energy case for hybrid datacenters. SIGOPS Oper Syst Rev 2010;44:76–80–. DOI: http://doi.acm.org/10.1145/1740390.1740408.

[94] Nathuji R, Isci C, Gorbatov E. Exploiting platform heterogeneity for power efficient data centers. 4th International Conference on Autonomic Computing, 2007. ICAC '07; 2007. p 5–5. doi: 10.1109/ICAC.2007.16.

[95] Filani D, He J, Gao S, Rajappa M, Kumar A, Shah R, Nagappan R. Dynamic data center power management: trends, issues and solutions. Intel Technol J 2008;12(01):59–68.

[96] Loukissas M, Al-Fares A, Vahdat A. A scalable, commodity data center network architecture. SIGCOMM '08: Proceedings of the ACM SIGCOMM 2008 Conference on Data Communication; Seattle (WA); 2008. p 63–74.

[97] Kliazovich D, Bounvry P, Audzevich Y, Khan SU. GreenCloud: A Packet-level Simulator of Energy-aware Cloud Computing Data Centers. IEEE Globecom; Miami, (FL); 2010.

[98] Greenberg A, Hamilton JR, Jain N, Kandula S, Kim C, Lahiri P, Maltz DA, Patel P, Sengupta S. VL2: a scalable and flexible data center network. SIGCOMM Comput Commun Rev 2009;39(4):51–62.

[99] Guo C, Wu H, Tan K, Shi L, Zhang Y, Lu S. DCell: a scalable and fault-tolerant network structure for data centers. SIGCOMM Comput Commun Rev 2008;38(4):75–86.

[100] Guo C, Lu G, Li D, Wu H, Zhang X, Shi Y, Tian C, Zhang Y, Lu S. BCube: a high performance, server-centric network architecture for modular data centers. SIGCOMM '09: Proceedings of the ACM SIGCOMM 2009 Conference on Data Communication; Barcelona, Spain; 2009. p 63–74.

[101] Wu H, Lu G, Li D, Guo C, Zhang Y. MDCube: a high performance network structure for modular data center interconnection. Proceedings of the 5th International Conference on Emerging Networking Experiments and Technologies (CoNEXT); Rome, Italy; 2009. p 25–36.

[102] Gyarmati L, Trinh TA. How can architecture help to reduce energy consumption in data center networking. e-Energy '10: Proceedings of the 1st International Conference on Energy-Efficient Computing and Networking; Passau, Germany; 2010. p 183–186.

[103] Mahadevan P, Sharma P, Banerjee S, Ranganathan P. Energy aware network operations. INFOCOM'09: Proceedings of the 28th IEEE International Conference on Computer Communications Workshops; Rio de Janeiro, Brazil; 2009. p 25–30.

[104] Heller B, Seetharaman S, Mahadevan P, Yiakoumis Y, Sharma P, Banerjee S, McKeown N. Elastic tree: saving energy in data center networks. 7th USENIX Symposium on Networked System Design and Implementation (NSDI); San Jose (CA); 2010. p 249–264.

[105] Valancius V, Laoutaris N, Massoulié L, Diot C, Rodriguez P. Greening the internet with nano data centers. CoNEXT '09: Proceedings of the 5th International Conference on Emerging Networking Experiments and Technologies. New York: ACM; 2009. p 37–48. DOI: http://doi.acm.org/10.1145/1658939.1658944.

[106] Gyarmati L, Trinh AT. Scafida: a scale-free network inspired data center architecture. SIGCOMM Comput Commun Rev 2010;40:5–12.

[107] Obler H. Energy efficient computer cooling. Heat Piping Air Cond Eng 1982;54(1):107–111.

[108] Green PA. A one-system, 'equipment first' cooling plan for computer installations. Heat Piping Air Cond Eng 1961;33(12):96–99.

[109] Grande FJ. How to select and integrate equipment for computer room air conditioning. Heat Piping Air Cond Eng 1963;35(7):96–98.

[110] Khoshhala A, Rahimia M, Alsairafib A. CFD investigation on the effect of air temperature on air blowing cooling system for preventing tube rupture. Int Commun Heat Mass Transfer 2009;36(7):750–756.

[111] Yoo S, Kim J, Kim T, Ahn S, Sung J, Kim D. A2s: automated agriculture system based on WSN. IEEE International Symposium on Consumer Electronics.

[112] Lea-Cox JD, Kantor G, Anhalt J, Ristvey AG, Ross DS. A wireless sensor network for the nursery and greenhouse industry. Southern Nursery Association Research Conference; 2007. p 454–458.

[113] Yang I-C, Chen S, Huang Y-I, Hsieh K-W, Chen C-T, Lu H-C, Chang C-L, Lin H-M, Chen Y-L, Lo C-C, Chen Y. Rfid-integrated multi-functional remote sensing system for seedling production management. ASABE Annual International Meeting.

[114] Ayers JM. Air conditioning needs of computers pose problems for new office building. Heat Piping Air Cond Eng 1962;34(8):107–112.

[115] CD-Adapco. Available at: http://www.cd-adapco.com/. Accessed 2014 Sep 29.

[116] ANSYS Fluent software. http://www.ansys.com

[117] Open Foam. Open CFD. Available at: http://www.openfoam.com/. Accessed 2014 Sep 29.

[118] Moore J, Chase J, Ranganathan P, Sharma R. Making scheduling "cool": temperature-aware workload placement in data centers. USENIX Annual Technical Conference.

[119] Tang Q, Gupta SKS, Varsamopoulos G. Energy-efficient thermal-aware task scheduling for homogeneous high-performance computing data centers: a cyber-physical approach. IEEE Trans Parallel Distrib Syst Arch 2008;19(11):1458–1472.

[120] Mukherjee T, Banerjee A, Varsamopoulos G, Gupta SKS, Rungta S. Spatio-temporal thermal-aware job scheduling to minimize energy consumption in virtualized heterogeneous data centers. Comput Netw Int J Comput Telecommun Netw 2009;53(7):2888–2904.

[121] Wang L, von Laszewskiand G Dayal J, He X, Younge AJ, Furlani TR. Towards thermal aware workload scheduling in a data center. Proceedings of the 10th International Symposium on Pervasive Systems, Algorithms and Networks.

7

ENERGY EFFICIENCY AND HIGH-PERFORMANCE COMPUTING

Pascal Bouvry,[1] Ghislain Landry Tsafack Chetsa,[2,3]
Georges Da Costa,[3] Emmanuel Jeannot,[4] Laurent Lefèvre,[2]
Jean-Marc Pierson,[3] Frédéric Pinel,[1] Patricia Stolf,[3] and
Sébastien Varrette[1]

[1]*Computer Science and Communication (CSC) Research Unit,
University of Luxembourg, Luxembourg*
[2]*INRIA, LIP Laboratory (CNRS, INRIA, ENS Lyon, UCB Lyon1),
University of Lyon, Lyon, France*
[3]*SEPIA Research Unit, Institute for Research in Informatics of Toulouse (IRIT),
University of Toulouse III, Toulouse, France*
[4]*Runtime Research Unit, INRIA Bordeaux Sud-Ouest, Bordeaux, France*

7.1 INTRODUCTION

Nowadays, high-performance computing (HPC) infrastructure can consume several megawatts. As of today, the world's fastest supercomputer, according to the Top'5000 list [1], is the Tianhe-2 and consumes more than 17 and 24 with cooling for almost 34 PFlops.

Without any progress in terms of energy efficiency, an Exascale infrastructure (1000 PFlops) would consume around 500 MW or between 10% and 20% of a modern nuclear reactor. To keep the energy consumption of an exascale machine below 30 MW,

Large-Scale Distributed Systems and Energy Efficiency: A Holistic View, First Edition.
Edited by Jean-Marc Pierson.
© 2015 John Wiley & Sons, Inc. Published 2015 by John Wiley & Sons, Inc.

TABLE 7.1. Main HPC Performance Metrics

Type	Metric
Computing capacity/speed	Floating point operations per seconds (Flops) 1 GFlops $= 10^9$ Flops 1 TFlops $= 10^{12}$ Flops 1 PFlops $= 10^{15}$ Flops
Storage capacity	multiples of *bytes* $= 8$ *bits* 1 GB $= 10^9$ bytes 1 GiB $= 1024^3$ bytes 1 TB $= 10^{12}$ bytes 1 TiB $= 1024^4$ bytes 1 PB $= 10^{15}$ bytes 1 PiB $= 1024^5$ bytes
Transfer rate on a medium	Mb/s or MB/s
I/O performance	Sequential versus random R/W speed, *IOPS*
Computing energy performance	Flops per watt

the energy efficiency of such a system must be multiplied by 16. To perform such progress, tremendous efforts must be carried out in many domains: hardware (e.g., energy-efficient processor or memory) and network, but it is expected that some effort must also be carried out on the software side. It is equally important to improve the energy efficiency of an application through the way it is programmed and executed.

In this chapter, we provide a state-of-the-art overview as regards energy efficiency in HPC facilities while describing the open challenges the research community has to face in the coming years to enable the building and usage of an exascale platform by 2020. In Section 7.2, we present an overview of HPC systems. Some research challenges and issues are reviewed in Section 7.3, while energy efficiency in clouds for HPC workload is discussed in Section 7.4. This chapter is finally concluded in Section 7.5.

7.2 OVERVIEW OF HPC COMPONENTS AND LATEST TRENDS TOWARD ENERGY EFFICIENCY

7.2.1 Architecture of the Current HPC Facilities

Since the advent of computer sciences, applications have been intrinsically restricted by the computing power available on execution. It led to a race to build more and more efficient supercomputers, opening the area of HPC. The main performance metrics used in this context are summarized in Table 7.1.

Computing systems used to evolve according to successive generations are summarized in Figure 7.1. As of today, computing systems are *multi-core* that is, they embed several computing units that operate in parallel. Also, the cloud computing (CC) paradigm opens new perspectives as regards to computing facilities, when mobile processors are considered to be the leading technology in the processor market for the coming years – the reasons for this market change will become self-explanatory by the end of this chapter.

Figure 7.2 illustrates a famous empirical law due to an engineer at Fairchild Semiconductor named Gordon Moore in the 1960s, stating that the density of transistors

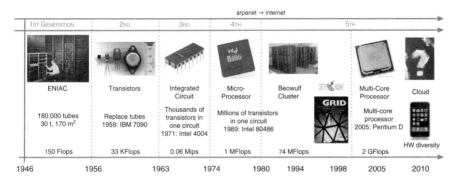

Figure 7.1. Evolution of computing systems.

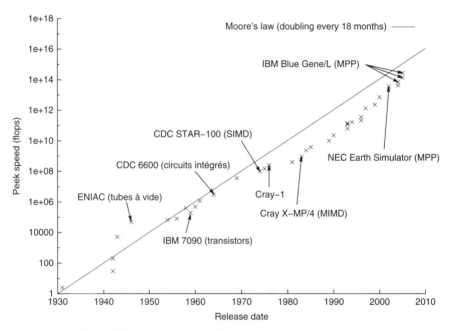

Figure 7.2. Moore's law illustrated on supercomputer.

in a microprocessor is doubling every 18 months. For a couple of years, this law has been reformulated as follows: the number of cores embedded in a microprocessor doubles every 18 months. Nonetheless, this law has been validated since the 1990s by the Top500 [1] Project, which ranks the world's 500 most powerful computers using the High-Performance Linpack (HPL) benchmark. We have the opportunity to describe this benchmark more precisely, together with its "green" derivative project named *Green 500* [2] later in this chapter. Nevertheless, it raises the set milestones of relevance for this chapter summarized in Table 7.2.

TABLE 7.2. Top500 Milestones (Gordon Bell Prize)

Date	Computing Capacity	High-Performance Computing (HPC) System	
1988	1 GFlops	Cray Y-MP	8 processors
1998	1 TFlops	Cray T3E	1024 processors
2008	1 PFlops	Cray XT5	$1.5 * 10^5$ processors
2018?	1 EFlops	n/a	

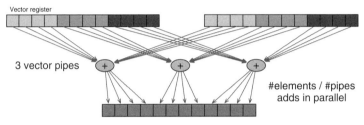

Figure 7.3.   MMX on x86 architectures.

Different hardware architectures used to permit these milestones to be reached. If we focus on today's systems relative to the seminal classification of Flynn [3], we are now relying on two architectures:

1. Single Instruction Multiple Data (SIMD), that is, vector machines.
2. Multiple Instruction Multiple Data (MIMD) with shared or distributed memory.

7.2.1.1   Vector Machines – General-Purpose Graphics Processing Unit (GPGPU).   This architecture is tuned to perform element-wise operations on entire vectors in a single instruction. For instance, Figure 7.3 illustrates a parallel reduction operated using the multimedia extension (MMX) on x86 architectures or the AltiVec on PowerPC.

These operations are now typically implemented in general-purpose graphics processing unit (GPGPU) cards (such as Nvidia Tesla or ATI Radeon cards) that offer impressive computing performances for a relatively low power consumption. For instance, in 2010, the ATI Radeon HD 5970 used to feature 3200 stream procs running at a frequency of 725 MHz (thus achieving a theoretical computing performance of 4.64 TFlops), for a maximum power consumption of 294 W. For some application, it may be worth to adapt to the capabilities of these devices to ensure large power savings – we have the opportunity to come back to this later in this chapter.

7.2.1.2   MIMD with Shared Memory: Symmetric Multi-Processors (SMPs).   Under this category falls symmetric multi-processors (SMPs) where all processors access the same memory and input/output (I/O). Thus it also applies to multi-core machines. Up to now, most HPC systems are built on such general-purpose

TABLE 7.3. TDP of the Top Four Processors Technologies Present in the Top500 List (November 2012)

Processor Technology	Top500 Count	Model Example	Maximum TDP	
Intel Nehalem	225 (45%)	Xeon X5650 6C 2.66 GHz	85 W	14.1 W/core
Intel Sandy Bridge	134 (26.8%)	Xeon E5-2680 8C 2.7 GHz	130 W	16.25 W/core
AMD x86_64	61 (12.2%)	Opteron 6200 16C "Interlagos"	115 W	7.2 W/core
IBM PowerPC	53 (10.6%)	Power BQC 16C 1.6 GHz	65 W	4.1 W/core

multi-core processors that use the x86 and power instruction sets (both to ensure backward productivity and enhance programmers productivity). They are mainly provided by three vendors: Intel (around 71% of the systems listed in the latest Top500 list,[1]) AMD (12%), and IBM (11%). While initially designed to target the workstation and laptop market, these processors admittedly offer very good single-thread performance (typically eight operations per cycle @ 2 GHz, i.e., 16 GFlops), yet at the price of a relative low energy efficiency. For instance, Table 7.3 details the Thermal Design Power (TDP) of the top four processors technologies present in the latest Top500 list.

Other systems, often referred to as Massively Parallel Processors (MPPs), feature a virtual shared memory with *global address space* over physically distributed memory. This type of architecture, generally quite expansive, corresponds to 16% of the computers present in the latest Top500 list.

7.2.1.3 MIMD with Distributed Memory: Clusters and Grids. A
low-cost alternative to MPPs features large-scale distributed systems such as clusters and grids. It corresponds to 83.4% of the systems listed in the latest Top500 list.

7.2.2 Overview of the Main HPC Components

At the heart of HPC systems rely the computing components, that is, central processing units (CPUs) (see Table 7.3) or GPGPUs. Another important component is the local memory that exists at different level as illustrated in Figure 7.4.

The interconnect backbone ensures high-performing communications between the resources of an HPC data center. The two key criteria at this level are the *latency* (i.e., the time to send a minimal (0 byte) message from A to B) and the *bandwidth* (the maximum amount of data communicated per unit of time). There exist several technologies, the main one being listed in Table 7.4. The most represented interconnect family in the latest Top500 list corresponds to the Infiniband technology (around 41%).

Of course, a software stack is mandatory to operate and exploit an HPC platform efficiently. Nearly every reasonable infrastructure features a Linux Operating System (OS) (95.2% of the systems ranked in the latest Top500 list). As regards the type of architecture deployed in HPC data centers, most of them corresponds to clusters (83.4% of the Top500 list). Computer clusters are generally organized in the configuration illustrated in Figure 7.5, thus features

[1] Top500 List of November 2012 – see http://top500.org.

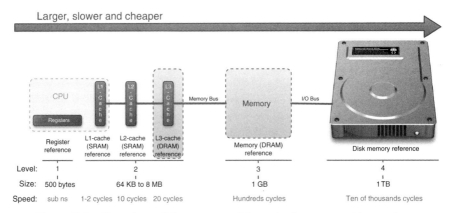

Figure 7.4.   Overview of the memory hierarchy in a computing system.

TABLE 7.4.   Overview of the Main Interconnect Technologies

Technology	Effective Bandwidth		Latency, μs
Gigabit Ethernet	1 Gb/s	125 MB/s	40–300
Myrinet (Myri-10G)	9.6 Gb/s	1.2 GB/s	2.3
10 Gigabit Ethernet	10 Gb/s	1.25 GB/s	4–5
Infiniband QDR	40 Gb/s	5 GB/s	1.29–2.6
SGI NUMAlink	60 Gb/s	7.5 GB/s	1

– an `access` server used as a Secure Shell (SSH) interface for the user to the cluster that grants the access to the cluster internals;
– a user `frontend` (eventually merged with the access node), used to reserve nodes on the cluster, etc.;
– an `adminfront`, often virtualized (typically over the Xen hypervisor [4]), which hosts the different services required to manage the cluster either to deploy the computing nodes or to manage various configuration aspects on the cluster such as the user authentication [generally via a Lightweight Directory Access Protocol (LDAP) directory] or the Resource and Job Management System (RJMS) (MOAB, OAR, SLURM, etc.);
– a shared storage area, typically over a network file system such as Network File System (NFS), General Parallel File System (GPFS), or Lustre, used for data sharing (homedirs, etc.) among the computing nodes and the user frontend;
– the computing nodes and the fast interconnect equipment (typically based on the technologies listed in Table 7.4).

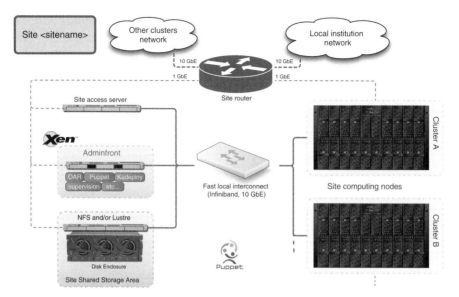

Figure 7.5. General organization of a computing clusters.

7.2.2.1 Data Center Cooling Technologies. One of the key factors to operate an HPC platform and obtain the expected performance is the cooling. There are many factors that must be considered before deciding on a cooling approach to use in a given data center. Energy usage, installation specifics such as the location of the data center itself (does it stand in a cold area etc.), the density of the data center on a per rack and kilowatt per square meter level, and other user-specific requirements will all impact this decision. The following reviews the literature with regards to cooling technologies.

Over the years, many methods have been used to cool information and technology (IT) loads in the data center environment.

7.2.3 HPC Performance and Energy Efficiency Evaluation

The way that performance is measured is critical, as it can determine if a server or other equipment will meet a consumer's needs or be eligible for utility rebates or required as part of federal or state procurement requirements. Developing performance metrics for even the simplest types of equipment can prove difficult and controversial. For this reason, in 1988, the System Performance Evaluation Cooperative (now named Standard Performance Evaluation Corporation, SPEC) was founded. It is a nonprofit organization that develops benchmarks for computers and is continuously working on energy-performance protocols – for small- to medium-sized servers. Currently, it is one of the more successful performance standardization bodies. It develops suites of benchmarks intended to measure computer efficiency, aimed to test "real-life" situations. They are publicly available for a fee covering development and administrative costs. Thanks to these standardized benchmarks, it is possible to compare the performance of different machines and rank them.

7.2.3.1 The High-Performance Linpack (HPL) Benchmark and the Green500 Challenge.

There are a few initiatives aimed at providing the list of computers in terms of performance or energy efficiency. One of the most popular is the TOP500 project [1] mentioned previously. Since 2003, twice a year it ranks the 500 most powerful computer systems in the world. The current fastest supercomputer, Tianhe-2, achieved a score which is 560,000 better than the fastest supercomputer in 1993.

The ranking itself relies on results obtained by running the High-Performance Linpack (HPL) reference benchmark [5]. HPL is a software package that solves a (random) dense linear system in double precision (64 bits) arithmetic on distributed-memory computers. This suit was chosen, thanks to it's widespread use. The result does not reflect the overall performance of a given system, but rather reflects the performance of a dedicated system for solving a dense system of linear equations. The list was often misinterpreted, and often regarded as a general rank that is valid for all applications. To fully examine the performance of the system, an approach consisting of different benchmarks, testing different parts of a supercomputer, is required.

One of the main advantages of Linpack is its scalability. It has been used since the beginning of the list, making it possible to benchmark systems that cover a performance range of 12 orders of magnitude. Moreover, it also measures the reliability for new HPC systems. Some systems were not able to run the Linpack benchmark because they were not stable enough.

Many of these supercomputers consume vast amounts of electrical power and produce so much heat that large cooling facilities must be constructed to ensure proper performance.

In parallel and for decades, the notion of HPC performance has been synonymous with speed (as measured in Flops). In order to raise awareness of other performance metrics than the pure computing speed (as measured in Flops for instance by the HPL suit), the Green500 project [6] was launched in 2005 to evaluate the "performance per watt" (PpW) and energy efficiency for improved reliability. More precisely, the PpW metric is defined as follows:

$$\text{PpW} = \frac{R_{\text{max}} \quad (\text{in MFlops})}{\text{Power } (R_{\text{max}}) \quad (\text{in W})}$$

This metric is particularly interesting because it is somehow independent of the actual number of physical nodes.

Currently, most energy-effective (Green500 list from June) supercomputer is Eurora, with 3208.83 MFlops/W. On the TOP500 list, it takes four hundred and sixty seventh place. By extrapolating its performance to exascale results, it would result in 312-MW machine. The electricity bills for such a system would be more than 300 million USD/year. As current requirements for such a system require the power draw not higher than 20–30 MW, it clearly shows the scale of the challenge that will be faced before building an exascale system.

Since the launch of the Green500 list, the energy efficiency of the highest-ranked machines has improved by only about 11%. Their performance has increased at a higher rate. It was due to the fact that for decades, there was an emphasis on speed as being the most important metric. The Green500 seeks to raise awareness of energy efficiency of supercomputers and treats them with equal importance as speed.

7.2.3.2 The [Green]Graph500 Benchmark Suit. Emerging large-data problems have different performance characteristics and architectural requirements than the floating point performance-oriented problems. Supercomputers are typically optimized for the 3D simulation of physics. For this reason, in 2010, the Graph 500 list was created to provide information on the suitability of supercomputing systems for data-intensive applications. Three key classes of graph kernels with multiple possible implementations were proposed: search, optimization, and edge oriented [7]. In parallel, the Green Graph 500 was created, to complement the Graph 500 list with an energy metric for data-intensive computing.

The emergence of such "green" lists clearly shows that greater importance is attached to the power consumed by computing systems. There have also been many metrics devised, which try to quantitatively describe the energy effectiveness of whole data centers. One of the most widely used is power usage effectiveness (PUE) [8]. It is the recommended metric for characterizing and reporting overall data center infrastructure efficiency. Its value indicates the relation between the fraction of power used only for components of the IT (servers, racks, etc.) and the complete power consumption of a data center.

7.2.3.3 The HPC Challenge (HPCC). Recently, the HPL benchmark has been integrated in a more general benchmark suite, named high-performance computing challenge (HPCC), which quickly became the industry standard suite used to stress the performance of multiple aspects of an HPC system, from the pure computing power to the disk/random access memory (RAM) usage or the network interface efficiency. More precisely, HPCC basically consists of seven tests:

1. HPL (the High-Performance Linpack benchmark), which measures the floating point rate of execution for solving a linear system of equations.
2. DGEMM – measures the floating point rate of execution of double precision real matrix–matrix multiplication.
3. STREAM – a simple synthetic benchmark program that measures sustainable memory bandwidth (in GB/s) and the corresponding computation rate for simple vector kernel.
4. PTRANS (parallel matrix transpose) – exercises the communications where pairs of processors communicate with each other simultaneously. It is a useful test of the total communications' capacity of the network.
5. RandomAccess – measures the rate of integer random updates of memory (giga-updates per second, GUPS).
6. FFT – measures the floating point rate of execution of double precision complex one-dimensional discrete Fourier transform (DFT).
7. Communication bandwidth and latency – a set of tests to measure latency and bandwidth of a number of simultaneous communication patterns.

7.2.3.4 I/O Performance Evaluation: IOZone and IOR. IOZone [9] is a complete cross-platform suite that generates and measures a variety of file operations.

IOZone is useful for performing a broad file system analysis of a given computing platform, covering tests for file I/O performances for many operations (Read, write, re-read, re-write, read backwards/strided, mmap, etc.)

IOR [10] is another I/O benchmark which is of interest when evaluating HPC data center components that generally feature shared storage based on distributed and parallel File System (FS) such as Lustre or General Parallel File System (GPFS). In this context, IOR permits to benchmark parallel file systems using POSIX, MPIIO, or HDF5 interfaces.

7.2.3.5 Measuring Data Center Energy Efficiency: The PUE Metric. A
key element for evaluating data center energy efficiency lies in the metrics used to assess this efficiency. Increased awareness of data centers' impact and increase in energy prices have stimulated the search for synthetic metrics to define and quantify energy efficiency. One of the first step was in 2003 when the Uptime Instituted proposed the Triton Coefficient of Effectiveness (total utility energy for the whole data center divided by the critical load in the computer room [11]).

Most classical metrics have raw performances as the sole focus, such as number of requests per second for services or Flops (floating point operations per seconds) for HPC systems. As the need for more eco-friendly metrics arose, several metrics were proposed. The Green Grid institution helped in making the PUE [12], which has been widely adopted since 2007. This metric is studied since 2013 to become a standard by governmental standardization bodies [13].

$$PUE = \frac{\text{Total data center energy consumption or power}}{\text{IT energy consumption or power}}$$

One of the limits of those metrics is that they do not take into account time and thus heat transfers. Metrics such as thermal imbalance [14] try to take into those elements.

7.3 BUILDING THE PATH TO EXASCALE COMPUTING

7.3.1 The Exascale Challenge: Hardware and Architecture Issues

There are a lot of challenges that need to be faced by the HPC community in the area of low-power computing devices. One of them is to build an exascale HPC system by 2020. The current fastest supercomputer featured in the top500 list, Tianhe-2 [1], consumes around 17 MW of power. Currently, the most efficient system needs 1–2 MW/PFlops. By multiplying it by 1000, to get the exascale, the required power becomes unaffordable. The most optimistic current predictions for exascale computers in 2020 envision a power consumption of 20–30 MW. It is, however, about 1 million times less power efficient than the human brain, which consumes 20–40 W. This comparison shows many challenges that the computing community needs to take on.

Current measures within a typical blade server estimate that 32.5% of its supplied power are distributed to the processor. Thus, some simple arithmetic calculations permit to estimate the average consumption per core in such an EFlops system: around 6.4 MW would be dedicated to the computing elements. Their number can be quantified by dividing the target computing capacity (1 EFlops) by one of the current computing cores (16 GFlops), thus leading to approximately 62.5×10^6 cores within an exascale system. Consequently, such a platform requires a maximal power consumption of 0.1 W/core.

To achieve this goal, alternative low-power processor architectures are required. There are two main directions currently explored: (i) relying on GPGPU accelerators and (ii) using the low-power processors. They are often combined, such as in the European Mont Blanc project [15], which aims at building an exascale HPC system. It plans to use ARM CPUs combined with Nvidia GPUs to achieve high-processing speed at low power consumption. The project aims at decreasing the power consumption at least 15- to 20-fold compared to current fastest supercomputers.

7.3.2 Energy Efficiency and Resource and Job Management System (RJMS)

The performance of an HPC system, and in particular its energy efficiency, is obviously determined by the unitary performance of the subsystems that compose it and also by the efficiency of their interactions and management by the middleware. In these kinds of systems, a central component called the Resource and Job Management System (RJMS) is in charge of managing the users' tasks (jobs) on the system's computing resources. The RJMS has a strategic position in the whole HPC software stack as it has a constant knowledge of both workload and resources.

RJMS middleware has to deal with several problems to be efficient. First, it has to be able to equitably distribute the computing resources to user applications. This is one of the prerequisites for user satisfaction. Then, it has to keep a fairly high level of utilization of the platform resources and avoid utilization "holes" as much as possible. In order to provide the best service to the users, RJMS configuration and scheduling policies have to reflect the user needs and their input workload. Also by its central position, the RJMS is key to operate energy-efficient decisions, assuming that the user workload is better modeled and characterized.

Actually, the understanding of users' workloads has motivated the study of production platform through the collection of traces from such systems and to the proposal of a standard: the Standard Workload Format (SWF) [16]. It is an initiative to make workload data on parallel machines freely available and to be presented in a common format. This work, along with workload data collection, is presented in the Parallel Workload Archive (PWA).[2] The idea is to collect and redistribute several traces from real production systems built from the logs of computing clusters. With SWF, one can work with several logs with the same tools and the format enables to be abstracted from the complexity of mastering different ad-hoc logs from batch schedulers. These contributions have enabled the study of numerous workload traces. This has also led to the construction of several models, based on the statistical analysis of the different workloads from the collection.

In many of the workloads provided in the PWA, it was observed that the system resources utilization showed unused periods and that the service rate is higher than the

---

[2]See http://www.cs.huji.ac.il/labs/parallel/workload.

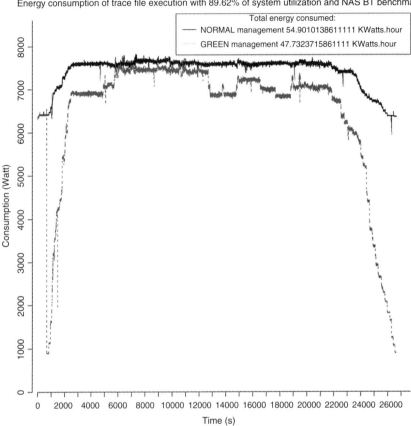

Figure 7.6.   Energy consumption for NAS BT benchmark upon a 32-node (biCPU) cluster with OAR. *Source*: Courtesy of Yiannis Georgiou [24].

arrival rate [17]. If the low utilization comes from a bad management of the resources, this will impact the users (and administrators) satisfaction. A platform not fully used while many jobs are still waiting to be granted for computing resources can be a symptom of this problem. If the low utilization is caused by an intrinsically low workload by the users, several techniques to take benefit of this underutilization can be used, such as energy saving, that idles unused resources and saves electrical power [18, 19]. The objective here is to define hibernation strategies that grant computing node to be powered off when idle during specific intervals. This mode is more and more present in recent RJMS such as OAR [20] (the RJMS used in Grid5000 or the UL HPC platform, for instance), the idea being to wake up *sleeping* nodes when there is a job that needs the "Powered OFF" resources. The benefit from such energy-saving techniques has already been proved by the GREEN-NET framework [19] works, as depicted in Figure 7.6. At this level, the intelligent placement of tasks and the shutdown of unused resources enabled an interesting energy gain, even with a high utilization of the platform.

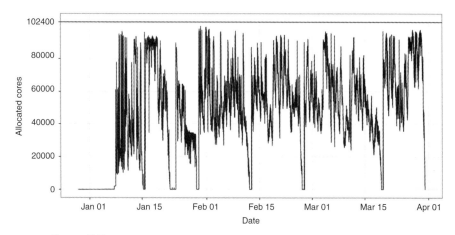

Figure 7.7. System utilization for TACC Stampede cluster *Source*: Ref. 25.

Compared to the state-of-the-art research, actual implementation in production RJMS is still thin. One of the most installed RJMS, Torque/Maui [21, 22], still only support simple hand-coded policies. Nevertheless, movements to support energy- and power-related policies are emerging. For example, Slurm [23] is now able to compute the expected power consumption of a node, given a particular workload, and is using such information to abide by a power budget. As previously described, OAR [20] is one of the most advanced RJMS in this sector, as it allows the user to submit tasks with power-related information such as maximum frequency and need of disks and using those information, tunes the hardware to reduce power consumption.

Research on this topic aims at building an energy-efficient scheduling through an accurate workload prediction model. Indeed, energy demand in cluster environment is directly proportional to the size of the cluster and the typical usage of the machines varies with time. This behavior is well visible in Figure 7.7, representing TACC Stampede[3] cluster system utilization in its first production months. During daytime, the load is likely to be more than that during night. Similarly, the load drastically decreases over the weekend. Of course, workloads can change upon different cluster configurations, and energy saving can occur if this pattern can be captured. Hence, a need for a prediction model arises and the research community currently focuses its effort on the characterization of this model. The objective at this level is to scan for current and future workload and tries to correlate it with the past load history to design an accurate energy-saving policy.

Nevertheless, having an accurate workload model is not enough to increase the acceptance level of the users when an energy-saving mode is activated. In practice, the hibernation strategy described earlier generally degrades the average slowdown of the platform. For a given job, this quantity corresponds for a given job to the ratio between the time spent by it in the system (wait time + run time) and the effective computation time (run time). A slowdown of 1 means that the job did not wait, a slowdown

---

[3]http://www.tacc.utexas.edu/resources/hpc/stampede.

Figure 7.8. Illustration of the two parameters to be continuously optimized when a hibernation strategy is in place.

of 2 means that the job waited as much as it ran. Thus the slowdown is affected by the delay required to wake up (i.e., boot) the computing resource. Improving the slowdown of a platform when an energy-saving mode is enabled assumes the continuous optimization of two key parameters associated to every computing resources of the platform: idle_time and sleep_time as illustrated in Figure 7.8. For a given resource, the first parameter affects the time to wait once the last job has finished before powering off the node. The second depicts how long the machine should remain in a sleeping state, that is, powered off. The key challenge is to avoid the next job scheduled on that resource to be penalized by a delay to powering up such that in the ideal case, the arrival of a new job is statistically anticipated to power up the machine even before the submission so as to make the resource available at the time of submission.

7.3.3   Energy-Aware Software

Being able to produce energy-aware software without reducing its testability, scalability, and security is a major goal of the high-performance community. In this context, a cutting-edge approach operates at the source-code level by means of Evolutionary Algorithms (EAs) to produced derived versions of that code which, once compiled, generate a program that consumes less energy when executed on a given computing platform.

Measuring this consumption is not easy, as it means an extrapolation of a process consumption once the global consumption of the computing platform is known.

7.3.4   A Methodology for Energy Reduction in HPC

Unlike hardware-based solution to the energy consumption issue in HPC, software-based initiative fails to find their way into real HPC deployments for reasons including their complex nature that often requires vast technical knowledge behind the proposed solution and/or applications at hand. Also, they fail to follow current trends; although the processor has traditionally dominated the energy consumption of a typical supercomputer, the tendency is being reversed. More precisely, projections indicate that the energy consumption of the processor will account for little in the global energy picture of an exascale system [26]. So all HPC subsystems from the memory to the processor to the communication and storage subsystems must be taken into account when designing energy reduction policies for HPC systems.

This section presents a general-purpose methodology for reducing the energy consumption of large-scale and distributed infrastructures focusing on HPC systems. Given that a typical HPC system is likely to experience periods wherein it is energy inefficient because of workload variability or variabilities within a specific workload. The proposed methodology lies on the fact that by observing a specific system while identifying periods wherein it is energy inefficient; one can make energy reduction decisions when the system experiences such periods again. To achieve that aim, our proposal breaks into three steps which we refer to, respectively, as (i) phase detection, (ii) phase characterization, and (iii) phase identification and system reconfiguration. There is no uniform definition of a phase; however, to ease the understanding of each of these steps, it is necessary to provide a clear definition of that term. We define a system phase as a region/period of execution of an application or a system relatively stable with respect to a given metric. Also, we use the term system to designate a single computing or storage node in an HPC system.

7.3.4.1   Phase Detection. Phase detection attempts to detect changes in the system's behavior that result from changes in the behavior of programs being executed. To accomplish this, we propose two complementary phase detection schemes: the power-based phase detection schemes [27] and the execution-vector-based phase detection scheme [28].

The power-based phase detection scheme, which is offline, makes use of the system power profile relying on two basic assumptions. The first one states that the power consumption of a system depends on the application being executed, while the second states that power consumption of the system under a specific type of workload can accurately be estimated or predicted using a specific set of variables. Using the just mentioned assumptions, the power-based phase detection detects changes in the system's behavior when a change occurs in the set of variables used to predict its power usage.

Suited to online use, the Execution-Vector (EV) based phase detection relies on the concept of execution vector. We define an execution vector as a column vector of sensors including hardware performance counters, disk read and write, and network byte sent/received counts. Hardware performance counters provide insights into the processor and memory activities, while network- and disk-related sensor provide information about disk and network activities, respectively. So, technically, an execution vector captures the system's behavior through resource utilization over a time unit. In using the concept of execution vector, a phase change occurs when the Manhattan distance, which is used here as a similarity metric, between consecutive execution vectors exceeds a threshold which varies throughout the system's life time.

7.3.4.2   Phase Characterization. Phase detection allows us to detect phase changes in the systems behavior, but because the objective of the whole methodology is to optimize the system when a known phase reappears again, it is necessary to know what happened during each and every detected phase. That purpose is served by the second step of our methodology, that is, phase characterization. It is the step where we associate useful information to known phases. The objective of phase characterization as defined herein is to group phases into classes so that similar phases from resource

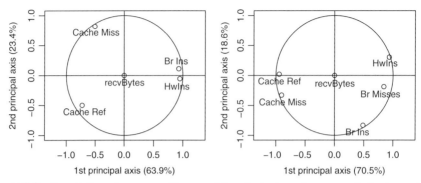

Figure 7.9. Correlation of sensors with respect to principal axes/components for two mixed workloads. (a) Fourier transform (FT) and (b) block tri-diagonal solver (BT).

utilization perspective appear under the same label. To accomplish this, we first define five labels in line with HPC applications: *compute intensive, memory intensive, mixed, communication intensive, and IO intensive*. These labels are self-explanatory except for the mixed label, which simply means that the phase is both compute intensive and memory intensive. Also, because in most systems sending data requires more processing than receiving the communication-intensive class can further be divided into network transmit and network received.

Second, as the effectiveness of the last step of the methodology lies on the accuracy of the characterization process, we propose three complementary characterization schemes at this stage. We refer the last-level cache references per instruction ratio (LLCRIR)-based phase characterization scheme and two statistical-based phase characterization schemes as principal component analysis (PCA)-based and sensor-based phase characterization, respectively. In this work, we only highlight the PCA-based phase characterization schemes. However, interested readers can refer to [29] for more details.

The aim of the principal component analysis bases or in short PCA-based characterization scheme is to discover patterns shared by workloads of the same category. To achieve that aim, we apply PCA to datasets made up of execution vectors collected when running workloads regarded as reference workloads. Figure 7.9 depicts the correlation of sensors with the first and second principal axis of PCA for two mixed workloads: Fourier transform (FT) and block tridiagonal solver (BT) from NAS parallel benchmark suite [30]. Note, the correlation of a variable/sensor with a principal component (PC) is defined as the value of that PC in the projection onto the plane of PCs. Figure 7.9 reveals that the first PC (first principal axis) opposes sensors related to the processor (hardware instruction, branch instructions, and branch misses) to those related to the memory (cache references and cache misses) in both cases. Therefore, we can postulate that for mixed workloads, the sensors related to the processor are opposed to those related to the memory. Also, given that the correlation of network- and IO-related sensors with PCs is nearly zero, we can claim that for mixed workloads, the correlation of IO- and network-related sensors with PCs is insignificant. A similar analysis can be waged for characterizing all categories of workloads.

7.3.4.3 Phase Identification and System Reconfiguration. As discussed earlier herein, the leading idea of our methodology is that by observing the system and identifying phases of execution wherein it is overprovisioned, we can accurately optimize that system for recurring phases. We have presented phase detection and phase characterization that allows us to find out points where the system changes its behavior and tell whether it needs to be optimized. Now, we are left with finding a way to identify recurring phases and perform system optimization accordingly. That purpose is served by the third and last step of our methodology.

It is actually the step wherein phase detection and phase characterization are exploited for reuse of optimal configuration information for recurring phases. However, at this point, we encounter two limiting factors. At the one hand, phases are often too large to efficiently represent and compare in the hardware. To overcome that limitation, we represent a phase with a single execution vector which we refer to as reference execution vector. The reference execution vector is defined as the closest EV to the centroid of the group of EVs belonging to the corresponding phase. With this representation, comparing two phases boils down to comparing their reference execution vectors.

On the other hand, a phase cannot be identified until it has completed. The literature suggests phase prediction; however, we cannot predict the next phase, as we do not have any useful information with regards to the system's workloads and it is likely to run multiple applications at the same time. Instead of predicting upcoming phases, we propose two alternatives to phase prediction: (i) *partial phase recognition and (ii) EV classification.* Partial phase recognition identifies an existing phase with an ongoing phase before its completion; it typically identifies a small portion of the phase and extrapolates the result to the remaining portion if successful; However, this does not work well when the two phases do not have the same length. The EV classification approach bypasses that limitation; instead of identifying a phase, it attempts to match each incoming EV to known phases and predicts the behavior of the system for the next sampling interval using a principle widely exploited by caching algorithms. The just mentioned principle can be formulated as follows: if at time t the system is in a specific phase, it is likely to remain in that very phase at time $t + 1$.

Thus far we have been focusing on techniques that allow us to reconfigure the system. At this point, we can reconfigure a system either for energy reduction or for performance improvement (reduction of applications' execution). In our case, all system reconfiguration decisions are destined to reduce the energy consumption of the system without significant performance degradation of applications' performance. We refer to reconfiguration actions that meet those criteria as power-saving schemes or green capabilities. Also, the term "significant performance degradation" being a relative term we use it to refer to a performance degradation higher than 10%. We next propose several power-saving schemes from management practices to actual system reconfiguration [29]. These include memory size scaling, CPU core switch on/off, and platform selection. Memory size scaling consists of switching off memory banks when they are suspected not to be used and back on when needed. Similarly, CPU core switch on/off consists of switching on/off one or more CPU cores depending on the computing demand. Speaking of platform selection, it boils down to selecting the most energy-efficient platform with respect to the application at hand.

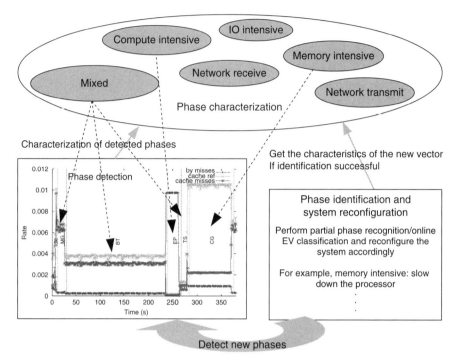

Figure 7.10. A summary of the methodology on a system that successively runs five different Multi-Grid (MG), BT, Embarrassingly Parallel (EP), Integer Sort (IS), and Conjugate Gradient (CG) from NAS parallel benchmark suite.

There also exists traditional power-saving schemes. They are traditional because they are loosely supported by existing hardware. Those include dynamic voltage and frequency scaling (DVFS), adaptive link rate (ALR), and disk-operating modes.

In summary, we have presented a complete methodology, summarized in Figure 7.10, that allows us to observe a system at runtime, detect phases, characterize them in order to determine whether system optimization will be required, and, finally, propose means for reconfiguring a system for energy-saving purposes relying on recurring phases identification.

7.3.4.4 Evaluation of the Methodology. To see how our proposal works in reality, we introduce a Multi-Resource Energy Efficient Framework (MREEF). MREEF implements our three-step methodology through two components: a coordinator and a system reconfiguration enforcer. The coordinator is responsible for all system-profiling-related tasks including phase detection, phase characterization, phase identification, and phase prediction. When it comes to the system reconfiguration enforcer, it is responsible for implementing power-saving schemes and reading execution vectors. By adopting a framework implementation, we leave users with the possibility of integrating their own power-saving schemes without worrying about all system-profiling-related tasks. Also one can think of several management strategies for the platform; for example, coordinated and decentralized. In its current development, MREEF is approximately 3000 lines of codes written in R, Python, and C.

We evaluate our methodology through MREEF, which we compare to Linux on-demand and performance configuration, on a 25-node cluster set up on the Grid'5000 [31] French large-scale and distributed platform. As test workload, we consider two real-life applications: the Advance Research Weather Research and Forecasting (WRF-ARW) [32] and molecular dynamics simulation (MDS) [33]. In a few words, molecular dynamics solves numerical Newton's equations of motion for the interaction of the many particles system, whereas WRF-ARW is a fully compressible conservative-form nonhydrostatic atmospheric model. It uses an implicit time-splitting integration technique to efficiently integrate the Euler equation.

The comparison with Linux on-demand and performance governors makes sense because they appear to be the closest energy reduction policies to our methodology. Speaking of system configurations, on-demand (respectively, performance configuration) means that the Linux on-demand (respectively, performance) governor is enabled on all nodes of the cluster of concern.

In this experiment, we are interested in reconfiguring multiple hardware including the processor, the disk, and the network interconnect (NIC). Reconfiguring the processor consists of scaling its frequency through DVFS, while reconfiguring the disk boils down to forcing it to sleep when it is suspected not to be in used. As far as the NIC is concerned, reconfiguring it consists of bringing the 1-Gb link down to 10 Mb when the NIC is suspected not to be in use and back to 1 Gb when needed.

Figure 7.11, which shows normalized energy consumption and execution time of WRF-ARW and MDS in each system configuration, offers an outline of the comparison of MREEF configuration with on-demand and performance configurations for our test workloads. We notice an energy reduction of up to 24% without a priori information about applications and with less than 4% performance degradation. Our analysis indicates that in that achievement, reconfiguring the disk and the NIC accounts for nearly 4%; further details can be found in [29]. What we learn from this experiment is that energy reduction in HPC systems can benefit from more than the "traditional" CPU

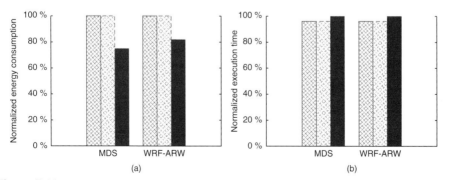

Figure 7.11. Normalized energy consumption and execution time of MDS and WRF-ARW in each of the three-system configurations. (a) Energy consumption and (b) execution time.

frequency scaling. To conclude this section, HPC systems can fully benefit from our MREEF and, therefore, from our methodology for reducing their energy consumption.

7.4   ENERGY EFFICIENCY OF VIRTUALIZATION AND CLOUD FRAMEWORKS OVER HPC WORKLOADS

Virtualization is emerging as the prominent approach to mutualize the energy consumed by a single server running multiple virtual machines (VMs) instances. However, little understanding has been obtained about the potential overhead in energy consumption and the throughput reduction for virtualized servers and/or computing resources, or if it simply suits an environment as high demanding as an HPC platform. Actually, this question is connected with the rise of CC increasingly advertised as THE solution to most IT problems. Several voices (most probably commercial ones) emit the wish that CC platforms could also serve HPC needs and eventually replace in-house HPC platforms.

The central component of any virtualization framework, and thus Cloud middleware, remain the *hypervisor* or VM manager. Subsequently, a Virtual Machine (VM) running under a given hypervisor is called a guest machine. There exist two types of hypervisors, either *native* or *hosted*, yet only the first class (also named bare-metal) presents an interest for the HPC context. This category of hypervisor runs directly on the host's hardware to control the hardware and to manage guest-operating systems. Among the many potential approaches of this type available today, the virtualization technology of choice for most open platforms over the past 7 years has been the Xen hypervisor [4]. More recently, the Kernel-based Virtual Machine (KVM) [34] and VMWare ESXi [35] have also known widespread deployment within the HPC community, unlike the remaining frameworks that are available (such as Microsoft's Hyper-V or OpenVZ).

In this context, a couple of recent studies demonstrate that the overhead induced by the Cloud hypervisors cannot be neglected for a pure HPC workload. For instance, in [36, 37], the authors proposed a performance evaluation and modeling over HPC benchmarks for the three most widespread hypervisors at the heart of most if not all CC middleware: Xen, KVM, and VMWare ESXi. At this level, the Grid'5000 platform [38] was used to perform the experimental study. Grid'5000 is a scientific instrument for the study of large- scale parallel and distributed systems. It aims at providing a highly reconfigurable, controllable, and monitorable experimental platform to support experiment-driven research in all areas of computer science related to parallel, large-scale, or distributed computing and networking, including the CC environments [39]. The study proposed in [37] is relevant to the computing and power performance of the different hypervisors when compared to a "bare-metal" configuration (also referred to as the `baseline` environment corresponding to classical HPC computing nodes) running in native mode, that is, without any hypervisor.

The scalability of each virtualization middleware is then evaluated under two perspectives:

1. For a fixed number of physical hosts that run an increasing number of VMs (from 1 to 12) – see Figure 7.12. It perfectly illustrates the obvious limitation raised by

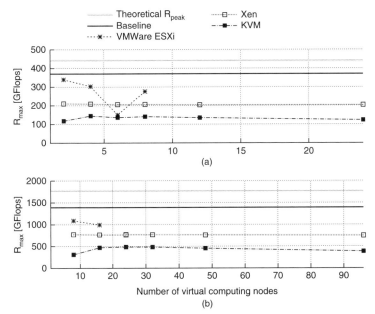

Figure 7.12. HPL performances for fixed numbers of physical nodes with increasing number of VMs per physical host. Baseline execution uses the number of actual physical nodes (a) Hypervisors running on two physical hosts and (b) hypervisors running on eight physical hosts.

a multi-VM environment as the performance is bounded by the maximal capacity of the physical host running the hypervisors. Also, we can see that for a computing application as demanding as HPL, the VMWare ESXi hypervisor performs generally better even if this statement is balanced by the fact that the VMWare environment appeared particularly unstable (it was impossible to complete successful runs for more than four VMs) when both Xen and KVM frameworks offer unmatched scalability.

2. For a fixed number of VM (between 1 and 12), increasing the number of physical hosts (between 1 and 8) – see Figure 7.13. It highlights a rather good scalability of the hypervisors when physical nodes are added.

Of importance in this chapter is the analysis using the virtual resources as a basis for the comparisons. It means hypervisor executions on N nodes with V VMs per nodes are compared to baseline executions on $N \times V$ physical nodes. As this approach might appear unfair as the hardware capabilities are not the same, this illustrates the point of view of the user who may not know the underlying hardware his/her application is running on in a virtualized environment. In particular, the best obtained results are displayed in the Figure 7.14, which demonstrates the fast degradation in the computing efficiency when the number for computing nodes is artificially increased through virtualization.

To highlight the relative performance of each computing node, the *isoefficiency* $ISO_{effic.}(n)$ metric was defined for a given number of computing nodes n. This measure is based on the following definitions:

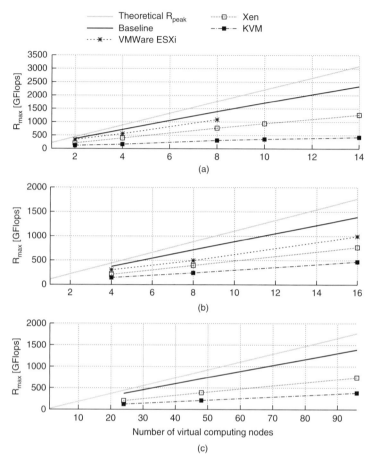

Figure 7.13. HPL Performances for fixed numbers of VMs with increasing number of physical nodes. Baseline execution uses the number of actual physical nodes (a) Hypervisors running 1 VM per physical host, (b) hypervisors running 2 VMs per physical host, and (c) hypervisors running 12 VMs per physical host.

- $\text{Perf}_{\text{base}}(n)$: HPL performance of the baseline environment involving n computing nodes;
- $\text{Perf}_{\text{base}}(1)$: Normalized performance of a bare-metal single node. For this study, as we only started our measures with two hosts, we approximate this value by $\text{Perf}_{\text{base}}(1) = \frac{\text{Perf}_{\text{base}}(2)}{2}$;
- $\text{Perf}_{\text{hyp}}(n)$: Maximal HPL performance of the virtualized environment based on the hypervisor hyp that feature a total of n computing nodes.

Then for a given hypervisor hyp,

$$\text{ISO}_{\text{effec.}}^{\text{hyp}}(n) = \frac{\text{Perf}_{\text{hyp}}(n)}{n \times \text{Perf}_{\text{base}}(1)}$$

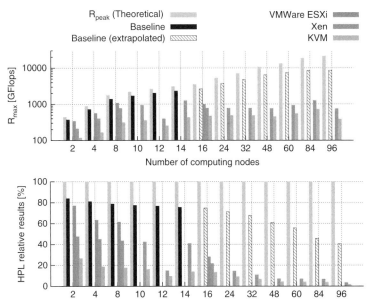

Figure 7.14. HPL efficiency of the considered hypervisors when compared to the baseline environment.

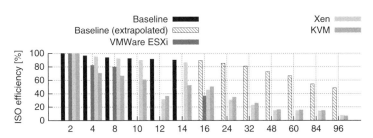

Figure 7.15. Isoefficiency evaluation for an increasing number of computing nodes.

This definition should not be confused with the classical isoefficiency metric used in parallel programs, the objective being here to simply normalize the hypervisor performance with regards to the best performance that can be obtained on a baseline environment, for example, $\text{Perf}_{\text{base}}(1)$. Figure 7.15 expounds the evolution of $\text{ISO}^{\text{hyp}}_{\text{effec.}}(n)$ with n. Again, this measure confirms that HPC workloads do not suit virtualized environments from a pure computing capacity point of view. The virtualized environment shows more available processors to the application. However, these computing resources have reduced performance compared to actual physical processors because they are shared for different VMs. This is perfectly highlighted by the HPL benchmark whose performance are mainly bounded by the performance of the processors.

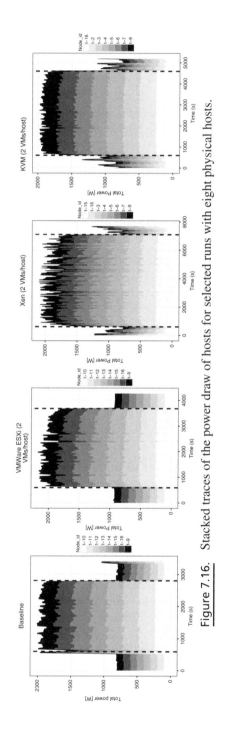

Figure 7.16. Stacked traces of the power draw of hosts for selected runs with eight physical hosts.

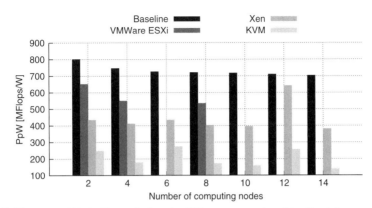

Figure 7.17. Green500 PpW metric for the HPL runs over the virtualized frameworks and comparison to the baseline environments.

All these performance evaluations confirm what other studies suggested in the past, that is, that the overhead induced by virtualized environments do not suit HPC workloads. Of interest in this chapter is the energy efficiency of the virtualized environments when running HPC workloads. For instance, Figure 7.16 illustrates the total power profile of a run involving each considered environment in a large-scale execution.

Figure 7.17 details the evolution of the PpW metric (as defined in the Green500 benchmark) over the baseline environment for an increasing number of computing nodes. We have compared these values with the cases where we have the corresponding PpW measure in the hypervisor environments. This figure outlines many interesting aspects. First of all, with a PpW measure comprised between 700 and 800 MFlops/W, the baseline platform would be ranked between the 93 and 112 position of the Green500 list. Although surprising at first glance, this result is easily explained by the usage of cutting-edge processors (Sandy Bridge) and the limited number of involved resources – the linear decrease is evident in the figure. The second conclusion that can be arrived from this figure is that virtualized environments do not even ensure a more energy-efficient usage during an HPC workload.

7.5 CONCLUSION: OPEN CHALLENGES

In this chapter, we presented an overview of the latest advances in energy-efficient computing systems. Current HPC facilities were described, together with the methods of evaluating their performance and energy efficiency. The research community is about to face many challenges on its way to build faster and more power-efficient systems. The road to exascale systems is still long. We presented some examples of technological and economical barriers that have to be overcome before building an exascale system.

ACKNOWLEDGMENTS

This work is partly supported by the INRIA large-scale initiative Hemera focused on "developing large-scale parallel and distributed experiments." Some experiments presented in this chapter were carried out using the Grid'5000 experimental testbed, being developed under the INRIA ALADDIN development action with support from CNRS, RENATER, and several universities as well as other funding bodies (see https://www.grid5000.fr). Some experiments presented in this chapter were carried out using the HPC facility of the University of Luxembourg.

REFERENCES

[1] The Top500 Project. [online] Available at: http://www.top500.org Accessed 2014 Sep 30.

[2] The Green500 Project. [online] Available at: http://www.green500.org Accessed 2014 Sep 30.

[3] Flynn M. Some computer organizations and their effectiveness. IEEE Trans Comput 1972;C-21:948–960.

[4] Barham P, Dragovic B, Fraser K, Hand S, Harris T, Ho A, Neugebauer R, Pratt I, Warfield A. Xen and the art of virtualization. Proceedings of the 19th ACM Symposium on Operating Systems Principles, SOSP '03. New York: ACM; 2003. p 164–177.

[5] Petitet A, Whaley C, Dongarra J, Cleary A, Luszczek P. HPL—A Portable Implementation of the High-Performance Linpack Benchmark for Distributed-Memory Computers; 2008.

[6] Sharma S, Hsu C-H, Feng W. Making a case for a Green500 list. 20th International Parallel and Distributed Processing Symposium, 2006. IPDPS 2006; 2006. p 8.

[7] Murphy RC, Wheeler KB, Barrett BW, Ang JA. Introducing the graph 500. Cray User Group; 2010.

[8] PUE (tm): A comprehensive examination of the metric. White paper, The Green Grid; 2012.

[9] Iozone Filesystem Benchmark. [online] Available at: http://www.iozone.org/ Accessed 2014 Sep 30.

[10] IOR HPC Benchmark. [online] Available at: http://sourceforge.net/projects/ior-sio/. Accessed 2014 Sep 30.

[11] Stanley JR, Brill KJ. Four metrics define data center 'greenness': Enabling users to quantify energy consumption initiatives for environmental sustainability and "bottom line" profitability. Technical report, Uptime Institute Inc.; TUI3009F; 2007.

[12] Malone C, Belady C. Metrics to characterize data center & IT equipment energy use. Proceedings of the Digital Power Forum; 2006.

[13] Force GMHT. Harmonizing global metrics for data center energy efficiency. Technical report, Global Taskforce Reaches Agreement on Measurement Protocols for PUE Continues Discussion of Additional Energy Efficiency Metrics; 2011.

[14] Laura S, Ramon BF, Assunta N, Jaume S, Georges DC, Eugen V, Andrew D. White paper on energy- and heat-aware metrics for computing modules. Technical report, CoolEmAll European Project; 2012.

[15] European Mont-Blanc Project. [online] Available at: http://www.montblanc-project.eu/. Accessed 2014 Sep 30.

[16] Chapin SJ, Cirne W, Feitelson DG, Jones JP, Leutenegger ST, Schwiegelshohn U, Smith W, Talby D. Benchmarks and standards for the evaluation of parallel job schedulers. In:

Feitelson DG, Rudolph L, editors. *JSSPP*. Volume 1659, Lecture Notes in Computer Science. Springer-Verlag; 1999. p 67–90.

[17] Feitelson DG, Tsafrir D, Krakov D. Experience with the parallel workloads archive. Technical report, School of Computer Science and Engineering, The Hebrew University of Jerusalem; 2012.

[18] Orgerie A-C, Lefèvre L, Gelas J-P. Save watts in your grid: green strategies for energy-aware framework in large scale distributed systems. 14th IEEE International Conference on Parallel and Distributed Systems (ICPADS); Dec 2008; Melbourne, Australia; 2008.

[19] Da-Costa G, Gelas J-P, Georgiou Y, Lefèvre L, Orgerie A-C, Pierson J-M, Richard O, Sharma K. The green-net framework: energy efficiency in large scale distributed systems. HPPAC 2009; 2009.

[20] Capit N, Da Costa G, Georgiou Y, Huard G, Martin C, Mounie G, Neyron P, Richard O. A batch scheduler with high level components. Cluster computing and Grid 2005 (CCGrid05); 2005.

[21] Staples G. Torque resource manager. Proceedings of the 2006 ACM/IEEE Conference on Supercomputing, SC '06. New York: ACM; 2006.

[22] Jackson D, Snell Q, Clement M. Core algorithms of the maui scheduler. *Job Scheduling Strategies for Parallel Processing*. Springer-Berlin Heidelberg; 2001. p 87–102.

[23] Yoo AB, Jette MA, Grondona M. Slurm: simple linux utility for resource management. *Job Scheduling Strategies for Parallel Processing*. Springer-Berlin Heidelberg; 2003. p 44–60.

[24] Georgiou Y. Contributions for resource and job management in high performance computing [PhD thesis]. Grenoble: LIG; 2010.

[25] Emeras J. Workload traces analysis and replay in large scale distributed systems [PhD thesis]. Grenoble: LIG; To be defended October 1st 2013. currently Available at: https://forge.imag .fr/docman/view.php/359/754/thesis_emeras_28aug13.pdf. Accessed 2014 Sep 30.

[26] Broekema PC, van Nieuwpoort RV, Bal HE. Exascale high performance computing in the square kilometer array. Proceedings of the 2012 Workshop on High-Performance Computing for Astronomy Date, Astro-HPC '12. New York: ACM; 2012. p 9–16.

[27] Tsafack G, Lefévre L, Pierson J, Stolf P, Costa GD. Exploiting performance counters to predict and improve energy performance of {HPC} systems. Future Gener Comput Syst 2013:118–125.

[28] Tsafack GL, Lefevre L, Pierson J-M, Stolf P, Da Costa G. A user friendly phase detection methodology for HPC systems' analysis. GreenCom 2013: The 2013 IEEE International Conference on Green Computing and Communications; Aug 2013. Beijing: IEEE; 2013.

[29] Chetsa GLT. System profiling and green capabilities for large scale and distributed infrastructures [PhD thesis]. École Normale Supérieure de Lyon; 2013.

[30] Bailey DH, Barszcz E, Barton JT, Browning DS, Carter RL, Fatoohi RA, Frederickson PO, Lasinski TA, Simon HD, Venkatakrishnan V, Weeratunga SK. The NAS parallel benchmarks. Technical report, The International Journal of Supercomputer Applications; 1991.

[31] Bolze R, Cappello F, Caron E, Daydé M, Desprez F, Jeannot E, Jégou Y, Lanteri S, Leduc J, Melab N, Mornet G, Namyst R, Primet P, Quetier B, Richard O, Talbi E-G, Touche I. Grid'5000: a large scale and highly reconfigurable experimental grid testbed. Int J High Perform Comput Appl 2006;20(4):481–494.

[32] Skamarock WC, Klemp JB, Dudhia J, Gill DO, Barker DM, Wang W, Powers JG. A description of the advanced research WRF version 2. NCAR Tech Note, NCAR/TN-468+STR; NCAR; Boulder, Colorado; 2005.

[33] Binder K, Horbach J, Kob W, Paul W, Varnik F. Molecular dynamics simulations. J Phys Condens Matter 2004;16(5):S429.

[34] Kivity A, Kamay Y, Laor D, Lublin U, Liguori A. KVM: the Linux virtual machine monitor. Ottawa Linux Symposium; 2007. p 225–230.

[35] Ali Q, Kiriansky V, Simons J, Zaroo P. Performance evaluation of HPC benchmarks on VMware's ESXi server. Proceedings of the 2011 International Conference on Parallel Processing, Euro-Par'11. Berlin, Heidelberg: Springer-Verlag; 2012. p 213–222.

[36] Guzek M, Varrette S, Plugaru V, Sanchez JE, Bouvry P. A holistic model of the performance and the energy-efficiency of hypervisors in an HPC environment. *Proceedings of the International Conference on Energy Efficiency in Large Scale Distributed Systems (EE-LSDS'13)*. Volume 8046, LNCS. Vienna: Springer-Verlag; 2013.

[37] Varrette S, Guzek M, Plugaru V, Besseron X, Bouvry P. HPC performance and energy-efficiency of Xen, KVM and VMware hypervisors. Proceedings of the 25th Symposium on Computer Architecture and High Performance Computing (SBAC-PAD 2013). Porto de Galinhas: IEEE Computer Society; 2013.

[38] Grid'5000. [online] Available at: http://grid5000.fr. Accessed 2014 Sep 30.

[39] Bolze R, Cappello F, Caron E, Desprez M, Daydé F, Jeannot E, Jégou Y, Lanteri S, Leduc J, Melab N, Mornet G, Namyst R, Primet P, Quetier B, Richard O, Talbi E-G, Touche I. Grid'5000: a large scale and highly reconfigurable experimental grid testbed. Int J High Perform Comput Appl 2006;20(4):481–494.

8

SCHEDULING AND RESOURCE ALLOCATION

Pragati Agrawal,[1] Damien Borgetto,[2] Carmela Comito,[3] Georges Da Costa,[2] Jean-Marc Pierson,[2] Payal Prakash,[1] Shrisha Rao,[1] Domenico Talia,[4] Cheikhou Thiam,[2] and Paolo Trunfio[4]

[1] *IIIT Bangalore, Bangalore, India*
[2] *IRIT, University of Toulouse, Toulouse, France*
[3] *ICAR, CNR, Rende, Italy*
[4] *DIMES, Università della Calabria, Rende, Italy*

8.1 INTRODUCTION: ENERGY-AWARE SCHEDULING

Scheduling is of course a well-known topic, having received extensive attention from practitioners as well as theoreticians. It is an important issue in operations research, as being of great importance in the management and operation of large chemical process systems, airlines, manufacturing equipment on a factory floor, etc. It is also studied by computer scientists, particularly in the context of chip-level processes and threads.

Almost all the work to date in scheduling has been concerned with reducing the makespan, that is, the time taken for a schedule of tasks to be completed (under given constraints). However, it is realized recently that reducing the energy consumed in completing a schedule is, in many contexts, a goal at least as worthy, and that time-minimal schedules need not be energy-minimal, so that energy-aware (EA) scheduling is a topic of study in its own right. With energy shortages, and rising costs of

Large-Scale Distributed Systems and Energy Efficiency: A Holistic View, First Edition.
Edited by Jean-Marc Pierson.
© 2015 John Wiley & Sons, Inc. Published 2015 by John Wiley & Sons, Inc.

energy, and other resources becoming a perennial reality across the globe, there is little doubt that scheduling and operations of systems at all sizes will perforce be required to be efficient not just in terms of the time taken to complete tasks but also in terms of the energy consumed thereby.

Most research in the past has dealt with scheduling on homogeneous systems to reduce the *makespan*, that is, the time taken to complete the schedule of tasks. However, scheduling problems become even more interesting and fruitful when we consider dissimilar machines while also taking into consideration that the total *energy* consumed in executing tasks should be reduced. EA scheduling is unfortunately at least as computationally intractable as minimum-makespan scheduling, which itself is known to be NP-hard. Even so, recent and ongoing work holds out promise that realistic and worthwhile approximation algorithms for EA scheduling, and protocols that apply them on practical systems, will be a reality in the near future, possibly within the next decade.

Therefore, in the present chapter, we look at some current directions and problems in EA scheduling. The first few sections consider some foundational issues, while the later ones discuss application of energy awareness and related concepts in specific application domains of some importance.

First comes a discussion on the use of linear programming (Section 8.2) in contexts where the problem size is not too large and then one of heuristics (Section 8.3) in cases where it is. We later compare allocation heuristics considering both makespan and energy reduction (Section 8.4).

The application contexts discussed are EA task allocation in mobile environments (Section 8.5), cloud computing (Section 8.6), and users of smart power grids (Section 8.7). Then we discuss (Section 8.8) some issues specific to EA operation of servers and data centers and offer some concluding remarks (Section 8.9) that we hope will show our vision for how this work can be carried forward.

8.2 USE OF LINEAR PROGRAMMING IN ENERGY-AWARE SCHEDULING

We start with a simple question: *How is one to characterize the quality of an allocation?*

Under this seemingly simple question lie numerous problems, mostly because the multiobjective optimization needed in the EA scheduling problem is conceived with incompatible objectives, namely, low-energy usage and high performance. That is why, instead of trying to resolve this question as a whole, we are forced to take another path. As we want to find allocations and schedules that are good, we instead need to ask ourselves not the quality of the solution as an absolute, but the quality of the solution in comparison with other solutions. That being said, one should note that this reasoning does not do away with the problem of finding the quality of a solution in an absolute sense.

8.2.1 Finding the Optimal Solution Using a Linear Program

In order to be able to compare two different algorithms, we have to either be able to actually quantify what the differences between the metrics of the solutions imply or else be able to rank them according to their respective distance from an optimal solution.

To do that, we chose to model the EA resource allocation problem using a set of linear constraints, in order to leverage linear program (LP) techniques to find a solution.

LP is a widely used technique [1, 2] for modeling problems and provides tools that allow us to describe a problem as two things: a set of linear constraints and an objective function to be either minimized or maximized. They allow to use several different methods to solve problems, such as the simplex method [3]. The fact that all constraints are linear gives the possibility to understand and model different aspects of the problem more easily and to test the validity of an allocation. For example, say we have a binary variable e_{jh} that represents the existence of a task j on a host h, meaning that $e_{jh} = 1$ if the task j is executing on the host h. We can model the set of constraints as

$$\forall j \quad \sum_j e_{jh} = 1. \tag{8.1}$$

Equation (8.1) then indicates that a task can only be executed on exactly one host, and we can use this simple linear constraint to test the validity of an allocation.

The set of linear constraints can sometimes contain both integer and rational variables. One should note here that using both integer and rational variables, a problem known as MIP (mixed integer program), is of significantly increased difficulty, on account of the noncontinuous aspects of integer variables.

In the case of the EA resource allocation problem, we have, for example, to represent the state of a machine, which is powered on or off, and this cannot be represented using a rational variable, because a host cannot be half powered on.

To begin with the LP, we have to describe our problem. This means that we have to write the set of linear constraints allowing us to describe and bound the behavior of the studied system.

We can then provide the different constraints as an input for LP solvers, such as Gurobi, CPLEX, or GLPK [4–6]. Those solvers solve the problem and give the optimal solution for the provided objective. The LP formalism has the advantage of the ability to describe a problem in a simple manner, using sets of linear constraints.

8.2.2   Benefits and Limitations of LP

With the use of such techniques, we are now able to answer the two questions: "Is this algorithm efficient?" and "Is this algorithm more efficient than another?" Moreover, it allows us to take into account the distance of a solution from the optimal. That way, we can say from experiments we conduct that an approximate solution is within a certain percentage range of the optimal.

There are, however, serious drawbacks to using LP to compare with an optimal solution. The main one is that due to the NP-hard nature of the resource allocation problem, the computation time increases exponentially with the size of the problem. As shown in Figure 8.1, it can on an average take rather long to solve even small instances (80 s on an average for instances of eight hosts and 16 tasks), but it can take even longer in the worst cases. There is a good chance that when we increase more than slightly the size of an instance of the problem, we cannot compute the results as we might want in a reasonable time. That is why the optimal solution is only computable and computed for small instances.

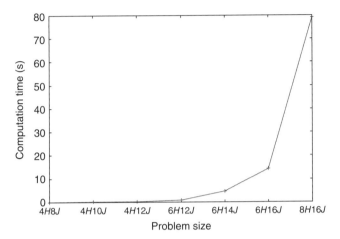

Figure 8.1. Mean time to compute the optimal solution for a system of *J* tasks and *H* hosts.

The small size of the problems that we can solve optimally become a problem as the complexity of the problem increases, because if the complexity increases too much, we might see that it reduces the size of the instance to a point where it is not relevant or to a point where the effects that we can observe do not apply for larger instances.

LP tools give us the ability to compute, in polynomial time, the rational upper bound on the optimal solution, given by relaxing all integer and binary variables into rational variables, thus yielding solutions that are not realistic (as when, e.g., a machine is half powered on).

The complications inherent in the resource allocation problem are also manifested when developing algorithms for it. This mostly means that for larger instances, meaning problem instances at the scale of real systems with hundreds of machines, one has to settle for an approximate solution computed using heuristics.

8.3   HEURISTICS IN LARGE INSTANCES

In this section, we describe how to adapt our algorithms for large-scale energy efficiency. For the resource allocation problem, there are numerous ways to model design algorithms. It can be as much a stochastic method as a multi-agent algorithm. In this section, we talk about manipulating algorithms called bin-packing algorithms. These algorithms aim to place volumes inside containers, in order to minimize the number of containers used.

Such a method means that we can reduce the resource allocation problem as a bin-packing problem, if we consider physical machines as containers and tasks as volumes. For tasks, each resource required [central processing unit (CPU), random access memory (RAM), etc.] corresponds to a dimension. In order to have an energy-efficient allocation, the resulting allocation should use a reduced amount of hosts.

To be able to handle large instances, we need to have efficient algorithms. As it means that we have to handle a large combinatorial space, the algorithms cannot be allowed to explore too large a portion of this space. The most intuitive and simplest algorithms that can be efficient are what we call greedy algorithms.

8.3.1 Energy-Aware Greedy Algorithms

There are several classical greedy resource allocation algorithms used in resource allocation field, such as First Fit, Best Fit, and Round Robin (RR).

First Fit aims at placing each volume in the first container on which it fits. If the volume cannot be contained in a container, then the algorithm tries the next one, and so on.

Best Fit functions similarly to the First Fit algorithm, but instead of placing in the first container, it tries to find the container in which the volume is best fitted, which means the container where there would be the least free space left over in the container after the volume is allocated to it.

RR functions as the name suggests. It attempts to allocate each volume on a different container and starts again on the first one when all containers have been used.

These resource allocation algorithms, even if they are able to work rather well in a single-dimensional environment, are not as well suited to use, as they are more complex resource allocation algorithms that are multidimensional and multiobjective in scope.

8.3.2 Vector Packing

We can design better algorithms to be able to tackle more complex problems. Such algorithms can, for example, be based on vector packing and thus be more suited for multidimensional environments.

In [7], an algorithm of vector packing is described, which performs really well with respect to consolidation of tasks in a high- utilization environment. The algorithm works as follows: first, separate tasks into as many different lists as there are dimensions, each list containing the tasks with the same highest dimension. This means that for an environment where we have CPU and RAM dimensions, we will have two lists: one with the tasks that have more CPU requirement than RAM and one with the tasks that have more RAM requirement than CPU. Second, allocate the tasks by choosing the first task that fits on a host in the list that counters the current imbalance of resource consumption of the host. This means that if we have a host that already has allocated tasks that consume more CPU overall than RAM, we choose the next task in the list where the tasks consume more RAM than CPU. Finally, we repeat this operation until there is either no task to allocate or no more host to fill. Variations of this algorithm have been studied elsewhere [2, 8] and have proven to consolidate tasks with good results, thus saving a lot of energy.

8.3.3 Improving Fast Algorithms

There is, however, a common denominator in all such greedy or meta-greedy algorithms: their performance as EA resource allocation algorithms relies heavily on the preliminary operations that we can make to improve their performance. This means, for example, that sorting tasks and hosts can greatly improve the performance of a resulting allocation, with respect to the problem domain we are in. For example, sorting the hosts in order to fill the most energy efficient first decreases the resulting power consumed. The power consumed by the system is, however, decided by the quality of the algorithm. So if sorting is paramount for good performances, we need an algorithm that is aware of both which hosts it will fill first and which tasks it will allocate in priority.

This awareness and the ability to make a good choice, at first attempt, in the allocation of a task, are what makes an algorithm stand out as the best. Although this is true for most algorithms, it is even harder to do in very large-scale environments, where the time to compute a solution cannot exceed certain values. There are lots of algorithms that yields good results but with poor performance with regard to computation time. For example, the algorithm based on the Monte Carlo method [9] gives good results both in terms of energy consumption and task performance but is hardly acceptable in terms of computation time as soon as we exceed a certain size of infrastructure. This is due to the fact that convergence of such probabilistic algorithms is slower the greater the size of the problem is, and this convergence is less precise if we bound the algorithm to compute in a reasonable amount of time.

8.4 COMPARING ALLOCATION HEURISTICS FOR ENERGY-AWARE SCHEDULING

This section starts with the formulation of the EA scheduling problem, as dealt with in depth elsewhere [10]. Two methods are presented so as to find a good schedule that reduces the total energy consumption of a system. Later subsections present comparisons with classical algorithms, given the system configuration and the tasks to be completed by it. The first algorithm considered is a genetic algorithm (Plain GA) and thus is basically a search method. Genetic algorithms have been used for makespan scheduling [11, 12]. The other algorithm, called efficiency-based allocation (EBA) uses a heuristic that tries to assign tasks to the most efficient machines available at the time of execution of the task. It is very fast but as it is based on a heuristic, it faces the same limitations as do other heuristic algorithms elsewhere.

These algorithms are tested on program graphs that are most commonly used by researchers in this field for testing their algorithms. The results give insights to the time-energy trade-offs found in many systems – as the number of machines are increased, the energy consumption may also increase while the makespan will decrease. The insights of results can enable system designers or users to choose the correct number of resources they want in their system, or the correct schedule, depending on the desired balance between makespan and energy.

8.4.1 Problem Formulation

The scheduling problem is generally modeled using a system graph and a program graph. The inputs to these algorithms are the *system graph*, the *program graph*, and the *energy specifications of the machines*.

The system graph specifies the connections between the machines of the system. The machines of the system are the units that perform the tasks. The program graph specifies the execution times and precedence relationships of the tasks. The power consumption of each machine while working as well as while being idle is to be specified as

TABLE 8.1. Terms Defined for Program Graph

Symbol	Meaning
i	Task i in program graph
$w(i)$	Weight of node i
$l(i,j)$	Weight of edge connecting i and j
$C(i)$	Machine that is assigned task i

inputs to the algorithms. The aim of these algorithms is to assign each task to a resource such that all the tasks are completed with a low overall energy expenditure; this is calculated by the *fitness function* which is a mapping from each schedule to the energy consumed by it.

The system model comprises a system graph, a program graph, and machine specifications.

8.4.1.1 System Graph.
A system is represented by an undirected unweighted graph called the system graph. Here, $\mathcal{V}_c$ is the set of nodes of the system graph representing machines with their local memories. The cardinality $|\mathcal{V}_c| = N_c$ specifies the number of machines in the system. Edges represent channels between machines and defines a topology of the multimachine system. In simulations, it is assumed that the topology is fully connected mesh topology.

8.4.1.2 Program Graph.
A parallel program is represented by a weighted directed acyclic graph $\mathcal{G}_p = (\mathcal{V}_p, \mathcal{E}_p)$ called a precedence task graph or a program graph. In the program graph,

- $\mathcal{V}_p$ is the set of nodes of the graph where each node represents an elementary task. The cardinality $|\mathcal{V}_p| = N_p$ specifies the number of elementary tasks in the program.
- $\mathcal{E}_p$ is the set of edges that specifies the precedence between the tasks.

The program graph specifies the execution times and precedence relationships of the elementary tasks.

The weight of a node represents the execution cost of the corresponding task, and the weight on an edge shows the transfer cost between two tasks if they are located at different machines. If they are located on the same machine, then the transfer cost is taken as zero. The weight $w(i)$ of node i describes the processing time needed to complete task i in a program graph. The weight $l(i,j)$ of an edge (i,j) describes the communication time between the pair of tasks i and j. If i and j are on the same machine, then it is 0. $C(i)$ denotes the machine that is assigned task i in a given schedule.

Table 8.1 describes the various parameters of a program graph.

8.4.1.3 Energy Specifications.
The power consumptions of each machine in working as well as in idle states are to be specified as inputs. The power consumption

TABLE 8.2. Power Consumption Specifications of the System

Symbol	Meaning
$\mu(C_u)$	Power consumption in working state by machine C_u
$k\mu(C_u)$	Power consumption in idle state by machine C_u, here $0 \leq k \leq 1$
$\tau_c(C_u)$	Time taken in working state by machine C_u
$\tau_i(C_u)$	Time taken in idle state by machine C_u

in the working state of machine C_u is denoted by $\mu(C_u)$ and the power consumption in the idle state of machine C_u is given by $k\mu(C_u)$, where $0 \leq k \leq 1$. If $k = 0$, it means the machine is effectively switched off when not under load and thus does not consume any power when idle. If $k = 1$, it means that in idle state with no load, the machine also consumes 100% of its full-load power. $\tau_c(C_u)$ is the time spent in the working state by machine C_u, and the time spent in the idle state by machine C_u is denoted by $\tau_i(C_u)$.

The total energy consumption of the system of all machines is denoted by E, and the total time taken by the system to complete a set of tasks is denoted by T.

8.4.1.4 Fitness Function. The aim of scheduling is to assign each node of the program graph (i.e., a task) to a node in the system graph (i.e., to a machine). In this section, we describe approaches to find schedules that reduce the total energy consumption of the system, given the energy specifications (power requirements) of each machine of the system, the system graph $\mathcal{G}_c$, and the program graph $\mathcal{G}_p$.

Suppose the power consumption specifications of the system are as indicated in Table 8.2.

The total energy consumption of the system is given by

$$E = \sum_{n=1}^{N_c} [\mu(C_n)\tau_c(C_n) + k\mu(C_n)\tau_i(C_n)]. \tag{8.2}$$

Hence, the aim is to find a schedule that minimizes the total energy E as given by Equation (8.2). As previously discussed, the classical scheduling problem that is similar to EA scheduling is minimum-makespan scheduling where T rather than E is minimized.

8.4.2 Allocation Heuristics

In this section, some classical algorithms and the proposed algorithms are discussed. Two methods for EA scheduling are then compared, each with its own strengths.

8.4.2.1 Classical Algorithms.

- *Greedy-Min* The task with the smallest execution time is scheduled first.
- *Greedy-Max* The task with the longest execution time is scheduled first.

8.4.2.2 *Efficiency-Based Allocation (EBA).* Among the types of algorithms generally used for scheduling are heuristic-based algorithms. Such algorithms have some heuristic at their core. The heuristic proceeds toward locally optimal results and it is hoped that with the combinations of locally optimal decisions, a globally optimal, or at least a good result can be obtained. Heuristic-based algorithms are very fast and have steady performances, but generally reach some sub-par solution. Search-based algorithms are slower but, on the other hand, do not get stuck in local minima, although they do not guarantee a good solution every time they are executed. Their success can only be measured statistically.

The first-in-first-out (FIFO) heuristic is used for scheduling in many single machine as well as multimachine systems. This algorithm is extended by using the knowledge of different power requirement of different machines. As soon as a task is ready to be executed, check which machines have an empty input queue. From the set of free machines, choose the one with the lowest working power and assign the task to that machine. If no machine is free, then the task is assigned to the machine with the least working power.

8.4.2.3 *Genetic Algorithm (Plain GA).* A genetic algorithm [13–15] (GA) is a heuristic for search, mimicking the natural evolution process. In a GA, a population of strings encoding candidate solutions evolve toward better solutions using mutation and crossover functions. The evolution usually starts from a random population of individuals and happens over multiple generations. In each generation, the fitness of every individual in the population is evaluated, multiple individuals are stochastically selected from the current population (based on their fitnesses), and modified (recombined and possibly randomly mutated) to form a new population. The new population is then used in the next iteration of the algorithm. Commonly, the algorithm terminates when either a maximum number of generations of candidate solutions are completed or a satisfactory fitness level is reached for the population.

Genetic algorithms have been used for makespan scheduling with good success [11, 12]. We present a method that instead uses this power of GAs to find energy-reducing schedules.

Initially, the EA scheduling problem is mapped to the GA domain. As a GA finds the strings that have good fitness values, we model schedules as strings and the energy values of the strings by the fitness function. Hence, a string in GA is a vector of length equal to the number of nodes in the program graph. Each element in that vector represents the machine corresponding to that node. The parents for mutation and crossover are chosen on the basis of the energies of the schedules in the current generation. A schedule is more likely to be chosen as a parent if its rank (in terms of lower energy consumption) is better than others. The mutation rule uses a Gaussian distribution with zero mean and a variance, which reduces the number of generations. The crossover is random, in the sense that it arbitrarily chooses the portions from the first and second parent. The search space of a GA depends on the number of machines as well as the number of elementary tasks in the program graph. The total number of possible solutions in a GA-based method is $N_p^{N_c}$.

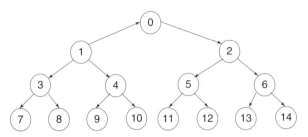

Figure 8.2. Program graph tree15.

8.4.3   Results

A number of simulations with standard program graphs have been conducted. These graphs are tree15, g18, gauss18, and g40, which are also used extensively in the literature (see, e.g., [16]).

The algorithms as well as the simulation setup allow for any number of machines, which can have different working state power consumptions and idle state power consumptions, to be used in the simulated systems. However, most existing scheduling algorithms consider fewer than eight-machine systems. The standard graphs that we have used are tested with eight-machine or smaller systems in other previous approaches. Hence, for illustrative purposes, we have used two-, four-, and eight-machine systems, so that it is easier to compare the algorithms with others. As has been previously discussed, prior state-of-the-art scheduling algorithms compute good schedules for minimizing makespan rather than energy. Although the algorithms are energy aware and work to reduce the energy rather than time, if we take the working power and idle power as being identical, then they provide the minimum-makespan schedules as well. Hence, for the sake of comparison with other systems, we have also calculated the schedules for makespan as well.

In the simulation, for the GA scheduling algorithm, we fixed the population size of the GA to be 20 and the maximum number of generations to be 100.

The schedules obtained from the GA algorithm will only tell us which task will be performed on which machine, and not the sequence of task execution. We have used a FIFO approach for scheduling of tasks assigned to the same machine, that is, the task that reaches the machine earlier is executed first.

The following section gives the explanation of the different program graphs that are used.

8.4.3.1   Program Graphs.   We consider four standard program graphs for simulation experiments: tree15, g18, gauss18, and g40. Tree15 is a binary tree with 15 nodes. All the working costs and communication costs in this program graph are the same and can be taken to be unity. The program graph for graph tree15 is shown in Figure 8.2.

The program graph g18 is displayed in Figure 8.3. It has 18 tasks with different computation costs as shown in the figure and the communication cost for all links equal unity.

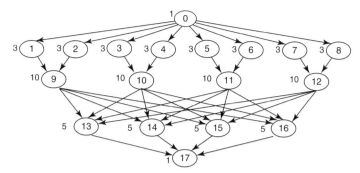

Figure 8.3. Program graph g18.

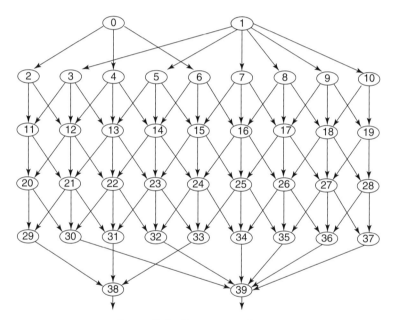

Figure 8.4. Program graph g40.

Figure 8.4 displays the program graph g40, which is also considered in simulation. This is a directed acyclic graph which has 40 nodes. The computation and communication costs of tasks are equal to 4 and 1, respectively.

Figure 8.5 displays the program graph gauss18. This is a directed acyclic graph that has 18 nodes. The computation and communication costs of tasks are as indicated in the figure.

8.4.3.2 *Comparative Performance of Algorithms.* We used an Intel i5 processor computer for these simulations. In Table 8.3, EBA refers to the efficiency-based allocation explained in Section 8.4.2.2. In the same table, GA refers

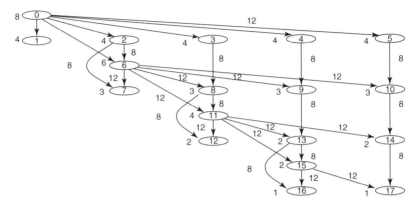

Figure 8.5. Program graph gauss18.

TABLE 8.3. Energy Comparison, with $C = 8$

Graphs	Plain GA	EBA	Greedy-Min	Greedy-Max
tree15	84, 0.71	76.8, 0.013	104, 0.048	104, 0.028
g18	412.8, 0.36	380.8, 0.006	652.8, 0.102	652.8, 0.07
gauss18	462.4, 1.23	834.4, 0.01	820.8, 0.086	820.8, 0.104
g40	761.6, 0.8288	786.4, 0.008	931.2, 0.372	931.2, 0.398

to the genetic-algorithm-based EA scheduling algorithm explained in Section 8.4.2.3. The greedy-min algorithm is a standard algorithm [17] that tries to first finish the jobs that can be finished sooner (i.e., the jobs with lower node weights) while honoring the program graph dependencies. In greedy-max algorithm, we give preference to first finish the jobs that take a long time to finish (i.e., the jobs with higher node weights) while adhering to the program graph dependencies.

Table 8.3 shows the energy requirements of all the algorithms considered, on an eight-machine system.

8.5   ENERGY-AWARE TASK ALLOCATION IN MOBILE ENVIRONMENTS

Recent advances in mobile computing technologies have paved the way for the arrival of new classes of distributed applications running on networks of mobile devices. Examples of mobile-to-mobile collaborations can be found in disaster relief, healthcare, and construction systems, in all of which mobile devices can act both as task requesters (clients) and task executors (servers) [18]. The basic principle behind such cooperative scenarios is that whenever a resource-limited mobile device has a task to execute, that task can be assigned to another mobile device that can handle its execution more effectively.

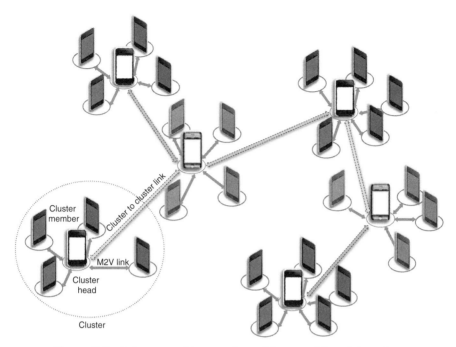

Figure 8.6. Reference architecture for mobile-to-mobile collaboration.

An issue that still prevents a wider implementation of distributed applications in mobile environments is the lack of task allocation strategies addressing both the energy constraints of wireless devices and the decentralized nature of mobile networks. This section focuses on such issues by describing an EA scheduling strategy for allocating computational tasks over a network of mobile devices in a decentralized but effective way. The main design principle of this scheduling strategy is finding a task allocation that prolongs the total lifetime of a mobile network and maximizes the number of functioning devices by balancing the energy load among them.

8.5.1 Reference Architecture

We consider a multi-hop wireless ad-hoc mobile network in which mobile *nodes* (i.e., *devices*) are divided into local groups, named *clusters*. Generally, geographically adjacent devices are assigned to the same cluster. Under a cluster-based structure, mobile nodes may be assigned different roles, such as *cluster-head* or *cluster member*. A cluster-head normally serves as the local coordinator for its cluster, performing intracluster transmission arrangements, data forwarding, and so on. A cluster member is a non-cluster-head node without any intercluster links.

In this work, we assume, as a reference, the cluster-based architecture of Figure 8.6, which is meant to support mobile-to-mobile (M2M) collaborations between mobile devices. Mobile nodes within a cluster interact through ad-hoc connections (e.g., Wi-Fi and Bluetooth), that we refer to as M2M links. Interactions between clusters (cluster-to-cluster links) take place through *ad-hoc* connections between the respective cluster heads.

The architecture is based on a fully distributed cluster formation algorithm in which nodes take autonomous decisions. The cluster formation algorithm has been presented elsewhere [19].

8.5.2   Task Allocation Strategy

Here we describe the EA task allocation strategy over the reference M2M network architecture introduced earlier. The main design principle of the EA strategy is that of finding a task allocation that prolongs the total lifetime of the network by balancing the energy load among all its devices.

The task allocation problem has been proven to be NP-complete in its general form [20]. Even though optimal algorithms have been proposed for some restricted versions of the problem, heuristic-based algorithms have been proposed for the more general versions of the problem, allowing to find good allocations in polynomial time [21].

Accordingly, we propose a two-phase heuristic-based decentralized task allocation strategy. When an assignment decision has to be made for a task, the first phase, referred to as *local assignment*, tries to assign the task locally to the cluster where the execution request has been generated, so as to maximize the cluster residual life. If local assignment fails because none of the devices within the cluster can execute the task, the cluster-head activates the second phase, referred to as *global assignment*, responsible for task arbitration among clusters. In this case, the task is assigned to the most suitable device, all over the network of clusters, that maximizes the overall network lifetime.

Before describing the strategy, we introduce some notation. We define the concept of *residual life* $RL_i(t)$ of device d_i at time t as follows:

$$RL_i(t) = RE_i(t)/P_i(t). \tag{8.3}$$

Similarly, we define *network lifetime* at time t, $RL_{net}(t)$, as the total residual life of the devices in the network. Therefore, the goal of our scheduling strategy is finding a task allocation that maps each task $t_i \in \mathcal{T}$ to a device $d_j \in \mathcal{D}$ so as to maximize $RL_{net}(t)$.

We formalize the problem of task allocation as an optimization problem. As said before, the goal is to maximally extend the network lifetime and the number of alive devices. To this end, tasks are allocated to devices so as to balance the load among them. We address the problem by iteratively trying to improve a candidate solution. A feasible allocation is optimal if the corresponding cluster residual life (in case of local assignment) or network lifetime (in case of global assignment) is maximized among all the feasible allocations.

A device d_i can be a candidate for the assignment of a task t_a, if it satisfies the following constraints:

1. d_i has enough memory to perform t_a over a data set of size s, that is, $EMC_i(t_a, s) < RE_i(t)$.
2. d_i has enough energy to perform t_a over a data set of size s, that is, $EEC_i(t_a, s) < RE_i(t)$.

During the local assignment phase, a cluster head, or the set of neighboring cluster heads in case of a global assignment, chooses the local node from among the ones satisfying the above constraints, in a manner that prolongs the life of the corresponding local group, by using the following objective function:

$$RL_{LG_j}(t) = \text{Max} \sum_{i=1}^{N_{LG_j}} \alpha_i RL_i(t), \tag{8.4}$$

where RL_{LG_j} denotes the residual life of local group LG_j, N_{LG_j} is the number of nodes within the local group LG_j, RL_i is the residual life of node d_i in the group, and parameter α_i takes into account the importance of d_i in the local group. The node associated with the maximum value of the objective function is selected by the cluster head as the candidate node. Note that throughout the experimental evaluation, the parameter α_i is set to 1; thus, all the nodes have the same role within the local group.

If the global assignment phase is activated, the final decision is taken by considering all the candidate nodes proposed by the neighboring clusters. The task is assigned to the local group that maximizes the network lifetime:

$$RL_{net}(t) = \text{Max} \sum_{j=1}^{N} \alpha_j RL_{LG_j}(t), \tag{8.5}$$

where N is the number of clusters in the network.

8.5.3 Task Allocation Algorithm

In this section, we describe the algorithm that implements the task allocation strategy introduced earlier.

Upon receiving a task allocation request, the cluster head triggers, through the method shown in Figure 8.7, the activation of the task allocation strategy to find the optimal assignment for that task. To this end, the cluster head verifies whether the residual life of its group is greater than the 20% of its peak value. If the check is successful, it starts up the local assignment phase. If the check is negative or if the local assignment fails because none of the nodes in the cluster can execute the task, the cluster head activates the global assignment phase. Note that in case of negative check on the threshold of the local group residual life, the global phase is activated only if there is a neighboring group whose residual life is greater than a given threshold. If this last condition is not satisfied, the local phase is activated anyhow. The choice of a low threshold value (20% in our case) is based on the experimental observation that the energy used in transmission is greater, by an order of magnitude, than that used in computation [22]. This is also the reason for first attempting a local optimum – doing so allows for reducing transmission costs.

The scheduling starts with the local assignment phase where the cluster head tries to assign the task to a node within the group that maximizes the cluster residual life (see Figure 8.8). In this way, the cluster head determines a candidate node in the group that meets the requirements for executing the task in terms of energy and memory

---

Method allocateTask
Input: task t, data set size s

---

begin
    localAssignmentFailed ← false;
    C ← determineNeighboringClusters();
    if (RL_{LG_i} > 20% **or** $C = \emptyset$) **then**
        < $d_{candidate}$, ERL_{LG_i} > ← localAssignment(t, s);
        if (< $d_{candidate}$, ERL_{LG_i} > ≠ $\emptyset$) **then**
            if ($d_{candidate}$ = this) **then**
                startTask(t, s);
            else
                $d_{candidate}$.executeTask(t, s);
            end
        else
            localAssignmentFailed ← **true**;
        end
    end
    if ((RL_{LG_i} ≤ 20% **or** localAssigmentFailed) **and** C ≠ $\emptyset$) **then**
        globalAssignment(t, s, C);
    end
end

Figure 8.7. Task allocation by the cluster head of local group LG_j.

Method localAssignment
Input: task t, data set size s
Output: candidate node $d_{candidate}$, estimated residual life
ERL_{LG_i} of local group LG_i if t is assigned to $d_{candidate}$

---

begin
    if (this = CH_i **or** (this ≠ CH_i **and** RL_{LG_i} > 30%)) **then**
        $RL_{LG_{curr}}$ ← 0;
        ERL_{LG_i} ← 0;
        $d_{candidate}$ ← $\emptyset$;
        foreach node d_i ∈ LG_i **do**
            if (d_i.hasSkill(t, s)) **then**
                RL_i ← d_i.estimateNodeResidualLife(t, s);
                $RL_{LG_{curr}}$ ← estimateGroupResidualLife(d_i, RL_i);
                if ($RL_{LG_{curr}}$ > ERL_{LG_i}) **then**
                    ERL_{LG_i} ← $RL_{LG_{curr}}$;
                    $d_{candidate}$ ← d_i;
                end
            end
        end
    end
    return < $d_{candidate}$, ERL_{LG_i} >;
end

Figure 8.8. Local assignment of task t within local group LG_j.

Method globalAssignment
Input: task t, data set size s, set of neighboring clusters C

---

begin
$\quad$ $\mathcal{D} \leftarrow \emptyset$;
$\quad$ **foreach** local group $LG_i \in C$ **do**
$\qquad$ $< d_{candidate}, RL_{LG_i} > \leftarrow CH_i.localAssignment(t, s)$;
$\qquad$ $\mathcal{D}.add(< d_{candidate}, RL_{LG_i} >)$;
$\quad$ **end**
$\quad$ $ERL_{net} \leftarrow 0$;
$\quad$ $d_{best} \leftarrow \emptyset$;
$\quad$ **foreach** node $d_i \in \mathcal{D}$ **do**
$\qquad$ $RL_{net} \leftarrow estimateNetworkResidualLife(d_i, RL_{LG_i})$;
$\qquad$ **if** $(RL_{net} > ERL_{net})$ **then**
$\qquad\quad$ $ERL_{net} \leftarrow RL_{net}$;
$\qquad\quad$ $d_{best} \leftarrow d_i$;
$\qquad$ **end**
$\quad$ **end**
$\quad$ $CH_{best} \leftarrow getClusterHead(d_{best})$;
$\quad$ **if** $(d_{best} = this)$ **then**
$\qquad$ startTask(t, s);
$\quad$ **else**
$\qquad$ **if** $(CH_{best} = this)$ **then**
$\qquad\quad$ $d_{best}.executeTask(t, s)$;
$\qquad$ **else**
$\qquad\quad$ $CH_{best}.requireTaskExecution(d_{best}, t, s)$;
$\qquad$ **end**
$\quad$ **end**
end

Figure 8.9. Global assignment of task *t*.

constraints. The local assignment phase can be executed both by the cluster head of the requesting node and by the cluster heads of neighboring clusters involved in a global assignment.

To limit the communication costs in the network, the global assignment phase (see Figure 8.9) only considers neighboring clusters at a distance of at most three hops from the requesting cluster head. Among such neighboring clusters only those having a residual life greater than a given threshold (set to 30%) are selected, so as to avoid overloading the local groups. This threshold is selected after some experiments, as a value that ensures a good balance between communication and computation costs. After that, in each of such local groups, including the one that originated the request, a candidate node that best performs the task is determined. Finally, among all candidate nodes, the task is assigned to the one that ensures the highest network lifetime.

8.5.4 Performance Results

Here we present some performance results of the proposed EA strategy, performed using a custom discrete-event simulator [23]. As a first step, the simulator builds a network composed of 100 mobile devices and groups them into clusters based on the algorithm

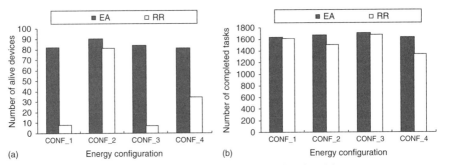

Figure 8.10. Number of (a) alive devices and (b) completed tasks with respect to energy configuration using EA and RR.

described in [19]. As a result of the clustering procedure, 20 devices act as cluster heads, with an average cluster size of 5. Then, an initial energy capacity ranging from 3000 to 11,000 J is assigned to each device, following a normal distribution. After the initial setup, mobile devices start generating a set of data mining tasks to be executed, which are allocated to the available nodes according to the EA strategy described earlier. The simulation is intended to study the behavior of the scheduler with respect to energy depletion and network lifetime. Accordingly, for performance metrics, we consider the number of functioning devices and the number of tasks completed at the end of the simulation.

To assess the effectiveness of the EA strategy, we compared its performance with the one achieved by the RR scheduling algorithm. We evaluated how the number of functioning devices and the number of completed tasks is affected by the distribution of the initial energy levels among nodes. In particular, we considered four energy configurations.

- *CONF_1*. The energy is assigned to the devices following a normal distribution with average at 40% of the peak value (this is also the default configuration used for the experiments presented earlier).
- *CONF_2*. All devices start with the same energy level, equal to 40% of the peak value.
- *CONF_3*. Energy is uniformly distributed in the range 15–65% of the peak value.
- *CONF_4*. Energy is assigned using a bimodal distribution, with local maxima at 30% and 75% of the peak value.

For all configurations, the total energy level available is constant and equal to about 700 kJ. The candidate task used for this evaluation is the J48 data mining algorithm running on a dataset of 200 kB. The results, obtained after the submission of 2500 tasks with $\lambda = 80$ tasks/h, are shown in Figure 8.10.

Figure 8.10a shows that EA keeps almost the same number of devices functional in all configurations. On the contrary, because RR assigns tasks to each device in equal portions and in circular order without taking into account their remaining energy, its effectiveness depends on the combination of the task to be allocated, and the device, at the beginning of the circular queue. In particular, we observe that the efficacy of RR is comparable with that of EA only when all devices have the same level of energy (CONF_2), which, however, is not a realistic situation as devices are usually heterogeneous in terms of their energy availability.

Figure 8.10b shows that EA completes almost the same number of tasks in all configurations considered, while in some cases, the number of completed tasks with RR varies significantly (see, e.g., CONF_3 versus CONF_4).

In conclusion, the experimental results discussed earlier demonstrated that a significant improvement can be achieved using EA as compared to RR in a distributed mobile scenario. In particular, the EA strategy is able to keep alive most mobile devices functioning, thanks to its energy load balancing strategy, without restraining the number of completed tasks.

8.6 AN ENERGY-AWARE SCHEDULING STRATEGY FOR ALLOCATING COMPUTATIONAL TASKS IN A FULLY DECENTRALIZED WAY

Given the increasing sizes of data centers, such systems are faced with challenges in terms of scalability, autonomy, and energy efficiency. In large-scale cloud systems, the centralized approach is difficult. First, centralized scheduling [24] requires accurate, centralized information about the state of the whole system. Second, sites forming the cloud may maintain some level of autonomy, yet classic algorithms implicitly assume a complete control over individual resources. Thus, many of the existing attempts to design and implement cloud systems are still based on centralized architectures, have limited autonomy, and lack energy saving mechanisms.

In contrast, a decentralized scheduler [25] overcomes the limitations of centralized structures with respect to fault tolerance, scalability, autonomy, and most importantly in being adequate for the cloud-computing environment. Jobs are submitted locally, but they can be migrated to another cluster if the local cluster gets overloaded. The targets of migration are chosen to ensure that migrated jobs do not overload their new host systems. A decentralized scheduling approach assumes that each entity is autonomous and has its own control that derives its scheduling decision based on its policies. However, if decisions are taken by several independent units, it might be the case that all these units aim at optimizing their own local objectives rather than the performance of the system as a whole. Such situations call for models and techniques that take the strategic behavior of individual units into account, and simultaneously keep an eye on the global performance of the system. In most cases, self-interested entities have to cooperate to achieve their respective objectives, but any cooperation must be self-enforcing and not merely enforced by binding agreements through third parties.

8.6.1 Decentralized Resources in Cloud: Overview

Generally, meta-scheduling solutions are classified into three categories: centralized, hierarchical, and decentralized. In a centralized scheduling architecture [24], scheduling decisions are made by a central controller for all virtual machines (VMs). The scheduler maintains all information about the VM and keeps track of all available resources in the system. A centralized scheduling organization is simple to implement and easy to deploy. However, such a centralized scheduling organization is not adequate for the cloud because of the nature of the cloud-computing environment. These centralized services are limited in their scalability.

In distributed scheduling, there is a central manager and multiple lower-level entities. The central manager is responsible for handling the complete execution of a VM and assigning the individual VMs to the low-level providers. Each lower-level entity scheduler is responsible for mapping individual tasks to cloud resources. Ranjan et al. [26] propose a meta-scheduling framework, where each resource consumer may value various resources differently depending on its quality of service (QoS)-based utility functions and may want to negotiate a particular price for using a resource based on demand, availability, and its budget. The failure of the central controller results in the failure of the entire system.

The decentralized meta-scheduling scheme allows each node to own a meta-scheduler that receives job submissions originated by local users and to assign such jobs to the local resource management system, that is, a local scheduler. Meta-schedulers of different nodes are capable of exchanging information and sharing jobs with one another in order to balance the resource load among participating nodes. Besides the issues of efficiency and overhead, the decentralized scheme brings better scalability, compared with other scheduling schemes. Comito et al. [27] proposed a task allocation scheme for mobile networks focusing on energy efficiency. To conservatively consume energy and maximize network lifetime, they introduced a heuristic algorithm that balances the energy load among all devices in the network. These authors referred to a cooperative EA scheduling strategy that assigns computational tasks over a network of mobile devices optimizing the energy usage. Huang et al. [28] proposed a decentralized dynamic scheduling approach named the community-aware scheduling algorithm (CASA). It makes job allocation decisions based on nodes' loads and real-time responses. In this case, each participating node needs to expose its resource utilization during its cooperation with other nodes. However, the problem has not been explored in the context of the need for optimization of energy consumption.

The cooperative scheduling anti-load balancing algorithm for cloud (CSAAC) extends CASA. CSAAC extends CASA by adding migration of VMs and the ability to avoid underload and overload of nodes. To save energy, CSAAC provides a holistic energy-efficient task placement algorithm. Particularly, it integrates migration of jobs and a mechanism that automatically switches off nodes, transitions them into a power-saving state (e.g., suspend), and wakes them up once required. The detection of underloaded and overloaded nodes is also performed. To remedy them, consolidation is used. Experimental results suggest that this algorithm is energy efficient.

8.6.2 Cooperative Scheduling Anti-Load Balancing Algorithm for Cloud (CSAAC)

8.6.2.1 Algorithm Description. CSAAC works by associating two threshold values with each host. When a host is underloaded (load < globally_defined_threshold), all its tasks are migrated to a comparatively more loaded host. The overload threshold ε, called saturation, is used to measure the saturation of a cluster. In dynamic load unbalancing schemes, the two most important policies are *selection policy* and *location*

policy. A selection policy concerns the choice of the host to unload, while a location policy chooses the destination host of these moved tasks. An important characteristic of a good selection policy is to prevent the destination host from becoming overloaded. Also, migration costs must be compensated by performance improvement.

As a multi-phase decentralized scheduling solution, the CSAAC is based on CASA [28]. CSAAC is comprises the job submission phase responsible for job dissemination, as well as the dynamic scheduling phase responsible for iterative scheduling improving. The job submission phase is the first phase of this CASA. Participating nodes only need to calculate estimated response time for a concerned job and bid for the job delegation using the calculated and promised job response times. CSAAC adds another criterion to evaluate the nodes' capabilities, the node load.

Each responder node computes an estimated completion time according to its current scheduling and resource status, calculates the necessary energy, and delivers the information by means of an ACCEPT message. In addition, the node load is also appended to the generated message, which can be utilized by the requester node for responder node evaluation and selection.

The selected node is the best candidate node based on several parameters, such as the promised time to complete, energy consumed, the node load between underload threshold and overload threshold, node weight due to historical interaction records, and so on. Furthermore, during the execution of the tasks, all the time the system verifies if there are underloaded or overloaded nodes.

CSAAC provides a task-scheduling strategy that dynamically migrates tasks among computing hosts, transferring tasks from underloaded hosts to loaded but not overloaded hosts. It balances the loads of computing hosts as far as possible in order to reduce programs' running times.

The decision-making algorithm behaves globally as follows:

- If total VM load on the host j of cluster $i > \varepsilon$, the host is overloaded.
- If total VM load on the host j of cluster $i < \gamma$, the host is underloaded.

Selection policies take into account the migration cost. The selected host (node j' in cluster i') is the one with the minimum energy consumed for the best execution time, weighed by the migration cost between the current position of the VM and the potential host. To reduce the load of an overloaded host, it begins to migrate the slowest task. The selection policy chooses the task that will stay the longest on the host.

This migration algorithm's goal is to minimize the energy. During the execution of the task, it may happen that a node is overloaded. In this case, VMs whose execution time remaining is greater are migrated.

The policy of localization then identifies the host that receives the task without exceeding its capacity (i.e., its load after migration to still be under ε). So this host is to be the new destination of the task.

8.6.3   Simulation Results

We now describe the simulation study conducted to evaluate the performance of CSAAC in terms of energy minimization as well as the execution time and the number

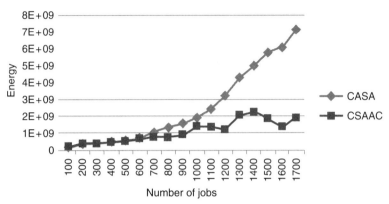

Figure 8.11. Energy of algorithms compared to CASA with sorted hosts by pmax. Lower is better.

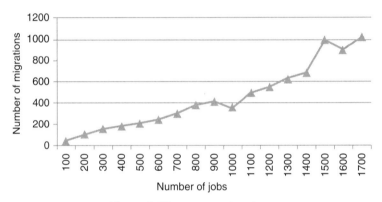

Figure 8.12. CSAAC: migration.

of migrations. CSAAC is compared with an implementation of CASA improved to produce energy-efficient schedules.

The first observation is that of the two algorithms, CSAAC consumes less energy than CASA (see Figure 8.11), when the number of jobs $T > 300$. For a small number of tasks, our algorithm leads to a significant reduction in energy consumption. The second observation is that CSAAC is able to reduce the energy consumption by 5–80% when the number of jobs increases from 300 to 1700. Figure 8.12 demonstrates the energy consumption and the number of migrations incurred by 1700 jobs. An obvious observation is that migrations are beneficial to save energy. The second phase of our algorithm calls into question the choices and, therefore, modifies the host loads over time. If at any time tasks are finished and there are several machines that are underloaded, they can be consolidated. In addition, jobs cannot be shared between neighbors to find a more efficient approach than neighboring nodes, starting step by step. The impact of migration, however, may not be large enough to dominate the total energy consumption when the number of jobs is less than 300.

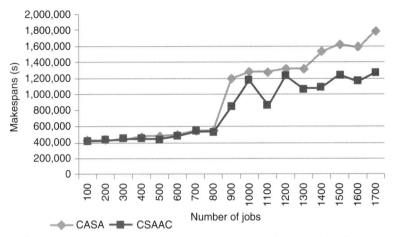

Figure 8.13. Makespans of algorithms compared to CASA with sorted hosts by pmax, where lower is better.

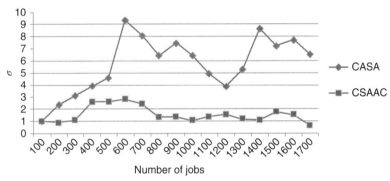

Figure 8.14. Comparison between two algorithms CSAAC and CASA, considering standard deviation σ of node load.

As CSAAC has more flexibility, given the possibility of migration, simulation showed that in all cases, the makespan of jobs with CSAAC is always lower than that with CASA (Figure 8.13).

Owing to the thresholds of CSAAC, it would be possible to further reduce the number of switched on hosts, but doing so would overload the remaining hosts. Those hosts could become hotspots (in a data center setting) and would have a negative impact on cooling. In order to prevent overloading, CSAAC adjusts load. Figure 8.14 also shows how widely host loads are dispersed from the average value (the mean). In previous results (Figures 8.11 and 8.12), CSAAC is in the lead in terms of energy gain and execution time, because in this algorithm, there is cooperation between schedulers, which allows an efficient consolidation in cloud. Figure 8.14 shows the standard deviation σ of the nodes load that confirms the good distribution of the load after consolidation. Thus Figure 8.14 shows that CSAAC gives a better (smaller) standard deviation than CASA, which is an indication of the good predictability of the performance of CSAAC. When the number of tasks increases, CSAAC perform even better.

8.6.4   Evaluation

The complexity of the cooperative scheduling problem is to optimize energy consumption, given task performance constraints. Energy consumption is to be taken in a broad way. As an example, hotspots are to be reduced, as they have a significant impact on cooling and cause equipment failures. CSAAC parameters lead to a family of heuristics that perform well in terms of energy savings while still leading to good task performance. It consolidates task on a subset of the cluster hosts, judiciously chosen depending on the characteristics and state of resources. This algorithm has a low-computational cost. It can thus be employed in practical settings. Overall, the proposed CSAAC algorithm can compute allocations effectively with an important energy gain.

The simulation results showed that our algorithm is capable of obtaining energy-efficient schedules using less optimization time. In particular, for the cases when jobs > 300, it is able to reduce the average energy consumption by about 10–80%. At the same time, the execution time of jobs is also reduced by 5–25% when number of jobs > 300, when compared to the CASA algorithm.

While showing less improvement than when using a centralized approach, cooperative scheduling can be used to reduce energy consumption for clouds while guaranteeing QoS.

8.7   COST-AWARE SCHEDULING WITH SMART GRIDS

Traditionally, scheduling problems concentrate on reducing the *makespan* (i.e., the time taken to complete a set of tasks). However, it stands to reason that time to completion is sometimes less significant, and it, instead, is more important to reduce the amount of money spent to complete a schedule of tasks. This new concept of emphasizing on reducing the amount of money spent to complete a schedule of tasks is termed *cost-aware scheduling* [29].

An important motivation for this class of scheduling problems is the advent of *smart grids* that have changed the traditional way of charging customers for electricity; time-varying electricity tariff rates, rather than fixed tariff rates, are the new norm.

If a smart electrical grid does not vary its tariff (i.e., behaves as a traditional fixed-price grid), then the cost-aware scheduling problem reduces to that of EA scheduling. A simple set of analyses can be done to show the hierarchy of scheduling problems proving that EA scheduling is a generalization of makespan scheduling and that cost-aware scheduling is in turn a generalization of EA scheduling [29].

8.7.1   Cost-Aware Scheduling

The scheduler's functionality is embedded into a controller that runs the proposed algorithm. The system model takes into account the deadline constraints of tasks and schedules them so as to minimize the cost (price paid for energy usage). The controller takes as inputs the number of tasks, the arrival time of each task, the deadline for each task, the duration of each task, the utility of each task, the power consumption of each machine, and, of course, the budget and cost-rate plan.

8.7.1.1   *Assumptions.*
A task is assumed to be an atomic unit of work, that is, a task can be completed when assigned the required resource, but it cannot be broken into subtasks. Tasks are independent of one another, and hence, a task can be scheduled any time between its arrival and deadline, irrespective of the completion of other tasks. No compound tasks are taken into consideration, that is, tasks are simple and do not have a dependency on other tasks.

Each task is characterized by a start time (time at which a task can possibly start execution) and a deadline (time before which a task should be completed). Tasks have dedicated types of machines which they can be assigned to. Each machine is able to perform only a specific type of task, that is, each machine has a different capability and all tasks cannot be completed on a general machine. For example, if the task is toasting of bread, then it can be done using only a toaster and not using a washing machine or any other machine. There are no substitutions and alternatives to tasks, so all tasks must be completed, or at least as many of them as possible must be completed to increase the utility while staying within the budget.

Tasks are assigned to machines, and each task can be executed on a machine dedicated to the task under consideration. The specification of a machine includes its rate of power consumption, taken as constant.

A cost-rate plan for power consumption is also necessary for total cost calculations. A variable cost-rate plan is chosen as input – that is, a tabulation of time slabs and the corresponding cost payable for energy consumption during that time slot.

The scheduling process is offline and all the necessary inputs are considered available before the application of the scheduling algorithm. The cost of scheduling is also assumed to be negligible, that is, the scheduling overhead should not play an important role for the application on which the model is used.

8.7.1.2   *System Model.*
The schematic view of the system described earlier is shown in Figure 8.15, whence it can be observed that the inputs to the systems are specified as tasks, machines, cost-rate plan, and budget. The output for the system is a schedule that is near optimal on the utility and obeys the constraints.

(i) *Machines.*

Tasks are to be scheduled on a set of machines $\mu = \{\eta_1, \eta_2, \dots, \eta_m\}$, where m is the total number of machines. Here, each task is predefined for a dedicated machine, and each task is independent of other tasks.

Machines are characterized by their power specifications $\kappa = \{P_1, P_2, \dots, P_m\}$, where P_i is the power consumption (energy usage per unit time) of the ith machine, $1 \le i \le m$.

(ii) *Tasks.*

Let $J = \{j_1, j_2, \dots, j_n\}$ be the set of tasks that are given to the system, where n is the total number of tasks in the system. The value of n is known

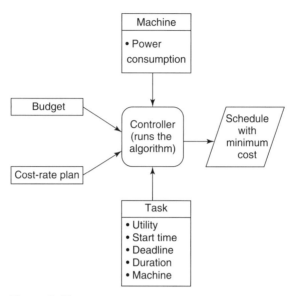

Figure 8.15. Schematic view of cost-aware scheduling.

a priori, which means that the size of the set of tasks to be completed is known in advance.

The total number of tasks can be greater than or equal to the number of machines that are present. The value of n is often much larger than that of m, that is, $n \geqslant m$, this means that many different but similar tasks can be performed on the same machine one after the other.

Each task $j \in J$ is given by the task specification $\Phi_j = \{\varphi(j), s_j, e_j, \tau_j, u_{j,t}\}$; here, φ is a function that maps tasks to the corresponding machines that are required to complete them, that is, $\varphi : J \to \mu$. It takes as input a task j and returns as output the machine η_i on which task j has to be performed, that is, $\varphi(j) = \eta_i$, where $j \in J$ and $\eta_i \in \mu$. This function is responsible for looking up the kind of task that is to be performed and to find an appropriate machine required to complete the task. s_j indicates the preferable time after which the jth task can be started, and e_j indicates the preferable time before which the jth task should be completed. τ_j indicates the duration of the jth task. $u_{j,t}$ is the time-varying utility (profit) that is obtained if jth task can be completed within specified time $s \leq t \leq (e - \tau)$.

A task must be scheduled to start after its indicated start time and completed before the indicated deadline. Thus a task, if scheduled, must be done so in the interval $[s, e - 1]$ [30], for all $j \in J$. A task can be assigned a time instance that belongs to the interval $[s, e - \tau]$ [31].

(iii) *Utility Function.*

The utility of a task is provided as a nonzero positive integer value. This represents the profit obtained on completing the task. One slightly different way of understanding utility could be that it indicates how important it is to complete a task. The utility of a task can also be indirectly considered to be the profit obtained on completing a task. Thus, if many instances of tasks with low cost are present, then the algorithm does not simply preferentially pick all of them simply because their cost to completion is less. The algorithm considers the utilities of other tasks with a higher value, so that tasks with higher profits are chosen.

(iv) *Cost of Completing a Task.*

The cost-rate plan for domestic or industrial consumers is denoted by $\mathfrak{R} = \{R_1, R_2, \ldots, R_T\}$ and T indicates the overall time period over which the plan is designed. Each R_k, where $1 \leq k \leq T$, indicates the cost per unit of energy a consumer has to pay for use of the electrical power supply during time interval k.

The cost of completing the jth task starting at a time instance t is represented by $C_{j,t}$. Here, $j \in J$, $s \leq t \leq (e - \tau)$ and s, t, τ should lie within the time period T.

$$C_{j,t} = \left(P_i \sum_{k=t}^{t+\tau_j} R_k \right),$$ where τ_j is a parameter of the jth task. R_k denotes the cost-rate plan over the duration τ_j. The function $\varphi(j) = \eta_i$ returns as output the machine η_i on which task j is performed, where $1 \leq j \leq n$ and $1 \leq i \leq m$. As each machine is associated with a power specification P_i, the jth task will use the same power specification for completion.

(v) *Optimization Problem.*

A schedule gives the list of tasks that have been chosen for completion. During the process of scheduling, a task may or may not be assigned the required energy source for completion. Hence, a heuristic is used to compute the costs for a subset of possible schedules and the one with minimum cost is picked and denoted as the optimal solution.

Let $\mathfrak{C}_l = \{C_{1,t_1} + C_{2,t_2} + \cdots + C_{n,t_n}\}$ represent the total cost needed to complete all tasks in a schedule and l be the schedule number. Now, $\mathfrak{C}_l = \{C_{1,t_1} + C_{2,t_2} + \cdots + C_{n,t_n}\}$ can also be represented as $\mathfrak{C}_l = \sum_{j=1}^{n} C_{j,t_j}$ where j indicates the task number.

The optimization problem can be stated as

$$\max \sum_{j=1}^{n} (u_{j,t} \cdot x_j)$$

Subject to   (8.6)

$$\mathfrak{C}_q \leq \beta, \text{ and } \mathfrak{C}_q \text{ is } \min\{\mathfrak{C}_l\}, \text{ where } l \in 1, 2, \ldots$$

$$s_j \leq (e_j - \tau_j), \forall j \in J.$$

Here, β is the total budget given for a period of time and for a specific set of tasks, $\min\{\mathfrak{C}_q\}$ returns a schedule with the minimum cost. Thus, the goal of the system is to maximize utility (profit obtained on completion of a task) such that a consumer obtains close to the maximum possible utility given a budget. Maximizing utility is of course a manifestation of the principle that the work done for a given expense should be maximized. x_j is a variable which takes

Boolean values, that is, $x_j \in \{0, 1\}$. If x_j takes the value 0, it indicates that a task has not been selected, and if x_j takes the value 1, it indicates that a task has been selected. If all the tasks can be completed within the specified budget, then the schedule with least cost should be chosen. If all the tasks cannot be completed within the specified budget, then tasks having greater utilities are given higher preferences. The deadline constraints for each task should also be taken into consideration while forming a valid schedule. A task j cannot be scheduled beyond its end time e_j, where $j \in J$.

8.7.2   Cost-Aware Scheduling Using DE

Mapping of differential evolution (DE) to the system model that has been described in Section 8.7.1 is presented here. The objective is to find a schedule using DE that minimizes the total cost. The problem has been solved using an approach that concentrates on trying to maximize utilities of tasks as described in the objective function that is formulated in Section 8.7.1 and is given by Equation (8.6).

The output is a schedule indicating the list of picked tasks and their start times, with the schedule being one that gives close to maximal utility over the tasks.

8.7.2.1   Decision Variables. The DE algorithm produces a solution vector as its output. The solution vector consists of a set of decision variables. The proposed algorithm uses a combination of binary and discrete DE [32] methods. The solution vector obtained should be understood to contain a valid schedule, and this is justified by adding a penalty whenever an invalid schedule is generated by the algorithm.

Given n tasks, the total number of decision variables required is $2n$, and these decision variables are represented as $x_1, x_2, \dots, x_{2n}$. Each decision variable is assigned its lower and upper bounds. The DE algorithm accordingly assigns a value that lies between the lower and upper bound of the corresponding decision variable.

The first n decision variables $x_1, x_2, \dots, x_n$ are finally assigned a Boolean value of 0 or 1. Decision variables $x_1, x_2, \dots, x_n$ are given their lower limit as 0 and upper limit as 2. DE algorithm used for continuous problems is used, and this generates a random value between 0 and 2. To convert these values into a binary value, the floor function of each of these decision variables (i.e., $\lfloor x_\xi \rfloor$, $1 \leq \xi \leq n$, is applied) is taken. A value of x_ξ, $1 \leq \xi \leq n$ as 0 indicates that the ξth task is not picked, and a value of 1 indicates that the ξth task is picked.

The second set of n decision variables $x_{n+1}, x_{n+2}, \dots, x_{2n}$ indicates the preferred starting time of appliance usage. Thus, $x_\vartheta \in [s_\xi, (e_\xi - \tau_\xi)]$, for $n \leq \vartheta < 2n$, and $1 \leq \xi \leq n$, where ξ indicates the ξth task.

8.7.2.2   Algorithm. The basic framework of the DE algorithm (for a single strategy) [33] used for cost-aware scheduling is described in Algorithm 8.1.

The terms weight factor (F), crossover rate (ζ), and dimension (D) used in the Algorithm 8.1 hold the same meaning as the standard terms used for any DE algorithm. The optimization function described in the system model is used in the evaluation function.

Line 1 of the algorithm initializes the variable *count* to 0. *count* keeps track of the number of iterations, and the algorithm runs for a maximum of Γ number of iterations.

Algorithm 8.1: Cost-aware scheduling using DE (for a single strategy)

$count \leftarrow 0$;
while $count \neq \Gamma$ **do**
    for $i \leftarrow 1$ **to** v **do**
        repeat
          | $a \leftarrow (rand\_uni() \times v)$
        until $(a \neq i)$;
        repeat
          | $b \leftarrow (rand\_uni() \times v)$
        until $((b \neq i) \& (b \neq a))$;
        repeat
          | $c \leftarrow (rand\_uni() \times v)$
        until $((c \neq i) \& (c \neq a) \& (c \neq b))$;
        $j \leftarrow (rand\_uni() \times D)$
        for $k \leftarrow 1$ **to** D **do**
          if $(rand\_uni() < \zeta \;||\; k == D)$ **then**
          $trial[j] \leftarrow (x1[c][j] + F \times (x1[a][j] - x1[b][j]))$
          else
          $trial[j] \leftarrow x1[i][j]$
          $j \leftarrow (j + 1)\%D$
        $score \leftarrow evaluate(trial)$;
        if $(score \leq cost[i])$ **then**
        for $j \leftarrow 0$ **to** D **do**
          | $x2[i][j] \leftarrow trial[j]$
         else
        for $j \leftarrow 0$ **to** D **do**
          | $x2[i][j] \leftarrow x1[i][j]$
    for $i \leftarrow 1$ **to** v **do**
        for $j \leftarrow 1$ **to** D **do**
          | $x1[i][j] \leftarrow x2[i][j]$
    $count \leftarrow count + 1$;

---

v is the number of samples in the initial population of the evolutionary algorithm. The **for** loop in line 3 indicates the start of a mutation/recombining step. Three vectors a, b, and c are picked randomly from the initial population and care is taken that none of the three are repeated nor are they the same as the vector for which the iteration is being carried out (a vector is a set of decision variables and values assigned to them). The decision variables are assigned values randomly such that their values lie between the minimum and maximum possible values that the variable can take, that is, the lower and upper bounds (as defined before).

    The function *evaluate(trial)* on line 21 takes the trial vector generated from mutation as input and evaluates the objective function that is given by Equation (8.6). The result

TABLE 8.4. Cost-Rate Plan for Winter (December to February)

Time of the Day	Cost (¢/kWh)
07:00 AM to 12:00 PM	16.435
12:00 PM to 04:00 PM	12.638
04:00 PM to 11:00 PM	16.435
11:00 PM to 07:00 AM	6.468

TABLE 8.5. Cost-Rate Plan for Non-winter (March to November)

Time of the Day	Cost (¢/kWh)
07:00 AM to 11:00 PM	12.638
11:00 PM to 07:00 AM	6.468

obtained is assigned to *score*. If the evaluated *score* is less than the previous value, then a new secondary vector created with this value is replaced with *score*. The algorithm assumes that the objective function is a minimization function (if it is a maximization function, one can easily convert it to a minimization function).

The above steps are followed for every vector in the population. Once all the vectors are exhausted in the initial population vector and Γ is not reached, the best solution of every iteration is saved locally and the best global solution is stored globally.

The complexity of the DE algorithm depends on the number of tasks.

As the number of tasks increases, the number of decision variables also increases by a factor of 2. DE algorithm can handle any number of tasks, thus making the algorithm dynamic and easily scalable. The algorithmic complexity depends on the dimension of decision variables and the population size. Thus, the algorithm has a complexity of $O(D \times v)$.

8.7.3 Comparison of DE with Other Approaches

A number of simulations imitating a putative standard home environment with the help of other standard input data have been carried out. The power consumptions of assumed machines are realistic, obtained from standard sources [34, 35]. However, the start times, end times, and durations of tasks are assumed arbitrarily. Here, a dataset refers to a set of tasks, machines on which those tasks are performed, utilities of tasks, start times, end times, and durations of the tasks. A sample of 365 datasets for simulations were generated for the year 2012. This constitutes the realistic part of data being used.

Real data for cost-rate plans are obtained from Nova Scotia Power [36], a Canadian power supply company, which formulates the cost-rate plan based on the time of energy consumption. A sample input cost-rate plan is shown in Tables 8.4 and 8.5.

We compared the performance of the DE algorithm with two major approaches, Particle Swarm Optimization (PSO) and Random Scheduling. Random scheduling indicates that the approach when the cost-rate plan has not been looked into and tasks are randomly assigned a time taking into account deadline constraints. PSO is nearly the

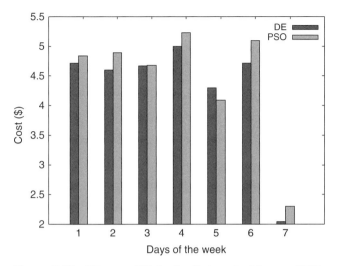

Figure 8.16. DE versus PSO for the first week of January 2012.

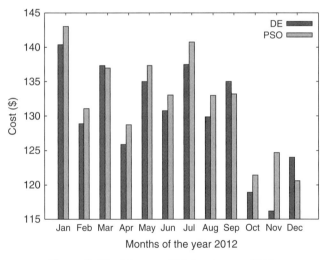

Figure 8.17. DE versus PSO for the year 2012.

best competing algorithm available (as others such as simple genetic algorithms do not do well in this problem domain), and random scheduling best represents the state of the practice – hence, the choice of these to present comparisons with.

A reduction in cost of 8–11% was seen when DE was used in place of PSO for the same input data. Figure 8.16 shows the daily performance of DE and PSO for the first week of January 2012. Figure 8.17 shows diagrammatically the overall monthly costs when DE and PSO were applied on a daily basis over the entire year 2012.

The proposed DE was also compared to PSO in terms of computational performance. (Although scheduling overhead is unlikely to be a serious issue in the context of cost-aware scheduling with smart grids, we can envision situations in other domains where it may be more significant.) DE was found to converge faster when experiments with the same number of iterations and the same population size were used. Also, DE was found to perform 13–20% better on a comparison done for computation time taken per iteration.

Using random scheduling, it can be seen that our algorithm performed significantly better, that is, it pays to schedule tasks after considering cost-rate plans rather than without considering them. Figure 8.18 shows the performance of DE and random scheduling for the first week of January 2012. Figure 8.19 shows diagrammatically the simulated

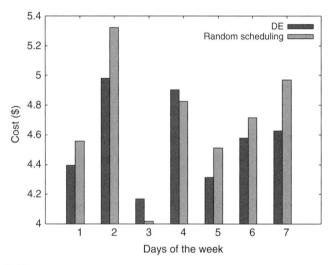

Figure 8.18.   DE versus random scheduling for the second week of January 2012.

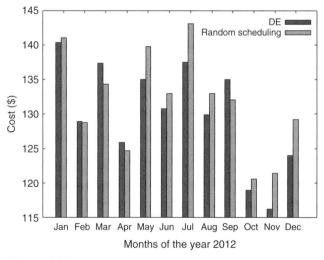

Figure 8.19.   DE versus random scheduling for the year 2012.

values when DE and random scheduling were performed on a daily basis over the year 2012. A percentage improvement of 15–17% was seen when DE was used in place of random scheduling for the same input data.

8.8 HETEROGENEITY, COOLING, DVFS, AND MIGRATION

EA resource allocation and scheduling is a difficult problem as it is, but as indicated in previous sections, it is a problem that can be effectively addressed, with suitable caution regarding computation time and objective function. However, we must take a step back to look at a broader picture. Recent techniques have offered us new ways to manage our infrastructures and more freedom to reach better solutions.

8.8.1 Lever Interactions

There have been significant changes in the levers we have to handle the resource allocation problem. These levers are even more important to enforce energy and power reduction in a distributed infrastructure. There is firstly the dynamic voltage and frequency scaling (DVFS), which allows us to modify the current voltage and frequency (and thus the computational speed and power consumption) of a processor. A lower speed consumes less power than a higher speed, while of course doing less computational work in a given time. However, when we are talking about tasks of fixed sizes, a lower speed does not necessarily mean that the energy consumed by the whole task to be lower, because we have to account for the power consumed over the whole task duration.

Secondly, there is the use of virtualization techniques. Such techniques, often used in cloud computing, also allow us to run a guest operating system in a VM. This makes it possible to have several different operating systems running different tasks on a same physical machine, in a completely separated environment. Common virtualization techniques also allow us to be able to migrate VMs from one host to another, either by stop-and-copy or by live migration, which means copying while the VM is still running, with almost no disruption of service, but higher transfer costs.

Lastly, in relation with the virtualization techniques, we have an increased need and ability for consolidation, thus reducing the number of hosts used to better match the current infrastructure utilization. There is a need to be able to power on and off physical machines often enough to manage the dynamic usages and movements of the VMs running tasks.

All these levers already feature complex interactions within the use of any single lever, and even more complex interactions with one another.

8.8.2 Infrastructures

When EA resource allocation is sought to be done in a large distributed system, it is interesting to take a step back and account for all the infrastructure. It can be interesting to take into account certain aspects of the system to better account for interactions and possible energy savings. We have to take into account, for example, the possible heterogeneity of the system and the cooling mechanisms.

In a modern data center, cooling equipment (such as air-conditioning units, fans, and pumps) account for a large percentage of the data center power consumption, which itself can easily be 30% of the total power consumption [37]. Such equipment, like almost all the equipments of a data center, can be used judiciously to effect energy savings. This means that there is a large potential for energy reduction if we take into account the cooling configuration in the allocation algorithms.

We can model, for example, the fact that we can act on the power state of the computer room air handler (CRAH, which handles the routing of the air inside a cluster), and power on or off some of them when they are needed or not.

There is also a need to take into account the possible heterogeneity of a data center for two reasons. First, if our infrastructure is geographically distributed, we might have several clusters that have not been built at the same time and thus have been using different types of servers. Secondly, inside a same cluster, over time, some machines may have been added to increase the capability or some machines may have been replaced. This means that there can be an intrinsic heterogeneity inside a cluster.

Such considerations imply that we have to take into account at the host level, and therefore, at the data center level, the energy efficiency of a machine, which gives rise to new problems because we need a knowledge of all the different machines and of the infrastructure as a whole.

There can be a difference in the interactions of the different aspects of an infrastructure that we must consider. For example, we cannot just minimize the number of running hosts to reduce power consumption – we may also have to reduce the usage of cooling equipment. This, while considering that the interactions induced by considering both objectives can be difficult to master, because we can imagine a case where switching off some cooling equipment would yield greater power reduction but cause problems because of increased hotspots, while powering off some computing equipment instead may increase the system's utilization but lead to a poor solution in terms of energy usage.

8.8.3 Resource Allocation as a Whole

In light of all the means of action we have to manage the infrastructure, it appears that the resource allocation is becoming a more complex problem. Allocating resources is not just deciding where to put a task any more – it is also the management of the machines, while taking into account all the means available after the allocation itself, such as the different frequencies of the chosen processor.

One should also note that there is a fundamental scale difference between the levers that implies different management styles needed. For example, the DVFS technique is at the processor, or even the core of the processor level while powering on or off a host is at the machine level, cooling a data center must be done at the cluster level, while migrating VMs will be done between a group of machines. We must have a multilevel approach taking into account the whole spectrum of possible approaches to improve performance and reduce energy consumption, from the data center level to the component level.

These new constraints make the EA resource allocation problem even more complex as some of the levers have conflicting interactions and requirements. Consider, for example, DVFS: we want to lower the frequency of a processor, which induces a lower power consumption of the host. However, we can easily imagine a case where there are other tasks that could have been executed by this host, if it was set to run at full speed, and thus may be switch off another host and further reduce the power consumption of the system. We would, therefore, have a discrepancy between the DVFS lever and the consolidation lever.

There can also be a negative effect within the usage of a lever. For example, if we consolidated our resource allocation too aggressively, we could have an effect on the provisioning of VMs, because it would be harder to increase the resources of a VM without affecting others. This happens without even considering the interferences between vVMs when they are allocated on a same host, which are due to the virtualization overhead itself [38].

The possibility of a negative effect does not, however, necessarily mean that it is not exceeded by the positive effects on the objective. It just means that to perform well, one has to account for the different aspects of the underlying infrastructure as much as possible.

However, accounting for as many different effects as possible can lead to more difficulties, such as in the modeling of the problem. Increasing the number of constraints on the system itself, if we are trying to model the resource allocation problem to be used in an LP, as mentioned in Section 8.2, would greatly increase the complexity of the LP, thus increasing the complexity of even writing the LP itself, as it would be harder to find sets of constraints that are linear (the larger the number of interactions between variables, the greater the chance that the model being nonlinear). This in turn drives up the complexity of solving the LP also, as a consequence of the increases in the numbers of constraints and variables.

The approximated solutions that we can compute using fast algorithms and heuristics have to account for such effects and aspects of the system. If not, the quality of the approximated solutions is too far removed from that of the optimal solution, and we end up not achieving anywhere close to the quantum of reduction possible in energy consumption.

Finally, it is paramount to take into account the migration of the VMs and the overhead in time and resource consumption that this implies. That means that instead of having resource allocation algorithms, we need to have resource allocation and reallocation algorithms, for the simple reason that we are usually unable to migrate a significant number of VMs at the same time, on account of likely bottlenecks in the network infrastructure.

8.9 CONCLUSIONS

While we have tried our best to cover as broad a range of issues as possible in relation to EA resource allocation and scheduling, it must be said that this is just the beginning and that many problems and issues remain, offering a rich range of possibilities for further research by both practitioners and theoreticians.

Among them, we may mention just a couple of importance: (i) in-depth theoretical studies of EA scheduling and (ii) unified practical approaches that permit the use of insights gained with EA scheduling in one application domain, in another.

With the first point, it must be noted that the state of the theory in EA task and resource allocation, and indeed in energy awareness in general, is very much in its infancy. Energy is an issue well understood by engineers and physicists in certain other contexts, but it is yet to receive much attention from theoreticians in applied mathematics, operations research, and computer science.

With the second point, but in a way still related to the first, there is also a pressing need for a general theory of EA scheduling that forestalls the need for practitioners in different domains to learn everything anew. Although different domains may operate at vastly different sizes and with very dissimilar sets of requirements and constraints, there is no reason to suggest that a more unified set of practical approaches, and best practices for energy efficiency in various domains, cannot be achieved.

If this chapter is able to foster growth in these ways, we will count it as successful.

REFERENCES

[1] Petrucci V, Carrera EV, Loques O, Leite JCB, Mosse D. Optimized management of power and performance for virtualized heterogeneous server clusters. Proceedings of the 2011 11th IEEE/ACM International Symposium on Cluster, Cloud and Grid Computing, Ser. CCGRID '11. Washington (DC): IEEE Computer Society; 2011. p 23–32. [Online] Available at: http://dx.doi.org/10.1109/CCGrid.2011.15. Accessed 2014 Sep 30.

[2] Borgetto D, Casanova H, Da Costa G, Pierson J-M. Energy-aware service allocation. Future Gener Comput Syst 2012;28(5):769–779, special section on Energy Efficiency in Large-Scale Distributed Systems. [Online] Available at: http://dx.doi.org/10.1016/j.future.2011.04.018. Accessed 2014 Sep 30.

[3] Horen J. In: Murty KG, editors. *Linear Programming*. New York: John Wiley and Sons; 1983. 482 pp; Networks 198515(2):273–274. [Online] Available at: http://dblp.uni-trier.de/db/journals/networks/networks15.html#Horen85. Accessed 2014 Sep 30.

[4] Gurobi Optimization. Reference Manual; 2013. [Online] Available at: http://www.gurobi.com

[5] IBM ILOG. ILOG CPLEX: high-performance mathematical programming solver for linear programming, mixed integer programming, and quadratic programming; 2013. Available at: http://www-01.ibm.com/software/commerce/optimization/cplex-optimizer/. Accessed 2014 Sep 30.

[6] GNU. GLPK (GNU linear programming kit); 2013. Available at: http://www.gnu.org/software/glpk/. Accessed 2014 Sep 30.

[7] Leinberger W, Karypis G, Kumar V. Multi-capacity bin packing algorithms with applications to job scheduling under multiple constraints. Proceedings 1999 International Conference on Parallel Processing; 1999. p 404–412.

[8] Stillwell M, Schanzenbach D, Vivien F, Casanova H. Resource allocation using virtual clusters. Proceedings of the 2009 9th IEEE/ACM International Symposium on Cluster Computing and the Grid, ser. CCGRID '09. Washington (DC): IEEE Computer Society; 2009. p 260–267. [Online] Available at: http://dx.doi.org/10.1109/CCGRID.2009.23. Accessed 2014 Sep 30.

[9] Borgetto D, Maurer M, Da Costa G, Brandic I, Pierson J-M. Energy-efficient and SLA-aware management of IaaS clouds (regular paper). ACM/IEEE International

Conference on Energy-Efficient Computing and Networking (e-Energy); 2012 May 09-11. Madrid; ACM DL; 2012 (electronic medium). Available at: http://portal.acm.org/dl.cfm. Accessed 2014 Sep 30.

[10] Agrawal P, Rao S. Energy-aware scheduling of distributed systems. IEEE Transactons on Automation Science and Engineering, 11(4), October 2014, 1163–1175.

[11] Kwok Y-K, Ahmad I. Efficient scheduling of arbitrary task graphs to multiprocessors using a parallel genetic algorithm. J Parallel Distrib Comput 1997;47(1):58–77.

[12] Zomaya A, Ward C, Macey B. Genetic scheduling for parallel processor systems: comparative studies and performance issues. IEEE Trans Parallel Distrib Syst 1999;10(8):795–812.

[13] Goldberg DE. *Genetic Algorithms in Search, Optimization, and Machine Learning.* Addison-Wesley Longman, Boston, MA: 1989.

[14] Davis LD, Mitchell M. *Handbook of Genetic Algorithms.* New York: Van Nostrand Reinhold; 1991.

[15] Srinivas M, Patnaik LM. Genetic algorithms: a survey. Computer 1994;27(6):17–26.

[16] Seredynski F, Zomaya A. Sequential and parallel cellular automata-based scheduling algorithms. IEEE Trans Parallel Distrib Syst 2002;13(10):1009–1023.

[17] Zomaya AY, Lee YC, editors. *Energy-Efficient Distributed Computing Systems.* Wiley-IEEE Press, Hoboken, NJ: 2012.

[18] Talia D, Trunfio P. *Service-Oriented Distributed Knowledge Discovery.* Chapman and Hall/CRC; Boca Raton, FL, 2012.

[19] Comito C, Talia D, Trunfio P. An energy-aware clustering scheme for mobile applications. Proceedings of the 11th IEEE International Conference on Computer and Information Technology (CIT 2011); Paphos, Cyprus; 2011. p 15–22.

[20] Garey MR, Grahams RL. Bounds for multiprocessor scheduling with resource constraints. SIAM J Comput 1975;4:187–200.

[21] Chang HWD, Oldham WJB. Dynamic task allocation models for large distributed computing systems. IEEE Trans Parallel Distrib Syst 1995;6(12):1301–1315.

[22] Comito C, Falcone D, Talia D, Trunfio P. Energy efficient task allocation over mobile networks. Proceedings of the 9th IEEE International Conference on Dependable, Autonomic and Secure Computing (DASC 2011); 2011 Dec 13; Sydney; 2011. p 380–387.

[23] Comito C, Falcone D, Talia D, Trunfio P. Efficient allocation of data mining tasks in mobile environments. Concurrent Eng Res Appl 2013;21(3):197–207.

[24] Yu J, Buyya R. Gridbus workflow enactment engine. In: Wang L, Jie W, Chen J, editors. *Grid Computing: Infrastructure, Service, and Applications.* Boca Raton (FL): CRC Press; 2009. p 119–146.

[25] Ranjan R, Rahman M, Buyya R. A decentralized and cooperative workflow scheduling algorithm. 8th IEEE International Symposium on Cluster Computing and the Grid, 2008. CCGRID'08. IEEE; 2008. p 1–8.

[26] Ranjan R, Harwood A, Buyya R. SLA-based coordinated superscheduling scheme for computational grids. 2006 IEEE International Conference on Cluster Computing. IEEE; 2006. p 1–8.

[27] Comito C, Falcone D, Talia D, Trunfio P. Energy efficient task allocation over mobile networks. 2011 IEEE Ninth International Conference on Dependable, Autonomic and Secure Computing (DASC). IEEE; 2011. p 380–387.

[28] Huang Y, Bessis N, Norrington P, Kuonen P, Hirsbrunner B. Exploring decentralized dynamic scheduling for grids and clouds using the community-aware scheduling algorithm. Future Gener Comput Syst 2013;29(1):402–415.

[29] Prakash P. Cost-aware scheduling using differential evolution for electricity consumers connected to a smart grid [Master's thesis]. International Institute of Information Technology Bangalore; 2013.

[30] Lee Z-J, Lee C-Y. A hybrid search algorithm with heuristics for resource allocation problem. Inf Comput Sci 2005;173(1–3):155–167.

[31] Venugopal S, Buyya R. A deadline and budget constrained scheduling algorithm for escience applications on data grids. 6th International Conference on Algorithms and Architectures for Parallel Processing (ICA3PP'05). Berlin, Heidelberg: Springer-Verlag; 2005. p 60–72.

[32] Lichtblau D. *Differential Evolution in Discrete and Combinatorial Optimization*. Mathematica Tutorial Notes, MathSource. Wolfram Research Inc.; 2010.

[33] Rohlfshagen P. Differential evolution and particle swarm optimisation; 2008. [Online] Available at: http://www.cs.bham.ac.uk/ pkl/teaching/2008/ec/. Accessed 2014 Sep 30.

[34] OKSolar.com. Appliance typical power consumption information. [Online] Available at: http://www.oksolar.com/technical/consumption.html. Accessed 2014 Sep 30.

[35] U.S. Department of Energy. Estimating appliance and home electronic energy use, department of energy. [Online] Available at: http://energy.gov/energysaver/articles/estimating-appliance-and-home-electronic-energy-use. Accessed 2014 Sep 30.

[36] Nova-Scotia Power. [Online] Available at: http://www.nspower.ca. Accessed 2014 Sep 30.

[37] Pelley S, Meisner D, Wenisch TF, Vangilder JW. Understanding and abstracting total data center power; 2009. p 2706–2710. [Online] Available at: http://web.eecs.umich.edu/~twenisch/papers/weed09.pdf. Accessed 2014 Sep 30.

[38] Nathuji R, Kansal A, Ghaffarkhah A. Q-clouds: managing performance interference effects for QOS-aware clouds. Proceedings of the 5th European conference on Computer systems, ser. EuroSys '10. New York: ACM; 2010. p 237–250. [Online] DOI: http://doi.acm.org/10.1145/1755913.1755938.

9

ENERGY EFFICIENCY IN P2P SYSTEMS AND APPLICATIONS

Simone Brienza,[1] Sena Efsun Cebeci,[2]
Seyed-Saeid Masoumzadeh,[3] Helmut Hlavacs,[3] Öznur Özkasap,[2]
and Giuseppe Anastasi[1]

[1]*Department of Information Engineering, University of Pisa, Pisa, Italy*
[2]*Department of Computer Engineering, Koç University, Istanbul, Turkey*
[3]*Research Group Entertainment Computing, University of Vienna, Vienna, Austria*

Peer-to-peer (P2P) systems and applications have achieved increasing popularity in the past years because of the characteristics of dynamicity and scalability of the P2P paradigm. Currently, P2P applications – especially file-sharing and file distribution applications – generate a remarkable portion of the overall Internet traffic. However, many common P2P protocols do not consider the energy problem. Frequently, hosts are requested to stay on and remain connected to the network for long times. Therefore, they are very energy consuming. In this chapter, we present a general taxonomy to classify possible approaches to the energy problem in P2P systems and applications. Then, we survey the main solutions available in the literature, focusing on two relevant classes of P2P protocols, namely, file-sharing/distribution protocols (e.g., BitTorrent and Gnutella) and epidemic P2P protocols.

Large-Scale Distributed Systems and Energy Efficiency: A Holistic View, First Edition.
Edited by Jean-Marc Pierson.
© 2015 John Wiley & Sons, Inc. Published 2015 by John Wiley & Sons, Inc.

9.1 INTRODUCTION

P2P systems have gained more and more importance in recent years. P2P file-sharing applications are among the most popular Internet applications and account for a large fraction of the overall Internet traffic [1]. According to an experimental study carried out in 2009 [2], the percentage of the Internet traffic originating from P2P file sharing ranges from 40% to 73%, depending on the considered geographic area. Also many distributed services such as reliable multicasting, aggregate computation, frequent items discovery, overlay topology construction, and failure detection rely on P2P systems.

Originally, P2P systems have been conceived without considering the energy problem. For instance, BitTorrent [3] – which is the most popular protocol for P2P file sharing – has no internal mechanism for energy efficiency. The main motivation for this design choice is that in P2P systems, energy consumption is distributed among a large number of peers, while in traditional client–server architectures, energy is mainly consumed at data centers. Hence, in P2P systems, energy costs are not supported by a single organization, instead they are shared by a large number of users. As the energy costs of P2P systems and applications keep increasing with their popularity and share of the overall Internet traffic – and awareness about energy and environmental issues increases – developing energy-efficient solutions for P2P systems has attracted more and more attention in recent years.

A number of solutions have been proposed in the literature. As energy consumption is distributed among several peers taking part in the application, providing energy-efficient solutions for P2P systems is generally more challenging than for traditional client–server scenarios. This issue is pointed out in [4] where it is shown that energy adaptation in P2P environments is more complex than in a traditional client–server environment. In this chapter, we classify the main approaches to energy efficiency in P2P systems and applications by introducing a general taxonomy. Then, we survey the main solutions proposed in the literature, with special focus on two main areas, namely, file-sharing/distribution and epidemic protocols.

The rest of this chapter is organized as follows. Section 9.2 discusses the main approaches to energy efficiency in P2P systems and applications and introduces a general taxonomy for them. Section 9.3 addresses energy efficiency in P2P file-sharing applications, while Section 9.4 focuses on energy efficiency in P2P epidemic protocols. Section 9.5 draws some conclusions.

9.2 GENERAL APPROACHES TO ENERGY EFFICIENCY

In this section, we provide a classification of energy-aware P2P approaches into three main classes, based on the techniques they use, namely, *sleep/wakeup*, *hierarchical*, and *resource allocation*. The taxonomy is illustrated in Figure 9.1.

9.2.1 Sleep/Wakeup Approaches

Sleep/wakeup is a commonly used energy efficiency technique in P2P systems, which is based on the idea of switching off some of the unused devices in the system and

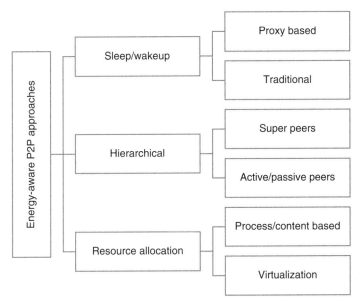

Figure 9.1. Classification of energy-aware P2P approaches.

waking them up when necessary. As availability has utmost importance in P2P systems, sleep/wakeup modes should be designed smartly. Furthermore, because of their dynamic nature, P2P systems require even smarter techniques. Sleep/wakeup approaches can be further divided into two subclasses, namely, *proxy based* and *traditional*, depending on whether, or not, they use proxy subsystems. The two alternative approaches are discussed in the following.

9.2.1.1 *Proxy-Based Sleep/Wakeup.* In proxy-based solutions, peers either completely hand over their tasks to a proxy or use the proxy only for the purpose of waking up. Proxy-based solutions for Gnutella P2P file sharing [5] have been proposed in [6] and [7]. In both cases, the idea consists in using a P2P proxy subsystem – embedded either in the network interface card (NIC) at the host or in another device such as a local area network (LAN) switch – that takes over the control when the host goes into a low-power mode.

EE-BitTorrent [8, 9] also leverages a proxy-based architecture for improving energy efficiency in BitTorrent [3]. The authors point out that energy waste could be avoided by switching off some peers and delegating the file download to their associated proxy. The proxy can be either a dedicated computer or a machine that has to be continuously powered on for providing other network services.

Download Sharing [10] also relies on proxying to reduce the energy consumption of P2P file sharing when dealing with unpopular files, that is, files for which very few copies are available on the overlay. As the number of seeders is very low, P2P file sharing tends to degenerate in a client–server file transfer and the download time (and energy consumption) increases significantly. In such conditions, it would be more convenient to combine the upload capacity of seeders and avoid semantically redundant download flows. To this end, in Download Sharing, a number of *active leechers* act as proxies and manage the download task on behalf of passive leechers, whose power mode is changed into sleep mode to ensure energy savings. Active leechers are selected among peers with the fastest links.

Proxy-based approaches are also used for P2P content sharing in wireless mobile systems [11–16]. All the previous proposals will be analyzed in detail in Section 9.3.

9.2.1.2 Traditional Sleep/Wakeup. In traditional sleep/wakeup approaches, peers do not use a proxy subsystem and the wakeup operation of a peer in sleep mode is done either by the peer itself or in cooperation with the other peers. An example study in this group aims at building an energy-efficient P2P storage system [17]. It argues that idle network resources are abundant in P2P systems and sleep mode can be utilized to save energy. Before entering the sleep mode, peers compute a future wakeup time. When this period of time passes, they wake up if there is no failure.

In the context of file sharing, *Green BitTorrent* [18] takes a traditional sleep/wakeup approach. It allows peers to sleep without being dropped from peer lists. By modifying the behavior of the BitTorrent client to flag a disconnecting peer as asleep, instead of removing its entry from the peer list, it is possible to maintain knowledge of sleeping peers throughout the swarm. If the resources of the sleeping peer are later needed, a peer can wake it up and restore the Transmission Control Protocol (TCP) connection. Green BitTorrent relies on the wake-on-LAN (WoL) technology [19]. A similar approach is also used in [20], where a set-top-box (STB) prototype for energy efficiency in BitTorrent is proposed. Like Green BitTorrent, it defines new peer states, including energy saving mode, uses WoL technology and relies on *hibernation* and *wakeup* messages.

An adaptive BitTorrent mechanism is proposed in [21], which relies on a *seed pool* method. The elements of the pool are servers with diverse upload capacities and power consumption rates. Sleep and active states are defined for all peers in the swarm. Peers in active state perform actions to serve the file download requests from other peers. For energy efficiency, seeders with high upload rates help peers with low upload rate to finish the download process quickly.

A model developed to reduce energy consumption in data centers is proposed in [22]. For this purpose, it uses a distributed algorithm, deployed over a P2P network of STBs. STBs are similar to small computers with hard drives, central processing unit (CPU), and even graphics processing unit (GPU) processors. In this study, the aim is to put unused STBs in standby mode without degrading the general service-level agreement (SLA). STBs are turned on only when clients request the service. The study discusses the potential advantages of turning STBs off and evaluations show energy consumption improvements.

9.2.2 Hierarchical Approaches

Hierarchical approaches introduce a structure in the overlay network. Not all peers are equal but some peers have a special role in the overlay. Hierarchical approaches can be further divided into two different classes, depending on whether they use *super peers* or not. Super peers are special peers that are advantageous in terms of energy efficiency and are preferable when compared to other peers. They are selected within the overlay to carry out some specific tasks. In hierarchical approaches that do not rely on super peers, referred to as hierarchical approaches with *active/passive peers* in our taxonomy, peers can be either active or passive. The aim of these approaches is to reduce the number of active peers in the system and, hence, the network overhead and resource usage.

9.2.2.1 Hierarchical Approaches Based on Super Peers.

An example of hierarchical solution based on super peers can be found in [23], where the authors propose an energy-efficient routing approach for *double-layered* mobile P2P systems aimed to improve the system lifetime. In a double-layered P2P system, there are two types of peers, namely, *super peers* and *subpeers*, and the search process is done mainly through super peers. Each super peer in the proposed system maintains a route table and a file routing table to keep the information regarding the routes and file lists, respectively.

Another example of solution based on super peers is presented in [24] and it develops a system where there exist multiple server computers each of which holds a file. A client computer sends a file transfer request to a load balancer (i.e., a logical process). Then, the load balancer selects one server computer s in the set S. There are two main conditions that must be considered when selecting the server computer. Firstly, it should satisfy the deadline constraint for the file transmission. Secondly, the power consumption of the selected server computer is also taken into account.

An energy-efficient P2P agreement protocol is presented in [25], which aims to reduce redundant transmissions without compromising reliability. For this purpose, it uses a mechanism, named TBMPR (*trustworthiness-based multipoint relaying*), which determines the trustworthiness of each peer by the number of successful transactions. Each peer sends a message to neighboring peers and only trustworthy neighbor peers forward that message.

9.2.2.2 Hierarchical Approaches Based on Active/Passive Peers.

Hierarchical approaches based on active/passive peers have been considered for energy efficiency in epidemic protocols. In [26] and [27], the authors investigate the power-awareness features of *flat* and *hierarchical* epidemic protocols. These studies propose a dominating set (DS)-based and power-aware hierarchical epidemic approach that eliminates a significant number of peers from gossiping. In contrast to previous works on hierarchical epidemics, the DS idea is used to construct a hierarchy and to choose peers performing gossip operation. In this adaptive approach, only a subset of peers is active in gossiping, forming an overlay consisting of DS peers, so that the other peers can switch to idle or passive state.

The hierarchical approach based on active/passive peers has been considered also for content sharing. The Smart Mobile Cloud (SMC) [28] is an energy-efficient cloud-based P2P content sharing solution for mobile devices. SMC uses a strategy for grouping mobile nodes (i.e., *helper nodes* act as active entities that manage the file download process and *seeker nodes* request file downloads as passive entities) close to each other based on their location. Serving file download requests by using resources of the nodes in the same group would then facilitate energy efficiency.

Another energy-adaptive technique for P2P file sharing in mobile devices is proposed in [29], where the idea is to gather mobile users according to their energy budget and to restrict their transmission capacity in order to achieve energy savings. In this technique, peers are grouped into *energy-sufficient* and *energy-constrained* peers. The download process differs from traditional BitTorrent protocol in the following aspects. When a file is requested, the tracker provides two neighbor lists to a peer. The first list contains information about peers belonging to the same energy group as the requester peer, while the second list contains information about energy-sufficient peers.

9.2.3   Resource Allocation

Resource allocation techniques have a significant effect on reducing energy consumption in P2P networks. These techniques are applied via various resource allocation mechanisms such as *process/content based* or *virtualization*. In the *process/content-based* approaches, the idea is to allocate system resources in an energy-efficient way. While some studies aim at reducing energy consumption of peers via efficient *process* allocation algorithms, others consider *content* file types as resources (e.g., polluted and unpolluted content) and conduct energy efficiency analysis for various system conditions. On the other hand, in *virtualization* approaches, system resources are managed by virtual machines (VMs) to perform tasks in an energy-efficient manner.

9.2.3.1   Process/Content-based   Resource   Allocation   Approaches.
In the category of content-based resource allocation, a model that considers content pollution for energy consumption is proposed in [30]. It is shown that deleting polluted file copies from stable systems and flash crowd systems yields energy savings. In the experimental analysis, the effects of leave rate of clean copies and delete rate of polluted copies on energy consumption are explored. The results show that increasing the delete and leave rates has a positive impact on energy savings. On the other hand, in the flash crowd case, results demonstrate that an increase in the leave rate of clean copies reduces energy consumption.

In the category of process-based resource allocation, computing the amount of electric power consumed to perform processes in each computer is addressed in [31]. It uses a macro-level model to show the relation between the amount of computation and the total power consumption of peer computers in order to perform Web types of application processes. In addition, the authors discuss the *laxity* concept for allocating a process to a computer so that the deadline constraint is satisfied and the total power consumption is reduced. In this system, there is a deadline constraint to allocate processes to computers. A deadline constraint on a process is issued by the application and the process has to be allocated to a computer so that it can terminate by the deadline. In laxity-based algorithm, the number of processes that do not satisfy the deadline constraint is reduced and evaluations show that the laxity-based process allocation algorithm is more efficient in reducing total power consumption when compared to the traditional round-robin algorithm.

9.2.3.2   Virtualization   Resource   Allocation   Approaches.   Some studies
propose a virtualization approach to conserve energy in P2P systems [32–34]. They are based on the idea of energy-efficient resource sharing among home networks interconnected via a P2P overlay, through virtualization of tasks. Virtualization of tasks means moving the VM responsible for a particular task from one virtual home environment

(VHE) to another VHE. Shifting load to a small number of computers provides that the relieved computers can be hibernated to save energy.

A task virtualization prototype for unpopular files has been developed in [10], where a VM that remotely takes care of managing the resources for file download is used. By using the VM, the download tasks are migrated to other machines. However, this approach has drawbacks in terms of privacy and security. The authors have developed scenarios to investigate the resource utilizations of CPU, memory, and NIC, and the results show that resource utilization grows linearly while the number of VMs involved in the system increases. Furthermore, the effects of load, upload bandwidth, and fairness on the energy consumption were demonstrated.

9.3 ENERGY EFFICIENCY IN FILE-SHARING APPLICATIONS

In this section, we focus on file-sharing/distribution applications, which are the most popular P2P applications and, according to a number of studies [1, 2], account for a large fraction of the overall Internet traffic. In Section 9.3.1, we compare, in terms of energy efficiency, the two main approaches to file sharing, that is, client–server and P2P. Then, we focus on P2P systems and present some techniques for optimizing the energy efficiency in P2P file sharing. Finally, we discuss energy efficiency in BitTorrent and in other popular P2P file-sharing protocols.

9.3.1 Client–Server versus P2P File Sharing

A major difference between client–server networks and P2P ones is the role of each node. In a typical client–server network, each node can be either a *client* or a *server*, but not both. On the contrary, in a P2P network, the role of each node is the same: it is both a client and a server at the same time. Each node is able to obtain and provide services from and to others simultaneously. With this in mind, in a P2P file-sharing system, the file is not offered at a single server location but is offered by a multitude of peers. Therefore, the load can be distributed among those peers. The increase in the number of clients and, consequently, the increase in file requests in a client–server approach can lead to performance degradations because of server overloading. The situation in a P2P system is less severe, because more clients not only mean more requests but also higher service capacity and better scalability [35]. On the other hand, the robustness of a P2P file-sharing system is also much stronger than that of client–server one, as each peer can be a file server and, consequently, failures of peers have less impact on the system than the failures of servers in client–server file-sharing systems.

To compare the energy consumption of P2P file-sharing systems to client–server systems, it is important to have an overall perspective of their architectures. Nedevschi et al. [36] addressed some important factors contributing to energy consumption of both architectures and investigated which architecture is more energy efficient. In the following, we take these factors into consideration. In a P2P file-sharing system, peers typically spend a high portion of the day fully powered up, while their average utilization is typically very low. This factor plays a significant role in energy consumption of P2P systems. Apart from this, a P2P file-sharing system makes much heavier use of the network than a client–server system. It arises from generating overhead traffic for peer discovery and searching, as well as for membership maintenance. The average path length between peers can be significantly longer than the average path length between a client and the central server. On the other side, in a client–server file-sharing architecture, the power consumed by cooling in data centers is the most important factor that reduces energy efficiency, while a P2P architecture is exempt from this cost because of its geographic distribution and the fact that peers are mostly home personal computers (PCs). Another factor is the high-baseline energy consumption of computers, that is, the amount of energy that a computer requires to be powered up. The baseline energy consumption is typically much higher than the additional energy consumed when the utilization increases. The difference between P2P and client–server file-sharing systems lies in the fact that a P2P service is only responsible for the resultant increase in the peer's power consumption and is not responsible for baseline energy consumption, while in client–server architecture, the data center is responsible for the entire power consumption. Nedevschi et al. [36] considered all the aforementioned factors in the energy consumption modeling and compared P2P and client–server architectures to each other. They concluded that from the point of view of end systems, P2P is likely to always win. However, this conclusion strongly depends on the assumption that baseline energy consumption at peers comes for free.

9.3.2 Energy Efficiency in P2P File Sharing

In this section, we discuss a couple of theoretical approaches that have been proposed for improving the energy efficiency of P2P file-sharing systems [37, 38]. Sucevic et al. [37] have proposed scheduling in order to power down peers. The authors proposed different strategies for distributing the file to peers (i.e., *descending*, *random*, *ascending* upload-capacity order) and compared them with simultaneous and sequential approaches. In the ascending upload-capacity-order strategy, the scheduling mechanism involves peers finishing their download in an increasing order of their upload capacity and then going offline as soon as their download has been completed. This mechanism guarantees that peers with high-request-serving capabilities remain online for a longer time. The authors presented a mathematical model and proposed an optimal strategy for a small network. Further, their results showed that the optimal strategies quickly become too complex as the number of peers grows. On the basis of the same concept, Andrew et al. [38] have proposed a scheduling strategy to turn peers off and on so as to minimize the total energy consumption. They have shown that the optimal case is achieved when peers are on only when they are downloading with the highest rate, while a small subset of energy-efficient peers might be needed to be on for the whole time of the transfer. The proposed strategy is centralized as the authors considered a central algorithm for scheduling, in contrast to the distributed–nature of P2P systems.

9.3.3 Energy Efficiency in BitTorrent

In this section, we survey the main solutions proposed for increasing the energy efficiency of BitTorrent that is the most popular platform for P2P file sharing. In order to facilitate the reader's understanding, we preliminarily provide a brief description of the BitTorrent protocol (details can be found in [3] and [39]).

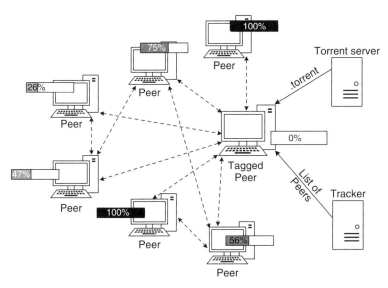

Figure 9.2. File distribution process.

BitTorrent implements an unstructured overlay network customized for file sharing. Nodes in the overlay are called *peers*, and the set of peers involved in the distribution of a file is referred to as *torrent* (or *swarm*). Each peer downloads the desired file, in *chunks*, from a multitude of other peers. While downloading missing chunks, peers upload to other peers in the same torrent the chunks they have already obtained. A peer can be either a *leecher*, if it does not have a complete copy of the file, or a *seeder*, if it has already achieved a complete copy of the file (seeders only upload chunks to other peers). For each torrent, there is a *tracker*, that is, a node that constantly tracks which peers are involved in the torrent. A peer that wants to join a torrent must register with the tracker and, then, it must periodically inform the tracker that it is still in the torrent. Figure 9.2 shows the different phases in the download process. As a preliminary step, a peer contacts the tracker and receives a random list of peers belonging to the torrent. It can thus open a TCP connection to a number of them and start exchanging chunks of the file. At any given time, the peer will be in contact with a set of other peers, called *neighbors*. The set of neighbors changes dynamically as peers join and leave the torrent. In addition, each peer preferentially selects, for downloading chunks, those peers from which it can achieve the highest download rate (see the following text). Finally, for every 30 s, the peer randomly selects a new peer from the list, as a way to discover new neighbors, and allows new peers in the torrent to start-up. At any given time, the peer has a subset of chunks composing the file. To figure out where missing chunks can be downloaded from, it periodically asks each of its neighbors for the list of chunks they have. Then, it uses the *Rarest First* strategy to decide the missing chunks to be requested first, that is, it gives priority to chunks that are less spread in the torrent. Finally, to decide which requests from other peers have to be served, the peer uses the *tit-for-tat* (*TFT*) strategy, that is, it gives priority to the peers from which it is downloading data at the highest rate.

Specifically, it measures the data rate it is achieving from each of its current neighbors and, then, selects the four neighbors with the highest data rate.

The BitTorrent protocol described earlier is not energy efficient. Peers have to stay active and connected to the overlay network for all the time required to download a file, which may take even several hours. Turning off peers is not a viable solution for the following reasons. If the peer is a leecher (i.e., it is still downloading chunks of the file), powering it off does not provide any benefit in terms of energy savings, as the download process immediately stops. If the peer is a seeder, powering it off is apparently a very good idea, as it has already obtained a complete copy of the file. However, if the number of seeders decreases, the average time for downloading a complete copy of the file becomes larger and larger, resulting in a corresponding increase in the average energy consumption of peers. Hence, powering off a seeder may also result in an increase in the overall system's energy consumption. Despite the previous remarks, a number of solutions have been proposed to increase the energy efficiency of BitTorrent. In the following, we discuss the most important of them.

Owing to the protocol popularity, the general problem of BitTorrent performance optimization has been thoroughly investigated – also using analytical techniques – and a number of solutions have been proposed. Most of these studies, however, are aimed at minimizing the *average download time*,[1] that is, the average time experienced by a peer to download a complete copy of the file [40–42]. Minimizing the average download time is a very important goal, especially from the user perspective. However, this is typically achieved by enforcing all (or a large number of) seeders to remain active all the time to continuously upload chunks, that is, at the cost of an increased system's energy consumption [38]. Hence, such strategies are inefficient from the energy consumption point of view. To make BitTorrent energy efficient, the *system energy consumption* (i.e., the total energy consumed by all the peers to achieve a complete copy of the file) should be minimized, instead of the average download time. To achieve this goal, the seeders should remain active for some time after getting a copy of the file. Hence, it is important to calculate the *optimal seeding time* that minimizes the system's energy consumption.

The optimal seeding time for popular files is calculated in [10], on the basis of the results derived in [40]. In [40], Qiu and Srikant referred to the scenario depicted in Figure 9.3 and developed a fluid model of the system, based on the following assumptions. Let $x(t)$ and $y(t)$ denote the number of leechers and seeders, respectively, at a given time t. New peers (i.e., leechers) arrive with a rate λ. Once a leecher turns into a seeder, it leaves the system with a rate γ, that is, it waits for a seeding time $\tau = 1/\gamma$ until it shuts down. As all peers are modeled equally, they are assumed to have a mean download rate of c and a mean upload rate of μ. In general, at a given point in time, uploading peers only have a part of the file and, hence, sometimes they may not be able to upload chunks to other peers. This is modeled through the *effectiveness* parameter η, that is, a real value in the range [0, 1] that represents the fraction of content already available at the peer. As seeders have the whole file, their effectiveness parameter is equal to 1. As shown in Figure 9.3, the total data flow is limited by either the total upload or download

---

[1]Another metric that is often used is the *last download time*, that is, the time taken by the last peer to get a complete copy of the file.

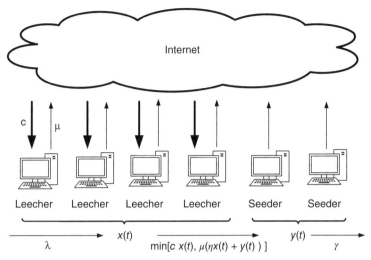

Figure 9.3. Fluid model consisting of uploads and downloads.

capacity. As a consequence, the actual data flow is given by the minimum of these two flows. Specifically, under the abovementioned assumptions, at a given time t the total download flow is $cx(t)$, while the total upload flow is $\mu[\eta \cdot x(t) + y(t)]$. It can be shown that the average download time T, which corresponds to the average time a leecher needs to turn into a seeder, is given by the following expression [40]:

$$T = \max\left\{\frac{1}{c}, \frac{1}{\eta}\left(\frac{1}{\mu} - \frac{1}{\gamma}\right)\right\}. \tag{9.1}$$

Equation (9.1) is exploited by Hlavacs et al. [10] to analyze the energy effectiveness of BitTorrent. They assume that each peer consumes one unit of power. Under this assumption, if λ leechers arrive each time unit, and each leecher needs, on an average, T time units to turn into a seeder, then the total energy consumed by all leechers is λT. Likewise, if τ denotes the average time a seeder waits until leaving the torrent (by definition, $\tau = 1/\gamma$), then the total energy consumed by all seeders is $\lambda\tau$. Hence, the average total energy E consumed by the system is

$$E = \lambda \cdot \max\left\{\frac{1}{c}, \frac{1}{\eta}\left(\frac{1}{\mu} - \tau\right)\right\} + \lambda\tau. \tag{9.2}$$

Figure 9.4 shows the average total energy E/λ as a function of the average seeding time τ. For low τ values, the average total energy consumed by the system tends to decrease as the average seeding time increases. This is because if there are more seeders uploading chunks, the download time experienced by peers – and the corresponding energy consumption – decreases. However, when the average seeding time becomes

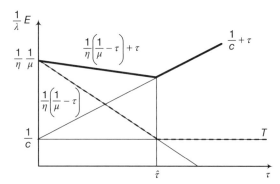

Figure 9.4. Average total power consumed by the system as a function of the average seeding time.

larger and larger, the additional energy consumed by seeders becomes predominant and it is not compensated anymore by the decrease in the average download time. Hence, the total energy consumption of the system increases. The optimal seeding time that minimizes the total energy consumption of the system can be derived from Equation (9.2). It yields

$$\hat{\tau} = \frac{1}{\mu} - \frac{\eta}{c}. \qquad (9.3)$$

On the basis of Equation (9.3), in order to minimize the energy consumption, ideally each seeder should remain active for a time equal to $\hat{\tau}$ after getting a complete copy of the file. In practice, the approach based on the optimal seeding time has a number of limitations that make it unpractical. First, the optimal seeding time depends on a number of parameters that are not under the user's control and, in addition, they also vary over time. Hence, it cannot be calculated by each peer. Besides, the user is typically *selfish* and *lazy*. He/she is mainly interested in getting a complete copy of the file (possibly with a minimum download time). He/she is not interested in minimizing the overall energy consumption of the system, especially if this is achieved at the cost of an increase in his/her personal energy consumption. In practice, the peer typically leaves the torrent *some time* after the file has been downloaded. The actual seeding time depends on user's convenience, not on energy considerations.

The optimal seeding time approach would be effective if it could be approximated so that the peer could calculate it at run time and automatically adjust the peer behavior in a transparent way for the user. This approach is exploited in *Green BitTorrent*, proposed in [18]. Green BitTorrent is an extended version of BitTorrent for energy efficiency and takes an approach classified as traditional sleep/wakeup, according to our taxonomy in Section 9.2. It allows peers to go to sleep when they are not downloading/uploading chunks, while remaining active members of the torrent. Green BitTorrent is backward compatible with the legacy protocol, that is, Green BitTorrent peers can operate with traditional BitTorrent peers, even if the latter ones experience some performance degradation. Basically, Green BitTorrent extends the legacy protocol by introducing the concept of *sleeping* peer. In the legacy protocol, peers establish TCP connections with their neighbors, which need to be always connected. In Green BitTorrent, a generic peer P in the torrent can appear to a tagged peer T in one of the following states [18]:

- *Connected.* Peer P has an active TCP connection with the tagged peer T. Hence, chunks can be uploaded and downloaded on the connection.
- *Sleeping.* Peer P has disconnected its TCP connection with the tagged peer T. The TCP connection must be reestablished before chunks can be uploaded or downloaded.
- *Unknown.* The tagged peer T has received P's address from the tracker; however, it does not know whether P is sleeping or awake.

To achieve its goals, Green BitTorrent relies on some additional mechanisms, namely, an *inactivity timer*, a *connection timer*, and uses *wakeup messages*. The inactivity timer is reset whenever a download/upload activity occurs, and it is used to decide when the peer can go to sleep. The connection timer is used to discover that a peer has disconnected. Finally, a wakeup message is a special message that is used to wake up a sleeping peer [43]. With reference to a tagged peer T in the torrent, the following events can occur, which are managed as described in the following (see [18] for details).

- *Detection of a Disconnected Peer.* Upon discovering that a peer P has closed its TCP connection, T sets P's state to sleeping.
- *Time-Out of the Inactivity Timer.* As soon as the inactivity timer expires, T closes all its TCP connections and enters the sleep state.
- *Reception of a Wakeup Message.* Upon receiving a wakeup message from a peer P, the tagged peer T waits until its TCP connection with peer P has been reestablished and, then, starts exchanging data with it.
- *Time-Out of Connection Timer.* On a timeout of the connection timer, the tagged peer T checks the number of connected peers. If it is below a predefined threshold *max_connect*, it randomly picks up a peer P from the list received from the tracker, sends a *wakeup* message to P, and tries to open a TCP connection with P. If the last step was successful, then P's state is set to connected. Otherwise, P is removed from the list.

It has been shown that Green BitTorrent can save about 25% of the energy, in comparison with legacy BitTorrent [18]. The drawback consists in an increased average download time experienced by peers which is, however, acceptable. Hence, Green Bit-Torrent is both practical and effective. However, it has a number of limitations. First, the wakeup message used by Green BitTorrent is typically implemented through a magic packet [43], which may not be available on some network technology (for instance, it may not be supported by WiFi NICs). In addition, there may be some privacy issues. For example, a remote peer is able to know whether your PC is active or sleeping. Also, a malicious user could wake up your PC, just to increase your energy consumption.

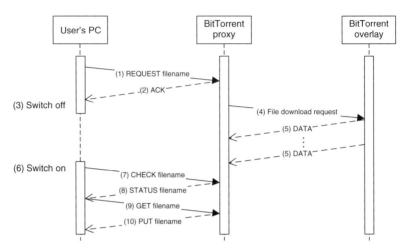

Figure 9.5. Action performed in the EE-BitTorrent protocol.

Finally, an attacker could suspend and wake up your PC with a high frequency to damage your hardware.

A completely different approach is used in *EE-BitTorrent* [8]. The proposed solution relies on a proxy-based architecture and, hence, belongs to the class of proxy-based sleep/wakeup systems, according to our taxonomy. It achieves energy efficiency by allowing a number of sleeping peers to be served by a *BitTorrent proxy*. Specifically, in EE-BitTorrent, peers delegate the download task to the associated proxy, which performs the task on their behalf. Most of the time, the requested file is already available on the proxy and can thus be immediately transferred to the user's PC. If this is not the case, the proxy participates in the BitTorrent overlay network as a regular peer and takes care of the overall process. Therefore, the user's PC can be switched off during the download phase. The file will be transferred from the proxy to the user's PC later, when the user reconnects.

Figure 9.5 shows the actions performed by the various actors of EE-BitTorrent. Upon receiving a request from the user, the user's PC contacts the proxy and requests the desired file (step 1). The proxy acknowledges the request (step 2). If the requested file is already available in the proxy's local cache, it is immediately transferred to the user. Otherwise, the proxy starts downloading the requested file from the BitTorrent overlay network, acting as a regular peer and following the legacy BitTorrent protocol (steps 4 and 5). The user's PC can be switched off just after receiving the acknowledgement from the proxy (step 3). Later, when the user reconnects (step 6), he/she can check the status of the download process at the proxy (steps 7 and 8). If the file is completely available, it can be transferred from the proxy to the user's PC (steps 9 and 10).

Experimental measurements have shown that EE-BitTorrent performs very well in an institutional scenario where the BitTorrent proxy is located on the same high-speed network of users' PCs [8], while in residential scenarios, the performance is strongly influenced by the uplink rate allowed by the access network [9]. When the uplink rate is low, the legacy BitTorrent protocol performs poorly, and EE-BitTorrent outperforms it

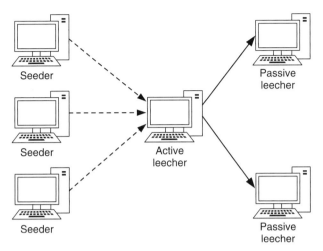

Figure 9.6. When the number of seeders is extremely low P2P file sharing may degenerate to a client–server file transfer.

in terms of average download time and energy consumption. The opposite occurs when the uplink rate is good. Motivated by these results, Giannetti et al. [9] have proposed an adaptive algorithm that dynamically selects the most efficient BitTorrent option (i.e., legacy or proxy-based), depending on the current operating conditions.

In terms of security, EE-BitTorrent is more robust than Green BitTorrent, provided that the BitTorrent proxy is a trusted machine. The basic idea of using a proxy for energy efficiency in BitTorrent has been highly influential in the design of later proposals, some of which are discussed in the following.

Download Sharing [10] also takes a proxy-based approach similar to that used in EE-BitTorrent, but it is mainly targeted to unpopular files. As well known, in BitTorrent, a file is simultaneously downloaded by a multitude of peers. However, in case of unpopular files, the number of seeders is very low and it may happen that there are as many leechers as seeders. Under such conditions, the P2P paradigm degenerates to a client–server file transfer, where a single seeder serves one or more leechers. Hence, there is dramatic performance degradation and a corresponding increase in the energy consumption. In such a case, it would be more convenient to combine the upload capacity of seeders and avoid semantically redundant download flows. The basic idea behind Download Sharing is to randomly select a subset of leechers to act as *proxies* and hibernate all the other leechers (see Figure 9.6). Proxies are called *active leechers*, as they represent other *passive* leechers hibernating in the meantime to save energy. Active leechers should be selected based on their network performance related to seeders, that is, the leecher with the fastest link to seeders should be selected as proxy. Once downloads are finished, active leechers may send the content to yet passive leechers with the full upload bandwidth. The analysis in [10] shows that Download Sharing reduces the energy consumption of the overall system when the uplink bandwidth of the proxies is much larger than the download rate achieved from the BitTorrent overlay (which, for unpopular file, is typically very low).

Proxy-based solutions have also been used for content sharing in a mobile environment [11–16]. The main goal here is to extend the lifetime of the mobile device. Different solutions have been proposed, which mainly differ in the location of the proxy. In [11], Kelenyi et al. proposed *CloudTorrent* where the proxy resides on a cloud server. It is shown that in comparison with a version of BitTorrent not using the proxy (*SymTorrent*), the proxy-based solution can significantly decrease the download time and reduce the energy consumption. In [12], the *router proxy* solution is presented where the proxy is hosted on the home router used by the user for residential Internet access. The home router is a good candidate for proxy because of its pervasiveness and stable energy consumption (i.e., independent from the operation load). The authors investigated the energy efficiency of the proposed approach by considering the memory limitation of the home router. It is shown that in both WLAN and 3G cellular networks, the download speed of the torrent and the chunk size affects the energy consumption. In the router proxy solution, the effect of chunk size on energy consumption and the effect of upload/download ratio on proxy download rate are investigated [16]. In this study, two types of peers, namely, limited (i.e., having limited repository) and regular peers (i.e., having sufficient repository) are defined. Then, the effect of increasing percentage of limited peers on the download time was analyzed.

In [13], a *distributed proxy* solution is proposed where multiple proxies are involved in the process of content download. In this solution, the aim is to increase the limited uplink rate of the home router, using multiple proxies, in order to meet the downlink capacity of mobile devices served. In the distributed proxy approach, the effect of increasing the number of proxies on energy consumption is investigated in [15]. It is shown that after a certain threshold, adding more proxies to the system is not convenient because the aggregate proxy upload rate meets the download rate of the mobile devices. Energy consumption for various upload/download ratios in single and multiple proxy settings have been explored. The experiments have shown that the energy consumption of multiple proxies slowly decreases while the upload/download ratio is low (i.e., 0.2–0.4) and then becomes stable once the aggregate proxy upload rate meets the download rate of the mobile devices.

In [14], the router proxy presented in [12] has been extended to overcome the memory limitation of the home router. In the overlay network, the router proxy behaves like an ordinary peer, but differently from the other peers, it is responsible for transferring the downloaded content to the mobile device. However, a problem arises due to limited memory of the router proxy. In the regular setting of the BitTorrent, when a peer downloads a chunk, it declares that chunk as available for downloading. In the case of mobile device, the router proxy erases the content transferred to a mobile device in order to reuse the memory. This introduces the problem of deleted content that is no longer available for other peers. To overcome these issues, the authors divided the memory available on the proxy into two buffers, namely, *upload* and *download buffers*. In the download buffer, downloaded chunks are kept but the content of the buffer is volatile. All the uploaded chunks available to download are stored in the upload buffer. Each downloaded chunk transferred to mobile device stays in the buffer and is accessible by the swarm. This router proxy approach outperforms the torrent client in the mobile device from energy efficiency and download time point of view.

9.3.4 Energy Efficiency in Other File-Sharing Protocols

After looking at the main solutions for increasing the energy efficiency in BitTorrent, in this section, we consider other P2P file-sharing protocols. *Gnutella* is another very popular protocol and, after BitTorrent, the one that has received the largest attention from the research community, in terms of proposals for increasing its energy efficiency. It uses *query flooding* to find files in the overlay network. The standard protocol version (version 4.0) defines five message types: *Ping*, *Pong*, *Query*, *QueryHit*, and *Push* [44]. The Ping message is used to discover Gnutella hosts in the neighborhood, and it is mainly used to build information about the neighborhood (reachable hosts, bytes shared, etc.). The Pong message is sent in response to a Ping. It includes information about the host sending it, such as uptime, amount of bytes shared, and whether it is willing to receive connections or not. The Query message is used to find files. It is sent by the host to its neighborhood and, in turn, the neighbors forward the message to their neighbors, for up to a maximum number of times specified in the Time-To-Live (TTL) field of the Query. The Query Hit message is the response from a Gnutella host that received the Query. It includes a file, or list of files, containing a combination of the keywords in the Query received. Finally, the Push message is used to download a file from a host that is behind a firewall. When a host receives a Push message, it opens a new TCP connection to the one that sent it. Through this connection, the host can request the file from the firewalled host and consequently download it.

After version 4.0, the version 6.0 was released. The main modification of this version is the introduction of *ultrapeers* [5]. In this Gnutella version, a peer can be either a *leaf* or an *ultrapeer*. A leaf connects to ultrapeers and shares with them the list of shared files. At first, and by default, all peers are leaf peers when they connect to the network. There are different ways to select peers to become ultrapeers in different Gnutella applications. The most common way is to use selection criteria such as the time the peer has been connected to the network, or the upload/download speed available to the peer. If the criterion is satisfied, then the peer advertises itself as an ultrapeer to the network.

A proxy-based solution for energy efficiency in Gnutella has been proposed in [6]. The authors designed a P2P power management proxy, operating in a low-power micro-controller. The proxy can be colocated within the host (e.g., on an Ethernet NIC) or in another device (e.g., a LAN switch). It supports a subset of a Gnutella host capabilities, including initiating and accepting connections to and from neighbors, receiving and for-warding Query messages, and generating QueryHit messages. As the proxy has limited capacity to store shared files, it wakes up the corresponding host in order to carry out file requests. For adequately maintaining the query messaging between the proxy and host, some state information is essential, such as power state of the host (i.e., powered on or sleeping), shared file names, and Internet Protocol (IP) addresses of the neighbor nodes. File names can be shared between the host and the proxy in the form of a Bloom filter [45]. TCP connections are transferred between host and proxy by reestablishment. Generally, the proposed method allows computers to go asleep when they are idle and be woken up by proxy when a request for file – in the form of a Hypertext Transfer Protocol (HTTP) GET – is received. The experimental results show that the proposed proxy-based approach outperforms the legacy approach, in terms of query forwarding rate and, in addition, the proxy-based approach provides significant energy savings. The authors claimed that if 25% of all P2P hosts in the United States were to adopt this method, a saving of over $38 million (in 2007 value) in energy costs could be achieved.

Another proxy-based solution for Gnutella has been presented in [7], where the authors proposed a method called *power-proxying* that consists of selectively proxying a subset of protocol semantics via a separate hardware controller on the NIC of each PC. When a PC is in standby state, the proxy handles all the Gnutella packets except the file upload requests. To deploy this approach in the real word, a specialized NIC needs to be developed, which is a major limitation of this work.

Energy-efficient solutions have been proposed also for wireless/mobile environments. As running P2P file-sharing applications in a wireless/mobile Internet entails different constraints compared with those in the traditional wired Internet, Neves da Hora et al. [46] proposed a message reduction approach to reduce the average energy consumption and delay of Gnutella on top of mobile ad hoc networks (MANETs). They employed a gossip protocol and used its inherent probabilistic forwarding behavior to reduce the number of messages. Furthermore, the authors proved that the lower load allowed the P2P network to consume up to 32% less energy. For the same environment, Mawji et al. [47] proposed a path selection algorithm for downloading files, using the Gnutella protocol, with constraints in energy costs and downloading time. The authors considered the problem of how client peers select not only which servers to download files from but also which transitional nodes to choose that constitute a path to reach the servers. To this end, they formulate a path selection algorithm that uses mixed integer linear programming to produce the optimal sets of paths for clients to select.

9.4   ENERGY EFFICIENCY IN P2P EPIDEMIC PROTOCOLS

Designing energy-efficient epidemic (gossip-based) protocols and services has become significant because of their wide usage in large-scale distributed systems. Several distributed services such as reliable multicasting [48–50], aggregate computation [51], frequent items discovery [52], overlay topology construction, failure detection, P2P streaming, and data dissemination use epidemic approaches. Key advantages of epidemic protocols are their simplicity, scalability, and high fault-tolerance properties. Moreover, all peers have equal responsibilities, and hence, the system is inherently load balanced. Energy awareness of epidemic protocols attracted attention and has been addressed in [26, 53–55].

An epidemic algorithm consists of periodical rounds. In each round, each peer contacts one or a few peers (i.e., neighbors) to exchange states. The algorithm finishes in multiple rounds, and data is disseminated to the network like an epidemic disease [48]. As depicted in Figure 9.7, in epidemic protocols, there are three communication styles used to exchange states, namely, *push-based*, *pull-based*, and *push–pull*. In the push-based model, each peer chooses random peer(s) to send its state. In the pull-based model, each peer chooses random peer(s) to receive their states, and in the push–pull model, each peer chooses random peers both to send and to receive states.

There exist two main classes of *epidemic algorithms*, namely, *flat* and *hierarchical*. Flat algorithms include *basic* and *neighborhood* epidemics. The basic epidemic requires global knowledge of peer population and performs uniform gossiping; therefore, it is

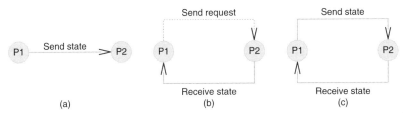

Figure 9.7. Communication styles in epidemic protocols. (a) Push based, (b) pull based, and (c) push–pull based.

not practical. On the other hand, neighborhood epidemic uses local knowledge which is more practical and performs gossiping with neighbors. Although neighborhood epidemic is better when compared to basic, it still has the problem of redundant communication. However, hierarchical epidemic makes use of structure among peers and aims to reduce communication overhead. In addition, it provides the possibility of active/passive peers to save energy.

In terms of their power usage, efficiency of the three abovementioned models of epidemic protocols (i.e., basic, neighborhood, and hierarchical epidemics) was first examined in [53]. Basic epidemics was found to be inefficient in its power usage. It has been shown that in neighborhood epidemics, the amount of peer's power consumption is independent of population size. On the other hand, for hierarchical epidemics, power usage increases with population size. However, this study evaluates different epidemics through simulations only and provides results only on latency and power (proportional to the gossip rate). Moreover, effects of gossip parameters such as fan-out and maximum gossip message size were not investigated.

In terms of energy efficiency, the reliability of epidemic protocols has been discussed in MANETs [54] and a gossip-based protocol has been proposed for wireless sensor networks [55]. In [54], based on packet delivery ratio, nodes with high delivery ratio are classified as active, and therefore, the energy consumption is affected significantly with less packet drops. In [55], low energy consumption and fault tolerance are achieved by early detection of the aggregation convergence independent of changes in the network topology.

A recent study addresses power-awareness features and develops energy cost model formulations for flat and hierarchical epidemics [26]. It also proposes energy cost models for generic peers using epidemic communication and examines the effect of protocol parameters to characterize energy consumption. A novel *hierarchical epidemic* approach that uses DS while constructing the hierarchy is proposed. It utilizes the benefits of both flat epidemic and hierarchical approaches. It uses only local knowledge and provides the possibility of active/passive peers to save energy. Robustness against peer failures is improved, and the message overhead is significantly reduced, thanks to the hierarchy. As a case study protocol, ProFID [52], an epidemic protocol for frequent items discovery in P2P systems, is used in [26]. Through large-scale simulations on PeerSim, the effect of protocol parameters on energy consumption is determined and comparison of flat and hierarchical epidemic approaches is performed.

In the hierarchical epidemic model [26], the DS idea is used to build a high-level overlay as illustrated in Figure 9.8. DS can be defined as a subset B of a graph $G = (VE)$

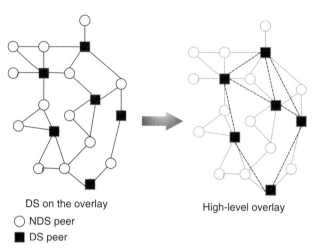

DS on the overlay   High-level overlay
○ NDS peer
■ DS peer

Figure 9.8. Construction of high-level overlay using dominating set.

such that every vertex in G is either in B or adjacent to a vertex in B. In this approach, a DS corresponds to a subset of peers such that a peer in the system is either in DS or a neighbor of a DS peer. There are two types of peers in the system, namely, *DS peer* and *non-dominating set (NDS) peer*. The aim is to save energy by reducing the number of peers performing gossip operation. NDS peers are excluded from gossip operation. DS peers collect local states of NDS neighbors. Consequently, DS peers form a high-level overlay topology on which gossiping is performed. There are two main advantages of this approach. First, NDS peers send their local state to one or multiple DS neighbors and, then, they switch to passive mode in which they just wait for the result to be announced by a DS neighbor. During this time period, they contribute reducing the energy consumption. Second, only DS peers participate in gossiping and, hence, the convergence time and message complexity of the epidemics reduces.

9.5 CONCLUSIONS

In this chapter, we have addressed the problem of energy efficiency in P2P systems and applications. Specifically, we have introduced a taxonomy that classifies the solutions proposed in the literature in three main classes, namely, *sleep/wakeup* approaches, *hierarchical* approaches, and *resource-allocation*-based approaches. In addition, we have analyzed in detail how energy issues have been addressed in two relevant areas in P2P systems, namely, file-sharing protocols and epidemic protocols. With reference to file-sharing protocols, we have emphasized the differences, in terms of energy consumption, between the P2P and client–server paradigms. In addition, we have discussed the main solutions proposed for addressing the energy efficiency of two very popular protocols for P2P file sharing, that is, BitTorrent and Gnutella. For epidemic protocols, we have analyzed the differences, in terms of energy efficiency, between different classes of epidemic protocols.

While a number of solutions are already available, we believe that there is still room for research activities and improvements in both considered areas. We briefly discuss in the following some limitations of existing solutions. Most of the previous studies rely on simple energy models. For an accurate modeling, the energy cost should not only consider the energy consumption of individual peers (baseline energy consumption, energy consumed for processing, communication, etc.) but also the energy consumption related to network communication (e.g., energy consumed by routers). Obviously, more energy-efficient protocols and applications could be implemented if the impact on the total energy consumption of the system was completely known.

Solutions proposed in the literature often exhibit limitations that reduce their applicability in a real environment. For instance, solutions that aim to determine the optimal behavior of peers in order to minimize the total energy consumption are not practical, as, in reality, there is no way to force users toward an optimal behavior. However, also adaptive solutions are not exempt from limitations. For instance, solutions based on sleep/wakeup mechanisms – to turn on/off peers when they are not necessary – are prone to security and privacy problems, as emphasized in Section 9.3. Finally, proxy-based solutions, although effective in certain scenarios, may not be very effective in other contexts. In the design of proxy-based techniques, a key point is the proxy location, which may significantly impact the energy efficiency of the overall system (as well as its robustness in terms of security/privacy). The use of low-power low-cost private proxies – instead of dedicated computers serving a large number of PCs – may be very appealing in certain contexts. We believe that the potentialities of such private proxies for energy efficiency in P2P have not been thoroughly investigated so far. However, a serious analysis would require considering economics costs in addition to energy efficiency.

REFERENCES

[1] Carlinet Y, Debar H, Gourhant Y, and Mé L. Caching P2P traffic what are the benefits for an ISP? In: Proceedings Ninth International Conference on Networks (ICN); 2010 Apr 11–16; Menuires, France.

[2] H. Schulze, K. Mochalski, IPOQUE – Internet Study 2008/2009; Leipzig, Germany.

[3] Bharambe AR, Herley C, and Padmanabhan VN. Analyzing and improving BitTorrent performance. Technical Report MSR-TR-2005-03; 2005 Feb.

[4] K. Kant, "Challenges in distributed energy adaptive computing", SIGMETRICS Performance Evaluation Review, Volume 37, pp. 3–7, 2010.

[5] Gnutella Protocol Specification Version 0.6. [Online]. Available at http://rfc-gnutella .sourceforge.net/src/rfc-0_6-draft.html. Accessed 2014 Sep 28.

[6] Jimeno M and Christensen K. A prototype power management proxy for Gnutella peer-to-peer file sharing. In: Proceedings of IEEE Conference on Local Computer Networks (LCN); 2007 Oct 15–18; Dublin, Ireland.

[7] Purushothaman P, Navada M, Subramaniyan R, Reardon C, and George A. Power-proxying on the NIC: a case study with the Gnutella file-sharing protocol. In: Proceedings 31st IEEE Conference on Local Computer Networks; 2006; no. 0519951; pp. 519–520; Tampa, USA.

[8] G. Anastasi, I. Giannetti, A. Passarella, "A BitTorrent proxy for green Internet file sharing: design and experimental evaluation, Comput Commun, Vol. 33, N. 7, pp. 794–802, 2010.

[9] Giannetti I, Anastasi G, and Conti M, Energy-efficient P2P file sharing for residential BitTorrent users. In: *IEEE Symposium on Computers and Communications (ISCC)*; 2012; pp. 524–529.

[10] H. Hlavacs, R. Weidlich, T. Treutner, "Energy efficient peer-to-peer file sharing", J Supercomput, 62 (3), 1167–1188. Available at http://dx.doi.org/10.1007/s11227-011-0602-8. Accessed 2014 Sep 28.

[11] Kelenyi I and Nurminen J. CloudTorrent – an energy-efficient BitTorrent content sharing for mobile devices via cloud service. In: Proceedings of IEEE Consumer Communications and Networking Conference (CCNC); 2010 Jan 9–12; Las Vegas, USA.

[12] Kelenyi I, Ludanyi A, Nurminen J, and Pusstinen I. Energy-efficient mobile BitTorrent with broadband router hosted proxies. In: Proceedings IFIP Wireless and Mobile Networking Conference (WMNC); 2010 Oct 13–15; Budapest, Hungary.

[13] Kelenyi I, Ludanyi A and Nurminen J. BitTorrent on mobile phones – energy efficiency of a distributed proxy solution. In: Proceedings International Green Computing Conference (IGCC); 2010 Aug 15–18; Chicago, USA.

[14] Kelenyi I, Ludanyi A and Nurminen J. Energy-efficient BitTorrent downloads to mobile phones through memory-limited proxies. In: Consumer Communications and Networking Conference (CCNC); 2011; Las Vegas, USA.

[15] Kelenyi I, Ludanyi A and Nurminen J. Distributed BitTorrent proxy for energy efficient mobile content sharing. In: *Wireless Personal Multimedia Communications (WPMC)*; 2011 Oct; pp.1–5; Brest, France.

[16] I. Kelenyi, J. Nurminen, A. Ludanyi, T. Lukovszki, "Modeling resource constrained BitTorrent proxies for energy efficient mobile content sharing, *Peer-to-Peer Networking and Applications (PPNA)*, vol. 5, pp. 163–177, 2012.

[17] Lefebvre G. and Feeley MJ. Energy efficient peer-to-peer storage. *Technical Report (TR-2003-17)*. Department of Computer Science, University of British Columbia; 2003.

[18] Blackburn J and Christensen K. A simulation study of a new green BitTorrent. In: *Proceedings of International Workshop on Green Communications (GreenComm)*; 2009 Jun; Dresden, Germany.

[19] Wake on LAN Technology. White Paper: Rev 2; 2006 Jun 1.

[20] Lee YJ, Jeong J-H, Kim HY, and Lee CH. Energy-saving set top box enhancement in BitTorrent networks. In: *Network Operations and Management Symposium (NOMS)*, IEEE; 2010 Apr; pp. 809–812; Osaka, Japan.

[21] Forshaw M and Thomas N. A novel approach to energy efficient content distribution with BitTorrent. In: *Computer Performance Engineering*; 2013. Berlin, Heidelberg: Springer. pp. 188–196.

[22] Jourjon, Rakotoarivelo T, and Ott M. Models for an energy efficient P2P delivery service. In: Parallel, Distributed and Network-Based Processing (PDP), 18th Euromicro International Conference; 2010 Feb; Pisa, Italy.

[23] Han J-S, Song J-W, Kim T-H, and Yang S-B, Double-layered mobile P2P systems using energy-efficient routing schemes. In: Telecommunication Networks and Applications Conference (ATNAC); 2008 Dec.

[24] Enokido T, Aikebaier A, and Takizawa M. A model for reducing power consumption in peer-to-peer systems, Systems J (ISJ), IEEE, vol. 4, no. 2, pp. 221–229, June 2010.

[25] Aikebaier A, Enokido T, Takizawa M, and Deen S, Energy-efficient agreement protocols in P2P overlay networks. In: Distributed Computing Systems Workshops (ICDCSW), IEEE 30th International Conference; 2010 Jun; Genova, Italy.

[26] O. Ozkasap, E. Cem, S. Cebeci, T. Koc, Flat and hierarchical epidemics in P2P systems: energy cost models and analysis. Future Generat Comput Syst, vol. 36, pp. 257–266, 2014.

[27] Koc T, Cem E, and Ozkasap O. Dominating-set based and power-aware hierarchical epidemics in P2P systems. In: Second International Conference on Energy-Efficient Computing and Networking; 2011; New York, USA.

[28] Chandrasekar A, Chandrasekar K, Ramasatagopan H, and Rafica AR. SMC: an energy conserving P2P file sharing model for mobile devices. In: *Data Engineering for Wireless and Mobile Access (MobiDE)*; 2012; New York; pp. 66–73.

[29] Raj M, Kant K, Das SK. Energy adaptive mechanism for P2P file sharing protocols. In: Volume 7640, *Euro-Par 2012: Parallel Processing Workshops*; Lecture Notes in Computer Science; 2013; pp. 89–99.

[30] Zhang P and Helvik BE. Towards green P2P: understanding the energy consumption in P2P under content pollution. In: IEEE/ACM International Conference on Green Computing and Communications & Int'l Conference on Cyber, Physical and Social Computing (GREENCOM-CPSCOM); 2010; pp. 332–337.

[31] T. Enokido, A. Aikebaier, and M. Takizawa, "Process allocation algorithms for saving power consumption in peer-to-peer systems, IEEE Trans Ind Electron, vol. 58, no. 6, pp. 2097–2105, 2011.

[32] Garcia AE, Weidlich R, de Lope LR, Hackbarth KD, Hlavacs H, and Leandro CS. Approximation towards energy-efficient distributed environments. In Proceedings of the 3rd International ICST Conference on Simulation Tools and Techniques (SIMUTools); 2010.

[33] Hlavacs H, Weidlich R, and Treutner T. Energy saving in future home environments. In: IFIP Wireless Days; 2008 Nov.

[34] H. Hlavacs, K. A. Hummel, R. Weidlich, A. M. Houyou, and H. De Meer, "Modelling energy efficiency in distributed home environments, Int J Commun Netw Distrib Syst, 4, 2, 161–182, 2010.

[35] K. Leibnitz, T. Hoßfeld, N. Wakamiya, and M. Murata, Peer-to-peer vs. client/server: reliability and efficiency of a content distribution service. In: Volume 4516, *Managing Traffic Performance in Converged Networks*; Lecture Notes in Computer Science; 2007; pp. 1161–1172.

[36] Nedevschi S, Ratnasamy S, and Padhye J. Hot data centers vs. cool peers. In: HotPower'08 Proceedings of the Conference on Power Aware Computing and Systems; 2008.

[37] A. Sucevic, L. L. H. Andrew, and T. T. T. Nguyen, "Powering down for energy efficient peer-to-peer file distribution," ACM SIGMETRICS Perform Eval Rev, vol. 39, no. 3, p. 72, 2011.

[38] Andrew L., Sucevic A., and Nguyen T. Balancing peer and server energy consumption in large peer-to-peer file distribution systems. In: Proceedings of IEEE Online Conference on Green Communications (GreenCom); 2011 Sep 26–29.

[39] Kurose J., Ross K., Peer-to-peer applications. In: *Computer Networking. A Top-Down Approach*, 4th ed., Addison-Wesley, Boston, USA, 2007.

[40] Qiu D, Srikant R. Modeling and performance analysis of BitTorrent-like peer-to-peer networks. In: *Proceedings of ACM Sigcomm*; 2004; Portland, Oregon; pp 367–378.

[41] Kumar R and Ross K. Peer-assisted file distribution: the minimal distribution time. In: Proceedings of IEEE Workshop on Hot Topics in Web Systems and Technologies; 2006.

[42] Ezovski G, Tang A, and Andrew L. Minimizing average finish time in P2P networks. In: *Proceedings of IEEE INFOCOM*; 2009 Apr 19–25; Rio de Janeiro, Brazil.

[43] Magic packet technology. White Paper, Publication# 20213, Rev: A, Amendment/0; 1995 Nov.

[44] Gnutella protocol specification, version 0.4, 2001. [Online]. Available at http://rfc-gnutella. sourceforge.net/developer/stable/.

[45] Jimeno M, Christensen K, and Roginsky A. A power management proxy with a new best-of-N bloom filter design to reduce false positives. In: IEEE International Performance, Computing, and Communications Conference; 2007; pp. 125–133.

[46] Neves da Hora D, Macedo DR, Nogueira JMS, and Pujolle G, Optimizing peer-to-peer content discovery over wireless mobile ad hoc networks. In: 9th IFIP International Conference on Mobile Wireless Communications Networks; 2007; pp. 6–10.

[47] Mawji A and Hassanein H. Optimal path selection for file downloading in P2P overlay networks on MANETs. In: *The IEEE symposium on Computers and Communications*; 2010 Jun; pp. 1133–1138.

[48] K. Birman, M. Hayden, O. Ozkasap, Z. Xiao, M. Budiu, Y. Minsky,"Bimodal multicast, ACM Trans Comput Syst 17 (2) pp. 41–88, 1999.

[49] O. Ozkasap, Z. Genc, E. Atsan, "Epidemic-based reliable and adaptive multicast for mobile ad hoc networks, Comput Network 53 pp. 1409–1430, 2009.

[50] P. Eugster, R. Guerraoui, S.B. Handurukande, P. Kouznetsov, A. M. Kermarrec, "Lightweight probabilistic broadcast, ACM Trans Comput Syst 21 (4) pp. 341–374, 2003.

[51] M. Jelasity, A. Montresor, O. Babaoglu, "Gossip-based aggregation in large dynamic networks." ACM Trans Comput Syst 23(3), pp. 219–252, 2005.

[52] E. Cem, O. Ozkasap, "ProFID: practical frequent items discovery in peer-to-peer networks, Future Generat Comput Syst, 29 (6), pp.1544–1560, 2013.

[53] van Renesse R. Power-aware epidemics. In: Proceedings of IEEE Symposium on Reliable Distributed Systems; 2002.

[54] S. Rajeswari, D. Y. Venkataramani, "An adaptive energy efficient and reliable gossip routing protocol for mobile ad hoc networks, Int J Comput Theor Eng, 2 (5), pp.740–745, 2010.

[55] Fauji S. and Kalpakis K. A gossip-based energy efficient protocol for robust in-network aggregation in wireless sensor networks. In: Pervasive Computing and Communications Workshops (PERCOM Workshops), IEEE International Conference; 2011; pp. 166–171.

10

TOWARD SUSTAINABILITY FOR LARGE-SCALE COMPUTING SYSTEMS: ENVIRONMENTAL, ECONOMIC, AND STANDARDIZATION ASPECTS

Christina Herzog,[1] Jean-Marc Pierson,[1] and Laurent Lefèvre[2]

[1] *IRIT, University of Toulouse, Toulouse, France*
[2] *INRIA, LIP Laboratory, Ecole Normale Supérieure de Lyon, University of Lyon, Lyon, France*

10.1 INTRODUCTION

During the previous chapters of this book, several advances have been demonstrated toward more energy-efficient distributed systems, from networks to data centers and clouds, high-performance computing or peer-to-peer systems. While these works are very important and valuable, we move the focus point slightly in this chapter and present a wider point of view.

Obviously, energy efficiency is only one side of the sustainability issue. All efforts toward energy efficiency do not mean that they all consider Green information technology (IT) as a whole. We want first to define precisely the link between sustainability and Green IT when the actions on computer systems can increase the economical, the societal, or the environmental values, but not necessarily the three aspects together.

Second, we want to outline the differences across the actors involved in the innovation circle in Green IT: their motivations, their approaches, and their outcomes can vary largely and that differences can accelerate or decrease the pace of Green IT adoption.

Recognizing the role of standardization and professional bodies toward greener IT, we examine, mainly in the data center area, the escalation of recommendations to potential regulations between the somehow concurrent but interleaved bodies.

Large-Scale Distributed Systems and Energy Efficiency: A Holistic View, First Edition.
Edited by Jean-Marc Pierson.
© 2015 John Wiley & Sons, Inc. Published 2015 by John Wiley & Sons, Inc.

Finally, we propose hereby a modeling of the actors, their interaction, and their mutual influence in the Green IT landscape. On the basis of this modeling, we demonstrate how its proper usage can help decision makers for assessing the investment in research projects, the development of technologies, and their wide acceptance.

10.2 GREEN IT FOR INNOVATION AND INNOVATION FOR GREEN IT

10.2.1 Defining Green IT and Its Link with Sustainability

Numerous definitions of Green IT have been proposed in the scientific and public press. Each of these definitions is taking different aspects into account and is more or less general or particular. Some of them are focused on server centers, not including economical thoughts, while others are only focused on energy management.

Already, Hilty [1] has given a definition of the life cycle. There is the use phase, the production, and the end of life. Green IT can join in every phase decreasing the ecological damages. In this definition of Green IT the real costs for production and also the "costs" for the environment, which we all have to pay are not taken into account. These costs will be paid – in reality – only by the producing countries, having a closer look the people producing servers/components and people living in these areas.

Green IT refers somehow to environmentally sustainable computing or IT. Murugesan [2] defines in the field of green computing as "the study and practice of designing, manufacturing, using, and disposing of computers, servers, and associated subsystems – such as monitors, printers, storage devices, and networking and communications systems – efficiently and effectively with minimal or no impact on the environment."

All the definitions are representing various ideas about Green IT and one reason might be that IT is in general a rather young topic, and green IT is even younger. Fifty years ago, the number of information technologies was that low that the impact on the environment was insignificant. The impact of IT on the environment during the past 5 decades increased because of the raise of IT-related devices. The interests and the requests of users and providers are changing dynamically and accordingly. Taking the example of the raising electricity costs, it is obvious that companies understood this impact and started setting up counter measures. These measures addressed energy reduction to reduce costs. This action, together with other actions related to the reduction of energy consumption in the field of IT, was summed up under the name of Green IT. In the past years, more companies, citizens, and governments were considering Green IT, leading to the fact that there is no final definition of Green IT under such changing interests. Following the work of others, we believe that three main reasons drive the interests for Green IT and its development: ecology, economy, and society.

10.2.1.1 Ecological Reasons. The first associated reasons for the usage of Green IT are ecological reasons. The following reasons do not only apply in the IT but also in other areas and lead at the end users and producers to an ecological awareness. Carbon dioxide emission is boosting the natural greenhouse effect causing the global warming. The worldwide estimated emission of carbon dioxide caused by IT is

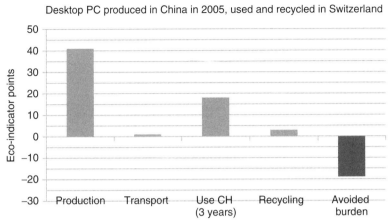

Figure 10.1. Comparing production, transport, usage, recycling, and loss for a typical PC Desktop. *Source:* Modified from Ref. [3].

600 million tons, still expected to grow up to 60% more in 2020. This is due to the high consumption of energy during the lifetime of the IT. Green IT can encourage low-power requirement if included in this phase.

The production of IT is polluting the environment. Many computers are produced in countries under inadequate ecological conditions. According to [1], the ecological damage through a production of a computer in China is almost the same than the ecological damage of the use of a computer during 6 years in Switzerland, as it can be seen from Figure 10.1.

In IT, there are three stages of the life cycle. Ecological pollution during the production has the highest impact. Rare metals such as indium are used for the production of IT. Not to reuse these metals means that the resources will soon be exhausted and not any more available for future generations and for future technologies. These productions mark the ecological damages, and also for workers and residents around production centers. Green IT cares that these metals are used efficiently and that there will be no lack in the future and it could reduce the damage of the environment.

Often misprized is the e-waste. The US Environmental Protection Agency (EPA) declared that Americans throw out more than 2 million tons of consumer electronics annually. This makes electronic waste one of the fastest growing components of the municipal waste stream. In the European Union (EU), the disposal of e-waste is regulated with guidance such as the WEEE (Waste Electrical and Electronic Equipment) guideline. Unfortunately, this rule is bypassed because of financial reasons and e-waste is sometimes transported to the developing world. There the waste is recycled in a very primitive way leading to a contamination of human beings and the environment. Green IT can point out these aspects and should insist that recycling is done in a "green way."

10.2.1.2 *Economic Reasons.* Beside ecological reasons, the industry is interested in Green IT because of multiple economic reasons. IT needs electricity, and this is an expense factor. Green IT can reduce the consumption of electricity used for IT in companies.

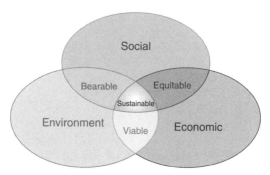

Figure 10.2. The place for sustainability. *Source:* Picture from Wikipedia, built from Ref. [4].

Companies invest annually a big amount of money in IT. But their memories, storage, and computing power and capacity are not well utilized. Often an expert would find cheaper and "greener" solutions in caring for more efficient usage of older equipment and a higher workload of new technologies.

10.2.1.3   Social Reasons.   Green IT has also a social aspect because each government (should) aims at preserving the environment and serving the country and its inhabitants. Green IT can bring governmental funding and tax advantages as some governments offer support for companies decreasing the environmental contamination.

10.2.1.4   Definition of Green IT.   On the basis of different definitions and motivations, a definition of Green IT is stated, which is for now the basis for this work. *"Green IT is the environmental and resource saving effort in the IT. The reason for using Green IT may arise from economically or ecologically interests. Actions can affect the whole lifecycle of information technology – meaning from the construction via utilization through to disposal."*

Green IT is, therefore, a movement toward sustainability. As shown in Figure 10.2, sustainability is at the cross between ecological, economic, and social aspects.

Let us analyze Green IT in respect with this definition and its role for sustainability. In best cases, Green IT is sustainable: Green IT is in the central "sustainable" area and stays there whatever are the operations on the system. For instance, buying not too much expensive hardware leads to a movement away from sustainability: indeed, from the economical point of view, a purchase is done, and from the ecological point of view, this new hardware had to be produced. But this can be compensated when this new hardware is consuming less electricity. It should be noted that making no efforts will lead the IT to move away of the sustainability area because of the obsolescence of the equipment.

In the general case, Green IT is represented as a direction toward the central area. For instance, calculating the price of the products including the financial costs for the e-waste before renewing equipment will move, within the social point of view, toward sustainability.

In the worst case, Green IT is unfortunately leaving away from the sustainable area to a border area, and it is not important toward which direction the movement is done.

For instance, a company can buy new hardware consuming more electricity than the older ones, but still consuming the minimum maximum (instead of minimum) electricity from the market, for the needed computing power. In that example, the movements in the environment and the economic directions are clearly not toward sustainability. But this company can still advertise some Green IT efforts.

Green IT is always moving, as there is always a development in one of these directions. Depending on the direction and how far it is moving to or from the sustainable area, it is possible to say if there is still a part of Green IT in it or not. With this view, it is possible to give a first label of Green IT. If all known components are filled, the result shows if there is Green IT or not.

10.2.2 Differences between Academia and Companies

In this section, we analyze the difference for handling Green IT research between the companies and the academics researchers. Firstly, it is important to set Green IT as a part of IT research, which has to be seen as a general research field, meaning it is also facing the same problems as other research areas do: each player (industry, researcher, university, etc.) has a different access and different aims for the development. This makes it difficult to cooperate and to have an efficient exchange of results. Moreover, the different parties may have difficulties in defining common research interests, even if they agree the scientific part but still there are different backgrounds.

The used definition of technology used here covers the knowledge of the appliance of scientific knowledge. Scientific cognizance stands in this case for all results and observations of activities in research and development. The constraint that these results had to be received with scientific methods is not taken into account when the transfer is done: scientific ambitions and also lucky consequences within practice may lead to new technology. Scientific knowledge encompasses both empirical and theoretical knowledge; it means all directed processes and methods, including their practical usage, and also material artifacts such as products, prototypes, and software.

Technology is special knowledge, know-how, in the sense of instructional knowledge and skills. Occasionally, knowledge is divided into know-how, know-why, know-what, and know-who, but simplifying all these definitions are summed up under the definition of know-how [5]. In the economical context, knowledge is seen as a resource with an important impact on the technical progress (e.g., the virtuous circle in the Green IT [6]) and the long-term development of companies. Compared to other production factors, technology can hardly be measured quantitatively compared to raw materials or capital. It is difficult – almost impossible – to evaluate the technical potential. Technology can never be consumed during the usage or dissemination, but it can lose importance in case the exclusive usage is lost and/or new knowledge is creating new technology. As a result of this, the value of technology may reduce. Green IT is a fast moving domain, and the development of new technology is going on quickly. This is also related to the fact that Green IT may be involved in a lot of different research fields of IT, and even outside only IT.

Changing the perspective toward usage of technology leads to another useful restriction. From this angle of view, technologies represent all results of research and development contributing to solutions of problems. The reference to the usage of technology suggests linking the term technology to the interaction between scientific–technical perception and the society.

A complete classification of interactions of parties in all sorts of technology transfers is not feasible as classifications can be done with different parameters (vertical, horizontal, product-oriented, procedure-oriented, infrastructure-oriented transfer, etc.)[7–9]. Innovation-oriented companies represent the academic research as a fundamental resource of external produced technologies. The more the industry is oriented toward novelties on the market and leadership in technology, the more the cooperation with public research institutes is interesting for it. And the more a public research institute is oriented toward the markets, the more it is interesting for it to have cooperation with companies. Academic institutes could be considered as the best partners as they have a wide experience in cutting-edge-research and they are mainly impartial – they should be! Despite this high synergetic potential, academic researcher and industry operate in unconnected systems.

Contracted research is a specific form of focused technology transfer with its challenges and chances for research projects and future cooperation between industry and research institutes. In the contracted research, there is the presumption that the company contracts a research to a university for implementing the result out of this contract in its organization, using this outcome and having an advantage in competition. The contracted research project is the instrument for the technology transfer. Contracted research is getting more important during the past years and it is influencing national and international research programs. The idea is to define certain criteria for this special way of transfer:

- The first point is the client–supplier relation, in which the client is a company and the supplier is a research institute.
- Second, it has to be mentioned that the primary purpose of this cooperation is the exchange of scientific knowledge. This exchange is interactive, organizational, service based, and focused mainly between two actors, without a third party involved.
- Third, the relation is contract based with a time limit and the obligation of providing a result, a solution. A particular issue of contracted research is when there is a funding organization involved, as in this case, the client–supplier relationship is supervised by this organization: progress reports have to be provided, and the parties have less opportunity in creating their relationship.

With a contracted research project, a temporary bridge is built between the system of economy and the system of science. To be successful elements, both contexts have to be taken into account and further stimulations have to be provided [10]. The interaction between partners with different background and a different environment is challenging. For a successful exchange, it is necessary to know the partner, its internal structure, and the general aims.

Different aspects of companies and academia are presented in the three parts of Figure 10.3. In the first part, all the different topics linked to research and innovation in IT are mentioned. In line A, the different core competences are presented, pointing out

			Academia	Industry
Research and Innovation process	A	Duties/responsibilities	Common welfare Extension of knowledge	Profit orientation Offering service and products for the market
	B	Core competence	Fundamental research in Software and Hardware User oriented research Experimental research	User oriented research Experimental research Product development
	C	Approach	Search and find General	Decide and act Concrete
	D	Priorities of topics	Personal interests Expected appreciation Financing	Strategic development of the company Portfolio of the products
	E	Selection of topics	Autonomic Funding relevant	Innovation management Top management
Criteria and dissemination	F	Criteria of efficiency	Scientific reputation	Profit and company value
	G	Criteria of quality of the work	Systematic production Reconstructable processes and results Big application area Explanatory contribution	Usability of the results Big effects for the clients usage Advantageous economic solution for a concrete application areal Production of an innovation leading to a temporary monopoly position
	H	Reference groups	Scientific community student	Clients Other units within the company
	I	Distribution of the results	Conferences Publications Patents	Products Internal processes Services Patents
Organization	J	Freedom of action	High Limited through resources (funding, staff, equipment, etc.)	Average limits through managment
	K	Funding	Non-performance related basic financing Calls of funding organizations Services for companies	Budget of the innovation management In-house accounting
	L	Organizational framework	Fixed and solid Influenced through scientific community Need safety concerning the expenses	Flexible Influenced through market needs, clients'needs Searching for information about efficiency and risk
	M	Relation with other units of the organization	Limited administrative support is offered Interaction within a given framework Parallel units with other fields of competences	Part of a chain within the company Targets given by the management

Figure 10.3. Different views from industry and academy.

that an exchange between academia and industry is needed to get a complex outcome. Product development can only be done if fundamental research is provided, and also if the approach is general. Like this, the industry has the opportunity to propose concrete solutions in answering to various demands concerning hardware and software, servers, data center, etc.

The second part deals with the criteria and the dissemination where there is also a gap. Academia mainly distributes their results within the scientific community while industry players need to address their clients. An actual topic has been server virtualization in cloud environment. Server virtualization decreases the number of needed servers to handle users' requests to services and, hence, decreases the usage of IT and opens doors for Green IT. But this system had to be developed, studied, and proved: measurements and simulations were needed. Only universities had the opportunity to invest time and knowledge and to test on a large platform. If there is an additional exchange with the industry about their clients' demands, the result will be achieved more quickly.

In the third part, the organization of the two parties is shown. The eventual difficulties in the cooperation can be seen. Both parties have to show some understanding concerning the framework of the other one. What is clearly an advantage of the academia is that they have existing cooperation with other research units within universities, while industry partner often have only one major experience or one major activity. Taking the example of cooling in server rooms, it may appear that the company is able to build efficient servers but they do not have the experience in modeling the airflow in a data center. Academics organize/participate in workshops on a large field of research, they exchange with others, invitation to conferences are sent where new results are presented. Academics are linked to other fields of research, and they are not in concurrence if they are in different research fields. Having a close link between industry and academic may help to find quick solutions in using the research network.

One possibility to build a bridge between different interests is the creation of a technology transfer office (TTO). These offices are dedicated to identify research having potential commercial interest and they develop strategies for exploitation.

10.2.3   Describing the Loop between Academia and Industry

Figure 10.4 shows the different links between the industry, the academia, and their ecosystems, being TTOs or business angels.

Companies and academia are linked in different ways – mainly within a scientific project funded by a public funding organization. A consortium is formed with a specific aim and linked for a certain time. During the project runtime, there is a strong exchange about scientific progress, research, and deliverables. Once the project is finished, the link between the partners loosens and finally disappears. Important knowledge (internal structure, research interests, etc.) about the other partner gets lost. For each new consortium, time is lost for the search of interested/interesting partners who can afford to participate in a funded cooperation. This is the same for academia looking for industrial partner as well as for the industry needing academia. Searching for a partner is even more difficult if you want to create a 1:1 project or cooperation. Time is wasted in the search for potential partners and academia as well as the industry has to rely on published information not knowing if these are really up to date.

In order to save resource of the industry and academia, TTOs should be created. In these offices, databases are created with data necessary to create a project/cooperation. In a TTO, there are experts of different fields working, who understand the needs of a client (= academia or industry) quickly and keep the database up to date. A start of a project/cooperation gets easier. Beside this, companies should use TTOs and angel

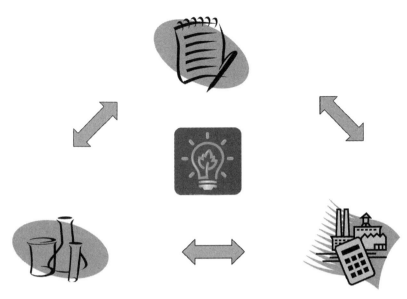

Figure 10.4.   The innovation circle.

investors for financing projects and collaborations – with the help of funding organizations and without the delay caused by waiting for open public calls.

In Green IT, there is still the advantage that there is a rather small community – but
growing quickly. Currently, it is possible to build up good databases on ongoing research
and to follow the innovation as the community is still manageable.

Standardization is also an important part in Green IT. As Green IT is involved in
different areas many standards are created or discussed. Saving natural resources and
protecting the environment are discussed topics, and Green IT can support these efforts.
Exactly, at the stage now, different parties have to participate in the discussion and in
the creation of standards, as these limits set now will be valid for future actions set in
the society. Already there are various existing initiatives for standardization, but still it
is possible to keep the overview and to follow or to participate in some. The aim should
be to link these initiatives and to coordinate their activities. This might not be possible
in some years when the research field of Green IT will have grown.

10.3   STANDARDIZATION LANDSCAPE IN GREEN IT

This section is describing the different standardization bodies and some contextualized
actions in the scope of large-scale distributed systems, focusing mainly on the data center
side. The reason for addressing this field is that (i) it illustrates quite clearly the possible
links between standardization and Green IT; (ii) one of the author participates in one of
these groups, giving an insight of their functioning; (iii) data centers are a major point
of energy consumption where actions have to be taken without delay.

TABLE 10.1. Classification of Standards Organizations

Standard Body Type	Nature of Standards	Example
International, regional and national and government-backed standards bodies	Highly structured standards, requiring some degree of certification/enforcement	ISO, UN ITU, IEC, CENELEC-CEN, ETSI National standards bodies, for example, AFNOR (France), AENOR (Spain), BSI (UK), DIN (Germany)
Institutes and professional bodies	Structured and de facto standards, metrics, and projects. Some certification required	BCS, IEEE, ASHRAE, Uptime Institute
Supplier and industry groups	De facto standards, projects and other initiatives.	The Green Grid, Open Compute Project
Technical initiatives, projects, supplier product development,	Loosely structured initiatives, published research, etc.	EC projects

10.3.1 Different Standardization Levels

The concept of standardization is a flexible term when applied to (Green) IT innovation. There are strictly managed standards existing (such as those managed by the International Organization for Standardization (ISO), the International Telecommunications Union (ITU), and the International Electrotechnical Commission (IEC), as well as a wide variety of other de facto initiatives, metrics, and frameworks being also classified as standards. Regulation also plays a role in the development of common approaches to (Green) IT.

Table 10.1 shows standard body types and their nature of standards and is giving some examples. The standard body-type section shows which kind of body it is and who can join; in the second colon, what these bodies are providing, how they are structured, and what they can provide for the standardization; and in the last colon, you find some examples of bodies, organizations, initiatives, and an example of an EC project, which can also be considered as having influence in the standardization of energy saving.

To help understand the relationships between these stakeholders, Figure 10.1 is sketching their links. Sustainability standards affect data centers in multiple ways. Some standards, such as green building certifications or European Code of Conduct, allow data centers to voluntarily demonstrate a certain level of environmental performance. Other standards, such as American Society of Heating, Refrigeration, and Air-conditioning Engineers (ASHRAE)'s temperature standards, can carry the force of de facto mandates or form the basis for true mandates later. Sustainability standards can affect how strongly data centers demand efficiency technologies, and sometimes even which technologies they choose. There are standards that address both IT and data center facilities. Some of them are discussed in the following.

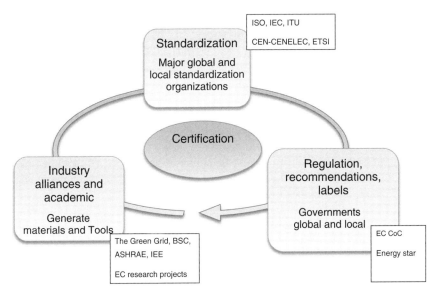

Figure 10.5. Existing links between standardization stakeholders [11].

In Figure 10.5, we can see that the first providers of materials and tools that may make their way to actual standards are industry alliances, academic researchers, or both in collaborative projects. Some of the proposed ideas may be presented in one standardization body and escalate toward standards. These standards can in turn be used by governments (national, federal, or European levels) as regulations in laws that must (and can) be enforced.

Governments can use directly the materials as regulations, recommendations, or labels. While the process for formal standardization takes a long time since a consensus has to be achieved between all members (especially states), the direct link with governments is sometimes more efficient.

Finally, it must be noted that some metrics, tools, and methods provided by industry and academia are used directly by final users and often become de facto standards.

The certification authority whose role is to certify that the measurements claimed by suppliers of technologies actually follow the standards, the labels or the recommendations is shown in the center of Figure 10.5.

10.3.2 Standardization Bodies

ISO is made up of numerous country-specific standards bodies. Inside ISO, TC207 is interested in environmental management.

ISO has developed a number of standards that may be relevant to the overall goals of the CoolEmAll project. For example, ISO 14064-1 is a standard for reporting on greenhouse gases (GHG) and makes use of the GHG protocol. It specifies the principles and requirements for design, development, management, and reporting of an organization's GHG inventory. The other standards apply to reporting at project level, to validation and verification, and to accreditation or other forms of recognition. ISO 14001 addresses the environmental impact of an organization in general.

The International Telecommunication Union (IUT-T) recommendations are defining elements in information and communication technologies (ICTs) infrastructure. Within ITU-T, Study Group SG5 is evaluating the effects of ICT on climate change and publishing guidelines for using ICTs in an eco-friendly way. An example is data center using direct current (DC), where ITU-T L.1200 specifies the DC interface between the power feeding system and ICT equipment connected to it. It also describes normal and abnormal voltage ranges and immunity test levels for ICT equipment to maintain the stability of telecommunication and data communication services. Another example comes with ITU-T L.1300 that describes best practices aimed at reducing the negative impact of data centers on the climate.

IEC is the leading global organization that publishes consensus-based international standards and manages conformity assessment systems for electric and electronic products, systems, and services, collectively known as electrotechnology. Within IEC, TC111 is interested in environmental standardization for electrical and electronic products and systems. It embeds the ecodesign, recycling/reuse, carbon, and GHG aspects.

Joint Technical Committees (JTC) are established between ISO and IEC in specific areas. JTC 1/SC 39 is the joint subcommittee on "Sustainability for and by Information Technology." The focus is on standardization related to the intersection of resource efficiency, and IT supporting sustainable development, application, operation, and management aspects is investigated. The activities of JTC1/39 have been developed, and drafts of the standard for metrics assessing the energy efficiency of data centers are on the way. At the moment, only the PUE (power usage effectiveness) standard is being developed in all its dimensions (taking into account the different possibilities to compute its value according to the energy used by the data center, e.g., mixed energy). The framework for describing other metrics is also on the move and must be considered when developing new metric for their standardization. Standards 30134-1 (General Requirements and Definitions) and 30134-2 (PUE) are related to these two aspects. Other metrics are in discussion, in particular, eITEE (information and technology equipment energy efficiency), ITEU (information and technology equipment utilization), CUE (carbon usage effectiveness), WUE (water usage effectiveness), and some more controversial such as GEC (where G is for Green, but what is Green?) or RES (renewable energy sources) that could not be supported by countries where the production is not renewable).

Another standard developed in this group is the 30133 on guidelines for resource-efficient data center. Discussions are on the way to figure out the possible overlap with the work of ITU-T L.1300 mentioned earlier.

The international bodies (ISO, ITU, and IEC) have some regional counterpart. For instance, the European Commission has established a standardization mandate. It requests that the three European standards bodies CEN, CENELEC, and ETSI develop standards that enable efficient energy use in fixed and mobile information and communication networks. Looking at a bird eye view, concerning European standardization activities on data centers, the network is done by ETSI, the power infrastructure by CENELEC, the IT management by CEN, the cooling by ASHRAE (not EU specific), and the monitoring by CEN/CENELEC. The need for having joint and coordinated groups is, therefore, obvious.

The establishment of the Coordination Group on Green Data Centers (CEN–ENELEC–ETSI) helps to harmonize initiatives. Its basic objectives are to coordinate standardization activities, to avoid duplication and conflicting content, and to define standardization landscape.

It particular, the definition of several items have been seen necessary in order to everyone can understand the scope of the potential standards. As an example, a data center is defined in this group as "a structure, or group of structures, dedicated to the centralized accommodation, interconnection, and operation of IT and network telecommunications equipment providing data storage, processing, and transport services together with all the facilities and infrastructures for power distribution and environmental control together with the necessary levels of resilience and security required to provide the desired service availability." This definition might be integrated by the ISO/IEC JTC 1 standard series.

Several agreements have been set up between regional and international bodies so that works done at one body can be used in the other ones.

10.3.3 Regulations

Established by the European Commission and parties from the IT industry in 2010, the ICT4EE forum focuses on two key aspects of eco-efficient IT: first, how the technology industry can curb its energy use; and second, how it can help other sectors do likewise. By mid-2010, four industry associations had signed up to represent the European, Japanese, and American ICT industries in the forum: DigitalEurope; Global e-Sustainability Initiative (GeSI); the Japanese Business Council Europe (JBCE); and TechAmerica Europe. Works may one day lead to worldwide regulations.

The European Code of Conduct (CoC) on Data Centers Energy Efficiency has been developed in response to the increase in energy consumption in data centers and the current needs to decrease the economic, environmental, and energy supply security impacts. The aim is to inform and foster the improvement of energy efficiency in the planning and operation of data centers. The CoC is not a legally binding document but a voluntary initiative with the objective of bringing stakeholders together. Parties signing up will be expected to follow this set of best practices recommendations and abide to the principles described therein. The code contains a comprehensive list of best practices as well as documentary aids and measurement procedures. If the code of conduct works well, it could be made mandatory under European law to encourage energy efficiency among nonparticipants; conversely, if it does not produce results, the European Commission might seek a tougher approach. This example shows the difficulty of regulations in the absence of metrics commonly accepted and standardized. The development of ISO/IEC standards such as the PUE (see previous section) is the key for enabling future noncontroversial regulations.

10.3.4 Industry Groups and Professional Bodies

Industries and professional groups are clearly also having an impact on standardization. These groups differ in several dimensions: some are country based, others are at European or global levels; some are activated by governments, while others are industry or professional based; some provides standards, others certifications. In this section, we detail some aspects of The Green Grid, the British BSC, and the US ASHRAE, among several other initiatives and groups that influence the Green IT area: IEEE, Uptime Institute, US Energy Star, Open Compute Project, the GHG protocol, US Green Building Council, BRE Global, etc. One can refer to [11] for more insights on this topic.

The most influential body in the scope of data center is The Green Grid, a non-profit, open industry consortium of IT suppliers, end users, policymakers, technology providers, facility architects, and utility companies. The aim is to promote the agenda of these suppliers and also unite global industry efforts, create a common set of metrics, and develop technical resources and educational tools. The Green Grid has expanded its mission from "energy-efficient IT" to "resource-efficient IT," meaning that it will begin looking at water, carbon, materials, and waste, in addition to just energy. The Green Grid has developed a number of metrics, frameworks, and initiatives in the domain of Data Center Energy Efficiency: PUE, WUE, and CUE, to name a few. These metrics assess the quality of a data center in terms of efficiency of the resource provided against the resources useful for the IT equipment. The PUE metric is also used in the European CoC. It should be stressed that there is no regulatory agency that monitors or certifies PUE ratings, and therefore, the figures, widely cited, have no legal status and are prone to distortion by technical and marketing staff. However, we can note that two task forces, namely, the Data Center Metrics Coordination Task Force (US Regional Task Force) and the Global Harmonization of Data Center Efficiency Metrics Task Force (Global Task Force), have confirmed PUE as the agreed-upon metric for measuring infrastructure energy efficiency in data centers. These task forces are composed of industry players and government agencies, from the United States and Japan. As already discussed, it can be noted that the PUE metric is currently being proposed for standardization at the ISO/IEC level and that the total timeline from the first mention of PUE to the ISO/IEC standard will be at least 8 years.

At a national level, one can cite the British Computer Society (BCS), which has a number of initiatives – particularly through its Data Center Specialist Group (DCSG). In collaboration with the UK Carbon Trust, the BCS DCSG developed open source software that can be used to model energy efficiency and carbon emissions in data centers on a per-service basis (leading and transferred to the commercial Prognose software). They also developed a set of metrics (DC-FVER, Data center Fixed to Variable Energy Ratio metric) that could be used, for instance, in a future iteration of the data center CoC and promoted at the standardization bodies level.

In United States, the ASHRAE is an influential standards group whose work impacts data centers in several ways. The most known ASHRAE guidelines describes the temperature and humidity ranges in which data center computer rooms should operate. Data centers are intended to operate most of the time within ASHRAE's fairly narrow "recommended" temperature and humidity ranges. Although ASHRAE standards do not have the force of law, many jurisdictions adopt them as part of mandatory building codes. In that sense, ASHRAE's 90.1 standards strongly affect new data center construction and major renovations.

10.3.5   Analysis of the Standardization Actors

The first obvious observation is the multiplicity of actors in standardization issues and the difficulty to have a global picture, despite the remarkable efforts through coordination in the past years (such as the Global Harmonization group or the Joint ISO/IEC Technical Committee JTC1/39). As one can see, the interaction between the different bodies is complex. An interesting point to outline is the influence of these groups in the standardization bodies. For instance, one can meet the same people at several meetings, at The Green Grid and the ISO/IEC meetings. It must, however, be noticed that most of the work is conducted by industries and that only a few academics are members of these bodies. Reasons might be the long-lasting enrolment to influence the groups, and the fact that for researchers, the participation to such group is not giving any benefit for the academic career. Big industry players are typically in these groups: their employers are paid for following and taking leaderships on some initiatives. In [12] and [16], we detailed those differences between academia and industries in the three dimensions detailed in Figure 10.3 and already discussed earlier.

10.4   MODELING ACTORS OF INNOVATION IN GREEN IT AND THEIR LINKS

As it has been described along the beginning of this chapter, a lot of interactions between several actors shape the Green IT field. To be able to understand correctly their different roles and their mutual influences, we propose in this section to model the main actors. This modeling is based on the previous observations and does not aim at being exhaustive. However, it represents a first step that would deserve more attention.

All actors are defined by several attributes that are evolving during their lifetime, according to their sole behavior and the interactions they will have with their environment, namely, the other actors in the system.

10.4.1   Researcher

- *Environmental Interest*. This value represents the willingness of one researcher to work in the Green IT field because of environmental interest. A high value is given to an active member while a null value describes a researcher not at all interested in the environmental impact of Green IT.
- *Social Interest*. This value represents the willingness of one researcher to work in the Green IT field because of social interest. A high value is given to an active member, while a null value describes a researcher not at all interested in the social impact of Green IT.
- *Economical Interest*. Opposed to the above two, but for economic interest.
- *Affiliation*. This attribute characterizes the working environment of the researcher. It is a link toward a university or an industry.
- Research fund dedicated to Green IT
- Number of publications in the Green IT field

- *Fellows*. This attribute is a list. It represents the links existing between researchers, recognized with joint publications.
- *Contracts*. This attribute is a list. It represents the contracted links between actors. One link may exist between researchers, between researchers and industry, between researcher and TTO, and so on.
- *Research Network*. This attribute represents the integration of the researcher in the scientific community.

10.4.2   Universities

- *Environmental Commitment*. This value represents the effort that is taken by a university toward sustainability. A high value represents a university involved in an active program for Green IT, for instance, favoring researchers working on this field.
- *Fellow Universities*. This attribute is a list. It represents the links existing between universities, recognized with contracts.
- *TTO*. This attribute represents the link with an existing TTO, or null if none is active
- *Legal Department*. This attribute represents how efficient the legal department is. Is it reactive in terms of creating patents, protecting new inventions, open source solutions, and so on?
- *Existing Memorandums of Understanding (MoU)*. This is a list of universities or companies with which it is easy to cooperate as no further documents have to be signed.

10.4.3   Technology Transfer Office (TTO)

- *Client Database*. This is a list of keywords expressing research interests of academia, industry, and names of contact persons
- *Arranged Cooperation*. This is a list showing the experience in finding partners, setting up agreements, and so on.
- *Existing MoU*. This is a list of partners (other TTOs, universities, etc.) with which no other agreement has to be signed before starting a business.

10.4.4   Industry

- *Existing Relations with Academia*. This list represents the interests of that industry, the knowledge of internal structures of academic partners, and so on.
- *Existing Relations with Companies*. This list shows the existing network, cooperation, and so on.
- *Existing Research Department*. This attribute represents the interest in the development, new technology, and willingness to invest money for being a step ahead compared to the concurrence.

- *Employed Scientists*. This attribute represents the understanding of academia and the efficiency in cooperation.
- *Size*. This number represents the resources being available for a cooperation.
- *Annual Turnover*. This number represents the stability of the partner within a project.

10.4.5   Funding Organization

- *Kind of Calls*. This is a list representing the different calls and their requirements, for example, if industrial partners have to be included, a product has to be presented at the end of the runtime.
- *What is Financed*. This is a list to see if already the start of cooperation can be financed: staff, lobbying, and so on.
- *How Often per Year*. This is a list to see how much pressure there is on a consortium to submit before a certain deadline.
- *Acceptance Rate*. This number is to compare different funding organizations and to evaluate the possibility of success.

10.4.6   Standardization Body

- *Member*. This list shows which different parties are involved and, therefore, which interests are mainly represented.
- *Internal Structure*. This graph shows the possibility to join the body, the possibility to become a member, its reactivity concerning new proposals or initiatives, and the possibility to work together with other bodies.
- *Cooperation*. This list shows the existing co-operations with other standardization bodies, de facto bodies, or initiatives as well as industry and academia.
- *Position in the Structure of Standardization Bodies*. This graph shows the influence of the body. Recommendations can be made at the word-wide level, European level, and so on.

10.4.7   Links between Actors

There are various links existing between these actors. They can be categorized in to direct and indirect links. Direct links exist between two partners without any intermediate, while indirect links involves one or more intermediate actors.

These links express the influence of one actor on the actors linked with it. These links are valued by two main influences: the internal behavior of one actor and the influence of its environment on its own development.

Taking some concrete example with the previously defined actors, one can develop, for instance, the impact of funding organizations on the actual development of research and the produced scientific papers from a researcher. This number of publications, an attribute from the researcher, is obviously influenced not only by the number of contracts this researcher raises but also on its internal willingness to develop the social, the economic, and the environment dimension of sustainability; on its research network; and so on. However, it is also obvious that the number of publications will increase because of the funding, as the researcher might be able to employ new collaborators. Giving this reasoning, a formula linking the number of publication to the other attributes can be constructed. And if one of these attributes evolves (more contracts, more funding, etc.) then the number of publications also evolves. This example represents a direct link.

Conversely, one can also consider that the number of publications has an impact on the number of contracts one researcher can get: funding agencies, TTOs, will probably favor those researchers with an already built reputation in Green IT than new comers. Hence, another researcher linked with this one will benefit indirectly from this reputation, being able to build a successful research project proposal with him. This represents an indirect link.

Another aspect to consider is the links with respect to a particular objective. Let us take as an example the increase of sustainability in the social dimension. An IT researcher might be more influenced by Green IT researchers on their usage of IT equipment than a researcher in another field. However, IT researchers have a stronger influence in general on the society (because they represent older links with society) than Green IT researchers (who are less numerous and less seen). This means that the indirect influence of Green IT researchers toward society benefit from their direct influence toward IT researchers.

For nonpointed research, given the passive diffusion of information, each actor influences regularly the adoption of Green IT technologies, knowingly or unknowingly. This means that the valuation of the interactions must be dynamic and reactive to possible feedback. For focused research, the Green IT researchers will influence directly and more strongly (higher valuation) only researchers (other Green IT, IT, and general) through contracts. In that scheme, the impact on society will only be indirect. It can be noted that the direct link between the IT researcher and the society is directly influenced by its link with the Green IT researchers. Also, focused research may produce freely available results, as, for instance, open source software, which may influence directly the society, creating a loose link between Green IT researchers and the society. This link strengthens indirectly the link between IT researchers and Green IT researchers (through Word of Mouth dissemination or facing the fact that such solutions exist). In [13], we examined several other examples of interactions between actors, directly coming from the previous analysis about the differences between actors (see Figure 10.3).

Using these small examples, one can see the difficulty of building and creating the direct and indirect influences in the network composed of the different actors.

10.4.8 Rating the Relationships between Actors

Considering simplistic situation is already a challenge. All interactions cannot be rated only with a 0/1 value. It is much more complex than limiting the scope to counting the number of interactions, and it depends on each individual actor itself. For instance, let us consider the previous case of publication. Counting the number of publications to express the reputation of one researcher is known to be prone to errors and do not reflect the quality of the research being conducted. There is a need to express the utility of one attribute depending on its usage and its combination with other. The number of

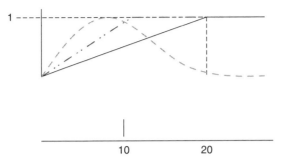

Figure 10.6. Utility as a function of the number of publication, for three profiles.

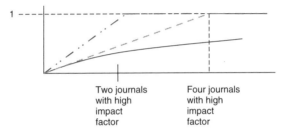

Figure 10.7. Utility as a function of the quality of publications, for two profiles.

publications can be enough to assess the quantity and the diversity of researches conducted that could be enough in some cases.

We propose to use normalized utility functions to map attribute values to utility values. In Figure 10.6, three profiles of utility functions have been defined. It is clear that the red profile will favor the number of publications much more than the black one: a lower number of publications are needed to get a higher utility value. A maximum is reached after a number of publications and the utility value is not increased anymore with further publications. The green profile favors a number of publications around 10 and starts decreasing after until 20 where the utility is null. This profile represents, for instance, a case where too many publications are not interesting, for example, let less time for developing industrial collaborations.

For the same case, Figure 10.7 shows the utility of the quality of the publications (for instance, based on international ranking such as the Australian CORE). Here, the utility function is high when the number of high-quality papers is high. The red profile considers two research papers in journals as sufficient, while the green profile asks for at least four. The black profile shows a case where the quality of the papers is never reaching a utility of 1, meaning that this criterion is not important for this case.

When the utility function for each attribute has been defined, they can be combined to value an objective that may differ from case to case. As for examples, the next section describes several objectives that could be achieved, thanks to this formalism.

10.5   USING THE MODELING FOR DECIDING

Following the current trend in modeling, the distributed interactions with multiagent systems, in particular, in the field of innovation diffusion [14], we propose in this section to use the modeling of the technological transfer between researchers and industry and its impact on Green IT.

The agents that will be used are the actors, their attributes, and links being defined from the previous section. Using multiagent system, one must concretize an optimization objective of the system. In the field of the development of Green IT, we foresee already the following objectives that could be valued and observed through the evolution of the multiagent system:

- For a funding agency, the impact of increasing the budget allocated to the Green IT theme could be assessed for the different dimensions of sustainability, social, environment, and economic, maybe with a stronger focus on one of these.
- For a business angel, the impact of funding a company in Green IT could be assessed in terms of return of investment.
- For a contract partner, the probability of success of a project proposal could be measured.
- For a researcher, the impact of his/her actions on a global value for Green IT.

It must be noticed that these objectives are very different. Obviously, the multiagent system has to be customized in order to reflect one objective. This parameterization is done, thanks to the utility functions sketched in the previous section.

An important aspect to consider is the network topology between the agents. As stated before, the research may or may not be spread out toward a selected number of early adopters. The impact of the topology of the links between the agents has been shown [15] in a number of previous works as very influential on the final spread of the product. Small-world and scale-free topologies are the most common ways of interactions used by the existing studies.

Changing the parameters and the behaviors of agents, we will be able to address a number of case studies by analyzing the change inside the system according to the objective functions.

10.5.1   Methodology to be Developed

We plan to derive our methodology in three steps: the first one will be to consolidate the multiagent systems, in particular in expressing more the different links and their mutual influences. The second step will be to actually develop the multiagent system on a suitable platform. However, when this system is developed, it is not useful if the data modeled are not realistic. In parallel to the theoretical work, we have developed an online survey to be filled by researchers and academic partners. Its results will feed the multiagent system in order to be able to extract statistics and to value some links between actors from these observations.

10.6 CONCLUSION

This chapter presented the landscape of Green IT, focusing on large-scale distributed systems. First, a definition of Green IT and its difference and links with sustainability was given. Then the differences in points of view for considering Green IT between academic and industry players were outlined, and the role of several actors were described: TTOs, standardization bodies, industries, and researchers. In the last part, a modeling of the actors is proposed and its usage for helping decision makers is sketched.

The landscape for Green IT innovation is complex and a lot of interdependent relationship can influence the impact of actual actions on the global aim for a greener and more sustainable IT. We believe that the works presented here are only a first step in order to better understand the landscape, so as to enhance the benefit from all the initiatives, funding, and interests around the world. And we hope that it will inspire governments, researchers, industries to tackle together the challenge for greening the IT.

ACKNOWLEDGMENT

This research work is partly supported by the European Commission under contract 288701 through the project CoolEmAll and by the COST (European Cooperation in Science and Technology) framework, under Action IC0804.

REFERENCES

[1] Hilty LM. Information Technology and Sustainability. Essays on the Relationship between ICT and Sustainable Development Books on demand, ISBN: 9783837019704, 2008

[2] S Murugesan. Harnessing Green IT: principles and practices. IT Prof 10, 1, 24–33. 2008.

[3] Eugster M, Hischier R, and Huabo D. Key environmental impacts of the Chinese EEE-industry – a life cycle study. St. Gallen and Bejing: Empa and Tsinghua University; 2007.

[4] Adams WM. The future of sustainability: re-thinking environment and development in the twenty-first century. Report of the IUCN Renowned Thinkers Meeting; 2006 Jan 29–31.

[5] R Garud: On the distinction between know-how, know-why, and know-what, Adv Strat Manag 14, p 81–101, 1997

[6] Herzog C, Lefèvre L, Pierson, JM. Green IT for Innovation and Innovation for Green IT: The virtuous circle. In: Human Choice and Computers (HCC10) International Conference (Technical Committee 9 – Relationship between Computers and Society, International Federation of Information Processing IFIP); 2012 Sep; Amsterdam. Springer.

[7] Brooks H. National science policy and technology transfer. In: *Conference on Technology Transfer and Innovation*; 1966; Washington, DC. pp. S53–S63.

[8] Auer M. (2000): *Transferunternehmertum. Erfolgreiche Organization des Technolietransfers*. Wiesbaden: Gabler; Deutscher Universitätsverlag (DUV Wirtschaftwissenschaft).

[9] Corsten H (1982): Der nationale Technologietransfer. *Formen, Elemente, Gestaltungsmöglichkeiten, Probleme*. Berlin: Schmidt (Technological economics, 7).

[10] Zissler, M.; *Technologietransfer durch Auftragsforschung*, Wiesbaden: Springer Gabler Verlag 2011. ISBN 978-3-8349-6131-0

[11] D7.6.2 Standardization Report 2, CoolEmAll project. Available at www.coolemall.eu. Accessed 2014 Sep 29.

[12] Herzog C. Green IT for standardization bodies, initiatives and their relation to Green IT focused on the data center side. In: Energy Efficiency in Large Scale Distributed Systems Conference, EE-LSDS 2013; 2013 Apr 22–24; Vienna, Austria. Springer; LNCS. ISBN: 978-3-642-40516-7 (Print), 978-3-642-40517-4.

[13] Herzog C, Pierson J-M, and Lefèvre L. Towards modelling the research in Green IT with agents. In: 27th International Conference on Environmental Informatics for Environmental Protection, Sustainable Development and Risk Management, EnviroInfo 2013; 2013 Sep 2–4; Hamburg, Germany. pp. 335–341.

[14] E Kiesling, M Günther, C Stummer, LM Wakolbinger, "Agent-based simulation of innovation diffusion: a review", Cent Eur J Oper Res, 2012, Volume 20, Issue 2, pp 183–230.

[15] Bass FM, "A new product growth for model consumer durables". Manag Sci. Vol 15 (5). pp 215–227. 1969.

[16] Herzog C, Pierson J-M, and Lefèvre L. Link between academia and industry for Green IT. In: International Conference on Information and Communication Technologies for Sustainability, ICT4S 2013; 2013 Feb 14–16; Zürich, Switzerland. pp 259–264. Conference Appendixes.

AUTHOR INDEX

Large-Scale Distributed Systems and Energy Efficiency: A Holistic View, First Edition.
Edited by Jean-Marc Pierson.
© 2015 John Wiley & Sons, Inc. Published 2015 by John Wiley & Sons, Inc.

SUBJECT INDEX

Large-Scale Distributed Systems and Energy Efficiency: A Holistic View, First Edition.
Edited by Jean-Marc Pierson.
© 2015 John Wiley & Sons, Inc. Published 2015 by John Wiley & Sons, Inc.

WILEY SERIES ON PARALLEL AND DISTRIBUTED COMPUTING
Series Editor: Albert Y. Zomaya

Computing for Numerical Methods Using Visual C++ / Shaharuddin Salleh, Albert Y. Zomaya, and Sakhinah A. Bakar

Architecture-Independent Programming for Wireless Sensor Networks / Amol B. Bakshi and Viktor K. Prasanna

High-Performance Parallel Database Processing and Grid Databases / David Taniar, Clement Leung, Wenny Rahayu, and Sushant Goel

Algorithms and Protocols for Wireless and Mobile Ad Hoc Networks / Azzedine Boukerche (*Editor*)

Algorithms and Protocols for Wireless Sensor Networks / Azzedine Boukerche (*Editor*)

Optimization Techniques for Solving Complex Problems / Enrique Alba, Christian Blum, Pedro Isasi, Coromoto León, and Juan Antonio Gómez (*Editors*)

Emerging Wireless LANs, Wireless PANs, and Wireless MANs: IEEE 802.11, IEEE 802.15, IEEE 802.16 Wireless Standard Family / Yang Xiao and Yi Pan (*Editors*)

High-Performance Heterogeneous Computing / Alexey L. Lastovetsky and Jack Dongarra

Mobile Intelligence / Laurence T. Yang, Augustinus Borgy Waluyo, Jianhua Ma, Ling Tan, and Bala Srinivasan (*Editors*)

Research in Mobile Intelligence / Laurence T. Yang (*Editor*)

Advanced Computational Infrastructures for Parallel and Distributed Adaptive Applicatons / Manish Parashar and Xiaolin Li (*Editors*)

Market-Oriented Grid and Utility Computing / Rajkumar Buyya and Kris Bubendorfer (*Editors*)

Cloud Computing Principles and Paradigms / Rajkumar Buyya, James Broberg, and Andrzej Goscinski (*Editors*)

Algorithms and Parallel Computing / Fayez Gebali

Energy-Efficient Distributed Computing Systems / Albert Y. Zomaya and Young Choon Lee (*Editors*)

Scalable Computing and Communications: Theory and Practice / Samee U. Khan, Lizhe Wang, and Albert Y. Zomaya (*Editors*)

The DATA Bonanza: Improving Knowledge Discovery in Science, Engineering, and Business / Malcolm Atkinson, Rob Baxter, Michelle Galea, Mark Parsons, Peter Brezany, Oscar Corcho, Jano van Hemert, and David Snelling (*Editors*)

Large Scale Network-Centric Distributed Systems / Hamid Sarbazi-Azad and Albert Y. Zomaya (*Editors*)

Verification of Communication Protocols in Web Services: Model-Checking Service Compositions / Zahir Tari, Peter Bertok, and Anshuman Mukherjee

High-Performance Computing on Complex Environments / Emmanuel Jeannot and Julius Žilinskas (*Editors*)

Advanced Content Delivery, Streaming, and Cloud Services / Mukaddim Pathan, Ramesh K. Sitaraman, and Dom Robinson *(Editors)*

Large-Scale Distributed Systems and Energy Efficiency: A Holistic View / Jean-Marc Pierson (*Editor*)